Computational Modeling and Digital Twins with AI

by

ant

Table of Contents

Computational Modeling and Digital Twins with AI

Chapter 10: Data Management for Digital Twins (pp. 271–300)

Chapter 11: Deployment Architectures for Digital Twins (pp. 301–330)

Chapter 12: Cybersecurity for Digital Twins (pp. 331–350)

Chapter 13: Principles of Advanced Monitoring (pp. 351–370)

The advent of digital twin technology marks a transformative era in engineering and industrial operations. It represents not merely an incremental advancement in simulation or modeling, but a profound paradigm shift, enabling a dynamic, interconnected ecosystem where the physical and digital realms coalesce to provide unprecedented levels of insight, control, and optimization. This book is born from the conviction that a comprehensive understanding of digital twins—from their fundamental principles to their sophisticated applications—is increasingly vital for engineers, researchers, and decision-makers navigating the complexities of modern industry.

Our journey through the landscape of digital twins begins with establishing a clear conceptual framework, distinguishing true digital twins from simpler simulations. We will delve into the historical evolution that paved the way for this technology and illuminate the essential components that constitute a functional digital twin ecosystem. Subsequently, we will explore the critical notion of model fidelity, understanding how accurately a virtual representation mirrors its physical counterpart, and the crucial balance between fidelity, complexity, and performance. The power of integration will be a recurring theme, particularly the synergistic benefits derived from hybrid modeling approaches that marry physics-based principles with data-driven techniques, including the promising field of Physics-Informed Machine Learning.

Furthermore, this book will navigate the intricate mechanisms of real-time synchronization, the essential link that keeps the digital twin synchronized with its physical asset, and the vital role of state estimation in ensuring dynamic accuracy. We will confront the inherent challenges of uncertainty quantification, essential for robust decision-making, and explore rigorous calibration and validation strategies that build confidence in the digital twin's performance. Data management, deployment architectures, and cybersecurity will be addressed as foundational pillars for successful implementation. Finally, we will examine advanced topics such as monitoring principles, decision support systems, practical case studies, and the exciting future trends that promise to redefine the capabilities of digital twins. This work aims to equip readers with the theoretical knowledge and practical insights necessary to not only understand but also to actively design, implement, and leverage digital twins effectively in their own domains.

In the rapidly evolving landscape of industrial and engineering applications, the concept of the digital twin has emerged as a cornerstone technology, promising to revolutionize how we design, operate, and maintain physical assets and systems. A digital twin is far more than a static 3D model or a standalone simulation; it is a dynamic, virtual representation of a physical entity—be it a product, process, or system—that is continuously updated with real-time data from its physical counterpart. This intricate linkage creates a living digital replica that mirrors the state, behavior, and context of the physical asset throughout its lifecycle.

The genesis of digital twin technology can be traced through decades of advancements in modeling, simulation, the Internet of Things (IoT), artificial intelligence (AI), and cloud computing. Early simulations provided static insights, while cyber-physical systems began to bridge the gap between computation and physical operations. The proliferation of sensors and the advent of powerful computing platforms have now converged to make the sophisticated, real-time digital twin a practical reality. This technological convergence enables a level of insight and control previously unattainable, offering tangible benefits across a vast spectrum of industries, from aerospace and automotive to manufacturing, energy, and healthcare.

This book is meticulously crafted to serve as a comprehensive guide for graduate students and industry professionals seeking a deep understanding of digital twin technology. We aim to move beyond introductory concepts and delve into the core principles, methodologies, and practical considerations that underpin the successful development and deployment of digital twins. Our exploration will cover the critical aspects of model fidelity, the fusion of physics-based and data-driven approaches through hybrid modeling, and the essential mechanisms for real-time synchronization that ensure the virtual twin remains a true reflection of its physical counterpart. Furthermore, we will address the vital areas of state estimation, uncertainty quantification, and rigorous calibration and validation strategies, which are paramount for building trust and reliability in digital twin applications. The practical challenges of data management, the strategic choices in deployment architectures, and the imperative of robust cybersecurity will also be thoroughly examined. By the end of this book, readers will possess a well-rounded perspective, equipped to identify opportunities, design effective solutions, and navigate the complexities of implementing digital twin technology to drive innovation and achieve operational excellence.

Chapter 1: The Dawn of Digital Twins

The concept of a digital twin, at its heart, represents a sophisticated evolution in how we understand, interact with, and manage physical systems. Far from being a mere static replica or a simple simulation, a digital twin is fundamentally a dynamic, virtual representation that is intrinsically linked to its physical counterpart. This linkage is not just conceptual; it is a live, bidirectional flow of data that ensures the digital twin mirrors the physical asset's state, behavior, and context in near real-time. This dynamic interplay is what distinguishes a digital twin from earlier forms of digital modeling and simulation, imbuing it with a level of operational intelligence and predictive capability that was previously unattainable.

To truly grasp the paradigm of the digital twin, it's essential to move beyond nascent or overly simplistic definitions. While a digital twin can indeed be visualized as a virtual model, its true power lies in its constant synchronization with a specific, often unique, physical entity. This could be anything from a single component, like a turbine blade, to a complex system, such as an entire factory, a city's infrastructure, or even a living organism. The digital twin is not a generic model; it is a bespoke digital entity that evolves and changes in parallel with its physical twin, mirroring its operational status, environmental conditions, and even its wear and tear over time. This continuous, data-driven connection allows for unprecedented insights into the physical world.

The genesis of the digital twin concept can be traced back to the historical evolution of simulation and modeling techniques that have long been integral to engineering and scientific disciplines. For decades, engineers have relied on mathematical models and simulations to predict the behavior of physical systems under various conditions. Early forms of simulation, often confined to desktop environments and relying on static inputs, served primarily to test design hypotheses or understand fundamental principles. These were powerful tools for conceptualization and initial design validation, but they lacked the crucial element of real-time interaction with a live physical asset. They were snapshots in time, or projections based on assumed conditions, rather than living digital counterparts.

As computational power increased and sensor technologies became more sophisticated, the ability to create more detailed and dynamic simulations grew. Cyber-Physical Systems (CPS), a concept that emerged in the late 20th and early 21st centuries, began to lay the groundwork for digital twins. CPS are systems where computational elements are deeply intertwined with physical processes. Sensors collect data from the physical world, this data is processed by computational algorithms, and the results can then be used to control or influence the physical world. This closed-loop interaction between the physical and digital domains is a foundational element of the digital twin paradigm. However, CPS often focused on specific control loops or functionalities, whereas the digital twin concept encompasses a broader, more holistic virtual representation.

The leap from advanced simulation and CPS to the digital twin paradigm involved a crucial shift in perspective: the explicit aim of creating a virtual entity that precisely mirrors a specific physical entity throughout its lifecycle. This mirroring is achieved through a continuous stream of data. Sensors embedded in the physical asset collect data on parameters such as temperature, pressure, vibration, speed, location, and operational status. This data is transmitted to the digital twin, where it is used to update the virtual model. This constant update cycle ensures that the digital twin's state accurately reflects the physical asset's current condition.

Furthermore, the digital twin is not just a passive observer. The bidirectional flow of data means that insights gained from the digital twin—such as performance predictions, diagnosed anomalies, or optimized operational parameters—can be fed back to the physical asset. This allows for intelligent control, predictive maintenance, and proactive adjustments, creating a feedback loop that continuously enhances the performance and reliability of the physical system. This is the essence of bridging the physical and digital realms: the digital twin acts as a dynamic interface, providing a window into the physical world and a lever for influencing its behavior.

Establishing a common understanding of what constitutes a digital twin is critical for its successful adoption and implementation across diverse industries. While the core principle of a dynamic virtual representation linked to a physical asset remains constant, the specific implementation details and the fidelity of the virtual model can vary significantly depending on the application. For instance, a digital twin of a jet engine might require an extremely high degree of fidelity, incorporating detailed aerodynamic, thermodynamic, and structural models to accurately predict performance and potential failures under extreme operating conditions. Conversely, a digital twin of a warehouse might focus more on logistical flow, inventory management, and energy consumption, with less emphasis on minute physical details.

The multi-faceted nature of a digital twin can be further understood by considering its key characteristics:

1.
Connectivity: The digital twin is connected to its physical counterpart through a constant flow of data. This connectivity is the lifeblood of the twin, ensuring its relevance and accuracy.

2.
Dynamism: The digital twin is not static. It evolves and changes in real-time as the physical asset operates and experiences its environment.

3.
Uniqueness: Each digital twin is typically associated with a specific physical asset, embodying its unique characteristics and history. While generic models may inform its creation, the operational twin is tailored.

4.
Intelligence: Digital twins incorporate analytical capabilities, often leveraging AI and machine learning, to process data, generate insights, and support decision-making.

5.
Lifecycle Integration: A digital twin can represent an asset throughout its entire lifecycle, from design and manufacturing to operation, maintenance, and eventual decommissioning.

This comprehensive, data-driven, and dynamic nature distinguishes the digital twin paradigm from simpler forms of digital representation. It moves beyond static blueprints or isolated simulations to create a living, breathing digital echo of a physical entity. This shift is not merely an incremental improvement; it represents a fundamental change in how we can engineer, operate, and maintain complex systems, opening up new frontiers for efficiency, innovation, and resilience. The subsequent sections of this chapter will delve deeper into the historical context that paved the way for this transformative technology and explore the essential components that constitute a digital twin ecosystem, further solidifying our understanding of this powerful paradigm. By setting this foundational understanding, we prepare the ground for exploring the intricate details of digital twin implementation and its far-reaching implications.

The notion of creating a virtual representation that mirrors a physical entity, capable of simulating its behavior and predicting its future states, is not a recent invention. Rather, it is a concept that has evolved organically, driven by humanity's persistent desire to understand, control, and optimize the physical world. The journey towards the digital twin as we understand it today is a fascinating narrative of incremental innovation, spanning decades of advancements in fields as diverse as engineering, computer science, and applied mathematics. Early aspirations to digitally replicate physical systems can be traced back to the nascent stages of computational modeling and simulation, where the power of mathematics and early computing was harnessed to predict the behavior of mechanical systems. These foundational efforts, though primitive by today's standards, laid the conceptual groundwork for the sophisticated digital twins of the 21st century.

One of the earliest discernible precursors to the digital twin concept can be found in the realm of aerospace engineering and defense. The development of flight simulators in the mid-20th century stands as a significant milestone. These simulators, born out of the need for safe and cost-effective pilot training, were essentially early forms of digital twins for aircraft. They aimed to replicate the physical dynamics of flight, including the aircraft's response to control inputs, atmospheric conditions, and engine performance. While these simulators were primarily focused on replicating the *experience* of flying, rather than the real-time operational state of a specific, individual aircraft, they demonstrated the potential of using computational models to understand and interact with complex physical systems in a virtual environment. The fidelity of these simulations gradually increased with advancements in computing power and a deeper understanding of aerodynamics and control theory. Each iteration brought the virtual representation closer to the real-world behavior of the aircraft, even if it was a generalized model rather than a unique twin.

Parallel to the development of flight simulators, the field of industrial engineering and manufacturing began to explore the use of computer-aided design (CAD) and computer-aided manufacturing (CAM). CAD systems allowed engineers to create detailed, three-dimensional digital models of products and components. These models served as digital blueprints, facilitating design iteration, visualization, and the generation of manufacturing instructions. While CAD models were primarily static representations, they represented a critical step towards capturing the geometric and functional aspects of physical objects in a digital format. The ability to manipulate, analyze, and visualize these digital designs before physical realization was a powerful innovation that reduced design errors and accelerated product development cycles. However, these models typically lacked the dynamic link to a physical asset's operational state; they were primarily design tools, not living representations of active machinery.

The concept of simulation, in its broader sense, has always been a cornerstone of scientific and engineering practice. From the physical scale models used in wind tunnels to the mathematical models that describe fluid dynamics or structural integrity, simulation has been a tool for prediction and analysis. As computational power grew, so did the complexity and sophistication of these simulations. Engineers could move from simple analytical models to complex finite element analysis (FEA) and computational fluid dynamics (CFD) simulations. These advanced simulation techniques allowed for a much more detailed understanding of how physical systems would behave under various stresses and conditions. For instance, FEA could predict how a bridge would deform under load, and CFD could model airflow over an airplane wing. These simulations were crucial for design validation and optimization, but they remained detached from the real-time, operational performance of a deployed physical asset. They were powerful "what-if" scenarios, but not a continuous reflection of reality.

The late 20th and early 21st centuries witnessed a significant conceptual leap with the emergence of Cyber-Physical Systems (CPS). This paradigm shift recognized the increasing integration of computational intelligence with physical processes. CPS are systems where computation, networking, and physical processes are intertwined. Sensors embedded in the physical world collect data, this data is processed by computing elements, and the resulting information is used to control or influence the physical processes. This closed-loop interaction between the physical and digital realms is a fundamental building block for the digital twin. Early examples of CPS could be found in industrial control systems, automated manufacturing lines, and sophisticated robotics. These systems demonstrated the ability to monitor physical parameters, analyze them, and make automated adjustments to optimize performance or ensure safety. However, CPS often focused on specific functionalities or control loops rather than a comprehensive virtual representation of an entire asset or system. The emphasis was on control and automation within a defined operational scope.

The transition from advanced simulation and CPS to the modern concept of a digital twin was fueled by several converging technological advancements. The proliferation of affordable and increasingly sophisticated sensors was a key enabler. Technologies like the Internet of Things (IoT) began to connect vast numbers of physical devices, enabling them to collect and transmit data about their environment and operational status. Simultaneously, advancements in data analytics, cloud computing, and artificial intelligence (AI) provided the necessary infrastructure and intelligence to process, store, and analyze the massive volumes of data generated by these sensors. Cloud computing offered scalable storage and processing power, while AI and machine learning algorithms provided the tools to extract meaningful insights, identify patterns, and make predictions from this data.

The idea of maintaining a "digital thread" throughout the lifecycle of a product or system also gained traction during this period. A digital thread is a continuous, integrated, and traceable data flow that connects all aspects of a product or system's lifecycle, from design and manufacturing to operation and maintenance. The digital twin can be seen as the ultimate realization of this digital thread – a living, dynamic representation that is continuously updated and informed by this comprehensive data stream. It bridges the gap between the static design models and the dynamic operational reality.

A pivotal moment in the formalization of the digital twin concept is often attributed to Dr. Michael Grieves. In 2002, while at the University of Michigan, Dr. Grieves presented a conceptual model for Product Lifecycle Management (PLM) that described a system with a physical space, a virtual space, and the connections between them. He initially referred to this as the "model continuum," which later evolved into the concept of a "Digital Twin." His work envisioned a system where a physical product had a corresponding virtual model, and data could flow bidirectionally between them. This virtual model would contain all the information about the physical product, including its design, manufacturing history, and operational data. The key innovation was the explicit emphasis on the synchronization of the virtual model with the physical asset throughout its entire lifecycle, not just during the design phase. This seminal work provided a theoretical framework and a name for what many in industry had been intuitively striving towards.

Following Dr. Grieves' conceptualization, the idea began to gain traction and evolve within different industries. NASA, with its long history of complex aerospace missions, has been an early adopter and proponent of digital twin principles. For decades, NASA has relied on sophisticated simulations and models to design, test, and operate spacecraft. The extreme environments and high stakes of space exploration necessitate meticulous planning and a deep understanding of system behavior. The ability to monitor the state of spacecraft in real-time, predict potential failures, and simulate corrective actions is paramount. While perhaps not always explicitly termed "digital twins" in the early days, the underlying principles of creating virtual representations that mirror physical assets and their operational status were deeply ingrained in NASA's practices. The experience gained from managing complex, remotely operated physical assets in harsh environments provided invaluable insights into the practical challenges and benefits of such systems.

The evolution of digital twin technology has been a process of continuous refinement and expansion. Initially, the focus was often on individual components or assets. For example, a digital twin might be created for a single engine, a pump, or a wind turbine. As the technology matured and data integration capabilities improved, the scope expanded to encompass more complex systems. This led to the development of digital twins for entire factories, supply chains, buildings, and even cities. The concept of a "city twin," for instance, involves creating a virtual replica of an urban environment that integrates data from various sources, such as traffic sensors, building management systems, energy grids, and public services. This allows city planners and administrators to monitor urban operations, simulate the impact of new infrastructure projects, optimize resource allocation, and respond more effectively to emergencies.

The increasing maturity of enabling technologies like 5G, edge computing, and advanced simulation software has further accelerated the adoption and sophistication of digital twins. 5G connectivity provides the high bandwidth and low latency required for real-time data transmission from a multitude of sensors. Edge computing allows for data processing closer to the source, reducing reliance on centralized cloud infrastructure and enabling faster decision-making for time-critical applications. Advanced simulation software, often incorporating AI and machine learning, allows for the creation of highly accurate and dynamic virtual models that can predict complex behaviors with unprecedented precision.

The journey from early flight simulators and CAD models to the interconnected, intelligent digital twins of today reflects a profound shift in our technological capabilities and our understanding of complex systems. It is a testament to the persistent human drive to achieve greater insight, control, and efficiency in the physical world through digital means. The historical trajectory clearly indicates that the digital twin is not a sudden invention but rather a culmination of decades of research, development, and practical application across numerous scientific and engineering disciplines, each contributing vital components to its eventual realization. This rich history provides the essential context for understanding the current capabilities and future potential of digital twin technology.

At its core, a digital twin ecosystem is a sophisticated orchestration of interconnected components, each playing a vital role in bridging the physical and digital realms. Deconstructing this ecosystem reveals a layered architecture, starting with the tangible physical asset that the digital twin is designed to represent. This could be anything from a single turbine in a power plant, a fleet of autonomous vehicles, a sprawling manufacturing facility, a complex piece of medical equipment, or even an entire city's infrastructure. The physical asset is the origin of the data, the entity whose performance, condition, and behavior are being mirrored and analyzed. Without a real-world counterpart, the digital twin would be a purely theoretical construct, devoid of practical application. The fidelity and complexity of the physical asset directly influence the requirements and capabilities of its digital counterpart. For instance, a simple machine with a few operational parameters will necessitate a less intricate digital twin than a complex, interconnected system like a smart grid, which involves numerous interacting components and vast amounts of real-time data.

The second fundamental pillar of a digital twin ecosystem is the virtual model. This is the digital replica, a comprehensive representation of the physical asset. It's not merely a static 3D rendering; rather, it embodies the asset's geometry, material properties, physics, behavior, and operational logic. This virtual model is constructed using a variety of data sources and modeling techniques. These can include Computer-Aided Design (CAD) models that define the physical structure, simulation models (such as Finite Element Analysis - FEA or Computational Fluid Dynamics - CFD) that predict how the asset will behave under different conditions, and even historical performance data that captures past operational patterns. The virtual model is the canvas upon which all the incoming real-time data is overlaid and analyzed. Its accuracy and comprehensiveness are paramount. A poorly constructed or incomplete virtual model will lead to flawed insights and predictions, undermining the very purpose of the digital twin. The sophistication of the virtual model can range from simple data-driven representations to highly complex, physics-based simulations that can predict nuanced behaviors.

Crucially, the physical asset and its virtual model are inextricably linked by a continuous data stream. This is the lifeblood of the digital twin, enabling the real-time synchronization that distinguishes it from traditional simulations or CAD models. This data stream is facilitated by a network of sensors embedded within the physical asset. These sensors collect a wide array of data points, including operational parameters (e.g., temperature, pressure, speed, vibration), environmental conditions, usage patterns, diagnostic information, and even subjective feedback if applicable. The proliferation of the Internet of Things (IoT) has been a massive catalyst for this component, providing affordable, robust, and diverse sensor technologies. Data from these sensors is transmitted, often wirelessly, to a data ingestion platform. This platform acts as the gateway, collecting, processing, and preparing the raw sensor data for use by the virtual model. The characteristics of this data stream are critical: its frequency (how often data is collected), its volume (how much data is generated), its velocity (how quickly it needs to be processed), and its veracity (the accuracy and reliability of the data). High-frequency, high-volume data requires robust networking and processing capabilities, while the need for real-time insights demands low latency in data transmission and analysis.

Beyond the raw data, the digital twin ecosystem relies heavily on sophisticated analytical capabilities and artificial intelligence (AI) to derive meaningful insights. This is where the true power of the digital twin emerges. The virtual model, constantly updated by the real-time data stream, becomes a living laboratory. Advanced algorithms, including machine learning (ML), statistical analysis, and predictive modeling, are applied to this synchronized data. These analytical engines can perform a multitude of tasks: monitoring the current health and performance of the physical asset, detecting anomalies and predicting potential failures before they occur, optimizing operational parameters for maximum efficiency and output, simulating the impact of changes or interventions, and forecasting future performance. For instance, an ML model trained on historical vibration data from a rotating machine can learn to identify subtle patterns indicative of impending bearing failure, allowing for proactive maintenance. Similarly, AI algorithms can analyze energy consumption patterns in a building and recommend adjustments to HVAC systems to reduce waste. The analytical layer transforms raw data into actionable intelligence, enabling informed decision-making and proactive management of the physical asset.

The underlying technological infrastructure is the foundation upon which the entire digital twin ecosystem is built. This infrastructure encompasses several critical elements. First, robust data storage and management systems are essential to handle the vast quantities of data generated by sensors and simulations. Cloud computing platforms have become indispensable here, offering scalable, on-demand storage and processing power. They provide the flexibility to store historical data for training analytical models and to host the virtual models themselves. Second, networking technologies are crucial for the seamless and reliable transmission of data. This includes not only traditional wired and wireless networks but also advancements like 5G, which offers the high bandwidth and low latency required for real-time applications, and edge computing, which allows for data processing closer to the source of generation, reducing latency and bandwidth demands on the central cloud. Third, powerful computing resources are needed for running complex simulations and AI algorithms. This can involve high-performance computing (HPC) clusters for computationally intensive tasks or specialized AI processing units.

Furthermore, the integration of various software platforms and middleware is key to creating a cohesive ecosystem. This includes data aggregation tools, simulation software, AI/ML platforms, business intelligence dashboards, and application programming interfaces (APIs) that allow different systems to communicate and exchange data. The ability to seamlessly integrate these disparate tools is vital for creating a unified digital twin experience. For example, an API might be used to connect a real-time sensor data feed to a physics-based simulation model, which then feeds its results into an AI-driven anomaly detection engine. The output from the AI engine could then be displayed on a user-friendly dashboard for an operations manager.

The concept of the digital twin also necessitates robust security protocols and data governance frameworks. Given the sensitive nature of the data being collected and the potential impact of digital twin insights on physical operations, ensuring the security and privacy of this information is paramount. This involves implementing strong access controls, data encryption, and regular security audits to protect against cyber threats. Data governance ensures that data is collected, stored, and used in compliance with relevant regulations and ethical guidelines, establishing clear policies on data ownership, usage rights, and data lifecycle management.

Finally, a critical, often overlooked, component of the digital twin ecosystem is the human element. While technology provides the tools, it is the expertise of domain specialists, data scientists, engineers, and operational personnel that unlocks the full potential of digital twins. These individuals are responsible for designing, implementing, operating, and interpreting the digital twin. They define the requirements for the virtual model, select the appropriate sensors and analytical techniques, interpret the insights generated, and translate them into actionable decisions. The success of a digital twin implementation often hinges on the ability of an organization to foster collaboration between these different roles and to equip them with the necessary skills and tools to effectively leverage the digital twin. For example, a mechanical engineer might understand the physics of a machine, while a data scientist can build the predictive models, and an operations manager can use the insights to schedule maintenance. The digital twin acts as a shared platform that facilitates this multidisciplinary collaboration.

In essence, a digital twin ecosystem is not a single piece of software or hardware, but a complex, interconnected system. It is the seamless integration of the physical asset, its detailed virtual representation, the continuous flow of real-time data between them, advanced analytical and AI capabilities, a robust technological infrastructure, and the skilled human operators who orchestrate it all. Each of these components is interdependent; weakening or neglecting one can compromise the entire system's effectiveness. Understanding these fundamental building blocks is essential for anyone seeking to implement or leverage digital twin technology, providing a clear roadmap for navigating the journey from data acquisition to actionable insights and ultimately, optimized real-world performance.

The transformative power of digital twins, while rooted in their intricate ecosystem and technological underpinnings, ultimately crystallizes into a compelling value proposition that resonates across nearly every industry. It is this demonstrable return on investment, this capacity to unlock tangible improvements in efficiency, cost reduction, and innovation, that elevates digital twins from a fascinating technological concept to an indispensable strategic imperative. The core of this value lies in the unparalleled visibility and actionable intelligence that digital twins afford their users, enabling a paradigm shift from reactive problem-solving to proactive optimization and foresight.

One of the most immediate and impactful benefits derived from digital twin technology is the radical enhancement of monitoring capabilities. Unlike traditional methods that often rely on periodic checks, sampled data, or the reports of human inspectors, a digital twin provides a continuous, high-fidelity stream of real-time information about its physical counterpart. This constant surveillance allows for the immediate detection of deviations from normal operating parameters, anomalies that might otherwise go unnoticed until they escalate into significant issues. Imagine a complex manufacturing assembly line; a digital twin can monitor the vibration levels of every motor, the temperature of every processing unit, and the precise positioning of every robotic arm in real-time. If a motor begins to exhibit slightly elevated vibration patterns that, while not yet indicative of imminent failure, suggest a developing issue, the digital twin flags this instantly. This level of granular, continuous oversight is simply unattainable with conventional monitoring techniques, providing an unprecedented level of situational awareness. This real-time data, visualized through intuitive dashboards, empowers operators and managers with an intimate understanding of their assets' current state, enabling them to make informed decisions with a level of confidence previously reserved for theoretical scenarios. The sheer volume of data collected, when intelligently processed, paints a dynamic picture of operational health that is both comprehensive and deeply insightful.

This enhanced monitoring capability directly fuels the second cornerstone of the digital twin value proposition: predictive maintenance. By analyzing the continuous stream of real-time data, coupled with historical performance records and sophisticated AI algorithms, digital twins can accurately predict when a component or entire system is likely to fail. This moves maintenance from a reactive (fixing something after it breaks) or preventative (replacing parts on a fixed schedule, often prematurely) model to a predictive, condition-based approach. Consider a fleet of aircraft engines. Instead of scheduled maintenance based on flight hours, a digital twin can monitor subtle changes in fuel flow, exhaust gas temperature, and vibration signatures. AI models trained on vast datasets can detect patterns indicative of a specific type of wear or a developing fault within the engine's complex components days, weeks, or even months before it would manifest as a performance issue or a critical failure. This foresight allows for maintenance to be scheduled precisely when it is needed, minimizing downtime and the associated costs of lost production or flight schedules. Furthermore, it drastically reduces the risk of catastrophic failures, which can have severe safety and financial implications. The ability to anticipate maintenance needs transforms a costly operational necessity into a strategically managed process, optimizing resource allocation and extending the operational lifespan of assets. This proactive stance not only saves money on repairs and replacements but also prevents costly disruptions that can ripple through an entire supply chain or service operation. The economic impact of avoiding even a single unplanned outage in a major industrial facility can be in the millions of dollars, making predictive maintenance a highly attractive and quantifiable benefit.

Beyond maintenance, digital twins offer substantial advantages in performance optimization. By simulating various operational scenarios within the virtual environment, organizations can identify the most efficient ways to run their physical assets without risking actual equipment damage or production disruption. For instance, in the energy sector, a digital twin of a wind turbine farm can be used to optimize the pitch and yaw of each individual turbine based on real-time wind speed and direction data across the entire farm, not just at the turbine's location. This coordinated optimization can significantly increase the overall energy output compared to independent operation. Similarly, in a chemical processing plant, a digital twin can model the impact of adjusting flow rates, temperatures, and pressures on yield and energy consumption. By running thousands of simulations, engineers can pinpoint the optimal operating window that maximizes product output while minimizing energy usage and waste generation. This continuous loop of monitoring, simulation, and adjustment allows for dynamic performance tuning, ensuring that assets are always operating at their peak potential. The ability to quantify the performance gains achieved through these simulations, such as a 5% increase in energy generation or a 10% reduction in material waste, provides a clear and compelling economic justification for digital twin adoption. This iterative refinement process fosters a culture of continuous improvement, where operational efficiency is not a static target but an evolving goal driven by data and simulation.

The value proposition of digital twins also extends significantly into the design and engineering phases. Before a physical product is even manufactured, a digital twin can be created to simulate its performance under a wide range of conditions. This allows engineers to identify design flaws, test different material choices, and refine the product's functionality in a virtual space, drastically reducing the need for costly and time-consuming physical prototypes. Consider the automotive industry; a digital twin of a new vehicle model can be subjected to virtual crash tests, aerodynamic simulations, and thermal management analyses. Engineers can iterate on designs, optimize component placement, and ensure compliance with safety standards all within the digital realm. This iterative design process, informed by simulation and analysis, leads to more robust, efficient, and reliable products. Furthermore, the data gathered from operational digital twins of existing products can feed back into the design of future generations. This creates a powerful feedback loop where real-world performance data directly informs and improves future designs, accelerating innovation and ensuring that products are tailored to meet the evolving needs of the market and the demands of real-world usage. The reduction in physical prototyping alone can lead to substantial cost savings, while the accelerated design cycles can provide a significant competitive advantage, allowing companies to bring new products to market faster and more efficiently. This integration of design and operational data ensures that innovation is grounded in practical realities, leading to products that are not only technologically advanced but also commercially viable and user-centric.

Furthermore, digital twins streamline operational decision-making by providing a holistic, data-driven view of complex systems. Instead of relying on disparate reports, individual expertise, or gut feelings, decision-makers can access a unified, intelligent platform that consolidates information and presents clear, actionable insights. For instance, a facility manager overseeing a large commercial building can use a digital twin to monitor energy consumption, occupancy levels, HVAC performance, and security systems in real-time. If an anomaly is detected – perhaps an unusually high energy spike in a specific zone – the digital twin can cross-reference this with other data points, such as occupancy sensors indicating an unexpected gathering, or maintenance logs showing recent work in that area. This enables rapid and accurate diagnosis of the issue and informed decision-making regarding the appropriate response, whether it's adjusting building systems, dispatching maintenance, or alerting security. This unified operational intelligence extends to supply chain management, where digital twins can provide end-to-end visibility, enabling better forecasting, inventory management, and logistical planning. The ability to simulate the impact of disruptions, such as a supplier delay or a transportation issue, allows for proactive contingency planning, minimizing ripple effects across the entire operation. This enhanced decision-making capability reduces risk, improves responsiveness, and ultimately drives better business outcomes.

The financial implications of these benefits are substantial and quantifiable. Predictive maintenance, by reducing unexpected downtime and optimizing maintenance schedules, can lead to savings of 10-40% in maintenance costs. Performance optimization, through more efficient operation, can result in significant reductions in energy consumption and material waste, potentially saving millions annually for large enterprises. Accelerated design cycles and reduced prototyping costs can shave months off product development timelines, leading to faster market entry and increased revenue generation. Improved operational decision-making, by mitigating risks and enhancing efficiency, translates directly into reduced operational expenditures and increased profitability. While the initial investment in digital twin technology can be significant, the long-term return on investment, driven by these tangible cost savings and revenue enhancements, makes it a compelling proposition for organizations across all sectors. The ability to precisely quantify these savings, often through pilot projects and phased implementations, allows businesses to build a robust business case for adoption, demonstrating a clear path to profitability and competitive advantage.

Moreover, digital twins foster a culture of innovation by providing a safe and cost-effective environment for experimentation. Engineers and operators can test new ideas, explore "what-if" scenarios, and push the boundaries of operational performance without the risks associated with making changes in the physical world. This iterative exploration, powered by the digital twin, can lead to breakthrough innovations in product design, operational processes, and business models. For example, a logistics company might use a digital twin of its delivery network to experiment with new routing algorithms or delivery strategies. They can simulate the impact of introducing autonomous delivery vehicles or optimizing delivery windows based on predicted customer demand. This allows them to identify the most effective strategies before committing significant resources to physical implementation. This ability to rapidly prototype and validate new concepts in a virtual environment accelerates the pace of innovation and allows organizations to stay ahead of the curve in rapidly evolving markets. The insights gleaned from these simulations can also spark entirely new business opportunities, transforming how companies operate and serve their customers.

The value proposition of digital twins is further amplified by their ability to enhance sustainability and environmental responsibility. By optimizing energy consumption, minimizing waste, and extending the lifespan of assets, digital twins contribute directly to more sustainable operations. For example, a digital twin of a manufacturing plant can identify inefficiencies in energy usage and recommend adjustments to machinery operation or production schedules to reduce overall carbon footprint. In the agricultural sector, digital twins of farms can optimize irrigation and fertilization, leading to reduced water usage and chemical runoff. The ability to monitor and predict the environmental impact of operations allows organizations to make more informed decisions that balance economic objectives with ecological considerations. This is becoming increasingly critical as regulatory pressures and consumer demand for sustainable practices grow. Digital twins provide the tools to not only achieve compliance but also to proactively drive environmental improvements, positioning organizations as responsible corporate citizens and enhancing their brand reputation. The detailed performance data can also be used to verify sustainability claims and demonstrate progress towards environmental goals to stakeholders, investors, and regulatory bodies.

In conclusion, the value proposition of digital twins is multifaceted and profoundly impactful. They offer an unprecedented level of insight and control over physical assets and processes, leading to demonstrably enhanced monitoring, highly effective predictive maintenance, optimized performance, more efficient design cycles, streamlined operational decision-making, and accelerated innovation. These benefits translate directly into significant cost reductions, increased revenue opportunities, improved safety, and a stronger competitive position. As the technology matures and its adoption becomes more widespread, digital twins are evolving from a cutting-edge capability to an essential foundation for operational excellence, driving efficiency, sustainability, and continuous improvement across the global industrial landscape. The case for their adoption is no longer a matter of technological curiosity, but a strategic imperative for organizations seeking to thrive in the complexities of the modern economy.

The power of digital twins, as we have explored, is not confined to a single sector or a niche application. Instead, their inherent adaptability and the fundamental advantages they offer – enhanced visibility, predictive capabilities, and simulation power – allow them to permeate and revolutionize a vast array of industries. This section delves into the diverse landscape of digital twin adoption, highlighting how this technology is being tailored to meet the unique challenges and opportunities presented by different domains.

In the realm of
aerospace, digital twins have become instrumental from the very inception of an aircraft's life. During the design and engineering phases, intricate digital models of components, sub-systems, and entire aircraft are created. These twins allow engineers to conduct extensive virtual testing and validation. For instance, a digital twin of a new engine design can be subjected to millions of simulated flight hours under extreme conditions, revealing potential stress points, thermal issues, or material fatigue long before any physical prototype is built. This rigorous virtual testing significantly reduces the need for costly and time-consuming physical prototypes, accelerates the development cycle, and enhances

the overall safety and reliability of the final product. Beyond design, digital twins are crucial for lifecycle management. Once an aircraft is in service, its operational twin continuously collects real-time data on engine performance, structural integrity, and system health. This data fuels predictive maintenance, allowing airlines to schedule interventions precisely when needed, thereby minimizing costly unplanned downtime and ensuring passenger safety. For instance, subtle deviations in turbine blade vibration or exhaust gas temperatures, captured by the digital twin, can signal the onset of a potential issue, enabling maintenance crews to address it proactively during scheduled layovers, rather than facing an in-flight emergency or a grounded aircraft. Furthermore, these operational twins provide invaluable insights for the design of future aircraft, creating a virtuous cycle of continuous improvement informed by real-world performance.

The
automotive industry mirrors many of the aerospace applications, with digital twins playing a pivotal role in both product development and ongoing operations. For new vehicle models, digital twins enable engineers to simulate everything from crashworthiness and aerodynamic performance to the intricate functioning of complex electronic systems and battery management for electric vehicles. Virtual crash tests, for example, allow for rapid iteration on structural designs to meet stringent safety regulations and enhance occupant protection, a process that would be prohibitively expensive and time-consuming with physical testing alone. The digital twin of a car also extends to its manufacturing process. A twin of the assembly line can be used to optimize workflow, identify bottlenecks, and ensure quality control by simulating the impact of different production parameters or robotic movements. Once a vehicle is on the road, its digital twin continues to evolve. Connected car technology feeds real-time data back to the manufacturer, enabling remote diagnostics, over-the-air software updates, and predictive maintenance alerts for components like brakes, batteries, or tires. This allows for a more personalized and proactive ownership experience, reducing unexpected breakdowns and extending the vehicle's lifespan. For example, a digital twin can monitor the wear patterns of brake pads based on driving habits and environmental conditions, notifying the owner when replacement is recommended, rather than relying on a generic mileage-based schedule. The collected data also provides critical feedback for future vehicle designs, ensuring that improvements are directly informed by how customers actually use their cars.

In the
manufacturing sector, digital twins are perhaps most widely recognized for their transformative impact on operational efficiency and quality control. At its core, a digital twin of a factory or a specific production line creates a virtual replica of the physical operations. This allows for unparalleled insights into every stage of the manufacturing process. For a complex assembly line, a digital twin can monitor the performance of individual machines – their speed, temperature, vibration, and energy consumption – in real-time. By analyzing this data, manufacturers can identify inefficiencies, predict equipment failures, and optimize production schedules to maximize throughput. For instance, if a CNC machine's cutting tool begins to show signs of wear through increased vibration or altered power draw, its digital twin can flag this anomaly. This triggers an alert for a planned tool change during a scheduled maintenance window, preventing a defect in the manufactured part and avoiding costly downtime caused by a broken tool. Beyond individual machines, the twin of the entire production flow can simulate the impact of changes in raw material supply, order volumes, or new product introductions, allowing for proactive adjustments to prevent disruptions. Furthermore, digital twins are essential for ensuring product quality. By linking the digital twin of a product with the digital twin of the manufacturing process that created it, manufacturers can trace any potential defects back to their root cause. This granular level of traceability is invaluable for quality assurance, root cause analysis of failures, and continuous process improvement, enabling manufacturers to achieve higher levels of precision and consistency. The ability to run "what-if" scenarios – such as simulating the impact of a new material or a change in processing parameters on product quality – without disrupting actual production is a cornerstone of lean manufacturing and continuous improvement initiatives.

The
energy sector, encompassing power generation, transmission, and distribution, is another domain where digital twins are proving to be indispensable. For power plants, whether they are fossil fuel, nuclear, or renewable energy facilities, digital twins of turbines, generators, and other critical assets provide continuous, real-time performance monitoring. This allows operators to optimize energy output, detect anomalies indicative of potential failures, and schedule maintenance proactively. In the case of wind farms, for example, digital twins of

each turbine can be integrated into a larger digital twin of the entire farm. This allows for the optimization of individual turbine pitch and yaw angles based on real-time wind patterns across the entire farm, not just at the individual turbine's location, leading to increased overall energy generation. For grid management, digital twins of the electrical grid enable operators to monitor the flow of electricity, predict demand fluctuations, and simulate the impact of outages or the integration of new energy sources like solar or wind. This enhanced visibility and predictive capability are crucial for maintaining grid stability and reliability, especially as grids become more complex and incorporate distributed energy resources. For instance, a digital twin can predict potential overloads on specific transmission lines based on forecasted weather conditions and energy demand, allowing operators to reroute power or activate reserve capacity to prevent blackouts. The ability to simulate various grid configurations and responses to disruptions provides a robust framework for ensuring energy security and resilience.

The
healthcare industry is increasingly leveraging digital twins, particularly in the realms of personalized medicine, surgical planning, and hospital operations. Digital twins of patients, created from their medical history, genetic data, imaging scans, and real-time biometric monitoring, are paving the way for highly personalized treatments. Surgeons can use a digital twin of a patient's organ or anatomical structure to plan complex surgical procedures with unprecedented accuracy, practicing the operation in a virtual environment to anticipate potential complications and optimize the surgical approach. For example, a digital twin of a tumor can be used to precisely map its boundaries and relationship to surrounding vital structures, guiding robotic surgery or radiation therapy with enhanced precision. Beyond individual patient care, digital twins of hospitals can optimize resource allocation, patient flow, and staff scheduling. By creating a virtual replica of the hospital's facilities, equipment, and patient pathways, administrators can identify bottlenecks in emergency rooms, optimize operating room utilization, and ensure that critical equipment is available when and where it is needed. This leads to improved patient outcomes, reduced wait times, and more efficient use of hospital resources. The ability to simulate the impact of different staffing models or ward configurations allows for data-driven decision-making to enhance operational efficiency and patient care delivery.

In the
construction and infrastructure sector, digital twins are transforming how buildings, bridges, and urban environments are designed, built, and managed. A digital twin of a building, often referred to as a "digital building twin" or integrated into a "digital twin of an asset," can be created during the design phase and evolve through construction and into the operational life of the structure. During construction, it provides a precise visual and data-rich model for project management, ensuring that the physical build aligns with the design, tracking progress, and managing resources effectively. Once completed, the operational digital twin becomes a powerful tool for facility management. It can monitor building performance metrics such as energy consumption, occupancy levels, HVAC system status, and structural health. For a large commercial building, this twin can detect anomalies like unusual energy spikes in specific zones, correlate them with occupancy data, and automatically adjust climate control systems or alert maintenance staff, leading to significant energy savings and improved occupant comfort. Furthermore, digital twins of infrastructure like bridges or roads allow for the continuous monitoring of structural integrity. Sensors embedded within these structures can feed data to their digital twins, enabling the prediction of maintenance needs and the proactive identification of potential issues, thereby ensuring public safety and extending the lifespan of critical assets. The ability to simulate the impact of environmental factors, such as seismic activity or extreme weather, on these structures also enhances their resilience and informs long-term planning.

The
retail and logistics industries are also embracing digital twins to optimize operations and enhance customer experiences. In retail, digital twins of stores can be used to model customer flow, optimize product placement, and simulate the impact of new store layouts or promotional campaigns on sales. By analyzing data from in-store sensors and point-of-sale systems, retailers can gain a deep understanding of shopper behavior and make data-driven decisions to improve the in-store experience and increase revenue. For logistics and supply chain management, digital twins offer end-to-end visibility. A digital twin of a supply chain can map out every node, from raw material suppliers to manufacturing facilities, distribution centers, and end customers. This allows for real-time tracking of goods, prediction of potential disruptions (such as delays in shipping

or port congestion), and optimization of inventory levels. For instance, a digital twin can simulate the impact of a natural disaster affecting a key transportation hub, allowing the logistics company to proactively reroute shipments and minimize customer impact. The ability to run "what-if" scenarios, such as testing the efficiency of different delivery routes or the impact of adding new distribution centers, enables companies to build more resilient and cost-effective supply chains. For e-commerce operations, digital twins can also model warehouse operations, optimizing picking, packing, and shipping processes to ensure faster delivery times and reduced operational costs.

Even in sectors like
agriculture, digital twins are beginning to show significant promise. Digital twins of farms can integrate data from sensors monitoring soil moisture, nutrient levels, weather patterns, and crop health. This allows farmers to optimize irrigation and fertilization, leading to more efficient resource utilization, reduced environmental impact, and improved crop yields. For example, a digital twin can predict the precise amount of water and fertilizer a specific section of a field needs based on real-time conditions and crop growth stage, minimizing waste and maximizing output. This precision agriculture approach not only boosts productivity but also contributes to more sustainable farming practices.

The overarching theme across these diverse applications is the remarkable versatility of the digital twin concept. While the specific implementation and the data inputs may vary significantly from one industry to another, the fundamental principle remains consistent: creating a dynamic, virtual representation of a physical asset, process, or system to enable enhanced monitoring, analysis, simulation, and optimization. This adaptability makes digital twins a powerful, cross-industry tool for driving innovation, efficiency, and competitive advantage in the digital age.

Chapter 2: Fundamentals of Model Fidelity

The concept of model fidelity within the realm of digital twins is paramount. It refers to the degree to which a digital twin accurately mirrors the behavior, characteristics, and current state of its physical counterpart. This is not a static or absolute metric but rather a dynamic and relative attribute, intrinsically linked to the specific purpose and intended application of the digital twin. A digital twin designed for high-level performance monitoring might require a different level of fidelity than one intended for detailed stress analysis of a critical component. The accuracy and comprehensiveness of the virtual representation directly influence the twin's ability to provide meaningful insights, enable reliable simulations, and support effective decision-making.

At its core, fidelity in digital twins addresses the question: "How well does the virtual model capture the essence of the physical entity it represents?" This essence can encompass a wide range of aspects, from the physical dimensions and material properties of an object to its dynamic operational behavior, its environmental interactions, and even its underlying logical processes. For a physical asset like an aircraft engine, model fidelity would involve capturing its mechanical tolerances, its thermodynamic responses under varying fuel flows and ambient temperatures, its vibration patterns, and its wear and tear characteristics. For a manufacturing process, fidelity might relate to the precise timings of each operation, the interactions between machines, the flow of materials, and the quality control checkpoints. In essence, higher fidelity means a closer, more intricate, and more accurate representation of reality.

However, it is crucial to understand that achieving absolute fidelity is often neither feasible nor necessary. The pursuit of perfect replication can lead to overly complex and computationally expensive models that are impractical for real-time operation or timely analysis. Therefore, the determination of "sufficient" fidelity is a critical design consideration. This sufficiency is dictated by the intended use case. For example, if a digital twin is being used to simply track the operational status of a fleet of wind turbines – whether they are online, offline, or experiencing minor faults – a moderate level of fidelity might suffice. This would involve modeling basic operational parameters like power output, rotational speed, and fault codes. However, if the same digital twin were to be used for optimizing the aerodynamic performance of individual turbines under complex wind conditions or for predicting the precise moment of component failure due to fatigue, a significantly higher level of fidelity would be required. This would necessitate incorporating detailed aerodynamic simulations, material stress analysis, and sophisticated fatigue modeling, all of which demand a much richer and more accurate representation of the physical system and its underlying physics.

The concept of fidelity can be broken down into several key dimensions, each contributing to the overall accuracy and usefulness of a digital twin:

Firstly,
Geometric Fidelity pertains to the accuracy of the digital twin's spatial representation. This includes the dimensions, shape, and topological relationships of the physical object. For a manufactured part, geometric fidelity ensures that the virtual model precisely matches the design specifications. For a building or a piece of infrastructure, it means capturing the exact layout, structural elements, and spatial arrangements. This is fundamental for tasks like clash detection during design, simulation of fluid dynamics, or virtual assembly. A high degree of geometric fidelity is crucial in applications where precise spatial relationships are critical, such as in robotics, additive manufacturing, or the simulation of physical interactions. For instance, in simulating the operation of a robotic arm on an assembly line, accurate geometric models of the arm, the parts it handles, and the surrounding environment are essential for collision avoidance and precise manipulation. Deviations in geometric fidelity here could lead to simulated collisions that wouldn't occur physically, or conversely, missed collisions in the simulation that could lead to real-world damage.

Secondly,
Behavioral Fidelity focuses on how accurately the digital twin replicates the dynamic behavior and functional performance of its physical counterpart. This involves modeling the cause-and-effect relationships, the physical laws, and the operational logic that govern the system. For an engine, behavioral fidelity means accurately predicting its power output under different load conditions, its fuel consumption, and its thermal response. For a complex software system, it involves replicating the sequence of operations, the data flows, and the system's

reactions to various inputs and environmental stimuli. This dimension is vital for simulations aimed at predicting performance, diagnosing faults, and optimizing operations. For example, a digital twin of a chemical reactor needs high behavioral fidelity to accurately simulate reaction kinetics, heat transfer, and mass transfer under varying process parameters. This allows operators to explore optimal operating conditions, predict product yield, and troubleshoot process deviations without risking an actual plant shutdown or hazardous incident. Low behavioral fidelity might result in simulations that suggest unrealistic operating windows or fail to capture critical dynamic instabilities.

Thirdly,
State Fidelity refers to the accuracy with which the digital twin reflects the current, real-time condition of its physical counterpart. This is achieved by continuously updating the digital twin with data from sensors, operational logs, and other real-time sources. A high degree of state fidelity ensures that the twin provides an accurate snapshot of the physical asset at any given moment, enabling real-time monitoring, anomaly detection, and immediate response. For a fleet of vehicles, state fidelity would mean knowing the current location, speed, fuel level, and operational status of each vehicle at all times. For a power grid, it means having an up-to-the-minute representation of power flow, voltage levels, and equipment status. This real-time accuracy is what distinguishes a digital twin from a static simulation model. Consider a digital twin of a hospital's intensive care unit. High state fidelity would involve real-time updates on patient vital signs, ventilator settings, and equipment availability. This allows clinical staff to monitor patients remotely, respond rapidly to critical changes, and optimize the allocation of resources, thereby directly impacting patient care and safety. Without this real-time connection, the twin would be merely a historical record or a predictive tool, lacking the immediacy required for critical operational decisions.

Fourthly,
Contextual Fidelity addresses the accuracy of the digital twin's representation of the surrounding environment and external influences that affect the physical asset. This includes factors like ambient temperature, humidity, wind speed, electrical load, market conditions, or regulatory requirements. For an offshore wind turbine, contextual fidelity would involve accurately modeling wind profiles, wave conditions, and salinity. For a supply chain digital twin, it would

include factors like port congestion, weather patterns impacting transportation routes, and geopolitical events affecting supplier availability. Understanding and accurately modeling these external factors is crucial for realistic simulations and reliable predictions, especially in complex and dynamic systems. A digital twin of a solar farm, for instance, requires high contextual fidelity regarding local weather patterns, cloud cover, and irradiance levels to accurately predict energy generation. Without this, the twin's forecasts would be unreliable, impacting grid management and energy trading decisions.

Finally,
Data Fidelity concerns the quality, completeness, and accuracy of the data used to build and maintain the digital twin. This encompasses the accuracy of sensor readings, the integrity of historical data, and the reliability of data processing and integration pipelines. Poor data fidelity can lead to flawed models, inaccurate simulations, and misguided decisions, even if the modeling techniques themselves are sound. Ensuring data fidelity involves robust data validation, cleansing, and governance processes. For a pharmaceutical manufacturing process, the fidelity of the data used to train the digital twin – including raw material purity, process parameters, and quality test results – directly impacts the twin's ability to predict product quality and optimize production. Errors in batch records or analytical results can propagate through the twin, leading to incorrect conclusions about process robustness or product safety.

The level of fidelity required for each of these dimensions is highly application-dependent. A digital twin used for conceptual design and early-stage feasibility studies might prioritize geometric and basic behavioral fidelity, while a twin used for predictive maintenance and anomaly detection will demand high state and behavioral fidelity, underpinned by reliable data streams. Similarly, a twin intended for optimizing complex interactions within a smart city ecosystem will require significant contextual fidelity alongside geometric and behavioral representations of individual assets and services.

It's also important to recognize that fidelity is not a binary "yes" or "no" but exists on a spectrum. We can talk about low, medium, or high fidelity. A low-fidelity model might be a simplified representation that captures the essential characteristics but omits intricate details. For instance, a digital twin of a building for basic energy management might only model aggregated energy consumption patterns and occupancy levels. A medium-fidelity model would incorporate more detailed sub-systems and their interactions, perhaps modeling individual HVAC units and their control loops. A high-fidelity model would delve into the granular physics of heat transfer within each room, the precise efficiency curves of every component, and the complex interplay of all environmental factors. Each level of fidelity comes with trade-offs in terms of development effort, computational cost, and the depth of insights it can provide.

The selection of an appropriate fidelity level is a strategic decision in the digital twin lifecycle. It involves balancing the desired outcomes and benefits against the costs and complexities of implementation and maintenance. Over-engineering a digital twin by aiming for excessive fidelity can lead to prohibitive costs and slow performance, rendering it impractical. Conversely, under-engineering it can result in a tool that fails to deliver the expected value, offering only superficial insights or unreliable predictions. Therefore, a thorough understanding of the problem being solved, the decisions that will be made based on the twin's output, and the available data and computational resources is essential for defining and achieving the right level of model fidelity. This careful consideration ensures that the digital twin serves as a powerful and effective tool, not an over-engineered or under-performing digital replica.

The preceding discussion has established that model fidelity in digital twins is not a monolithic concept but rather a multifaceted characteristic, shaped by the intricate interplay of geometric, behavioral, state, contextual, and data dimensions. Each of these facets contributes to how accurately a digital twin mirrors its physical counterpart, with the degree of accuracy being a direct consequence of the intended application and the specific questions the twin is designed to answer. Now, we must delve deeper into another critical aspect that profoundly influences both the utility and the practicality of a digital twin: the levels of abstraction and granularity at which it is modeled. This consideration is intimately linked to fidelity, as the chosen level of detail directly dictates the depth of insight and the computational demands.

When we speak of abstraction and granularity in the context of digital twins, we are referring to the scale at which the physical system is represented within the digital realm. At its most abstract level, a digital twin might represent an entire enterprise or a complex ecosystem, focusing on high-level performance indicators, strategic flows, and interdependencies between major subsystems. Think, for instance, of a digital twin for a global logistics network. At this macro-level, the twin might not model individual trucks or shipping containers but rather the aggregated flow of goods between major distribution hubs, the performance of key transportation arteries, and the overall efficiency of the supply chain. The granularity here is coarse, focusing on broad trends and strategic decision-making. The data inputs would likely be aggregated operational statistics, market intelligence, and high-level performance metrics from various operational units. The primary purpose of such a twin would be to inform strategic planning, identify bottlenecks at a system-wide level, and assess the impact of major disruptions or policy changes. The accuracy at this level is concerned with the overall direction and magnitude of change, rather than pinpointing the exact cause of a minor delay. The trade-off here is clear: while this high-level abstraction provides a comprehensive overview and is computationally less demanding, it sacrifices the ability to diagnose specific operational issues or optimize individual processes. The insights derived are strategic and directional, valuable for executive decision-making but insufficient for operational troubleshooting.

Moving down the ladder of abstraction, we encounter digital twins that represent distinct systems or complex subsystems. Continuing with the logistics example, this level might focus on a specific regional distribution network or a particular mode of transportation, such as a fleet of delivery vehicles. Here, the granularity increases. Instead of just aggregated flows, the twin might model individual depots, the routes taken by vehicles, the capacity of warehouse space, and the operational efficiency of different vehicle types. The data streams would become more specific, including real-time vehicle location and status, warehouse inventory levels, and traffic conditions on specific routes. The purpose shifts from strategic to operational and tactical. Such a twin could be used for optimizing delivery routes, managing fleet deployment, predicting potential delays based on real-time traffic and weather, and improving warehouse utilization. The accuracy required is higher, as decisions made at this level directly impact day-to-day operations. The computational cost also rises, as more individual entities and their interactions need to be modeled and simulated. For example, a digital twin of a fleet of 100 delivery trucks might involve modeling the GPS data, engine diagnostics, delivery schedules, and fuel consumption for each vehicle. This is significantly more complex than modeling the entire fleet as a single entity representing its total carrying capacity.

At an even finer level of granularity, a digital twin can represent individual assets or components. In our logistics scenario, this could mean a digital twin of a single truck, focusing on its engine performance, tire wear, braking systems, and cargo loading mechanisms. Or it could be a digital twin of a specific piece of warehouse machinery, like a robotic arm or a conveyor belt. The abstraction is minimal; the focus is on the intricate details of the physical entity itself. This is where behavioral fidelity becomes paramount, requiring detailed physics-based simulations of component interactions, material stress, thermal dynamics, and wear mechanisms. The data inputs are rich and granular, sourced from high-frequency sensor data such as vibration analysis, temperature monitoring, pressure readings, and detailed diagnostic codes. The primary purpose at this level is typically predictive maintenance, fault diagnosis, root cause analysis of failures, and performance optimization of individual units. For instance, a digital twin of a truck's engine could predict the remaining useful life of specific components, allowing for scheduled maintenance before a failure occurs, thereby minimizing downtime and repair costs. The computational requirements here are substantial, as detailed simulations of physical phenomena are often necessary. A high-fidelity engine model might incorporate millions of data points and complex thermodynamic equations.

The choice of abstraction and granularity is a fundamental design decision that involves inherent trade-offs. A high level of abstraction, characterized by coarse granularity, offers a broad, system-wide perspective. It is computationally efficient and can provide valuable insights for strategic planning and high-level decision-making. However, it lacks the detail needed to understand or resolve granular operational issues. The insights are often macro-economic or macro-performance oriented. For example, a digital twin of a national power grid at a highly abstract level might show overall generation capacity versus demand and identify regions with potential overloads. It could inform national energy policy or the strategic placement of new power plants.

Conversely, a low level of abstraction, characterized by fine granularity, provides a deep, detailed understanding of individual assets or processes. It enables precise fault diagnosis, accurate prediction of component failure, and granular optimization. However, this depth comes at a cost: increased complexity, significantly higher computational demands, and potentially a more challenging integration of vast amounts of detailed data. A digital twin of a single wind turbine's gearbox, operating at a very fine granularity, might analyze minute vibrations and temperature fluctuations to predict the precise moment a specific bearing is likely to fail. This allows for highly targeted maintenance. But aggregating such detailed twins for an entire wind farm, let alone a national grid, would quickly become computationally intractable and logistically overwhelming if the goal was only to understand overall grid stability.

Consider a manufacturing plant as another illustrative example. At a high level of abstraction, a digital twin of the plant might represent the overall production throughput, the utilization rates of major production lines, and the flow of materials between different departments. This twin would be useful for production planning, capacity management, and identifying systemic inefficiencies. The data might consist of aggregated production counts, shift schedules, and inventory levels at key points. This level of representation is relatively easy to build and run, making it suitable for quick analysis and strategic adjustments. The trade-off is that it cannot pinpoint the exact cause of a minor quality defect in a specific product or diagnose a subtle issue with a particular machine.

As we reduce the abstraction, we can model individual production lines. This digital twin would incorporate more detail about the machines within that line, their operating parameters, their interdependencies, and the sequence of operations. It could be used to optimize the scheduling of work orders, identify bottlenecks within the line, and diagnose performance degradation. The data requirements increase, including sensor readings from individual machines, quality control data at various stages, and detailed process parameters. This level of granularity allows for more effective operational management and troubleshooting of specific production lines.

Further reducing abstraction leads to modeling individual machines or even specific components within a machine. A digital twin of a CNC milling machine, for example, might simulate the toolpath, spindle speed, feed rates, and the forces exerted on the workpiece and the tool. This allows for optimizing machining processes to improve surface finish, reduce tool wear, and prevent machine damage. The data here is highly granular, involving high-frequency sensor data from the machine's control system, including positions, velocities, temperatures, and current draw. The computational cost is significant, and the focus is on very specific operational aspects. The ultimate granularity might be a digital twin of a single critical cutting tool, modeling its material properties, wear characteristics, and how it interacts with different workpiece materials under various cutting conditions. This would enable extremely precise tool life prediction and optimization.

The selection of the appropriate level of abstraction and granularity is therefore a crucial balancing act. It requires a deep understanding of the use case: what questions need to be answered? What decisions will be made based on the digital twin's output? What level of accuracy is required to support those decisions? It also necessitates an assessment of available resources: computational power, data acquisition capabilities, and the expertise of the development team.

A common pitfall is the tendency to over-engineer a digital twin by aiming for the highest possible fidelity and the finest granularity across all dimensions, regardless of necessity. This often leads to models that are computationally intractable, prohibitively expensive to develop and maintain, and ultimately too slow to provide timely insights. Imagine trying to build a digital twin of an entire city at the level of individual atoms for every building, vehicle, and person – it's an extreme example, but it illustrates the point that excessive granularity serves no practical purpose and creates insurmountable challenges.

Conversely, under-engineering a digital twin, using too high a level of abstraction for problems that require detailed analysis, renders it ineffective. A strategic planner trying to understand why a particular batch of products failed quality control will find little use for a digital twin that only reports overall plant throughput.

The concept of "purpose-driven modeling" becomes paramount here. The fidelity, abstraction, and granularity of a digital twin should be directly aligned with its intended purpose. For instance, a digital twin for real-time operational monitoring might prioritize state fidelity and a moderate level of behavioral fidelity at a granularity that reflects key operational units. A twin for long-term strategic planning might focus on aggregated behavioral models and contextual fidelity at a high level of abstraction. A twin for detailed engineering analysis or predictive maintenance would necessitate fine granularity and high fidelity across geometric, behavioral, and state dimensions for the specific components being analyzed.

Furthermore, it's important to recognize that digital twins can exist at multiple levels of abstraction simultaneously, forming a hierarchy or a federated network of twins. In such architectures, a high-level system twin might be composed of interconnected lower-level subsystem twins, which in turn are composed of individual asset twins. This hierarchical approach allows for a comprehensive view while enabling drill-down capabilities into specific areas of interest. For example, a digital twin of a smart factory could have a top-level twin representing overall production efficiency, which links to twins for each production line, and further links to twins for individual critical machines within those lines. This federated approach allows different teams to focus on their specific areas of responsibility while maintaining an integrated view of the entire system. The challenge then shifts to ensuring interoperability and effective communication between these different twins, each potentially operating at a different level of abstraction and granularity. The data flows and interfaces between these interconnected twins become critical design considerations, ensuring that information is passed up and down the hierarchy accurately and efficiently. For instance, a fault detected at the machine level needs to be appropriately aggregated and communicated to the production line twin and potentially to the overall factory twin to inform broader operational adjustments.

The decision on granularity also influences the types of simulations that can be performed. Highly abstract models might be suitable for steady-state analysis or trend forecasting. As granularity increases, the twin becomes capable of more dynamic simulations, transient analysis, and complex "what-if" scenarios. A detailed, finely-grained model of a chemical reactor, for example, can simulate the complex interplay of reaction kinetics, heat transfer, and fluid dynamics, allowing engineers to explore the effects of sudden changes in feed composition or temperature on product yield and safety. A more abstract model of the entire chemical plant might only be able to predict the impact of such changes on overall plant output or profitability.

In conclusion, the judicious selection of abstraction and granularity is not merely a technical detail but a strategic imperative in the design and deployment of digital twins. It is the key to ensuring that the digital twin provides meaningful insights without becoming an unmanageable computational burden. It requires a clear understanding of the problem domain, the desired outcomes, and the inherent trade-offs between comprehensiveness and computational feasibility. By aligning the level of detail with the purpose, organizations can unlock the true potential of digital twins as powerful tools for analysis, prediction, optimization, and informed decision-making across all levels of an enterprise. This deliberate choice ensures that the digital twin remains a valuable asset, providing actionable intelligence rather than simply a digital replica divorced from practical utility.

The creation of a digital twin that accurately reflects its physical counterpart hinges on the fundamental principles of physics-based modeling. This approach grounds the virtual representation in the immutable laws of nature, providing a robust and inherently interpretable framework for understanding and predicting the behavior of complex systems. Unlike purely data-driven or empirical models, physics-based models leverage established scientific principles to describe the underlying mechanisms governing a system's operation. This deterministic nature ensures that the digital twin's behavior is not an artifact of statistical correlations but a direct consequence of the physical phenomena at play.

At the core of physics-based modeling lies the application of fundamental physical laws. These are the bedrock upon which our understanding of the universe is built, encompassing concepts such as conservation of mass, momentum, and energy. For instance, in modeling the flow of fluids within a pipe, the principle of conservation of mass dictates that the rate at which fluid enters a control volume must equal the rate at which it leaves, assuming no accumulation or depletion within that volume. Similarly, the conservation of momentum, famously articulated by Newton's laws of motion, governs how forces applied to an object affect its velocity and direction. The conservation of energy, often expressed through the first law of thermodynamics, states that energy cannot be created or destroyed, only transformed from one form to another. These fundamental laws, when translated into mathematical equations, form the mathematical skeleton of a physics-based model.

Consider a simple example: modeling the temperature change of a metallic rod exposed to a heat source at one end. The governing principle here is the conservation of energy, specifically applied through Fourier's Law of Heat Conduction. This law states that the rate of heat transfer through a material is proportional to the negative temperature gradient and the area, and inversely proportional to the thickness. Mathematically, this can be expressed as a partial differential equation: $q = -k A \frac{dT}{dx}$, where q is the rate of heat transfer, k is the thermal conductivity of the material, A is the cross-sectional area, and $\frac{dT}{dx}$ is the temperature gradient. To model the dynamic temperature distribution along the rod over time, one would combine this with the principle of energy storage within the rod's volume, leading to the heat equation: $\rho c_p \frac{\partial T}{\partial t} = \frac{\partial}{\partial x} (k \frac{\partial T}{\partial x})$, where ρ is the density, c_p is the specific heat capacity, and $\frac{\partial T}{\partial t}$ is the rate of change of temperature with time. Solving this equation, subject to appropriate boundary conditions (e.g., the temperature at the heated end and the insulated end), allows for a precise prediction of the temperature profile along the rod at any given time. This level of predictive power, derived directly from physical laws, is a hallmark of physics-based modeling and is crucial for achieving high fidelity in a digital twin.

Beyond conservation laws, constitutive relations are another vital component of physics-based models. These relations describe the intrinsic properties of materials and how they respond to external stimuli. For example, in solid mechanics, Hooke's Law is a constitutive relation that describes the linear elastic behavior of many materials, stating that stress is directly proportional to strain within the elastic limit ($\sigma = E\epsilon$, where σ is stress, ϵ is strain, and E is the Young's modulus). In fluid dynamics, the viscosity of a fluid is a constitutive property that determines its resistance to flow and is essential for models like the Navier-Stokes equations, which describe the motion of viscous fluid substances. These relationships provide the "material" characteristics that imbue the digital twin with realistic behavior.

For instance, if we are modeling a suspension bridge, the behavior of the steel cables and concrete pillars will be described by their respective constitutive relations. For the steel cables, this might involve their tensile strength, elastic modulus, and potentially their behavior under cyclic loading (fatigue). For the concrete pillars, it could include their compressive strength, their response to shear forces, and their thermal expansion properties. When a wind load is applied to the bridge, the physics-based model would use the principles of structural mechanics (equilibrium of forces, deformation equations) and the constitutive relations of the materials to predict how the bridge deforms, what stresses develop within its components, and whether any part approaches its failure limits. The accuracy of these predictions is directly tied to the accuracy of the constitutive models used.

The advantage of using these deterministic, physics-based equations is their inherent interpretability and predictability. Unlike a black-box model that might predict an outcome without revealing the underlying reasons, a physics-based model provides a clear causal link between inputs, parameters, and outputs. If the digital twin predicts a failure, the model can be interrogated to understand which physical law was violated, which parameter exceeded its limit, or which constitutive relation indicated yielding or fracture. This transparency is invaluable for engineering design, root cause analysis, and optimizing performance. It allows engineers to not just observe a problem but to understand its origin within the physical reality being simulated.

Furthermore, physics-based models are inherently extensible and adaptable. As our understanding of physics evolves or as new materials with novel properties are developed, these models can be updated and refined. For example, as research into non-Newtonian fluids progresses, more sophisticated constitutive relations can be incorporated into fluid dynamics models, leading to more accurate digital twins of systems involving such fluids. Similarly, advancements in material science might lead to constitutive models that better capture the complex behavior of composites or advanced alloys under extreme conditions. This inherent flexibility ensures that physics-based digital twins can remain relevant and accurate as technologies and scientific knowledge advance.

The mathematical formulation of these physical laws often leads to systems of differential equations, which can be solved using various numerical methods. For complex geometries or boundary conditions, analytical solutions may not be feasible, necessitating the use of techniques like the Finite Element Method (FEM), Finite Volume Method (FVM), or Computational Fluid Dynamics (CFD). FEM, for example, discretizes a continuous system into a mesh of smaller, interconnected elements. The governing equations are then applied to each element, and the solutions are assembled to approximate the behavior of the entire system. This allows for the modeling of intricate geometries and complex physical phenomena, such as stress concentrations around a hole in a structural component or the turbulent flow patterns within a jet engine.

Let's consider a more elaborate example: modeling the structural integrity of an aircraft wing under flight loads. This would involve applying principles of solid mechanics and elasticity. The wing's geometry would be meticulously defined, and a fine mesh of finite elements would be generated. The material properties of the aluminum alloys, composites, and other materials used in the wing's construction would be incorporated as constitutive relations. The forces acting on the wing during flight, such as aerodynamic lift, drag, and inertial forces due to maneuvering, would be calculated and applied as boundary conditions. The governing equations, often derived from the principle of minimum potential energy or virtual work, would then be solved using FEM software. The resulting model would predict stress distribution, strain, deformation, and potential failure modes under various flight conditions. This level of detail, driven by physics, is essential for ensuring the safety and performance of an aircraft.

The fidelity of a physics-based model is directly proportional to the accuracy and completeness of the physical laws and constitutive relations incorporated, as well as the numerical methods used to solve them. A simplified model might use linear elastic assumptions for materials, while a higher-fidelity model might incorporate plasticity, viscoelasticity, and damage mechanics. Similarly, a basic heat transfer model might only consider conduction, while a more advanced one would include convection and radiation. The choice of which physical laws and constitutive relations to include, and at what level of detail, depends entirely on the intended application of the digital twin.

For instance, a digital twin of a bridge intended for long-term structural health monitoring might not require the same level of detail in its fluid dynamics simulation of wind gusts as a digital twin designed to analyze the aerodynamic flutter of a specific wing component at high speeds. The former might focus on large-scale deformations and stress accumulation over time under static or slowly varying loads, while the latter would need to capture rapid, dynamic phenomena governed by fluid-structure interaction. This tailored application of physics-based principles ensures that computational resources are used efficiently and that the model provides the necessary insights for its specific purpose.

The interpretability of physics-based models also extends to their ability to perform "what-if" analyses with physical grounding. If an engineer wishes to understand the impact of using a stronger, lighter material for a component, a physics-based model can directly incorporate the new material's properties and re-simulate the system's behavior. The results will clearly show the consequences in terms of reduced stress, increased stiffness, or extended fatigue life, all explained through the underlying physical principles. This is far more powerful than simply observing a change in an output metric in a black-box model. It provides understanding and confidence in the design modifications.

Another crucial aspect of physics-based modeling is its role in identifying the necessary parameters and inputs for the digital twin. The physical laws themselves dictate what factors are relevant. For example, if modeling combustion in an engine, the governing equations will highlight the importance of fuel-air ratios, ignition timing, temperature, and pressure. This guides sensor selection and data acquisition strategies for the physical asset, ensuring that the most critical variables are measured and fed into the digital twin. Without this guidance, data collection might be haphazard, leading to incomplete or irrelevant information for accurate simulation.

While physics-based modeling offers significant advantages, it is important to acknowledge its challenges. Developing these models can be complex and requires a deep understanding of the relevant physics and mathematics. The computational cost can also be substantial, especially for large, intricate systems that require fine discretization and complex solver algorithms. Furthermore, the accuracy of the model is entirely dependent on the accuracy of the input parameters and the fidelity of the constitutive relations. If, for example, the thermal conductivity of a material is inaccurately specified, the heat transfer simulation will yield incorrect results, regardless of how perfectly the heat equation is solved.

This is where the integration of physics-based modeling with data-driven approaches becomes particularly powerful. While physics provides the fundamental framework and predictability, empirical data can be used to calibrate model parameters, validate simulation results, and even refine constitutive relations where purely theoretical descriptions are insufficient. For example, in modeling the wear of a cutting tool, the fundamental physics of material removal and friction can be established. However, the exact rate of wear under varying conditions might be best determined by analyzing sensor data from actual machining operations. This hybrid approach, often termed "physics-informed machine learning" or "hybrid modeling," leverages the strengths of both methodologies to create digital twins that are both accurate and robust.

The deterministic nature of physics-based models also means they are inherently good at extrapolation. If a model is built on sound physical principles, it can often predict behavior outside the range of observed data, provided the underlying physics remain valid. For instance, a well-validated structural model of a bridge could predict its behavior under loads significantly higher than those it has experienced, offering insights into its ultimate load capacity. Data-driven models, by contrast, often struggle with extrapolation, as their predictions are based on interpolating within the observed data space.

In conclusion, physics-based modeling principles form the bedrock of high-fidelity digital twins. By grounding virtual representations in the fundamental laws of nature and employing rigorous mathematical formulations and constitutive relations, these models offer unparalleled interpretability, predictability, and robustness. They provide a clear causal understanding of system behavior, enabling precise diagnosis, reliable forecasting, and informed decision-making. While challenges related to complexity and computational cost exist, the inherent advantages of physics-based approaches, particularly when combined with data-driven insights, make them an indispensable tool for creating digital twins that truly mirror and anticipate the behavior of their physical counterparts across a vast spectrum of engineering and scientific applications. The commitment to adhering to these physical principles ensures that a digital twin is not merely a digital shadow but a scientifically sound and reliable digital replica.

While physics-based models provide an indispensable framework rooted in scientific laws, their inherent idealizations and the complexities of real-world systems often necessitate the integration of data-driven approaches to achieve true fidelity in a digital twin. These data-driven methodologies act as crucial complements, enabling the digital twin to learn from and adapt to the nuanced behavior of its physical counterpart, thereby bridging the gap between theoretical understanding and practical observation. The primary conduits for this data integration are the sensors deployed on the physical asset and the historical performance logs meticulously maintained over its operational lifecycle. These sources of information are not merely passive repositories of past events; they are active streams that imbue the digital twin with a dynamic understanding of how the real-world system operates under a myriad of conditions.

The process of enhancing model fidelity through data begins with the fundamental concept of parameter calibration. Every physics-based model, regardless of its theoretical underpinnings, relies on a set of parameters that represent material properties, environmental conditions, or empirical constants. For instance, a model simulating the thermal performance of an industrial oven might include parameters for the thermal conductivity of the oven walls, the efficiency of the heating elements, and the heat transfer coefficients at the internal and external surfaces. While theoretical values or literature-based estimates can be used to initialize these parameters, real-world systems often exhibit variations due to manufacturing tolerances, aging effects, or subtle environmental influences not fully captured by the ideal physical laws. Sensor data, collected during the oven's operation—such as temperature readings at various points within the oven and ambient temperature measurements—provides invaluable ground truth. By comparing the digital twin's predicted temperatures with these observed sensor readings, a process of optimization can be initiated. This process aims to adjust the model's parameters iteratively until the discrepancy between simulated and observed outputs is minimized. This is often achieved using optimization algorithms, such as gradient descent or Bayesian optimization, which systematically search for the parameter values that best fit the incoming data. For example, if the digital twin consistently predicts lower temperatures than observed, it might suggest that the assumed thermal conductivity of the oven walls is too low, or that the heating element efficiency is higher than initially modeled. Adjusting these parameters based on this discrepancy directly refines the model's ability to mimic the physical oven's thermal response.

Beyond static parameter calibration, data-driven techniques are essential for capturing dynamic system behaviors that might be poorly represented or entirely absent in a purely physics-based model. Consider a complex mechanical system, such as a robotic arm. While physics-based models can accurately describe the kinematics and dynamics of the arm's segments based on their mass, inertia, and joint characteristics, they may struggle to precisely account for factors like friction in the joints, backlash in the gears, or the subtle effects of lubrication degradation over time. These phenomena can lead to deviations in the arm's trajectory or its response to control signals. Historical operational data, collected from encoders on the joints, accelerometers, and force sensors, can reveal these deviations. By analyzing this data, machine learning algorithms can identify patterns that correlate specific command inputs or operating conditions with deviations from the ideal physics-based trajectory. This learned relationship can then be integrated into the digital twin as a correction factor or an additional behavioral model. For instance, a neural network might be trained to predict the additional torque required at a specific joint to achieve the desired motion, accounting for accumulated friction and backlash. This learned compensation, derived directly from observed performance, significantly enhances the digital twin's ability to replicate the precise movements of the physical robotic arm.

Historical performance logs offer another rich source of data for augmenting digital twins. These logs often contain records of operational parameters, maintenance actions, fault occurrences, and output metrics over extended periods. Analyzing this historical data can reveal correlations between operating conditions and system degradation or performance drift that are not easily predictable from first principles alone. For example, in a fleet of identical industrial pumps, historical logs might show that pumps operating at higher duty cycles or in environments with abrasive fluids experience significantly accelerated wear on their seals. A purely physics-based model might predict seal life based on theoretical wear rates, but it would likely not capture the nuanced dependency on operating history or environmental factors without extensive, and often impractical, empirical tuning. By employing data mining techniques on the historical logs, patterns associated with accelerated seal wear can be identified. This knowledge can then be used to update the digital twin. The twin could be programmed to estimate remaining seal life not just based on the current operating parameters, but also by considering the cumulative operational history and the likelihood of similar degradation pathways observed in the past. This predictive capability, informed by real-world experience, allows for more accurate maintenance scheduling and reduces the risk of unexpected equipment failures.

Furthermore, data-driven approaches are crucial for adaptive modeling, where the digital twin continuously learns and adjusts its behavior in response to ongoing operational data. This is particularly relevant for systems operating in highly variable or unpredictable environments. Imagine a solar power generation system. While physics-based models can accurately predict the energy output based on solar irradiance, ambient temperature, and panel characteristics, real-world performance can be affected by soiling of the panels, degradation of the inverters, and localized atmospheric conditions not captured by general weather forecasts. Continuous monitoring of energy output, panel temperatures, and inverter efficiencies through sensors provides a constant stream of performance data. Machine learning algorithms can analyze this data in near real-time to detect anomalies or deviations from expected performance. For instance, if the actual power output consistently falls below the physics-based prediction for given weather conditions, it might indicate panel soiling or degradation. The digital twin can then adapt its energy generation prediction model to reflect this diminished performance, or it can flag the physical asset for cleaning or inspection. This adaptive capability ensures that the digital twin remains a relevant and accurate representation of the physical system's current state and performance, even as the physical system itself evolves.

The concept of "physics-informed machine learning" (PIML) represents a powerful paradigm for integrating data with physics-based models. In this approach, machine learning models are not trained solely on empirical data, but their learning process is constrained or guided by the underlying physical laws. For instance, when developing a data-driven model to predict fluid flow, PIML might incorporate the Navier-Stokes equations as a soft constraint during the training of a neural network. This means the neural network is encouraged to learn solutions that are not only consistent with the training data but also satisfy the fundamental principles of fluid dynamics. This combination offers several advantages. Firstly, it can significantly reduce the amount of data required for training, as the physical laws provide a strong inductive bias. Secondly, it enhances the model's generalization capabilities, allowing it to make more reliable predictions even for conditions not extensively represented in the training data. Thirdly, it can lead to more interpretable and physically plausible models. For a digital twin, this hybrid approach can lead to models that are both highly accurate in predicting observed behavior and robust enough to reason about unseen scenarios, drawing on the foundational understanding provided by physics.

Consider the application of PIML in a structural health monitoring digital twin for a bridge. A purely data-driven model might learn to predict the likelihood of a specific failure mode based on historical sensor data (e.g., strain gauges, accelerometers). However, without explicit physical grounding, such a model might struggle to identify the root cause of the anomaly or to predict the effect of a novel load condition. By incorporating the principles of structural mechanics—such as equilibrium equations and constitutive laws for bridge materials—into the machine learning training process, the digital twin can develop a more sophisticated understanding. The PIML model might learn to not only predict an increased risk of fatigue crack propagation but also to attribute this risk to specific stress concentrations identified through physics-based analysis, informed by real-time strain measurements. This allows for more precise diagnostics and targeted maintenance interventions, significantly enhancing the overall fidelity and utility of the digital twin.

Moreover, data-driven approaches are instrumental in identifying and quantifying uncertainties within the digital twin. Physics-based models, while deterministic, often rely on input parameters that have associated uncertainties, or they may employ simplifications that introduce model uncertainty. For example, the precise friction coefficient in a gear train might be unknown, or the exact microstructural properties of a material might not be fully characterized. By analyzing the variance in sensor data or the residual errors between the physics-based model predictions and observed data, probabilistic machine learning techniques can be employed to estimate the uncertainty associated with the digital twin's outputs. Techniques like Gaussian Processes or Monte Carlo Dropout in neural networks can provide not just a point estimate of a predicted value (e.g., temperature, stress), but also a measure of confidence or a range of plausible values. This probabilistic output is crucial for informed decision-making, as it highlights the situations where the digital twin's predictions should be treated with caution, prompting further investigation or data acquisition. For high-fidelity applications, understanding and quantifying these uncertainties is as important as achieving accurate point predictions, as it directly impacts the reliability and trustworthiness of the digital twin.

The continuous influx of data from the physical asset enables a perpetual cycle of refinement for the digital twin. This feedback loop is central to maintaining high fidelity over the lifespan of the asset. As the physical system undergoes wear and tear, operational changes, or environmental variations, its behavior will inevitably diverge from a static, physics-based model. Data-driven techniques, applied iteratively, allow the digital twin to adapt to these changes. This might involve periodic retraining of machine learning components, recalibration of physics-based parameters, or even the identification of the need to update the underlying physics-based model itself if significant and persistent discrepancies arise. For instance, if a manufacturing process undergoes a significant change that alters the material properties of a key component, sensor data will eventually reflect this change in the system's performance. A data-driven component of the digital twin can detect this shift, perhaps by observing changes in vibration patterns or energy consumption. This detection can then trigger an alert to re-evaluate the physics-based model, potentially leading to an update in the material constitutive relations or the introduction of new physical phenomena previously not considered. This dynamic self-correction ensures that the digital twin remains a faithful representation, capable of providing accurate insights and predictions even as the physical world evolves.

The integration of data-driven methods also opens avenues for detecting subtle anomalies that might escape the notice of a purely physics-based model. Physics-based models are typically designed to simulate expected behavior. While they can predict deviations based on known failure modes, they may not readily identify unexpected or novel failure signatures. Machine learning algorithms, particularly unsupervised learning techniques like anomaly detection, can sift through large volumes of sensor data to identify patterns that deviate significantly from normal operational behavior, even if the exact cause is not immediately apparent from first principles. For example, a sudden, slight increase in the power consumption of a motor coupled with a subtle change in its acoustic signature might be detected as an anomaly by an anomaly detection algorithm. While a physics-based model might not have explicitly predicted this specific combination of symptoms leading to a particular failure, the anomaly detection system can flag it as a precursor to potential trouble, prompting an engineer to investigate. This early warning capability, powered by data analysis, is a critical aspect of proactive maintenance and operational optimization, directly contributing to the overall fidelity and value of the digital twin.

In essence, the journey towards a high-fidelity digital twin is a symbiotic one, where the theoretical rigor of physics-based modeling provides the essential structure and causal understanding, while the empirical insights derived from data-driven approaches imbue the twin with the nuanced realism and adaptive capacity required to reflect the complexities of the physical world. By leveraging sensor data and historical logs to calibrate parameters, learn dynamic behaviors, predict degradation, and quantify uncertainties, these data-driven methodologies ensure that the digital twin is not merely a static representation but a living, breathing digital counterpart that accurately mirrors and anticipates the behavior of its physical twin across its entire lifecycle. This fusion of physics and data transforms a static simulation into a dynamic, intelligent, and continuously evolving digital entity, capable of driving significant value in operational efficiency, predictive maintenance, and design optimization.

The pursuit of a digital twin that flawlessly mirrors its physical counterpart is inherently a balancing act, a sophisticated negotiation between achieving unparalleled model fidelity, managing the escalating complexity that such fidelity demands, and maintaining the computational performance necessary for practical, real-time applications. This interplay is not merely theoretical; it forms the bedrock of effective digital twin deployment. A model that is too simplistic, while computationally light, will inevitably fail to capture the subtle nuances of the physical system, rendering its predictions unreliable and its insights superficial. Conversely, a hyper-detailed model, meticulously accounting for every conceivable physical phenomenon, might achieve exquisite fidelity in a laboratory setting but become computationally intractable when faced with the demands of operational deployment. The challenge, therefore, lies in identifying and striking that crucial sweet spot where the model is sufficiently detailed to be accurate and predictive, yet lean enough to be executed efficiently and effectively in the operational environment.

This optimization is fundamentally an engineering trade-off, one that permeates every stage of digital twin development. Consider the simulation of fluid dynamics within a complex industrial pipe network. A fully resolved computational fluid dynamics (CFD) model, employing extremely fine mesh elements (adaptive meshing), might capture every turbulent eddy, every micro-vorticity, and the precise interaction of the fluid with the pipe walls down to the microscopic level. Such a model would offer exceptional fidelity, allowing for accurate predictions of pressure drop, flow distribution, and even potential erosion points. However, the computational resources required to solve the governing equations (e.g., Navier-Stokes equations) for such a finely discretized domain, especially in a transient simulation, would be astronomical. Running such a model in real-time, perhaps to inform operational adjustments to pump speeds or valve positions, would be entirely infeasible with current mainstream hardware.

The decision of "how detailed is detailed enough" is therefore critical. It requires a deep understanding of the specific use case and the criticality of the predictions being made. For a digital twin focused on long-term asset health monitoring, where minute-by-minute accuracy might be less paramount than understanding degradation trends, a coarser model might suffice. This could involve using larger mesh elements in CFD, simplifying material properties, or neglecting certain secondary physical effects. The trade-off here is a reduction in temporal and spatial resolution for a significant gain in computational speed. The resulting model, while less "faithful" in an absolute sense, might still provide sufficient accuracy for its intended purpose—predicting the likelihood of component failure over months or years, or optimizing long-term operational strategies.

Conversely, if the digital twin is intended for real-time control of a high-speed manufacturing process, where milliseconds matter, then a higher degree of fidelity and a correspondingly more computationally intensive model might be unavoidable. In such scenarios, the focus shifts to optimizing the computational process itself. Techniques like domain decomposition, where the problem is broken down into smaller, manageable parts that can be solved in parallel across multiple processors or even multiple machines, become indispensable. Advanced numerical solvers that employ adaptive time-stepping—adjusting the simulation timestep dynamically based on the rate of change of system variables—can also significantly reduce computational load without sacrificing accuracy in critical phases of the simulation.

The concept of "multi-fidelity modeling" is a powerful strategy for navigating this delicate balance. Instead of relying on a single, monolithic model of extreme detail, multi-fidelity approaches employ a hierarchy of models, each with a different level of fidelity and associated computational cost. A high-fidelity model, perhaps a detailed physics-based simulation, might be used sparingly, for instance, during design validation or for deep-dive analysis of specific critical events. Simultaneously, one or more lower-fidelity models—which could be simplified physics-based models, empirical models derived from historical data, or even surrogate models trained on the outputs of the high-fidelity model—are used for routine, real-time operations.

For example, consider a digital twin of an aircraft engine. A full-fidelity, highly detailed CFD-thermodynamic model could simulate the combustion process with intricate detail. However, this would be too slow for continuous monitoring. Instead, a lower-fidelity model, perhaps a simplified thermodynamic cycle model or even a machine learning surrogate trained on data from the high-fidelity model and real flight data, could be used for real-time prediction of engine performance and remaining useful life. This lower-fidelity model would be computationally efficient, allowing for continuous updates based on sensor readings from the actual engine. When specific anomalies are detected or when a detailed investigation is required, the system could then invoke the high-fidelity model for a more in-depth analysis, correlating its findings with the ongoing predictions from the lower-fidelity operational model. This layered approach ensures that computational resources are used judiciously, applying the most resource-intensive models only when absolutely necessary, while maintaining a continuous, responsive digital representation through less demanding means.

Adaptive meshing, while mentioned earlier in the context of CFD, is a broader principle applicable to various simulation types. In a finite element analysis

(FEA) for structural mechanics, for instance, adaptive meshing involves automatically refining the mesh density in regions where stress gradients are high or where significant deformation is occurring, while keeping the mesh coarser in areas of relatively uniform stress. This means the computational effort is concentrated precisely where it is most needed to capture critical behaviors, such as crack initiation or localized buckling. This dynamic adjustment of the computational grid, guided by the evolving state of the simulation, allows for a more efficient allocation of computational resources, achieving higher accuracy in critical zones without the prohibitive cost of uniformly high-density meshing across the entire model. The digital twin can dynamically re-mesh critical areas as the simulated physical state evolves, ensuring that high-fidelity representations are maintained in regions of interest while computational load is managed elsewhere.

The choice between different modeling paradigms also directly impacts this balance. Purely physics-based models, while offering a strong foundation in first principles, can become computationally prohibitive as the complexity of the phenomena to be modeled increases (e.g., non-linear material behavior, complex geometries, transient multiphysics interactions). Data-driven models, such as neural networks or Gaussian processes, can often be significantly faster to evaluate once trained. However, they may lack the inherent physical interpretability and may struggle to extrapolate to conditions far beyond their training data. The advent of physics-informed machine learning (PIML) seeks to bridge this gap. By embedding physical laws as constraints or regularization terms within the training of machine learning models, PIML aims to achieve models that are both data-driven and physically consistent. This can lead to models that are more data-efficient, more robust to unseen conditions, and potentially faster to evaluate than their purely physics-based counterparts, all while retaining a degree of physical plausibility. The decision to employ a purely physics-based model, a pure data-driven model, or a hybrid PIML approach is a strategic one, directly influencing the trade-off between fidelity, complexity, and performance.

Furthermore, the fidelity requirement itself is not static; it can and should evolve over the lifecycle of the digital twin and the physical asset. In the initial stages of design and validation, a very high-fidelity model might be essential to prove the concept and understand fundamental performance envelopes. As the asset enters its operational phase, the fidelity requirements might shift. For routine monitoring, a moderately faithful model might be sufficient, focusing on capturing trends and detecting deviations. However, if a critical failure event occurs, or if the asset is subjected to unusual operating conditions, the need for a higher-fidelity diagnostic or predictive model might resurface. A well-architected digital twin system should be capable of dynamically adjusting its modeling fidelity based on the operational context and the specific task at hand. This might involve switching between different pre-trained models, activating more computationally intensive simulation modules, or even initiating a process to re-train or refine a model based on new data that highlights performance deficiencies at the current fidelity level.

The communication overhead and data management aspects also play a significant role in the overall performance. A highly detailed model, even if computationally feasible on its own, might generate an overwhelming volume of data. If this data needs to be streamed in real-time to a central processing unit or a cloud platform, network latency, bandwidth limitations, and data storage costs can become performance bottlenecks. Therefore, strategies for data reduction, aggregation, and intelligent filtering at the source (i.e., close to the physical asset) are crucial. This can involve on-device processing, edge computing, and the use of techniques that extract only the most relevant features or summaries of the data rather than transmitting raw, high-resolution streams. The fidelity of the digital twin is thus not just about the accuracy of its internal models, but also about the efficiency of its entire data pipeline, from sensor acquisition to actionable insight generation.

In summary, balancing fidelity, complexity, and performance in digital twin development is an ongoing engineering challenge. It necessitates a pragmatic approach, grounded in the specific application requirements and the available computational resources. Strategies such as multi-fidelity modeling, adaptive meshing, intelligent model selection, and efficient data management are not mere optimizations; they are fundamental pillars that enable the creation of digital twins that are not only scientifically accurate but also operationally viable. The goal is to construct a digital replica that provides maximum value—accurate predictions, insightful diagnostics, and robust forecasting—without succumbing to the paralysis of computational intractability or the superficiality of oversimplification. This dynamic equilibrium ensures that the digital twin remains a powerful, agile, and indispensable tool throughout the lifecycle of its physical counterpart.

Chapter 3: Hybrid Modeling: The Power of Integration

The relentless pursuit of digital twins that can truly mirror their physical counterparts, capturing every nuance and anticipating every behavior, invariably leads us to the limitations inherent in any single modeling approach. For decades, engineers and scientists have relied on two dominant paradigms: physics-based modeling and data-driven modeling. Physics-based models, rooted in fundamental scientific principles and established physical laws (like Newton's laws of motion, thermodynamics, or Maxwell's equations), offer a profound level of interpretability and extrapolative power. They provide a deep understanding of *why* a system behaves as it does, allowing for predictions even in scenarios not encountered in historical data. However, as systems grow in complexity, incorporating intricate geometries, non-linear material properties, multi-physics interactions, and transient phenomena, the computational burden of solving these first-principles equations can become astronomical. The mathematical models can become analytically intractable or require immensely fine discretization for numerical solutions, pushing the boundaries of what is computationally feasible for real-time applications.

Conversely, data-driven models, particularly those leveraging machine learning and artificial intelligence, have revolutionized our ability to learn complex patterns directly from observed data. These models, such as neural networks, support vector machines, or Gaussian processes, excel at identifying correlations and predicting outcomes based on historical inputs and outputs. Once trained, they can often provide rapid predictions, making them ideal for applications requiring high throughput and real-time responsiveness. Furthermore, they can capture subtle, emergent behaviors that might be difficult to articulate or even discover through first-principles derivations, especially in highly complex or poorly understood systems. The significant drawback, however, lies in their potential lack of interpretability and their limitations in extrapolation. Data-driven models are fundamentally interpolative; their predictive accuracy can degrade significantly when faced with operational conditions that fall outside the range of their training data. They also offer little insight into the underlying physical mechanisms driving the observed phenomena, making it difficult to diagnose root causes of failure or to trust predictions made under novel circumstances.

This dichotomy—the interpretability and extrapolative power of physics-based models versus the speed and pattern-recognition prowess of data-driven models—presents a fundamental challenge for constructing truly comprehensive and robust digital twins. A purely physics-based model might offer unparalleled accuracy under well-defined conditions but be too slow for continuous monitoring or real-time control. A purely data-driven model might be lightning-fast and adept at pattern recognition but lack the trustworthiness to operate beyond its training envelope or provide deep diagnostic insights. The limitations of each approach become starkly apparent when we consider the dynamic, often unpredictable, and inherently complex nature of the physical world.

It is within this context that the concept of hybrid modeling emerges not merely as an alternative, but as a superior strategy. Hybrid modeling, at its core, is about integration; it is the deliberate and synergistic combination of different modeling paradigms to leverage their respective strengths while mitigating their individual weaknesses. The goal is to create a unified modeling framework that is more comprehensive, more accurate, more robust, and more computationally efficient than any single paradigm could achieve on its own. This integration is not simply about running two models in parallel; it involves creating deep connections and feedback loops between different types of models, allowing them to inform and enhance each other.

The rationale behind hybrid modeling is rooted in the understanding that complex systems often possess characteristics that are best captured by different approaches. For instance, a critical component in a mechanical system might have its mechanical behavior and failure modes well-understood through established physics-based principles (e.g., stress, strain, fracture mechanics). However, its interaction with surrounding systems, the influence of environmental factors that are difficult to model precisely, or the subtle degradation patterns that emerge over long operational periods might be more effectively captured by analyzing historical sensor data. A hybrid model can use the physics-based component to simulate the fundamental structural integrity and material response, while a data-driven component can learn from real-world operational data to predict the probability of failure due to these less precisely defined or emergent factors.

Consider a complex chemical process. The core chemical reactions and thermodynamics might be governed by well-established physical laws, lending themselves to accurate simulation with physics-based models. However, the efficiency of these reactions can be heavily influenced by factors such as catalyst degradation, impurities in feedstock, or minute variations in flow rates that are difficult to model from first principles due to their complexity or lack of complete understanding. A data-driven model, trained on historical process data, can learn these subtle influences and predict deviations from ideal behavior. By coupling a physics-based model of the chemical kinetics with a data-driven model that learns from sensor readings to adjust parameters or predict performance anomalies, the hybrid approach can achieve a level of accuracy and responsiveness unattainable by either model in isolation. The physics-based model provides the foundational understanding, while the data-driven model provides the adaptive intelligence to account for real-world complexities and deviations.

This synergistic benefit is crucial for digital twins aiming to represent intricate system dynamics. Purely physics-based models can struggle with complex, emergent phenomena that are not easily expressible through differential equations. For example, the behavior of a biological system, or the complex interactions within a smart grid, often involve a multitude of feedback loops and non-linear relationships that are difficult to map out with perfect fidelity using only first principles. Data-driven models excel at uncovering these complex relationships from data, but without a physical grounding, their predictions might be spurious or untrustworthy. Hybrid models can bridge this gap. A physics-informed machine learning (PIML) approach, for instance, embeds physical laws as constraints or regularization terms within the training objective of a machine learning model. This guides the data-driven model to learn patterns that are not only consistent with the observed data but also physically plausible. Such models often require less data to train effectively and exhibit better generalization capabilities compared to purely data-driven counterparts.

Another powerful manifestation of hybrid modeling is the use of surrogate models, which are themselves often data-driven, to accelerate computationally expensive high-fidelity physics-based simulations. A high-fidelity physics model might be used to generate a dataset of system responses under various operating conditions. This dataset is then used to train a simpler, faster surrogate model (e.g., a neural network or a polynomial response surface). Once trained, the surrogate model can provide near-instantaneous predictions that closely approximate the results of the complex physics-based simulation. This allows for rapid exploration of the design space, real-time parameter tuning, or continuous performance monitoring where the full physics simulation would be prohibitively slow. The surrogate model acts as a data-driven approximation of the physics, enabling a level of computational efficiency that would otherwise be impossible. The fidelity of this hybrid approach is derived from the accuracy of the initial high-fidelity simulations used for training, combined with the speed of the data-driven surrogate.

The integration can also occur at different levels of abstraction. A system might be decomposed into subsystems, where each subsystem is modeled using the most appropriate paradigm. For example, in a complex robotic system, the rigid body dynamics and kinematics of the robot arm might be accurately modeled using physics-based principles. However, the interaction of the robot's end-effector with a delicate object, which involves complex contact mechanics and material deformation, might be better handled by a data-driven model trained on experiments or more detailed finite element simulations. The overall digital twin then orchestrates these different models, passing information between them as needed.

Furthermore, hybrid approaches can significantly enhance the predictive capabilities of digital twins. By combining the explicit knowledge encoded in physics-based models with the implicit knowledge learned from data, the digital twin becomes more resilient to uncertainty and better equipped to handle novel situations. For instance, a predictive maintenance digital twin for an industrial pump might use a physics-based model to simulate the wear and tear on specific components under known operating conditions. Concurrently, a data-driven model, analyzing vibration signatures, temperature fluctuations, and historical failure data, can identify subtle anomalies that might indicate the onset of a failure mode not fully captured by the physics model. The digital twin can then fuse the information from both models. If the physics model predicts a certain failure probability and the data-driven model detects an anomaly that aligns with that prediction but also indicates an unusual pattern, the twin can issue a more urgent or specific warning, prompting a more detailed investigation. This fusion of explicit and implicit knowledge allows for more nuanced and accurate predictions, moving beyond simple extrapolations to informed estimations of future system states.

The development of hybrid models is an iterative process. Often, a physics-based model serves as a starting point, providing a foundational understanding of the system. Data from the physical asset is then collected and used to calibrate and refine the physics model, or to train complementary data-driven models. In cases where the physics is poorly understood or too complex to model accurately, data-driven models might be developed first, and then physics-informed techniques are applied to imbue them with greater physical consistency and interpretability. The insights gained from the data-driven component can also lead to refinements in the underlying physics model itself, potentially uncovering new physical phenomena or relationships that were previously overlooked. This co-evolution of physics-based and data-driven components is a hallmark of sophisticated hybrid modeling.

The potential applications for hybrid modeling in digital twins are vast and continually expanding. In aerospace, a hybrid model of an aircraft engine could combine detailed thermodynamic and fluid dynamics simulations with machine learning models trained on flight data to predict engine performance degradation, optimize fuel efficiency in real-time, and forecast component lifetimes with unprecedented accuracy. In the automotive industry, hybrid models for vehicle dynamics could integrate precise physics-based simulations of suspension and tire behavior with data-driven models that learn from driver behavior and road conditions to enhance active safety systems and optimize autonomous driving algorithms. For smart grids, hybrid models can merge physics-based power flow equations with machine learning models that predict energy demand, renewable energy generation intermittency, and potential grid instabilities, enabling more resilient and efficient energy management.

In essence, hybrid modeling represents a paradigm shift towards more intelligent, adaptable, and trustworthy digital twins. By acknowledging that no single modeling technique holds a monopoly on capturing the complexities of the physical world, hybrid approaches embrace a philosophy of integration. They combine the rigor of scientific principles with the pattern-recognition power of data, creating a more complete and dynamic digital representation. This allows for digital twins that are not only faster and more accurate but also more insightful, providing a deeper understanding of system behavior and enabling more effective decision-making in a wide array of engineering applications. The move towards hybrid modeling is thus a critical step in realizing the full potential of digital twins, transforming them from mere digital replicas into sophisticated, learning, and predictive tools that can profoundly impact how we design, operate, and maintain complex physical systems.

The crucial step in realizing the promise of hybrid modeling lies in the practical implementation of integrating established physics-based models with empirical data. This integration is not a mere conceptual exercise; it involves a suite of rigorous techniques to ensure that the virtual representation accurately reflects the behavior of its physical counterpart. The synergy between theoretical understanding and real-world observation is what elevates a digital twin from a static replica to a dynamic, predictive tool. When we combine the well-defined principles of physics with the messy, nuanced realities captured by sensor data, we unlock a level of fidelity and trustworthiness that neither approach can achieve in isolation. The physics-based model provides an indispensable scaffolding of fundamental knowledge, a robust framework that dictates the plausible behaviors of a system. However, this framework, derived from idealized conditions or simplified assumptions, often fails to account for the myriad of subtle influences, unforeseen interactions, and material degradations that occur in the real world. It is here that empirical data, meticulously collected from the physical asset, plays its transformative role.

Parameter estimation is a cornerstone of this integration process. Most physics-based models, even those derived from fundamental laws, contain parameters that are not precisely known a priori or that may vary over time or with operating conditions. These parameters might represent material properties that deviate from textbook values due to manufacturing tolerances or aging, coefficients of friction that are influenced by lubrication and environmental factors, or even subtle geometric imperfections. Traditionally, engineers might rely on expert judgment, literature values, or separate laboratory experiments to estimate these parameters. However, these methods can be time-consuming, costly, and may not accurately represent the specific instance of the physical asset being twinned. The integration of empirical data offers a powerful alternative: using the measured outputs of the physical system under specific inputs to infer the most likely values of these unknown parameters. Techniques such as least-squares fitting, maximum likelihood estimation, and Bayesian inference are commonly employed. For instance, in modeling the thermal behavior of an electronic device, a physics-based model might describe heat conduction and convection. However, the exact thermal conductivity of the interface materials or the effective heat transfer coefficient to the ambient air might be uncertain. By monitoring the device's temperature response to controlled power inputs (empirical data), these parameters can be estimated to best match the observed temperatures with the simulated ones. This process effectively "tunes" the physics model to the specific characteristics of the physical asset, moving it closer to an accurate representation.

Calibration, a closely related concept, involves adjusting the parameters and even the structure of a physics-based model so that its outputs align closely with observed data. While parameter estimation focuses on quantifying unknown constants within a given model structure, calibration can encompass a broader adjustment. It might involve fine-tuning coefficients, modifying constitutive relationships, or even introducing empirical correction terms to account for phenomena not explicitly modeled. Consider a structural dynamics model of a bridge. A physics-based model would incorporate material properties (Young's modulus, Poisson's ratio), geometric dimensions, and boundary conditions. However, real-world bridges experience effects like soil-structure interaction, aerodynamic forces that are difficult to predict precisely, and minor damage accumulation over time, all of which can alter their vibrational characteristics. By instrumenting the bridge with accelerometers and measuring its response to ambient vibrations or controlled excitation (empirical data), the model can be calibrated. This calibration process aims to minimize the discrepancy between the measured vibration frequencies and amplitudes and those predicted by the physics model, thereby enhancing the model's predictive accuracy for scenarios like seismic events or the passage of heavy loads. The calibration ensures that the model not only respects the underlying physics but also "learns" the specific deviations and emergent behaviors of the real bridge.

Model validation is the indispensable final step, ensuring that the hybrid model is not just a good fit for the calibration data but also generalizes well to new, unseen data. This involves holding back a portion of the collected empirical data, which was not used during the parameter estimation or calibration phases, and then evaluating the hybrid model's performance against this validation dataset. Metrics such as root-mean-squared error (RMSE), mean absolute percentage error (MAPE), R-squared values, and visual comparison of time series plots are used to quantify the agreement between the model's predictions and the actual measurements. A robust hybrid model should exhibit low prediction errors on the validation data, demonstrating its ability to capture the essential physics while adapting to real-world complexities without overfitting to the specific noise or idiosyncrasies of the calibration dataset. For instance, if a hybrid model of a manufacturing process is calibrated using data from a week of normal operation, it must be validated against data from subsequent weeks, potentially including periods with different raw material batches, minor equipment drift, or variations in environmental conditions. Successful validation builds confidence that the digital twin will provide reliable insights and predictions during its operational life.

The synergistic interplay between physics and data can manifest in several powerful ways. One common approach is to use the physics-based model to provide a baseline prediction and then use a data-driven model to correct or refine this prediction. For example, in predicting the trajectory of a projectile, a physics-based model using Newtonian mechanics can provide a good initial estimate. However, this model might not account for air resistance, wind variations, or subtle aerodynamic effects, especially for complex shapes. A machine learning model, trained on data that includes the influence of these factors (e.g., from experimental firings or simulations incorporating atmospheric data), can then learn to predict the deviation from the idealized physics-based trajectory. This hybrid model would combine the physical understanding of projectile motion with the data-driven ability to capture complex, often non-linear, environmental influences, leading to significantly more accurate predictions over longer ranges or in varied conditions.

Another potent integration strategy is the use of data to inform the selection of appropriate physics-based models or model components. In highly complex systems, the exact physical phenomena governing behavior might not be fully understood, or multiple physical mechanisms might be at play, each dominant under different operating regimes. Data-driven analysis of system behavior can help identify these regimes and guide the selection or activation of the corresponding physics-based models. For example, in modeling the performance of a battery, its electrochemical behavior can be described by a complex set of partial differential equations. However, at different states of charge or discharge rates, different physical processes might become limiting. By analyzing historical charge/discharge data and correlating it with measured voltage and temperature profiles, a machine learning model can predict which regime the battery is operating in and thus which set of physics-based equations are most relevant and accurate for simulation at that moment. This regime-switching approach allows for a more nuanced and accurate representation of battery performance across its entire operational spectrum, leveraging physics where it is most applicable and using data to navigate the transitions.

Furthermore, the iterative refinement loop between physics and data is crucial for continuous improvement. As the physical asset operates, it generates new data. This new data can be used not only to validate the existing hybrid model but also to further refine its parameters, update its calibration, and even identify potential shortcomings in the underlying physics model itself. If the model consistently underpredicts a certain behavior, or overpredicts another, and this discrepancy is not resolved by adjusting parameters, it might indicate that the physics model is missing a key phenomenon. The empirical data then serves as a powerful diagnostic tool, pointing towards areas where theoretical understanding or the chosen physical laws may need to be revisited or augmented. This continuous learning cycle ensures that the digital twin remains a relevant and accurate representation of the physical asset throughout its lifecycle, adapting to changes, degradation, and evolving operating conditions.

Consider the application in predictive maintenance for rotating machinery, such as industrial turbines or pumps. A detailed physics-based model can simulate the mechanical stresses, fatigue life, and potential failure modes of critical components like bearings or seals based on operating parameters like speed, load, and temperature. However, this model might assume ideal material properties and perfectly uniform operating conditions. Empirical data from vibration sensors, acoustic emission sensors, and thermal cameras can reveal subtle anomalies that deviate from the physics model's predictions. For instance, the physics model might predict a slow, predictable wear rate for a bearing. However, vibration data might show the emergence of higher-frequency oscillations, indicative of developing micro-cracks or localized wear. A data-driven component, perhaps a neural network trained on historical vibration signatures correlated with known failure modes, can detect these anomalies. The hybrid twin then fuses these two sources of information. The physics model provides the projected lifetime under nominal conditions, while the data-driven anomaly detection flags deviations that suggest accelerated degradation or an imminent failure not captured by the first-principles simulation. This combined insight allows for more precise and proactive maintenance scheduling, preventing costly unplanned downtime.

In the realm of complex fluid dynamics, such as modeling flow through a porous medium in a reservoir or within a biological tissue, purely physics-based models can be computationally prohibitive due to the intricate pore structures and multi-phase flow phenomena. These models, often based on Navier-Stokes equations or Darcy's law coupled with conservation equations, require extremely fine discretization to capture the detailed geometry. Empirical data, obtained from core samples, well tests, or imaging techniques like micro-CT scans, provides crucial information about the effective properties of the medium (porosity, permeability) and the overall flow behavior. Hybrid modeling can address this by using a simplified physics-based model (e.g., homogenized properties) and then employing a data-driven surrogate model or a machine learning technique to capture the deviations caused by the complex micro-structure. The surrogate model, trained on high-fidelity simulations or experimental data, can then predict the flow behavior much faster than solving the full physics equations. This allows for rapid simulation of different reservoir management strategies or drug delivery scenarios, while still being grounded in the fundamental principles of fluid flow.

The integration process itself necessitates careful consideration of data quality and experimental design. The empirical data used for parameter estimation, calibration, and validation must be accurate, representative, and sufficiently informative. This means addressing issues such as sensor noise, calibration drift, missing data, and the choice of sampling rates and operating points during data acquisition. A well-designed experiment will aim to excite the system in a way that maximally informs the unknown parameters or validates the model's behavior across a wide range of operating conditions. For instance, when calibrating a suspension system model for an autonomous vehicle, simply collecting data during highway driving might not be sufficient. Data must also be collected during cornering, braking, and over different road surfaces to ensure the model's robustness and accuracy in diverse scenarios. The quality of the empirical data directly dictates the quality of the resulting hybrid model.

Moreover, the "black box" nature of some data-driven models can be mitigated through physics-informed machine learning (PIML) approaches. In PIML, the governing physical equations are incorporated directly into the loss function of the machine learning model during training. For example, a neural network might be trained to predict the temperature distribution in a heated object, but its training objective would include a term that penalizes deviations from the heat equation. This forces the neural network to learn a solution that is not only consistent with the training data but also physically plausible, even in regions where data might be sparse. This integration imbues the data-driven model with a degree of interpretability and better extrapolation capabilities, as it is constrained by known physical laws. The empirical data then serves to refine the specific parameters or boundary conditions within this physically consistent framework, leading to a highly effective hybrid model.

In summary, the process of integrating physics-based models with empirical data is a multi-faceted endeavor that is central to the creation of accurate and trustworthy digital twins. Through techniques such as parameter estimation, calibration, and rigorous validation, the inherent strengths of theoretical understanding are amplified by the nuanced insights derived from real-world measurements. This synergy allows for digital twins that not only embody fundamental physical laws but also adapt to the specific characteristics, complexities, and evolving states of their physical counterparts. The resulting hybrid models offer enhanced predictive capabilities, improved robustness, and a deeper understanding of system behavior, paving the way for more intelligent design, operation, and maintenance of complex physical systems.

The landscape of modeling and simulation has been dramatically reshaped by the advent of machine learning (ML). Traditionally, engineering disciplines have relied heavily on physics-based models—mathematical formulations derived from fundamental scientific laws such as Newton's laws of motion, Maxwell's equations for electromagnetism, or the laws of thermodynamics. These models offer a deep understanding of system behavior, are often interpretable, and can, in principle, provide accurate predictions across a wide range of conditions, even those not encountered during development. However, constructing these models can be a laborious and knowledge-intensive process. It requires a profound understanding of the underlying physics, significant expertise in formulating complex differential equations, and considerable computational resources for their solution, particularly for intricate or non-linear systems. Furthermore, real-world applications often introduce complexities—material imperfections, environmental variations, or interactions not fully captured by idealized physical laws—that can lead to discrepancies between model predictions and actual system performance.

In parallel, data-driven machine learning models have emerged as powerful tools for uncovering complex patterns and relationships directly from observational data. Techniques like neural networks, support vector machines, and random forests excel at learning from vast datasets, identifying correlations, and making predictions without explicit prior knowledge of the underlying physical mechanisms. This empirical approach has proven highly effective in domains where physics is poorly understood or where data is abundant. However, purely data-driven models often suffer from significant limitations when applied to engineering problems. They can be "black boxes," making it difficult to understand *why* a particular prediction is made, which is crucial for trust and validation in safety-critical applications. Perhaps more importantly, these models typically require substantial amounts of training data to achieve acceptable accuracy and often struggle to generalize to conditions outside the range of their training set. Extrapolation is a notorious weakness; predicting behavior under novel operating regimes or stresses can lead to wildly inaccurate or physically impossible results. This reliance on data can also be a bottleneck, as acquiring sufficient, high-quality data for complex systems can be expensive, time-consuming, or even impossible.

The convergence of these two powerful paradigms—physics-based modeling and machine learning—has given rise to a new era of hybrid modeling, seeking to harness the strengths of both while mitigating their weaknesses. Among the most promising and rapidly developing approaches within this hybrid framework is Physics-Informed Machine Learning (PIML). PIML represents a sophisticated integration strategy where the governing principles of physics are not merely used to generate training data or to post-process model outputs, but are fundamentally woven into the fabric of the machine learning model itself during the training process. This integration is achieved by augmenting the standard loss function of a machine learning model with terms that penalize violations of known physical laws.

Consider, for instance, training a neural network to predict the temperature distribution within a solid object subject to heat transfer. A standard supervised learning approach would involve feeding the network input data (e.g., boundary conditions, material properties, heat sources) and corresponding target output data (e.g., measured temperature values at various points). The network would then adjust its internal parameters to minimize the difference between its predictions and the ground truth temperatures (e.g., using a mean squared error loss). In a PIML approach, however, the loss function would include not only this data-fitting term but also an additional term designed to measure how well the network's predicted temperature field satisfies the heat equation—a fundamental partial differential equation describing heat diffusion. This "physics loss" term is typically calculated by evaluating the residual of the differential equation when the network's output (its prediction of temperature as a function of space and time) is substituted into it. By minimizing a combined loss that includes both data fidelity and physical consistency, the neural network is implicitly constrained to learn solutions that are not only accurate with respect to the observed data but also obey the fundamental physics of heat transfer.

This embedding of physical laws directly into the learning process yields several profound advantages, particularly for engineering and scientific applications. Firstly, it significantly enhances the model's generalization capabilities. Because the model is forced to adhere to physical constraints, it is much more likely to produce physically plausible results even when predicting in regions of the input space where training data is sparse or entirely absent. Unlike purely data-driven models that might extrapolate erratically, a PIML model is guided by the underlying physics, providing a more robust and reliable prediction of unseen phenomena. This is immensely valuable in situations where experimental data is limited, expensive to acquire, or where exploring extreme operating conditions is necessary but risky. For example, in simulating the behavior of novel materials or predicting the performance of a system under extreme loads, where real-world data is scarce, PIML can provide more trustworthy insights than a purely empirical model.

Secondly, PIML can drastically reduce the amount of labeled training data required. When the physics loss term strongly guides the learning process, the model can learn a correct representation of the system's behavior with far fewer data points than would otherwise be necessary. The physical laws act as a powerful form of inductive bias, effectively informing the model about the structure of the solution space. This is a game-changer for many complex systems where obtaining a comprehensive dataset is a major challenge. For instance, in modeling fluid dynamics or complex chemical reactions, where experimental measurements are difficult and costly, PIML can leverage existing physical knowledge to build accurate models from limited experimental observations, significantly accelerating the discovery and design cycle.

Furthermore, PIML models often exhibit improved interpretability. While a deep neural network can still be complex, the explicit inclusion of physical equations can make its behavior more understandable. The model is not just matching data points; it is learning a representation that respects physical laws. In some formulations, the network's outputs or internal layers can be directly related to physical quantities, making it easier for domain experts to assess the model's predictions and to diagnose potential issues. This bridges the gap between the "black box" nature of traditional ML and the interpretability of physics-based models.

The formulation of PIML can take various forms, but a common thread is the incorporation of differential equations into the training objective. Let us consider a general system governed by a set of partial differential equations (PDEs) of the form:

$N(u(x, t; \theta)) = 0$

where $u(x, t; \theta)$ represents the unknown solution (e.g., temperature, velocity, pressure) as a function of spatial coordinates x and time t, parameterized by the model's trainable parameters θ. The operator N encodes the physical laws, and the equation must hold over a specific domain Ω and time interval $[0, T]$.

In a PIML framework, a neural network is typically used to approximate the solution $u(x, t; \theta)$. The network takes x and t as inputs and outputs the predicted value of u. To train this network, a composite loss function L is defined:

$L(\theta) = L
{data}(\theta) + \lambda L{PDE}(\theta)$

Here, $L
*{data}(\theta)$ is a standard data-fitting loss (e.g., mean squared error) computed using available observed data points $(x*i, t*i, u*i^{obs})$, where $u*i^{obs}$ is the observed value at $(x*i, t_i)$:

$L
{data}(\theta) = \frac{1}{N{data}} \sum*{i=1}^{N*{data}} (u(x*i, t*i; \theta) - u_i^{obs})^2$

The term $L
*{PDE}(\theta)$ represents the physics loss, which penalizes deviations from the governing PDE. It is computed by sampling points within the domain and time interval, evaluating the PDE operator N using the network's output, and then calculating a measure of the residual error. For instance, if $N(u) = \frac{\partial u}{\partial t} - \nu \nabla^2 u$ (the heat equation, with ν being thermal diffusivity), the PDE residual at a sampled point $(x*j, t*j)$ would be $r*j = \frac{\partial u(x*j, t*j; \theta)}{\partial t} - \nu \nabla^2 u(x*j, t*j; \theta)$. The physics loss would then be an aggregation of these residuals:

$L
{PDE}(\theta) = \frac{1}{N{PDE}} \sum*{j=1}^{N*{PDE}} r_j^2$

The parameter λ is a hyperparameter that balances the importance of fitting the data versus satisfying the physical laws. Derivatives required for the PDE residual (e.g., $\frac{\partial u}{\partial t}$, $\nabla^2 u$) are efficiently computed using automatic differentiation, a standard feature in modern deep learning frameworks.

Beyond the governing equations, boundary conditions (BCs) and initial conditions (ICs) are also critical components of physical models. PIML readily incorporates these into the loss function as well. For instance, if a Dirichlet boundary condition $u(x_b, t) = g(t)$ must hold on a boundary $\partial \Omega$, a boundary loss term can be defined as:

$L
{BC}(\theta) = \frac{1}{N{BC}} \sum{k=1}^{N{BC}} (u(x{b,k}, tk; \theta) - g(t_k))^2$

where $(x
{b,k}, tk)$ are sampled points on the boundary. Similarly, initial conditions $u(x, 0) = h(x)$ can be enforced via an initial loss term $L_{IC}(\theta)$. The total loss function then becomes a comprehensive objective that encourages the network to satisfy the PDE, boundary conditions, initial conditions, and data fidelity simultaneously.

The ability of PIML to leverage physical laws makes it particularly well-suited for problems involving complex material behaviors, fluid dynamics, solid mechanics, heat transfer, and even biological processes. For example, in computational fluid dynamics (CFD), traditional methods like Finite Element Method (FEM) or Finite Volume Method (FVM) discretize the computational domain and solve the Navier-Stokes equations numerically. While accurate, these methods can be computationally very expensive, especially for large domains, turbulent flows, or when many simulations are needed for design optimization or uncertainty quantification. PIML offers an alternative by training a neural network to directly approximate the velocity and pressure fields. By including the Navier-Stokes equations, continuity equation, and relevant boundary conditions in the loss function, the neural network learns a solution that satisfies these physical constraints. This can lead to significantly faster prediction times once the network is trained, making it viable for applications where real-time or near-real-time simulations are required, such as control systems or interactive design tools. Furthermore, PIML can be beneficial in situations where the geometry is complex or changes dynamically, as neural networks can naturally handle unstructured inputs and can be more adaptable than mesh-based methods in certain scenarios.

In structural mechanics, PIML can be employed to predict stress and strain distributions in complex structures. A physics-based model would typically involve the equations of elasticity or plasticity, along with load and boundary conditions. Training a neural network with PIML would incorporate these governing equations into the loss function. This allows the model to predict how a structure will deform and respond to applied forces, even for geometries that are difficult to mesh or for material models that are highly non-linear. The resulting PIML model could then be used for rapid structural analysis, design iteration, or to identify potential failure points with greater efficiency than traditional solvers.

Another compelling application area is in modeling phenomena where the underlying physics is not fully understood or where multiple competing physical effects are at play. In such cases, traditional physics-based models might be incomplete or require extensive parameter fitting. PIML can help by providing a framework where the known physics is enforced, and the data helps to resolve the unknowns or the nuances of the system. For instance, in modeling complex biological systems, such as the spread of a disease or the dynamics of a biochemical reaction network, where precise kinetic parameters or interaction strengths are hard to measure, PIML can use observed data (e.g., infection rates, concentration levels) alongside the known conservation laws or reaction kinetics to learn a more accurate and predictive model. The network effectively learns to bridge the gap between the idealized physical description and the observed reality.

The development of PIML is closely tied to advancements in deep learning architectures and automatic differentiation. The ability to compute high-order derivatives of complex functions with respect to their inputs and parameters, which is essential for evaluating PDE residuals, is provided by automatic differentiation libraries like TensorFlow and PyTorch. This has democratized the implementation of PIML, allowing researchers and engineers to experiment with integrating physical laws into their machine learning models without needing to develop custom numerical differentiation schemes.

However, it is important to acknowledge that PIML is not a panacea, and challenges remain. The training process can still be sensitive to hyperparameters, such as the weighting factor λ for the physics loss. Finding the right balance between fitting the data and satisfying the physics is crucial and often requires careful tuning. Additionally, for very complex or stiff PDEs, the training can become numerically challenging, requiring advanced optimization techniques. The computational cost of evaluating the PDE residual during training, especially for higher-order PDEs or in high-dimensional spaces, can also be significant. Research is ongoing to develop more efficient sampling strategies for PDE residuals and to design neural network architectures that are better suited for representing solutions to differential equations.

Despite these challenges, Physics-Informed Machine Learning represents a significant leap forward in hybrid modeling. By directly incorporating physical laws into the machine learning framework, PIML models are endowed with a degree of physical consistency, robustness, and data efficiency that is difficult to achieve with purely data-driven or purely physics-based approaches alone. This paradigm shift promises to accelerate scientific discovery, enhance the design and operation of complex engineering systems, and enable more reliable predictive modeling in a wide array of domains. It embodies the core principle of hybrid modeling: leveraging the complementary strengths of theoretical understanding and empirical observation to create models that are more powerful, trustworthy, and versatile than either approach can offer independently. The future of digital twins and advanced simulation will undoubtedly be shaped by the continued evolution and application of physics-informed machine learning.

The successful implementation of Physics-Informed Machine Learning (PIML) hinges on two critical pillars: the choice of appropriate model architectures and the strategic design of training methodologies. These elements work in concert to ensure that the machine learning model not only learns from data but is also intrinsically guided by the fundamental physical principles governing the system under study.

When selecting neural network architectures for PIML, the goal is to choose a structure that can effectively represent the solution of physical phenomena, often governed by differential equations, and facilitate the computation of necessary derivatives. Traditionally, feedforward neural networks (FNNs), also known as multi-layer perceptrons (MLPs), have been the workhorse for PIML. An FNN, consisting of multiple layers of interconnected nodes, takes spatial coordinates and potentially time as input and outputs the physical quantities of interest (e.g., temperature, velocity, displacement). The continuous, differentiable nature of these networks, combined with the power of automatic differentiation, makes them ideal for calculating the residuals of partial differential equations (PDEs) required for the physics loss term. For instance, a network might be configured with input layers representing $x, y, z,$ and t, and output layers corresponding to $u(x, y, z, t), v(x, y, z, t),$ and $w(x, y, z, t)$ for fluid velocity components, or $\phi(x, y, z, t)$ for a scalar field like temperature or pressure. The depth and width of these networks—the number of hidden layers and the number of neurons per layer—are hyperparameters that need to be tuned, often in relation to the complexity of the underlying physics and the dimensionality of the problem. Deeper networks can potentially learn more complex functions, while wider networks can represent more intricate relationships within a layer.

However, for certain types of physical problems, more specialized architectures might offer advantages. For spatio-temporal problems, recurrent neural networks (RNNs) and their variants, such as Long Short-Term Memory (LSTM) networks, can be employed. While primarily known for sequence modeling, LSTMs can be adapted to handle spatio-temporal dynamics by processing spatial information sequentially or by incorporating spatial features into their recurrent state. Another architectural consideration arises in problems with inherent symmetries or specific structural properties. Convolutional Neural Networks (CNNs), typically used for image processing, can be adapted for PIML, particularly for problems defined on regular grids or for tasks where local spatial correlations are dominant, such as in certain fluid dynamics or solid mechanics applications. If the physics exhibits specific invariances (e.g., translation, rotation), geometric deep learning approaches, including graph neural networks (GNNs) or more specialized equivariant networks, can be designed to incorporate these symmetries directly into the architecture, potentially leading to more efficient learning and better generalization. GNNs, for example, are adept at modeling systems defined on irregular domains or networks, making them suitable for problems where mesh-based methods are traditionally used but where a data-driven, meshless approach is desired.

The core of PIML training lies in its tailored loss functions. As previously

outlined, the total loss is typically a weighted sum of terms reflecting data fidelity, adherence to PDEs, and satisfaction of boundary and initial conditions. The data fidelity term, $L
{data}$, is usually a standard regression loss, such as Mean Squared Error (MSE) or Mean Absolute Error (MAE), comparing the network's predictions with available observational data. The physics loss term, $L*{PDE}$, is where the integration of physical laws truly occurs. This term is calculated by sampling points within the computational domain and time interval and evaluating the residual of the governing differential equations. For a PDE like $\frac{\partial u}{\partial t} + \mathcal{L}(u) = 0$, where $\mathcal{L}$ is a differential operator, the residual at a point (x, t) is $r(x, t) = \frac{\partial u(x, t; \theta)}{\partial t} + \mathcal{L}(u(x, t; \theta))$. The $L*{PDE}$ is then typically the MSE of these residuals over a set of sampled points: $L{PDE} = \frac{1}{N*{PDE}}
\sum*{i=1}^{N*{PDE}}* r*(xi, ti*)^2$. Similarly, boundary conditions (e.g., $u=*ub$ on $\partial\Omega$) and initial conditions (e.g., $u=u*0$ at $t=0$) are incorporated as loss terms, $L*{BC}$ and L_{IC}, penalizing deviations from these prescribed values at the respective boundaries and initial times.

The weighting coefficients for these loss terms, particularly λ for L_{PDE}, are crucial hyperparameters. A high λ emphasizes physical consistency, potentially at the expense of fitting sparse data, while a low λ prioritizes data fitting, which might lead to physically implausible results if data is insufficient or noisy. Balancing these terms is a key challenge. Adaptive weighting strategies have been proposed, where the weights are adjusted dynamically during training based on the relative magnitudes of the different loss components or their gradients, aiming to achieve a more harmonious convergence. For instance, techniques like multi-objective optimization or loss landscape balancing can be employed to navigate this trade-off more effectively.

Managing computational costs is paramount, especially for complex systems or high-dimensional problems. Evaluating the PDE residual, which involves computing derivatives via automatic differentiation, can be computationally intensive. Strategies to mitigate this include:

1. **Sampling Strategies:** Instead of evaluating the PDE residual at every possible point, intelligent sampling techniques can be employed. This might involve adaptive sampling that focuses on regions where the residual is high, or quasi-random sampling (e.g., using Sobol sequences) to ensure better coverage of the domain with fewer points compared to purely random sampling.
2. **Reduced-Order Modeling:** For systems with dominant low-dimensional dynamics, reduced-order models can be learned in conjunction with PIML. This involves projecting the high-dimensional state onto a lower-dimensional latent space, where the PIML model operates, and then reconstructing the full-state prediction.
3. **Efficient Architectures:** Architectures designed for computational efficiency, such as using shallower networks where possible, or employing specialized layers that encode physical symmetries, can reduce the burden of derivative calculations.
4. **Transfer Learning and Pre-training:** If similar physical systems have been modeled, pre-training a PIML model on related data or using a pre-trained network as a starting point can significantly accelerate convergence and reduce the overall computational effort.

Ensuring convergence during PIML training often requires careful selection of optimization algorithms and learning rate schedules. Standard optimizers like Adam, RMSprop, or SGD with momentum are commonly used. However, the complex, multi-component nature of the PIML loss function can lead to challenges such as vanishing or exploding gradients, or getting stuck in suboptimal local minima. Techniques like gradient clipping, learning rate warm-up, and cyclical learning rates can help stabilize the training process. For problems with stiff differential equations, where different physical processes occur on vastly different time scales, specialized solvers and optimization techniques that handle stiffness are necessary.

Furthermore, the type of physical laws being incorporated influences the training strategy. For conservation laws (e.g., mass, momentum, energy conservation), specific formulations of the physics loss can be derived to directly enforce these principles. For example, if the divergence of a vector field (representing flux) must be zero, the L_{PDE} term can directly penalize the discrete divergence computed from the network's output. For systems exhibiting symmetry, as mentioned, network architectures can be designed to reflect these symmetries. Problems involving stochasticity can be handled by using PIML to learn probability distributions or by incorporating stochastic differential equations (SDEs) into the loss function, often requiring sampling-based approaches to estimate the drift and diffusion terms.

A practical consideration in implementing PIML is the handling of different types of physical constraints. Beyond PDEs, boundary conditions are paramount. Dirichlet (prescribed value), Neumann (prescribed derivative), and Robin (linear combination of value and derivative) boundary conditions can all be incorporated into the loss function. For Neumann conditions, for instance, if $\frac{\partial u}{\partial n} = g$ on $\partial\Omega$, the loss term would penalize the difference between the network's computed normal derivative (obtained via automatic differentiation) and g. Similarly, initial conditions are crucial for time-dependent problems. The loss function effectively becomes a multi-objective optimization problem, forcing the network's parameters θ to satisfy:

$$ \min{\theta} \left(\alpha L{data}(\theta) + \beta L{PDE}(\theta) + \gamma L{BC}(\theta) + \delta L_{IC}(\theta) + \dots \right) $$
where $\alpha, \beta, \gamma, \delta, \dots$ are weighting coefficients that balance the contribution of each loss component. Determining these weights is often an empirical process, requiring experimentation and validation against ground truth or known physics. Sensitivity analysis on these weights can reveal how robust the solution is to variations in physical constraint enforcement versus data fitting.

Moreover, the concept of "soft" versus "hard" constraints is relevant. While PIML primarily enforces constraints through the loss function (soft constraints), there are ongoing research efforts to develop methods for enforcing "hard" constraints, where the network's output is guaranteed to satisfy the constraints by design, for example, through specific architectural choices or output transformations. For instance, if a quantity must always be positive, the network's output layer might employ a non-negative activation function, or a transformation to ensure positivity.

The integration of PIML also benefits from advancements in interpretable AI. While standard ML models can be black boxes, the explicit inclusion of physical equations provides a degree of interpretability. By analyzing how the physics loss contributes to the overall error, one can infer where the model is struggling to adhere to physical laws. Furthermore, if the network outputs directly correspond to physical quantities (e.g., velocity components, stress tensors), domain experts can more readily validate the model's behavior. Techniques like sensitivity analysis of the network's output with respect to physical parameters can also offer insights into the system's behavior as predicted by the PIML model.

The choice of how to discretize the domain for sampling points in the PDE and boundary condition loss terms is also an architectural and strategic decision. While many PIML approaches are meshless, relying on sampling points within the continuous domain, the density and distribution of these points can significantly impact training. For problems with sharp gradients or singularities, a higher density of sampling points in those regions might be necessary. This can be informed by a preliminary analysis of the problem or by adaptive strategies that refine the sampling based on the evolution of the residual during training.

In summary, PIML architectures and training strategies are sophisticated. They typically involve differentiable neural networks capable of approximating complex solutions, and loss functions that rigorously incorporate data fidelity with physics-based terms derived from governing equations, boundary conditions, and initial conditions. The successful application of PIML requires careful consideration of network design, balancing various loss components through appropriate weighting, efficient computational strategies to manage derivative calculations, robust optimization techniques to ensure convergence, and thoughtful selection of sampling methods. By mastering these architectural and training paradigms, engineers and scientists can unlock the full potential of PIML to develop more accurate, robust, and data-efficient models for a wide range of scientific and engineering challenges.

The preceding discussion has established the foundational principles of Physics-Informed Machine Learning (PIML) and the broader concept of hybrid modeling, emphasizing their synergy in leveraging both data-driven insights and fundamental physical laws. Having delved into the architectural considerations and training methodologies that underpin these integrated approaches, it is now imperative to illustrate their practical efficacy through concrete examples. This section will showcase how hybrid models, and PIML specifically, have been deployed across diverse engineering disciplines, yielding tangible improvements in simulation fidelity, predictive capabilities, and the efficiency of design processes. These case studies are not merely academic exercises; they represent real-world applications that underscore the transformative power of combining physical understanding with machine learning's pattern recognition prowess.

One prominent domain where hybrid modeling has made significant inroads is **Computational Fluid Dynamics (CFD)**. Traditional CFD methods, while powerful, can be computationally prohibitive, especially for complex geometries, turbulent flows, or when numerous design iterations are required. PIML offers a compelling alternative or complementary approach. For instance, researchers have successfully employed PIML to accelerate the solution of the Navier-Stokes equations. In a specific application involving the simulation of laminar and turbulent flow over airfoils, a PIML framework was developed to predict the velocity and pressure fields. The neural network was trained not only on sparse experimental data but also on the residuals of the incompressible Navier-Stokes equations. This ensured that the network's predictions remained physically consistent, even in regions where data was scarce. The physics-informed loss function, incorporating the continuity and momentum equations, acted as a strong regularizer, guiding the network towards physically plausible solutions. The outcome was a model capable of generating high-fidelity flow fields with a fraction of the computational cost typically associated with high-resolution CFD simulations. Furthermore, by embedding the governing equations directly into the training process, the PIML model demonstrated remarkable generalization capabilities, performing well on unseen geometries and flow conditions after sufficient training. This enabled rapid exploration of the design space for airfoil optimization, leading to the identification of novel shapes with improved aerodynamic performance.

Beyond direct simulation, PIML has also been instrumental in **turbulence modeling**, a notoriously challenging aspect of CFD. Traditional turbulence models often rely on empirical closures or simplified assumptions that may not hold across all flow regimes. Hybrid models can enhance these by learning corrections or sub-grid scale models from data while being constrained by physical principles. One notable application involved developing a data-driven Reynolds-averaged Navier-Stokes (RANS) model. Instead of relying solely on pre-defined algebraic expressions or differential equations for the turbulent viscosity, a neural network was trained to predict the turbulent stresses. This network was trained using high-fidelity Direct Numerical Simulation (DNS) data, which provides a more accurate representation of turbulence, and crucially, its training was regularized by enforcing physical constraints such as the realizability conditions for Reynolds stresses (e.g., ensuring that the turbulent kinetic energy is non-negative and that certain components of the stress tensor are physically consistent). This physics-informed data-driven approach resulted in a RANS model that captured turbulent behavior more accurately across a wider range of flows compared to conventional models, particularly in complex separated or transitional flows. The ability to learn from DNS data and adhere to physical realizability conditions allowed for more robust and accurate predictions in situations where traditional RANS models often falter.

In the realm of **structural mechanics and solid mechanics**, hybrid models are similarly revolutionizing simulation and design. Finite Element Analysis (FEA) is the cornerstone of structural design, but it can be computationally intensive, especially for nonlinear materials, large deformations, or probabilistic analyses. PIML offers a path to create surrogate models that are orders of magnitude faster while retaining high accuracy. For instance, consider the problem of predicting stress and strain distributions in complex mechanical components under various loading conditions. A hybrid model might involve a neural network trained on experimental data (e.g., strain gauge measurements) and augmented by the principles of elasticity or plasticity. The physics-informed loss would include terms related to equilibrium equations, compatibility conditions, and constitutive material laws. In one successful implementation, a PIML model was used to predict the deformation and stress fields in a composite material structure. The model was trained on limited experimental data from material testing and was enforced to obey the equations of linear elasticity and strain-displacement compatibility. The results showed that the PIML model could accurately predict the stress concentrations and failure modes under static and dynamic loads, outperforming purely data-driven models that often struggled with extrapolation beyond the training data range. The physical constraints ensured that the learned model inherently respected fundamental mechanical principles, leading to more reliable predictions and a significant reduction in the computational burden for design iterations and sensitivity studies. This enabled engineers to explore a much wider design space and optimize structural integrity more efficiently.

Another significant application in structural analysis involves **damage detection and prognosis**. Identifying and predicting the evolution of structural damage (e.g., cracks, delamination) in real-time is critical for safety and maintenance. PIML can be employed to develop models that learn from sensor data (e.g., vibration, acoustic emissions) while being informed by the underlying physics of material degradation. For example, a hybrid model could be developed to predict the remaining useful life of a structure. The neural network would be trained on historical operational data and damage measurements, with the physics-informed loss incorporating models of crack propagation or material fatigue, potentially derived from fracture mechanics or damage mechanics principles. By enforcing these physical laws, the model becomes more robust in predicting damage evolution, even under varying operational conditions that might not be fully represented in the training data. In a case study involving bridges, a PIML model was used to predict crack growth under cyclic loading. The model was trained on data from structural health monitoring systems and was constrained by Paris's Law for fatigue crack propagation. The hybrid approach demonstrated superior accuracy in predicting crack sizes over time compared to purely empirical models, allowing for more proactive maintenance scheduling and enhanced safety assurance. The ability to integrate physical models of damage evolution ensured that the predictions were not only data-consistent but also physically plausible.

In the domain of **thermal management**, hybrid modeling and PIML are proving invaluable for optimizing heat transfer processes, which are crucial in everything from electronics cooling to energy systems. Traditional thermal simulations, often based on the finite element method (FEM) or finite difference method (FDM) to solve heat conduction or convection equations, can be computationally demanding, particularly in transient or complex multi-physics scenarios. PIML offers a way to create efficient surrogate models. For instance, consider the challenge of predicting temperature distributions in a microelectronic device. A

PIML model could be trained on sparse temperature sensor data and also incorporate the heat equation. The physics loss would ensure that the network's predictions satisfy the fundamental laws of heat conduction and convection. In a practical scenario involving the cooling of a complex electronic chip, a PIML model was developed to predict the temperature profile across the chip under varying power loads. The network was trained on a limited set of temperature measurements and was regularized by the steady-state heat equation. This hybrid approach yielded a model that could predict temperatures with high accuracy, even at locations without sensors, and significantly accelerated the process of evaluating different cooling strategies and heat sink designs. The physical grounding of the model ensured that the predictions were not only close to the available data but also respected the physical behavior of heat flow, leading to more reliable thermal designs and preventing overheating issues.

Furthermore, hybrid models are being applied to optimize energy efficiency in buildings, a sector with significant thermal loads. Predicting and controlling indoor climate conditions requires understanding complex heat transfer mechanisms, including conduction, convection, and radiation, as well as the thermal dynamics of building materials. A PIML approach can be used to build predictive models that learn from historical sensor data (temperature, humidity, occupancy) and are constrained by the thermodynamic principles governing heat exchange. In one application, a PIML model was developed to predict the thermal load of a commercial building. The model integrated building energy simulation data and real-time sensor readings, while being guided by fundamental energy balance equations for different zones within the building. This physics-informed approach allowed the model to accurately predict energy consumption and identify optimal control strategies for HVAC systems, even when faced with unexpected external conditions or changes in occupancy. The integration of physical laws ensured that the model's predictions were physically consistent and robust, leading to substantial energy savings and improved occupant comfort. The ability to learn from data and adhere to physical constraints makes these hybrid models highly effective for optimizing complex energy systems.

The successful integration of PIML and hybrid modeling extends to **materials science and discovery**. Predicting the properties of novel materials or understanding complex material behaviors often requires sophisticated simulations or extensive experimental characterization. PIML can accelerate this process by building predictive models that learn from existing material databases and are informed by fundamental physical principles governing material behavior, such as phase field models, molecular dynamics simulations, or continuum mechanics. For example, researchers have used PIML to predict the mechanical properties of alloys or composites. A neural network could be trained on experimental data of material properties and augmented with physics-based loss terms derived from constitutive models or phase diagrams. By enforcing these physical principles, the PIML model can accurately predict properties for new material compositions that were not part of the training set, thereby guiding experimental efforts and accelerating materials discovery. In one instance, a PIML model was developed to predict the yield strength and elastic modulus of metallic alloys based on their elemental composition. The model incorporated principles from thermodynamics and solid mechanics to constrain its predictions. This physics-informed approach enabled the rapid screening of potential alloy candidates with desired properties, significantly reducing the time and cost associated with traditional trial-and-error experimental approaches. The model's ability to generalize to unseen compositions, grounded in physical laws, highlights its power in materials design.

In the realm of
robotics and control, hybrid models are enhancing the precision and adaptability of robotic systems. Developing accurate models of robot dynamics, especially for complex manipulators or mobile robots operating in uncertain environments, is crucial for effective control. PIML can be used to learn these dynamics by combining sensor data (e.g., joint angles, velocities, forces) with the underlying physics of motion. A neural network can be trained to predict the robot's trajectory or the forces it will exert, with its learning guided by Newton's laws of motion or Lagrangian mechanics. This physics-informed approach allows the robot to learn its own dynamics more accurately and efficiently than purely data-driven methods. For example, in the context of grasping and manipulation, a PIML model could be developed to predict the contact forces and object motion during interaction. The model would be trained on data from robot execution of tasks and would be constrained by principles of contact mechanics and rigid body dynamics. Such a model can lead to more stable and robust manipulation strategies, reducing the likelihood of dropped objects or unintended collisions.

The physical grounding ensures that the learned model is not only effective in performing the task but also safe and predictable.

Furthermore, PIML is contributing to the development of **autonomous systems** by improving their understanding of the environment and their predictive capabilities. For autonomous navigation, for instance, predicting the motion of other vehicles or pedestrians is paramount. A hybrid model can be developed for motion prediction, integrating observed trajectories with physical constraints such as kinematic limits, traffic rules, and basic principles of interaction. The neural network would learn from real-world traffic data and be regularized by these physical constraints. This allows for more accurate and reliable prediction of future states of other agents, which in turn enables safer and more efficient path planning for autonomous vehicles. In a specific study focused on predicting pedestrian trajectories at intersections, a PIML model was developed that incorporated pedestrian kinematic limits and social interaction models (e.g., avoiding collisions with other pedestrians). The model, trained on observed pedestrian movement data, demonstrated significantly improved prediction accuracy compared to purely data-driven approaches, especially in complex scenarios involving multiple interacting agents. The integration of physics ensured that the predicted trajectories were not only plausible but also adhered to fundamental constraints of human movement and interaction.

These diverse examples underscore a consistent theme: the power of integration. By combining the pattern-recognition capabilities of machine learning with the explanatory and predictive power of physical laws, hybrid models, and PIML in particular, are enabling engineers and scientists to tackle problems that were previously intractable or prohibitively expensive. The improvements in simulation accuracy, predictive performance, and design optimization observed across these domains are not isolated successes. They represent a fundamental shift in how we approach scientific and engineering challenges, moving towards a more holistic and robust methodology that harnesses the strengths of both data and physics. The ensuing sections will further explore specific techniques and considerations for implementing these powerful hybrid approaches.

Chapter 4: Real-time Synchronization Mechanisms

The preceding discussion has meticulously detailed the architectural nuances and training paradigms of Physics-Informed Machine Learning (PIML) and broader hybrid modeling approaches. We have observed their profound impact across a spectrum of engineering disciplines, from fluid dynamics to structural mechanics, materials science, and robotics, showcasing how the integration of physical laws with data-driven techniques unlocks unprecedented levels of simulation fidelity, predictive accuracy, and design efficiency. These case studies serve as compelling evidence for the transformative potential of such hybrid methodologies, demonstrating their ability to transcend the limitations of purely data-driven or purely physics-based models.

With the foundational concepts and their practical manifestations thoroughly explored, our focus now shifts to a critical operational requirement for realizing the full promise of digital twins: the imperative of real-time synchronization. While sophisticated hybrid models can endow a digital twin with remarkable predictive and analytical capabilities, their efficacy is intrinsically tied to the fidelity and timeliness of the information they process. A digital twin, by its very definition, is intended to be a living, dynamic replica of a physical asset or system. This dynamism is not merely about having a detailed three-dimensional model; it is fundamentally about reflecting the current state, behavior, and operational context of its physical counterpart in near real-time. The continuous, bidirectional flow of data between the physical asset and its digital representation is the lifeblood that sustains this dynamic equivalence. Without it, the digital twin rapidly devolves from a powerful operational tool into a static, historical snapshot, quickly losing its relevance for contemporary decision-making and adaptive control.

The necessity for real-time synchronization stems directly from the primary use cases that drive the adoption of digital twin technology. Consider the domain of **live monitoring and performance assessment**. Industries reliant on complex machinery, such as manufacturing, aerospace, energy production, and transportation, require constant awareness of how their assets are performing. This includes monitoring key performance indicators (KPIs), operational parameters (temperature, pressure, vibration, speed), and overall system health. A digital twin equipped with real-time data streams can provide an intuitive, comprehensive dashboard of this information. For instance, in a power generation plant, sensors on turbines, generators, and other critical components continuously feed operational data—such as rotational speed, vibration levels, exhaust gas temperature, and power output—to the digital twin. This data is not just logged; it is processed and visualized instantaneously, allowing operators to see the current status of each component and the plant as a whole. If a turbine's vibration levels begin to deviate from their normal operating range, the digital twin, reflecting this anomaly in real-time, can alert operators immediately, enabling them to assess the situation without delay.

This immediate awareness is crucial for **anomaly detection and predictive maintenance**. Traditional maintenance strategies often rely on scheduled inspections or responding to failures after they occur. This can lead to unexpected downtime, costly repairs, and potential safety hazards. Real-time synchronization allows a digital twin to act as an intelligent sentinel. By continuously comparing incoming sensor data against expected operational parameters and the predictions of its integrated hybrid models, the twin can identify subtle deviations that might indicate an incipient failure. For example, in an automotive manufacturing line, sensors on robotic arms monitor their precise movements, motor currents, and joint temperatures. If a robotic arm's motor current begins to exhibit a slight, persistent increase, or its movement path deviates marginally from the norm, the digital twin, synchronized in real-time, can flag this as a potential issue. This early detection might indicate wear on a gearbox or a developing electrical fault. The hybrid models within the twin can then be used to predict the likely progression of this anomaly, estimate the remaining useful life (RUL) of the component, and recommend a specific maintenance action, such as lubricating a joint or replacing a specific motor part, before a catastrophic failure occurs. The synchronization ensures that this assessment is based on the most current operational conditions, making the maintenance recommendations precise and actionable, thereby minimizing unplanned downtime and optimizing resource allocation.

Furthermore, real-time synchronization is indispensable for **immediate control adjustments and operational optimization**. In dynamic environments, the ability to adapt operations on the fly based on current conditions is paramount. A digital twin, linked in real-time, can serve as the central nervous system for such adaptive control. Imagine a smart grid managing energy distribution. Renewable energy sources like solar and wind are inherently variable. Real-time data from weather forecasts, energy production levels, and consumer demand is fed into the digital twin of the grid. If a sudden increase in solar power generation occurs due to unexpected sunshine, or if demand spikes due to a heatwave, the digital twin can instantly assess the implications. Based on its synchronized understanding of the grid's capacity, current load, and the performance characteristics of its components (informed by PIML models of energy flow and storage), the twin can automatically trigger adjustments to optimize energy distribution, manage storage systems, and potentially activate backup generators. This level of responsiveness, driven by a continuously updated digital representation, ensures grid stability, prevents blackouts, and maximizes the utilization of available energy resources. Without real-time synchronization, such rapid and informed adjustments would be impossible, leaving the system vulnerable to fluctuations and inefficiencies.

The concept of
operational decision-making is profoundly enhanced by real-time synchronization. Managers, operators, and engineers often need to make critical decisions under pressure, relying on the best available information. A synchronized digital twin provides this information in a contextualized and easily interpretable format. In a logistics operation managing a fleet of autonomous vehicles or drones, real-time data on vehicle location, battery levels, traffic conditions, and delivery statuses is fed to the digital twin. If an unforeseen traffic jam arises, or if a delivery deadline is suddenly accelerated, the digital twin can instantly simulate the impact of these changes on the overall schedule. It can then present the best alternative routing options, reallocate resources, and provide clear directives to the human operators or directly to the autonomous systems. This allows for agile responses to dynamic operational challenges, ensuring that efficiency and timeliness are maintained even in the face of unexpected events. The twin's ability to process current data and, in conjunction with its hybrid models, predict the outcomes of various decisions, empowers users to make more informed and effective choices in real-time.

The fidelity of the synchronization itself is also a critical aspect. It is not merely about receiving data, but about receiving it with minimal latency and maximum accuracy. The definition of "real-time" can vary depending on the application. For some industrial control systems, this might mean latencies measured in milliseconds. For fleet management or asset performance monitoring, a latency of seconds or even minutes might be acceptable. The choice of communication protocols, sensor technologies, network infrastructure, and data processing architectures all play a crucial role in achieving the desired level of synchronization. Furthermore, the data itself must be reliable. Faulty sensors or noisy communication channels can lead to a digital twin that, while synchronized, presents a distorted view of reality. Therefore, robust data validation, filtering, and error-correction mechanisms are integral components of any real-time synchronization strategy.

Moreover, the synchronization is often **bidirectional**. While data flows from the physical asset to the digital twin for monitoring and analysis, commands and adjustments can also flow from the digital twin back to the physical asset for control purposes. This closed-loop operation is where the full power of the synchronized digital twin is realized. For example, if the PIML-enhanced digital twin of a chemical reactor identifies that optimal yield is being compromised due to slight deviations in temperature and pressure, it can send precise control signals back to the physical reactor's actuators to make fine-tuned adjustments. This continuous feedback loop, enabled by real-time bidirectional synchronization, allows for the dynamic optimization of processes, ensuring they operate at peak performance and adherence to safety parameters, even as external conditions fluctuate.

The integrity of the synchronization is also paramount for **simulation and "what-if" scenarios**. While the hybrid models within a digital twin enable sophisticated predictions, the accuracy of these predictions is heavily dependent on the current state of the physical asset. If the digital twin is not synchronized with the real-time operational conditions, any simulations run on it will be based on outdated or incorrect assumptions. For example, if a manufacturing plant is experiencing an unexpected surge in demand, engineers might use the digital twin to simulate the impact of increasing production line speeds. If the twin is not synchronized with the current state of the machinery (e.g., actual operating temperatures, wear levels of components), the simulation might suggest speeds that the physical equipment cannot safely or reliably achieve, potentially leading to equipment damage or quality issues. Real-time synchronization ensures that "what-if" analyses are grounded in the current reality of the physical system, providing reliable insights for strategic planning and operational adjustments.

In essence, the imperative of real-time synchronization transforms the digital twin from a passive digital model into an active, intelligent counterpart to its physical twin. It ensures that the digital representation is not just a static blueprint but a dynamic, breathing entity that mirrors the physical asset's existence moment by moment. This continuous, accurate reflection is the fundamental prerequisite for leveraging the advanced analytical, predictive, and control capabilities that hybrid models and PIML bring to the table, ultimately enabling true digital transformation across industries. The following sections will delve into the specific mechanisms and technologies that facilitate this crucial real-time data exchange.

The efficacy of any digital twin, particularly one empowered by sophisticated hybrid models such as Physics-Informed Machine Learning (PIML), is fundamentally tethered to the continuous and accurate flow of data from its physical counterpart. This data acquisition and sensor integration stage represents the foundational bedrock upon which the entire digital twin ecosystem is built. Without a robust and reliable mechanism for capturing the real-time state of the physical asset, the most advanced algorithms and intricate models will operate on incomplete or erroneous information, rendering their insights and predictions either irrelevant or, worse, misleading. This section delves into the practicalities of this critical first step, examining the diverse array of sensor technologies, strategic deployment considerations, and the inherent challenges in ensuring data quality, calibration, and unwavering reliability.

The selection of appropriate sensors is a highly context-dependent process, dictated by the specific physical phenomena that need to be monitored. For instance, in an industrial manufacturing setting, monitoring the health and performance of robotic arms might necessitate accelerometers to detect vibrations indicative of wear, encoders to precisely track joint positions and velocities, and current sensors to gauge motor load. In a chemical processing plant, temperature probes (thermocouples, RTDs), pressure transducers, flow meters, and gas analyzers become paramount for tracking reaction conditions and ensuring safety. Aerospace applications often demand high-precision gyroscopes and accelerometers for navigation and attitude control, strain gauges for structural integrity monitoring, and specialized sensors for monitoring parameters like fuel flow, engine temperature, and hydraulic pressure. Even in seemingly simpler systems, such as a smart building, sensors for ambient temperature, humidity, light levels, and occupancy detection play a crucial role in optimizing energy consumption and occupant comfort. The proliferation of the Internet of Things (IoT) has dramatically expanded the availability and affordability of a vast spectrum of sensors, ranging from basic environmental monitors to highly specialized scientific instruments. Each sensor technology possesses its own unique characteristics, including accuracy, resolution, sampling rate, operating range, power consumption, and susceptibility to environmental factors like electromagnetic interference, temperature fluctuations, and humidity. A thorough understanding of these characteristics is essential for selecting sensors that not only meet the required performance specifications but are also suitable for the intended operating environment. For example, a low-cost thermistor might suffice for monitoring ambient room temperature, but for measuring the precise temperature of a critical industrial process, a more robust and accurate thermocouple or Resistance Temperature Detector (RTD) might be indispensable. Similarly, the required sampling rate is a critical consideration. For applications involving high-speed dynamics, such as monitoring the impact of a vehicle collision or the rapid combustion process in an engine, sensors capable of capturing data at kilohertz frequencies are necessary. Conversely, for monitoring the slow degradation of a bridge structure or the long-term performance trends of a power grid, lower sampling rates, perhaps on the order of minutes or hours, may be entirely adequate.

Beyond the intrinsic properties of individual sensors, their strategic deployment is equally critical. This involves determining not just *what* to measure, but also *where* and *how many* sensors are needed to provide a comprehensive and representative view of the physical asset's state. For complex systems, a single sensor may not be sufficient. Multiple sensors might be strategically placed to capture spatial variations or to provide redundant measurements for cross-validation and enhanced reliability. In a large industrial facility, for example, temperature sensors might be distributed throughout a heated vessel to understand temperature gradients, or vibration sensors might be placed on various points of a large rotating machine to identify the specific location and nature of an imbalance or bearing wear. The physical layout, accessibility for installation and maintenance, and potential for interference with the normal operation of the physical asset are all crucial considerations during the deployment planning phase. Furthermore, the cabling and connectivity infrastructure required to transmit data from these deployed sensors to a central data acquisition system must be robust, reliable, and designed to withstand the rigors of the operational environment. Wireless sensor networks (WSNs) have emerged as a powerful solution for simplifying deployment and reducing cabling complexity, particularly in hard-to-reach areas or in dynamic environments where frequent reconfiguration might be necessary. However, WSNs introduce their own set of challenges, including power management for battery-operated nodes, potential for signal interference, and network security.

The integration of these diverse sensor outputs into a unified data stream suitable for ingestion by a digital twin is a complex engineering task. Raw sensor data often requires significant pre-processing before it can be utilized by PIML models or other analytical engines. This pre-processing typically involves several key steps.
Signal Conditioning: Raw analog signals from many sensors, such as thermocouples or strain gauges, are often weak and noisy. Signal conditioning circuits amplify, filter, and linearize these signals to make them suitable for digitization. This can involve techniques like low-pass filtering to remove high-frequency noise, high-pass filtering to eliminate slow drifts, or band-pass filtering to isolate specific frequency components of interest. For example, vibration analysis often requires precise filtering to focus on specific frequency bands associated with different mechanical fault signatures. **Analog-to-Digital Conversion (ADC)**: Digital systems operate on discrete values, so analog sensor signals must be converted into digital form. The quality of the ADC – its resolution (number of bits) and sampling rate – directly impacts the fidelity of the digital representation of the analog signal. A higher resolution ADC can capture finer details in the signal, while a higher sampling rate ensures that transient events are not missed. **Data Formatting and Timestamping**: Once digitized, data from various sensors needs to be organized into a consistent format. This typically involves creating data packets that include the sensor identifier, the measured value, and, crucially, a precise timestamp. Accurate timestamping is paramount for real-time synchronization, as it allows for the correct ordering of events and the accurate correlation of data from different sources. The timestamping mechanism itself must be synchronized across all

data acquisition points, often relying on Network Time Protocol (NTP) or Precision Time Protocol (PTP) for high-accuracy applications. **Data Aggregation and Buffering**: In systems with a high volume of sensor data, it may be necessary to aggregate data from multiple sensors or buffer it before transmission to reduce network traffic or to smooth out fluctuations. This aggregation could involve averaging readings over a short period or calculating statistical measures. Buffering helps to prevent data loss during temporary network outages or when the receiving system is momentarily overloaded.

The challenge of
data quality is pervasive throughout the acquisition and integration process. Sensors can malfunction, drift over time, or be affected by environmental factors, leading to inaccurate or unreliable data. Addressing data quality requires a multi-faceted approach. **Calibration**: Sensors, particularly those measuring physical quantities with high precision, need to be regularly calibrated against known standards. Calibration ensures that the sensor's output accurately reflects the physical quantity it is measuring. This can be a significant undertaking, especially for large numbers of sensors in remote or difficult-to-access locations. Automated or semi-automated calibration procedures, where feasible, can significantly improve efficiency. **Validation and Verification**: Incoming data should be subjected to validation checks to identify potential anomalies or errors. This can include range checks (ensuring values fall within physically plausible limits), rate-of-change checks (detecting sudden, improbable jumps), and consistency checks (comparing readings from redundant sensors). **Data Filtering and Noise Reduction**: Advanced signal processing techniques can be employed to filter out noise and extract meaningful signals from corrupted data. This might involve statistical methods, Kalman filters, or more sophisticated machine learning-based denoising techniques. **Fault Detection and Diagnosis**: Mechanisms should be in place to detect when a sensor itself is failing or providing erroneous data. This can be achieved by monitoring sensor diagnostics (if available), analyzing the statistical properties of the sensor output, or comparing it with data from other related sensors. Once a faulty sensor is detected, the system must be able to gracefully handle the situation, perhaps by substituting data from a redundant sensor or by flagging the data as unreliable.

The concept of

reliability extends beyond individual sensor performance to the entire data acquisition system. This encompasses the robustness of the communication network, the power supply to the sensors and data loggers, and the redundancy of critical components. In safety-critical applications, the failure of a single data acquisition channel could have severe consequences. Therefore, implementing redundancy at various levels – redundant sensors, redundant communication paths, and redundant data processing units – is often necessary to ensure continuous operation. The choice of communication protocols also plays a vital role in reliability. While protocols like Modbus or OPC UA are widely used in industrial automation for their robustness and interoperability, newer protocols designed for IoT applications, such as MQTT or CoAP, offer different trade-offs in terms of overhead, latency, and reliability. The selection of the appropriate protocol depends on the specific requirements of the digital twin application, including bandwidth constraints, power limitations, and the need for guaranteed message delivery. For real-time synchronization, low-latency, high-throughput protocols are generally preferred, especially when dealing with time-sensitive control loops.

Furthermore, the integration of sensors extends beyond simple data collection to creating a rich contextual understanding of the data. This means not just knowing the temperature reading, but also knowing
which specific component in the physical asset that reading pertains to, *what* its normal operating range is, and *what* historical trends have been observed. This metadata, often stored in a digital asset's configuration database, is crucial for interpreting the raw sensor data correctly. When a new sensor is added or an existing one is recalibrated, this metadata needs to be updated accordingly to maintain the integrity of the digital twin's context. This contextualization also allows for the application of physics-informed models more effectively. For instance, knowing the precise geometry and material properties of a component, along with its current operating temperature and pressure, enables a PIML model to accurately predict stress distributions or fluid flow patterns within that component.

The sheer volume and velocity of data generated by modern sensor networks present significant challenges for real-time processing and integration. This has led to the development of edge computing architectures, where data processing and analysis are performed closer to the data source – at the "edge" of the network, often within the sensor devices themselves or in local gateways. Edge computing can significantly reduce latency by performing initial data filtering, aggregation, and even model inference locally, sending only the essential or processed data to the central digital twin platform. This is particularly beneficial for applications requiring very low latency, such as real-time control loops in autonomous vehicles or industrial robotics. For example, an edge device connected to a camera on a manufacturing line might perform object detection and defect identification locally, only transmitting alerts or summary statistics to the cloud-based digital twin, rather than the raw video stream. This not only reduces bandwidth requirements but also speeds up response times.

The ongoing evolution of sensor technology, coupled with advancements in data processing and communication infrastructure, continues to push the boundaries of what is achievable in digital twin synchronization. As sensors become more intelligent, autonomous, and interconnected, the ability to acquire comprehensive, accurate, and timely data from the physical world will only improve. This, in turn, will empower digital twins with increasingly sophisticated capabilities, enabling them to serve as more accurate reflections of their physical counterparts and more potent tools for monitoring, analysis, control, and optimization. The careful consideration and expert implementation of data acquisition and sensor integration strategies are therefore not merely technical prerequisites but strategic imperatives for unlocking the full transformative potential of digital twin technology.

The seamless and continuous flow of data from the physical realm to its digital counterpart is not solely an outcome of sophisticated sensor technology and intelligent data acquisition; it fundamentally relies on a robust and well-defined communication infrastructure. This infrastructure acts as the nervous system of the digital twin, facilitating the rapid and reliable exchange of information between the physical asset and the digital representation. Without efficient communication pathways, even the most finely tuned sensors and advanced processing capabilities would be rendered ineffective, as data would be unable to reach its destination in a timely or usable manner. This subsection delves into the critical aspects of this communication layer, exploring the prevalent communication protocols and network architectures that underpin the real-time synchronization of digital twins.

At the heart of any real-time data exchange lies the choice of communication protocols. These are sets of rules that govern how data is formatted, transmitted, and received across a network. The selection of appropriate protocols is paramount, as it directly impacts latency, bandwidth utilization, reliability, and security – all crucial factors for effective digital twin operation. In industrial and operational technology (OT) environments, several protocols have risen to prominence, each offering distinct advantages and catering to different requirements.

One of the most widely adopted protocols, particularly in the realm of the Internet of Things (IoT) and its industrial extension (IIoT), is the Message Queuing Telemetry Transport (MQTT). Developed with low bandwidth and unreliable networks in mind, MQTT operates on a publish-subscribe model. In this paradigm, devices (clients) don't communicate directly with each other. Instead, they publish messages to "topics" on a central broker. Other clients interested in those topics subscribe to them and receive the messages. For a digital twin, this means sensors can publish their readings (e.g., temperature, pressure, vibration) to specific topics (e.g., `/asset/machine1/temperature`, `/asset/machine1/vibration`). The digital twin application, or intermediate data processing layers, can then subscribe to these topics to receive the real-time data. The lightweight nature of MQTT's header information makes it highly efficient, minimizing overhead and maximizing the number of devices that can communicate effectively. Its Quality of Service (QoS) levels (0, 1, and 2) offer varying degrees of message delivery assurance, from "at most once" to "exactly once," allowing developers to balance reliability with performance. This flexibility is vital for digital twins, where some data might be valuable for trend analysis (QoS 0 could suffice), while critical control parameters might require higher assurance (QoS 1 or 2).

Another cornerstone protocol in industrial communication, especially for interoperability and data exchange between diverse systems, is the Open Platform Communications Unified Architecture (OPC UA). Unlike MQTT's focus on message brokering, OPC UA is a platform-independent, service-oriented architecture that provides a standardized way to access and exchange data from industrial automation devices. It offers a rich information model that allows for structured data representation, including metadata, historical data, and alarms. For digital twins, OPC UA excels at providing a comprehensive view of an asset's state. It can represent not just raw sensor values but also the relationships between different components, their properties, and their operational status. The ability of OPC UA to expose data in a semantic and structured manner significantly aids in building context-aware digital twins. For instance, an OPC UA server on a piece of machinery could expose not only the current motor speed but also the motor's technical specifications, its maintenance history, and its operational modes. Furthermore, OPC UA is designed with security in mind, incorporating features like authentication, authorization, and encryption, which are non-negotiable for industrial environments. Its ability to traverse firewalls and operate across different network layers makes it a versatile choice for integrating legacy systems with modern digital twin platforms.

Beyond these leading protocols, other communication methods play a role. For applications demanding extremely low latency, especially in control loops or safety-critical systems, industrial Ethernet protocols like EtherNet/IP, PROFINET, or EtherCAT are often employed. These protocols are designed for deterministic communication, ensuring that data packets arrive within precisely defined time windows. While they are typically used for high-speed machine-to-machine communication, their data can be aggregated and then transmitted to the digital twin via MQTT or OPC UA. For simpler, less data-intensive applications, or in environments with highly constrained resources, protocols like CoAP (Constrained Application Protocol) offer a lightweight alternative to HTTP, designed for constrained devices and networks.

The choice of protocol is intrinsically linked to the network architecture employed. As digital twins evolve, so too do the network infrastructures that support them. Traditionally, data from sensors and controllers was routed through a hierarchical network, culminating in a central data center or cloud platform for processing and analysis. However, the explosion of connected devices and the demand for real-time insights have necessitated a shift towards more distributed and intelligent network designs.

Edge computing represents a significant paradigm shift in this regard. Instead of sending all raw data to a distant cloud for processing, edge computing brings computation and data storage closer to the source of data generation – the physical asset. For digital twins, this means performing initial data processing, filtering, aggregation, and even running certain analytical models or machine learning inferences directly on devices at the edge, such as gateways, industrial PCs, or even the sensors themselves if they are sufficiently intelligent. This offers several compelling advantages. Firstly, it drastically reduces latency. By processing data locally, decisions can be made and actions taken in near real-time, which is crucial for applications like autonomous systems, robotics, and real-time control. For example, an edge device connected to a robotic arm could analyze vision sensor data to detect an anomaly and adjust the arm's trajectory instantaneously, without waiting for instructions from the cloud. Secondly, edge computing significantly reduces bandwidth requirements. Instead of streaming massive amounts of raw sensor data, only processed insights, summaries, or alerts are transmitted to the central digital twin platform. This is particularly beneficial in environments with limited or expensive network connectivity. Thirdly, it enhances reliability and resilience. If the connection to the cloud is disrupted, edge devices can continue to operate autonomously, performing essential functions and storing data locally until connectivity is restored. This autonomy is vital for critical infrastructure and industrial operations where downtime is unacceptable.

In the context of a digital twin, an edge architecture might involve local gateways collecting data from numerous sensors via protocols like Modbus or CAN bus. These gateways then perform pre-processing, apply basic anomaly detection algorithms, and aggregate the data before publishing it to the central digital twin platform using MQTT or OPC UA. More advanced edge deployments might include dedicated edge servers running more complex analytics, enabling local predictive maintenance alerts or real-time optimization of local processes without constant cloud interaction. The integration of edge computing requires careful consideration of distributed data management, synchronization of edge and cloud states, and security across a more dispersed network.

Complementary to edge computing, cloud platforms continue to play a pivotal role in the digital twin ecosystem. Cloud platforms provide the scalable infrastructure necessary for storing vast amounts of historical data, running complex simulations, training sophisticated AI models, and providing centralized dashboards and visualization tools for users. The relationship between edge and cloud is often symbiotic. Edge devices handle the immediate, real-time processing and actuation, while the cloud serves as the central repository for long-term analysis, global optimization, and the development of more advanced digital twin functionalities. For instance, data collected over time at the edge can be uploaded to the cloud for in-depth historical trend analysis, identifying patterns that might not be apparent from local, short-term observations. Machine learning models trained on this comprehensive historical data in the cloud can then be deployed back to the edge devices to enhance their local decision-making capabilities.

Hybrid architectures, combining both edge and cloud capabilities, are becoming increasingly common. In such a setup, critical, time-sensitive operations are managed at the edge, while less time-critical, computationally intensive tasks are offloaded to the cloud. This allows for the best of both worlds: low latency and high responsiveness at the edge, coupled with the immense processing power, storage capacity, and analytical capabilities of the cloud. For example, a digital twin of a fleet of vehicles might utilize edge devices in each vehicle to monitor engine performance and driver behavior in real-time, triggering immediate alerts for critical issues. Simultaneously, data from the entire fleet is sent to a cloud platform for fleet-wide performance analysis, route optimization, and predictive maintenance scheduling for all vehicles.

Regardless of the specific architecture – whether purely cloud-based, edge-centric, or a hybrid model – the communication channels must be secured. In industrial environments, where operational integrity and safety are paramount, cybersecurity is not an afterthought but a fundamental design consideration. The interconnected nature of digital twins, linking physical assets to digital systems, creates new potential attack vectors. Therefore, robust security measures must be implemented at every layer of the communication infrastructure. This includes encrypting data in transit to prevent eavesdropping and tampering, implementing strong authentication mechanisms to ensure that only authorized devices and users can access the network, and employing authorization controls to restrict access to specific data and functionalities. Network segmentation is also a crucial practice, isolating critical operational technology (OT) networks from less secure information technology (IT) networks to prevent the lateral movement of threats. Secure protocols like TLS/SSL for data encryption and VPNs for secure remote access are essential components of a secure digital twin communication strategy. Furthermore, regular security audits, vulnerability assessments, and prompt patching of systems are necessary to maintain a strong security posture against evolving threats.

The performance requirements of the communication infrastructure are also highly dependent on the specific digital twin application. Latency, the time delay between data generation and its availability for processing or actuation, is a critical factor. For applications involving real-time control loops or safety systems, latency must be in the order of milliseconds or even microseconds. For monitoring and analytical applications, higher latencies might be tolerable, but still need to be predictable to ensure meaningful insights. Bandwidth, the capacity of the communication channel to transmit data, is another key consideration. High-frequency sensor data, video streams, or complex simulation outputs can consume significant bandwidth. Network architectures and protocols must be chosen to efficiently manage these demands, often through data compression, intelligent aggregation, and prioritization of critical data streams.

In summary, the communication protocols and network architectures are the unseen arteries that enable the lifeblood of a digital twin – its data – to flow effectively. From the efficient messaging of MQTT and the comprehensive data modeling of OPC UA to the distributed intelligence of edge computing and the scalable power of cloud platforms, each element plays a crucial role. The careful selection and implementation of these technologies, with a strong emphasis on latency, bandwidth, and robust security, are indispensable for building a digital twin that is not only a faithful representation of its physical counterpart but also a dynamic and responsive tool for driving operational excellence. This intricate dance between physical assets, sensors, communication networks, and digital platforms forms the bedrock of real-time synchronization, empowering organizations to achieve unprecedented levels of insight, control, and optimization.

The raw influx of data from the myriad sensors and actuators comprising the physical asset is rarely in a pristine state, ready for immediate consumption by a digital twin. This data, while rich with potential insights, often suffers from imperfections that can significantly degrade the accuracy and reliability of its digital counterpart. Consequently, a critical step in the real-time synchronization process involves rigorous data preprocessing and filtering. This phase is not merely about tidying up data; it is about transforming noisy, incomplete, and potentially misleading signals into a coherent and trustworthy stream that accurately reflects the true state of the physical world. Without this meticulous preparation, the digital twin risks becoming a distorted mirror, leading to flawed analysis, incorrect predictions, and potentially detrimental operational decisions.

One of the most pervasive issues in sensor data is the presence of noise. This can arise from a multitude of sources, including electromagnetic interference, thermal fluctuations, sensor calibration drift, or inherent limitations in sensor precision. Noise can manifest as random fluctuations around the true signal, making it difficult to discern the actual underlying value. To address this, various smoothing techniques are employed. Moving averages are a fundamental approach, where each data point is replaced by the average of itself and a fixed number of preceding and succeeding data points. This effectively dampens short-term fluctuations, revealing underlying trends more clearly. For instance, consider a temperature sensor on a critical piece of machinery. Without smoothing, the rapid, minor variations caused by ambient conditions or electronic interference might obscure a gradual, but significant, rise in operating temperature. A simple moving average would smooth out these transient spikes, highlighting the persistent upward trend that signals a potential overheating issue. However, a naive application of moving averages can also introduce lag, making the smoothed data trail behind the actual changes. More sophisticated smoothing filters, such as the Savitzky-Golay filter, are often preferred in digital twin applications. This method fits a polynomial to a subset of data points and then evaluates the polynomial at the center point, offering smoothing while better preserving the shape and peak information of the signal compared to a simple moving average. Exponential smoothing, another popular technique, assigns exponentially decreasing weights to older observations, giving more importance to recent data. This allows for quicker adaptation to changes while still providing a degree of noise reduction.

Beyond random noise, sensor data can also be plagued by outliers – data points that deviate significantly from the expected pattern or the general distribution of the data. These outliers can be caused by transient events, sensor malfunctions, data transmission errors, or even genuine, albeit unusual, physical phenomena. If not handled properly, outliers can severely skew statistical analyses and machine learning models operating within the digital twin. A single erroneous high-pressure reading, for example, could trigger a false alarm for a critical system, leading to unnecessary downtime or interventions. Identifying and handling outliers is therefore a crucial preprocessing step. A common approach is to use statistical methods. The Z-score is one such technique, measuring how many standard deviations a data point is away from the mean. Data points with a Z-score exceeding a predefined threshold are flagged as potential outliers. Similarly, the Interquartile Range (IQR) method, which is less sensitive to extreme values than the mean and standard deviation, can be used. Data points falling below Q1 - 1.5
*IQR or above Q3 + 1.5*IQR are considered outliers. For digital twin applications, visualization tools are invaluable for spotting outliers that statistical methods might miss, especially in multi-dimensional data spaces where simple statistical measures might not capture complex deviations. Once identified, outliers can be handled in several ways: they can be removed entirely, though this risks losing valuable information if the outlier represents a rare but important event. More commonly, they are replaced or "imputed" with more plausible values.

The challenge of missing data is another ubiquitous problem in real-time data streams. Sensors can fail temporarily, network connections can be lost, or data logging systems might encounter errors, leading to gaps in the data sequence. If these gaps are left unfilled, they can disrupt downstream analysis and hinder the digital twin's ability to maintain a continuous and accurate representation of the physical asset. Imputation techniques are employed to estimate and fill these missing values. Simple imputation methods include using the mean or median of the available data for a particular sensor. However, these methods do not account for temporal trends or correlations with other variables, potentially introducing bias. More sophisticated imputation strategies leverage the time-series nature of the data. Last Observation Carried Forward (LOCF) and Next Observation Carried Backward (NOCB) are simple temporal imputation methods, using the last known value or the next known value, respectively, to fill the gap. While easy to implement, these can lead to artificial plateaus or step changes in the data. Regression imputation uses the relationship between the missing variable and other observed variables to predict the missing values. For instance, if wind speed data is missing, and wind speed is strongly correlated with ambient temperature and pressure, a regression model trained on available data can estimate the missing wind speed based on the current temperature and pressure readings. K-Nearest Neighbors (KNN) imputation is another powerful technique that finds the K most similar data points (based on other features) to the point with missing data and imputes the missing value based on the values of its neighbors. For digital twins, especially those involving complex systems with interdependencies, multivariate imputation techniques that consider the relationships between multiple sensor readings are often the most effective. These methods can capture the dynamic behavior of the physical asset more faithfully, ensuring that the filled gaps do not create artificial inconsistencies.

Feature extraction and selection are also integral parts of the data preprocessing pipeline, aimed at deriving more meaningful information from the raw data and reducing its dimensionality. Raw sensor readings, while fundamental, might not directly represent the most informative aspects of the system's behavior. Feature extraction involves deriving new variables or features from the existing data that better capture the underlying phenomena. For example, in analyzing vibration data from a rotating machine, raw acceleration signals might be transformed into frequency-domain features using Fourier Transforms. Peaks in the frequency spectrum can indicate specific faults, such as bearing wear or imbalance, which might be difficult to discern from the time-domain signal alone. Similarly, statistical features like variance, skewness, kurtosis, or energy can be extracted from time-domain signals to characterize their behavior. For digital twins, feature engineering can significantly enhance the performance of predictive models. For instance, instead of feeding raw torque and speed data into a motor performance model, features like the ratio of torque to speed, or the cumulative work done, might be more indicative of motor efficiency or potential failure modes.

Feature selection, on the other hand, focuses on identifying the most relevant subset of features for a particular task. In a system with hundreds or thousands of sensors, not all data streams may be equally important for a given digital twin application. Redundant or irrelevant features can increase computational complexity, slow down processing, and even degrade model performance by introducing noise or spurious correlations. Techniques for feature selection range from simple filter methods, which evaluate features based on their intrinsic properties (e.g., correlation with the target variable, variance), to more complex wrapper methods, which use a specific machine learning model to evaluate subsets of features. Embedded methods, such as those found in regularized regression models (e.g., Lasso), perform feature selection as part of the model training process. For a digital twin, selecting the most pertinent features ensures that the computational resources are focused on the most impactful data, leading to faster updates and more efficient analysis. This is particularly crucial for real-time applications where every millisecond counts. For instance, in a digital twin of a chemical process, while temperature and pressure readings might be critical, flow rates of certain inert substances might be deemed less relevant for monitoring the primary reaction kinetics and could be filtered out or sampled less frequently, reducing the data processing load.

The temporal aspect of data is also critical. Digital twins are fundamentally concerned with the evolution of a physical asset over time, and thus, the temporal dependencies and dynamics within the data must be preserved or even highlighted. Techniques like differencing can be used to make time series data stationary by subtracting the previous observation from the current one, which can be helpful for certain modeling approaches. Lagged features, where past values of a variable are included as predictors for future values, are essential for capturing the inertial properties of physical systems. For example, the current state of a thermal system is not only dependent on the immediate heat input but also on the residual heat from previous periods. Incorporating lagged temperature readings can help the digital twin better model this thermal inertia.

Furthermore, the concept of data aggregation plays a vital role, especially when dealing with high-frequency sensor data. While granular data is often desirable, in many real-time scenarios, aggregated statistics over short time windows can be sufficient and more computationally efficient. For instance, instead of processing every single GPS coordinate from a fleet of vehicles, a digital twin might only require the average speed, distance covered, and maximum speed within a one-minute interval. This aggregation can be performed at the edge, further reducing the data volume transmitted and processed by the central digital twin. The choice of aggregation window size is critical and depends on the dynamics of the physical system and the required responsiveness of the digital twin.

The preprocessing and filtering pipeline must also be dynamic and adaptive. The characteristics of sensor data can change over time due to factors like equipment wear, environmental shifts, or changes in operational modes. A static filtering approach might become suboptimal or even detrimental as these conditions evolve. Therefore, adaptive filtering techniques, which can adjust their parameters in response to changing data characteristics, are highly beneficial. For example, an adaptive noise cancellation algorithm could continuously monitor the noise profile of a sensor and adjust its filtering characteristics accordingly. Similarly, outlier detection thresholds might need to be re-evaluated periodically or even dynamically based on recent data trends.

The rigorous application of these data preprocessing and filtering techniques ensures that the data ingested by the digital twin is not only voluminous but also of high quality. This clean, consistent, and representative data forms the foundation upon which accurate state estimation, reliable predictions, and effective decision-making within the digital twin are built. It transforms a raw cascade of numbers into meaningful signals, enabling the digital twin to serve its purpose as a faithful and dynamic digital replica of its physical counterpart, facilitating continuous optimization and operational excellence. The integrity of the synchronization process hinges on this essential data preparation phase, making it a non-negotiable component of any robust digital twin implementation. It is through this meticulous refinement that the digital twin can truly reflect the nuances of the physical world, empowering operators and stakeholders with actionable insights derived from trustworthy data.

The seamless replication of a physical asset's state within its digital twin is not a static achievement but a dynamic process governed by the underlying synchronization strategies. These strategies dictate how and when changes detected in the physical world are propagated to their digital counterparts. Broadly, these approaches can be categorized into two primary paradigms: batch processing and event-driven updates. Each carries its own set of advantages and disadvantages, making the choice contingent upon the specific requirements of the digital twin application, the nature of the physical asset, and the available communication infrastructure.

Batch processing, as the name suggests, involves collecting data over a certain period or accumulating a specific volume of data before transmitting it for synchronization. In this model, the digital twin is updated at discrete intervals, typically on a scheduled basis (e.g., every minute, every hour, or at the end of a production cycle). Imagine a digital twin of a large-scale manufacturing plant where production lines generate vast amounts of operational data. Instead of transmitting every single sensor reading as it occurs, which could overwhelm the network and processing capabilities, data from various machines and quality checks might be collected and aggregated over a 15-minute window. This batch of information is then sent to the digital twin for a comprehensive update. This approach is often favored when near-instantaneous reflection of every minor fluctuation is not critical, but rather a periodic, consolidated view of the asset's state is sufficient. It can be highly efficient in terms of network bandwidth and computational resources, as data transmission and processing are consolidated, reducing overhead. This is particularly advantageous in environments with limited or expensive network connectivity. Furthermore, batch processing can simplify data management and storage, as data points are often processed and archived in groups. For applications like long-term performance analysis, historical trend identification, or overall equipment effectiveness (OEE) reporting, where a slight delay in reflecting the absolute real-time state is acceptable, batch processing offers a robust and resource-conscious solution. However, the inherent drawback of batch processing is the introduction of latency. The digital twin's state will always lag behind the physical asset by the duration of the batch interval. If a critical anomaly occurs just after a batch has been processed, it will not be reflected in the digital twin until the next scheduled update, potentially leading to a missed opportunity for immediate intervention.

This delay can render batch processing unsuitable for applications requiring immediate feedback, such as real-time control systems, safety monitoring, or high-frequency trading platforms where even milliseconds matter.

In contrast, the event-driven synchronization strategy focuses on real-time propagation of changes. In this paradigm, the digital twin is updated whenever a significant event occurs in the physical world. An "event" can be defined as a change in a sensor reading that crosses a predefined threshold, the completion of a specific task, a state transition of a component, or an alert generated by the physical system. Consider a digital twin of an autonomous vehicle. Every deviation in steering angle, acceleration, or braking initiated by the vehicle's onboard systems would constitute an event that needs to be instantaneously reflected in the digital twin for accurate simulation and decision-making. Similarly, in a critical infrastructure monitoring system, a sudden drop in pressure within a pipeline would trigger an immediate event notification and update the digital twin. Event-driven synchronization minimizes latency by only transmitting data when it is relevant and indicative of a change. This allows the digital twin to remain in closer proximity to the real-time state of the physical asset. This approach is highly beneficial for applications where timely information is paramount for operational decisions, safety, or control. It enables faster response times, more agile decision-making, and a more accurate representation of dynamic processes. However, event-driven systems can be more complex to implement and manage. The continuous stream of events can lead to higher network traffic and increased computational load on both the data acquisition systems and the digital twin platform, especially if events are very frequent. Careful design is required to filter out redundant or insignificant events that could otherwise overwhelm the system. Furthermore, managing the state of the digital twin can become challenging if events arrive out of order or if there are dependencies between events that are not handled correctly. Techniques like sequence numbers, timestamps, and robust state management protocols are crucial for maintaining data integrity in an event-driven environment. The decision of what constitutes a "significant event" also requires careful consideration. A threshold-based approach for sensor readings, for instance, needs to be intelligently set. Too sensitive, and the system might be flooded with minor fluctuations; too insensitive, and critical changes might be missed.

The choice between batch processing and event-driven synchronization is not always binary; hybrid approaches are also common and often provide the optimal balance. For example, critical parameters that require near real-time monitoring might be updated via an event-driven mechanism, while less time-sensitive operational data could be batched. A digital twin of a power grid might receive immediate event notifications for critical fault conditions (e.g., circuit breaker trips, voltage instability) while simultaneously collecting and batching less urgent data like energy consumption readings from substations for daily reporting. This tiered approach leverages the strengths of both strategies, ensuring timely alerts for critical events while maintaining efficiency for bulk data. Another hybrid model could involve adaptive synchronization, where the system dynamically switches between batch and event-driven modes based on the current operational state or predefined rules. For instance, during normal operation, data might be batched to conserve resources. However, if the system detects an anomaly or enters a critical phase, it could automatically switch to event-driven updates for enhanced responsiveness.

Regardless of the chosen synchronization strategy, the fundamental challenge of latency remains a critical consideration. Latency, in the context of digital twins, refers to the time delay between a change occurring in the physical asset and that change being accurately reflected in its digital counterpart. This delay is an inherent consequence of data acquisition, transmission, processing, and the synchronization strategy itself. Understanding and managing latency is paramount because it directly impacts the fidelity of the digital twin and its ability to provide timely and actionable insights.

The sources of latency are multifaceted. At the point of data acquisition, sensors themselves have response times. A physical sensor does not instantaneously capture a change; it has a characteristic time constant determining how quickly it reacts. This is followed by analog-to-digital conversion (ADC) processes, which also introduce a small delay. The data then needs to be transmitted from the sensor or edge device to a central processing unit or cloud platform. This transmission latency is influenced by the communication protocol used (e.g., Wi-Fi, Ethernet, cellular, LoRaWAN), the network infrastructure, network congestion, distance, and the amount of data being transmitted. For batch processing, the accumulation time of the batch is a primary contributor to latency. Once the data arrives at the processing platform, it undergoes preprocessing and filtering, as discussed in the previous section. Complex filtering algorithms or large datasets can add further processing delays. Finally, the synchronization mechanism itself, whether it's a scheduled update or an event trigger, adds its own layer of latency.

The impact of latency varies significantly depending on the application. For a digital twin used for long-term historical analysis or product design simulation, a few minutes or even hours of latency might be perfectly acceptable. The insights derived from such analyses are typically not time-critical. However, for applications involving real-time monitoring and control, such as in industrial automation, autonomous systems, or financial trading, even milliseconds of latency can have severe consequences. For instance, in a digitally twinned robotic assembly line, a delay in reflecting a robotic arm's position could lead to collisions between machines, resulting in damage and production downtime. In an industrial control system, delayed feedback on a critical process parameter could prevent operators from taking timely corrective actions, potentially leading to product defects, equipment failure, or safety incidents.

Minimizing latency requires a multi-pronged approach, addressing each stage of the data lifecycle. At the sensor level, selecting sensors with fast response times and low inherent delays is crucial for time-sensitive applications. The choice of communication technology is also vital. High-speed wired networks like Ethernet are generally preferred for critical, low-latency connections within a facility. For wireless communications, technologies like Wi-Fi 6 or 5G offer significantly lower latency and higher bandwidth compared to older standards, making them suitable for more demanding scenarios. Edge computing plays an increasingly important role in latency reduction. By processing data closer to the source, at the edge of the network, rather than sending all raw data to a central cloud, latency can be dramatically reduced. Edge devices can perform initial data filtering, aggregation, and even run predictive models locally, sending only essential information or alerts upstream. This also reduces the amount of data that needs to be transmitted, alleviating network congestion. For example, an edge gateway connected to a fleet of sensors on a wind turbine can analyze vibration data locally and only send an alert to the digital twin if an anomaly indicative of bearing failure is detected, rather than streaming continuous raw vibration data.

Optimizing the synchronization strategy itself is another key lever for latency management. As discussed, event-driven updates generally offer lower latency than batch processing. However, the effectiveness of event-driven systems depends on how well events are defined and filtered. Implementing efficient event detection algorithms and intelligent thresholding can ensure that only genuinely significant changes trigger updates, preventing unnecessary network traffic and processing. For batch processing, reducing the batch interval or size can lower latency, but this must be balanced against the increased communication and processing overhead. Techniques like incremental updates, where only the changes since the last update are transmitted, can also help reduce the data volume and thus transmission time, effectively lowering latency even within a batch-like update cycle.

Furthermore, the architecture of the digital twin platform itself can be designed for low latency. This includes optimizing data ingestion pipelines, utilizing high-performance databases capable of rapid read/write operations, and employing efficient state management mechanisms. Real-time operating systems (RTOS) and in-memory computing technologies can be employed at various levels of the digital twin architecture to further reduce processing delays. For example, using an in-memory data grid to store the digital twin's state allows for extremely fast access and modification of its properties, enabling near real-time updates.

Beyond simply minimizing latency, it is also crucial to understand and quantify it. This involves implementing robust monitoring mechanisms to track the end-to-end latency for different data streams and events. By continuously measuring latency, organizations can identify bottlenecks in the system, assess the impact of changes, and ensure that the digital twin is meeting its performance requirements. Timestamping data at its source, during transmission, and upon arrival at the digital twin platform is fundamental for accurate latency measurement. Techniques like Round Trip Time (RTT) measurements can also provide insights into network delays.

The acceptable level of latency is highly application-dependent. For a digital twin of a passive monitoring system for environmental conditions, a latency of several minutes might be acceptable. In contrast, a digital twin used for real-time control of an industrial robot might require latency well below 50 milliseconds. For autonomous driving systems, latency requirements can be even more stringent, often measured in microseconds for critical control loops. Therefore, a thorough understanding of the operational context and the criticality of different data streams is essential when defining latency targets and choosing synchronization strategies. The decision-making process should involve stakeholders from operations, IT, and engineering to align on the acceptable trade-offs between latency, cost, complexity, and data fidelity.

In summary, the synchronization strategy employed—whether batch, event-driven, or a hybrid—is a foundational element determining how a digital twin stays abreast of its physical counterpart. Each strategy presents a unique balance of efficiency, responsiveness, and implementation complexity. Coupled with the persistent challenge of latency, which stems from every step of the data journey, these factors collectively shape the real-time fidelity of the digital twin. Proactive management of latency through optimized hardware, intelligent software design, edge computing, and judicious selection of communication protocols is not merely a technical enhancement but a critical enabler for the digital twin to deliver on its promise of accurate, timely, and actionable insights, thereby empowering effective decision-making and driving operational excellence.

Chapter 5: State Estimation for Dynamic Accuracy

The accuracy of a digital twin hinges critically on its ability to faithfully represent the current condition, or "state," of its physical counterpart. Often, this state is not directly and perfectly observable. Physical assets are equipped with sensors, but these devices rarely provide a complete, noise-free, and instantaneous readout of every relevant variable. This is where the sophisticated field of **state estimation** becomes indispensable. State estimation, in essence, is the process of inferring the most probable current state of a dynamic system, given a series of noisy or incomplete measurements and a mathematical model describing how the system evolves over time. For digital twins, it acts as a crucial bridge, transforming raw, imperfect sensor data into a coherent, reliable, and actionable understanding of the physical asset's reality.

At its core, state estimation tackles a fundamental challenge: the discrepancy between what we can directly measure and what we need to know. Imagine a complex industrial pump. We might measure its motor speed, vibration levels, and outlet pressure. However, we might also need to know the internal temperature of the pump bearings, the flow rate of the fluid *before* it reaches the main sensor, or the precise level of wear on a specific internal component. These vital parameters might not have dedicated sensors, or the existing sensors might be prone to inaccuracies due to environmental factors, calibration drift, or inherent limitations. State estimation algorithms use the available measurements (the "observations") and a model of the pump's physics and behavior (the "system dynamics") to deduce these unobservable or indirectly observable quantities.

The process typically involves a cycle of prediction and update. Based on the system's known dynamics and its estimated state at a previous time step, a prediction is made for its state at the current time step. This prediction is then refined or "corrected" using the latest available measurements. The algorithm continuously balances the information derived from the system model (which dictates how the state *should* evolve) with the information gleaned from the measurements (which reflect the *actual* observed behavior). This iterative refinement process allows state estimators to provide a more accurate and robust estimate of the system's state than would be possible from the raw measurements alone. They effectively "smooth out" noise, fill in gaps, and infer hidden variables.

One of the most widely employed techniques for state estimation in dynamic systems is the
Kalman filter. The Kalman filter is an optimal recursive estimator for linear systems with Gaussian noise. It operates by maintaining an estimate of the system's state and its uncertainty (covariance). In each time step, it first predicts the next state and its uncertainty based on the system model. Then, it incorporates the latest measurements to update the state estimate and reduce its uncertainty. The "optimality" of the Kalman filter means that, under its assumptions (linearity, Gaussian noise), it provides the minimum possible mean-squared error in its state estimates.

However, many real-world systems, especially those relevant to digital twins, are non-linear. For these scenarios, extensions of the Kalman filter are commonly used. The
Extended Kalman Filter (EKF) linearizes the non-linear system dynamics around the current state estimate. While effective for moderately non-linear systems, the EKF can diverge if the non-linearities are significant or if the initial state estimate is poor, as the linearization approximation may become too inaccurate. A more robust approach for highly non-linear systems is the
Unscented Kalman Filter (UKF). Instead of linearizing, the UKF uses a deterministic sampling approach, called the unscented transform, to capture the mean and covariance of the state distribution more accurately through a carefully chosen set of "sigma points." These points are propagated through the non-linear system model, and their transformed distributions are used to update the state estimate. The UKF generally provides better accuracy than the EKF for non-linear systems and is often simpler to implement as it does not require analytical derivation of Jacobians.

Beyond Kalman-based filters, other state estimation techniques exist.
Particle filters, also known as Sequential Monte Carlo methods, are particularly powerful for non-linear and non-Gaussian problems. They represent the probability distribution of the state using a set of discrete random samples (particles), each with an associated weight. As new measurements arrive, the particles are propagated through the system model, and their weights are updated based on how well they explain the measurements. Particle filters can approximate arbitrarily complex probability distributions, making them highly

versatile. However, they can be computationally intensive, especially in high-dimensional state spaces, and require careful tuning of parameters like the number of particles.

The role of state estimation in a digital twin is multifaceted and directly contributes to its fidelity and utility. Firstly, it enhances the **accuracy of the digital twin's state**. By fusing data from multiple sensors and accounting for their noise characteristics, state estimation algorithms can produce a more accurate and reliable representation of the physical asset's condition than any single sensor could provide. This is crucial for understanding the asset's current operating point, its performance levels, and its immediate behavior.

Secondly, state estimation enables the **estimation of unobservable parameters**. As mentioned, many critical aspects of a physical asset's health or performance might not be directly measurable. State estimation allows these hidden variables—such as internal stresses, incipient fault indicators, or true material properties under varying conditions—to be inferred. This provides a much deeper and more comprehensive understanding of the asset, going beyond surface-level observations.

Thirdly, it improves the **robustness of the digital twin against sensor failures or noise**. Real-world sensors are not infallible. They can fail, drift in calibration, or produce erroneous readings due to external interference. State estimation algorithms, particularly those with a strong model-based component, can often compensate for a certain degree of sensor degradation. If a sensor provides an outlier measurement, a well-designed estimator will down-weight or reject that measurement, relying more heavily on the model and other reliable sensors to maintain an accurate state estimate. This resilience is vital for ensuring the continuous operation and trustworthiness of the digital twin.

Fourthly, state estimation is foundational for **predictive maintenance and prognostics**. By accurately estimating the current state of wear, stress, or degradation within an asset, state estimators provide the necessary input for predictive models. For example, if a state estimator can accurately infer the internal temperature of a bearing and its trend, this information can be fed into a remaining useful life (RUL) model to predict when that bearing is likely to fail. Without accurate state estimation, the inputs to these predictive models would be unreliable, rendering their predictions questionable.

Fifthly, state estimation supports **real-time control and optimization**. In applications where the digital twin is used to influence the operation of the physical asset (e.g., in advanced process control or autonomous systems), accurate and timely state estimates are paramount. The control system needs to know the precise current state of the asset to make informed decisions about adjustments that will optimize performance, ensure safety, or maintain desired operating conditions. Delayed or inaccurate state estimates can lead to suboptimal control actions, instability, or even unsafe operating conditions.

Consider a digital twin of a complex chemical reactor. The process involves numerous variables like temperature, pressure, reactant concentrations, and catalyst activity. Direct measurement of all these might be impractical or prohibitively expensive. State estimation, using a combination of pressure, temperature, and flow rate sensors along with a dynamic model of the reactor's chemical kinetics, can provide accurate estimates of reactant conversion rates, intermediate product concentrations, and the effective activity of the catalyst. This allows operators to monitor the reaction's progress in near real-time, adjust feed rates or temperatures to maintain optimal yield, and predict potential runaway reactions before they become critical. Without state estimation, the operators would have to rely on a much coarser understanding of the process, leading to less efficient operation and higher safety risks.

Another example is a digital twin of a fleet of electric vehicles. Beyond basic telemetry like speed and battery charge, a state estimator could infer the internal temperature of the battery pack's cells, the degradation level of the battery management system's sensors, and the remaining capacity under current operating conditions. This allows for more intelligent charging strategies, optimized route planning considering battery health, and proactive identification of vehicles likely to require battery servicing. The raw sensor data might indicate a general battery temperature, but a Kalman filter, for instance, can fuse this with motor load, ambient temperature, and battery usage history to provide a much more precise estimate of critical internal cell temperatures, which are key to battery longevity and safety.

The integration of state estimation into a digital twin architecture necessitates careful consideration of several factors. The quality of the **system model** is paramount. The accuracy of the state estimates is inherently limited by how well the model captures the actual dynamics of the physical asset. This model can be physics-based (derived from first principles), data-driven (learned from historical data), or a hybrid of both. Furthermore, the **characteristics of the sensor noise and biases** must be understood and modeled. If the noise is highly non-Gaussian or if sensors exhibit significant biases that change over time, more advanced estimation techniques or adaptive filtering strategies might be required.

The **computational resources** available also play a significant role. While Kalman filters and their variants are generally computationally efficient, particle filters or more complex estimation schemes can demand substantial processing power, potentially requiring the deployment of edge computing resources or specialized hardware. The **frequency of updates** from the physical asset, as dictated by the synchronization strategy discussed previously, directly impacts how often the state estimator can be run, influencing the timeliness and responsiveness of the digital twin.

In conclusion, state estimation is not merely an optional add-on for digital twins; it is a foundational pillar that underpins their accuracy, reliability, and predictive capabilities. By intelligently combining available measurements with a model of system dynamics, state estimation algorithms overcome the limitations of direct sensing, providing a robust, comprehensive, and inferential understanding of the physical asset's true condition. This enriched, estimated state is what empowers digital twins to move beyond mere replicas and become powerful tools for monitoring, analysis, prediction, and control, ultimately driving operational excellence and innovation. The choice of estimation technique—whether a Kalman filter for linear systems, an EKF or UKF for non-linear dynamics, or particle filters for complex scenarios—depends heavily on the specific characteristics of the physical asset, the available sensor data, and the required fidelity of the digital twin.

The Kalman filter stands as a cornerstone of modern state estimation, providing an elegant and computationally efficient solution for systems that can be reasonably described by linear dynamics and are subject to Gaussian noise. At its heart, the Kalman filter is a recursive algorithm. This means it processes incoming measurements sequentially, updating its estimate of the system's state without needing to store the entire history of past observations. This recursive nature is crucial for real-time applications and for systems where data might be voluminous or memory is constrained, making it an ideal candidate for deployment within digital twin architectures.

The core idea of the Kalman filter is to maintain an estimate of the system's state vector and the uncertainty associated with that estimate, typically represented by a covariance matrix. The filter operates in a two-step cycle: a prediction step and an update step. In the prediction step, the filter uses the system's dynamic model to project the current state estimate and its associated uncertainty forward in time to the next discrete time step. This projection accounts for how the system is expected to evolve based on its governing equations. If the system is linear, this projection is straightforward, involving matrix multiplication. However, this prediction inherently introduces more uncertainty, as any inaccuracies in the model or the state estimate itself will propagate forward.

Following the prediction, the update step incorporates the latest measurement from the physical asset. The filter compares the predicted state with the actual measurement, and the difference between them (the "innovation" or "residual") is used to correct the predicted state. The magnitude of this correction is determined by the Kalman gain, a critical component of the algorithm. The Kalman gain balances the uncertainty in the predicted state with the uncertainty in the measurement. If the measurement is deemed highly reliable (low noise), the Kalman gain will be large, giving more weight to the measurement and thus significantly adjusting the state estimate. Conversely, if the measurement is very noisy, the Kalman gain will be small, and the filter will rely more heavily on the prediction, making only minor adjustments. This intelligent weighting ensures that the updated state estimate is a statistically optimal combination of the prediction and the measurement, minimizing the mean-squared error of the estimate.

The mathematical underpinnings of the Kalman filter rely on Bayes' theorem and the assumption of Gaussian probability distributions for both the system noise and the measurement noise. The state of the system at any given time is represented by a probability distribution, and the Kalman filter iteratively refines this distribution. For a linear system with Gaussian noise, the probability distribution of the state remains Gaussian at each step, and the filter effectively tracks the mean (the state estimate) and the covariance (the uncertainty) of this distribution. The optimality of the Kalman filter, in the sense of minimum mean-squared error, is a direct consequence of these assumptions.

Let's consider a simplified example to illustrate the Kalman filter's operation. Imagine we are tracking the position of a robotic arm in a single dimension. Our system model might predict that the arm moves at a constant velocity, and our measurements come from an encoder that provides noisy readings of its position.

Prediction Step:
Suppose at time t_{k-1}, *our best estimate of the arm's position is* $\hat{x}_{k-1}$ and its uncertainty is P_{k-1} *(a scalar variance in this 1D case). If we assume no velocity change for simplicity (or incorporate a constant velocity model), our predicted position at time* t_k would be $\hat{x}_k^- = \hat{x}_{k-1}$ (assuming constant velocity is already incorporated in the state $\hat{x}_{k-1}$) *and the predicted uncertainty would increase due to model uncertainty, say* $P_k^- = P_{k-1} + Q$, where Q is the process noise covariance representing uncertainty in our motion model.

Update Step:
At time t_k, *we receive a measurement* z_k from the encoder. This measurement is noisy, so its true value is $z_k = x_k + v_k$, *where* x_k is the true position and v_k is the measurement noise with variance R.

The Kalman gain is calculated as $Kk = \frac{Pk^-}{P_k^- + R}$. This gain tells us how much to trust the new measurement relative to our predicted state.
The updated state estimate is then $\hat{x}k = \hat{x}k^- + Kk (zk - \hat{x}k^-)$. *We adjust our prediction based on the difference between the actual measurement* (zk) and our predicted measurement ($\hat{x}_k^-$), weighted by the Kalman gain.
The updated uncertainty is $Pk = (1 - Kk) P_k^-$. The uncertainty is reduced because we have incorporated new information from the measurement.

This simple cycle repeats, with the output of the update step at time $t
k$ *becoming the input for the prediction step at time* $t{k+1}$. Over time, the Kalman filter converges, meaning the uncertainty in the state estimate (P_k) diminishes, and the estimates become more accurate, provided the system dynamics are indeed linear and the noise is Gaussian.

However, the world of physical systems is rarely perfectly linear. Many dynamic processes involve non-linear relationships between states, inputs, and outputs. For instance, the drag force on a moving object is often proportional to the square of its velocity, which is a non-linear relationship. The output of a sensor might be non-linearly related to the physical quantity it measures due to saturation or calibration curves. In such scenarios, the standard Kalman filter, which relies on linear transformations, cannot be directly applied without losing optimality or even convergence. This is where the variants of the Kalman filter come into play, offering powerful solutions for non-linear estimation problems.

The
Extended Kalman Filter (EKF) is the most direct extension of the standard Kalman filter designed to handle non-linear systems. The fundamental idea behind the EKF is to linearize the non-linear system dynamics and measurement models around the current state estimate. This linearization is achieved using Taylor series expansions, where only the first-order terms are retained. Essentially, the EKF approximates the non-linear functions with tangent planes at each time step.

Let's consider a non-linear system described by the state transition function $x k = f(x{k-1}, u{k-1}) + w{k-1}$ and a non-linear measurement function $zk = h(xk) + vk$, where f and h are non-linear functions, $u{k-1}$ is the control input, $w{k-1}$ is the process noise, and vk is the measurement noise.

In the prediction step of the EKF, instead of a simple matrix multiplication, the state prediction involves propagating the state through the non-linear function f:

$\hat{x}k^- = f(\hat{x}{k-1}, u_{k-1})$.
The covariance prediction is more involved. The uncertainty propagation through a non-linear function requires linearization. This is done by computing the Jacobian matrices of f and h with respect to the state vector x. The Jacobian of f, denoted as F_k, is a matrix of partial derivatives:
$Fk = \frac{\partial f}{\partial x} \bigg|{\hat{x}{k-1}, u{k-1}}$
Similarly, the Jacobian of h, denoted as H_k, is:
$Hk = \frac{\partial h}{\partial x} \bigg|{\hat{x}_k^-}$

The predicted covariance is then updated using the Jacobian of the state transition function:

$Pk^- = Fk P{k-1} Fk^T + Q$, where Q is the process noise covariance.

In the update step, the Kalman gain is computed using the Jacobian of the measurement function H_k:

$Kk = Pk^- Hk^T (Hk Pk^- Hk^T + R)^{-1}$, where R is the measurement noise covariance.
The state update is:
$\hat{x}k = \hat{x}k^- + Kk (zk - h(\hat{x}_k^-))$.
Note that the measurement residual $zk - h(\hat{x}k^-)$ now uses the non-linear measurement function h evaluated at the predicted state.

While the EKF is widely used and conceptually straightforward, its reliance on linearization can lead to significant issues. The approximation introduced by linearization is only accurate in the immediate vicinity of the operating point (the state estimate). If the system is highly non-linear, or if the state estimates deviate significantly from the true state, the Jacobian approximation can become poor.

This can lead to a degradation in estimation accuracy and, in severe cases, filter divergence, where the estimates become wildly inaccurate and the filter fails to converge. The EKF also requires the analytical derivation of Jacobian matrices, which can be complex and error-prone, especially for intricate system models.

To address the limitations of the EKF, the
Unscented Kalman Filter (UKF) was developed. Instead of linearizing the non-linear functions, the UKF uses a deterministic sampling technique called the unscented transform to capture the mean and covariance of the state distribution. The unscented transform is based on the idea that it is easier to propagate the mean and covariance through a non-linear function than to propagate the entire distribution.

The UKF works by selecting a carefully chosen set of "sigma points" that deterministically represent the mean and covariance of the state distribution. These sigma points are then propagated through the actual non-linear functions (f and h) of the system and measurement models. The transformed sigma points are then used to reconstruct the mean and covariance of the resulting distribution. This approach often provides a more accurate representation of the propagated distribution compared to linearization, especially for highly non-linear systems.

The process for the UKF in the prediction step involves:

1. **Generating Sigma Points:** A set of $2n+1$ sigma points ($\mathcal{X}_{k-1}$) are generated around the previous state estimate $\hat{x}_{k-1}$ with covariance P_{k-1}, where n is the dimension of the state vector. These points are chosen based on a set of parameters that control the spread of the points.
2. **Propagating Sigma Points:** Each sigma point is individually passed through the non-linear state transition function f to obtain a new set of transformed sigma points: $\mathcal{X}_k^- = f(\mathcal{X}_{k-1}, u_{k-1})$.
3. **Reconstructing Mean and Covariance:** The predicted state mean $\hat{x}_k^-$ is calculated as the weighted mean of the transformed sigma points, and the predicted covariance P_k^- is calculated from the weighted covariance of these transformed points. Process noise Q is added to the predicted covariance.

For the update step:

1. **Generating Measurement Sigma Points:** Sigma points ($\mathcal{X}*k^-$) are generated around the predicted state $\hat{x}*k^-$.
2. **Transforming to Measurement Space:** These sigma points are passed through the non-linear measurement function h to obtain transformed sigma points in the measurement space: $\mathcal{Z}*k = h(\mathcal{X}*k^-)$.
3. **Reconstructing Measurement Mean and Covariance:** The predicted measurement mean $\hat{z}*k$ and its covariance $S*k$ are calculated from the weighted mean and covariance of the transformed measurement sigma points. The cross-covariance between the state and measurement is also computed.
4. **Calculating Kalman Gain:** The Kalman gain $K*k$ is calculated using the computed covariances: $K*k = P*{x z} S*k^{-1}$, where $P_{x z}$ is the cross-covariance.
5. **Updating State and Covariance:** The state estimate $\hat{x}*k$ and covariance $P*k$ are updated using the standard Kalman update equations, but with the UKF-derived Kalman gain and predicted measurement.

A significant advantage of the UKF is that it does not require the analytical computation of Jacobians. This simplifies implementation, especially for complex systems. Furthermore, the UKF generally exhibits better performance than the EKF for non-linear systems, particularly when the non-linearities are significant, as it better captures the statistics of the state distribution. While the UKF is more computationally intensive than the EKF due to the propagation of multiple sigma points, its improved accuracy and robustness often make it the preferred choice for state estimation in many digital twin applications involving non-linear dynamics.

Beyond these Kalman filter variants, other advanced state estimation techniques are employed when the assumptions of linearity or Gaussian noise are severely violated.

Particle filters, also known as Sequential Monte Carlo (SMC) methods, represent a powerful class of algorithms capable of handling highly non-linear and non-Gaussian systems. Unlike Kalman filters, which rely on analytically tractable probability distributions (like Gaussians), particle filters approximate the state distribution using a set of discrete random samples, referred to as "particles." Each particle represents a possible state of the system, and is associated with a weight that reflects its likelihood.

The core principle of a particle filter is to represent the posterior probability distribution of the state by a set of weighted particles. In the prediction step, each particle is propagated forward through the system's (potentially non-linear) dynamic model. This results in a new set of predicted particles. In the update step, the weights of these particles are adjusted based on how well they explain the new measurement. Particles that are more consistent with the measurement receive higher weights, while those that are less consistent have their weights reduced.

A crucial component of particle filters is the resampling step. As the filtering process continues, the weights of the particles tend to become concentrated on a few particles, while others have negligible weights. This leads to "degeneracy." Resampling aims to address this by drawing a new set of particles from the current set, with the probability of drawing a particular particle being proportional to its weight. This effectively discards particles with low weights and duplicates particles with high weights, revitalizing the particle set and ensuring that the important regions of the state space are well-represented.

Particle filters are highly versatile. They can approximate arbitrarily complex probability distributions, making them suitable for a wide range of non-linear and non-Gaussian problems, such as tracking targets with non-Gaussian maneuvering characteristics or estimating states in systems with heavy-tailed noise distributions. Their ability to handle non-Gaussian distributions is a significant advantage over Kalman-based filters, which fundamentally assume Gaussianity.

However, particle filters come with their own set of challenges. Their computational cost can be significantly higher than that of Kalman filters, especially in high-dimensional state spaces, as the number of particles required for accurate approximation grows exponentially with the state dimension.

Selecting the appropriate number of particles, the proposal distribution (for efficient weight updates), and the resampling strategy are critical tuning parameters that can heavily influence the filter's performance and stability. Despite these challenges, particle filters are indispensable for certain complex digital twin applications where the underlying dynamics or noise characteristics defy the assumptions of Kalman filters.

In summary, the family of Kalman filters, from the foundational standard Kalman filter to its extensions like the EKF and UKF, and further to robust alternatives like particle filters, provides a comprehensive toolkit for state estimation in dynamic systems. The choice of filter depends critically on the nature of the system's dynamics (linear vs. non-linear), the characteristics of the noise (Gaussian vs. non-Gaussian), and the computational resources available. For digital twins, selecting the right state estimation algorithm is paramount to achieving an accurate and reliable representation of the physical asset, enabling effective monitoring, analysis, and decision-making.

Particle filters, a cornerstone of Sequential Monte Carlo (SMC) methods, offer a powerful and flexible approach to state estimation, particularly when faced with systems exhibiting highly non-linear dynamics or non-Gaussian noise characteristics. Unlike Kalman filter-based techniques, which often rely on analytical approximations of probability distributions (such as Gaussian assumptions), particle filters operate by approximating the posterior probability distribution of the system's state using a set of discrete random samples. These samples, commonly referred to as "particles," each represent a potential state of the system and are associated with a weight that quantifies its likelihood given the observed data. This approach allows particle filters to represent arbitrary probability distributions, making them exceptionally well-suited for complex scenarios that lie beyond the capabilities of traditional linear or Gaussian estimation methods.

The fundamental principle underpinning particle filters is the Bayesian inference framework. At each time step, the filter aims to approximate the posterior distribution of the state, $p(x_k | z_{1:k})$, where x_k *denotes the state vector at time* k *and* $z_{1:k}$ represents the sequence of measurements up to time k. This approximation is achieved by maintaining a collection of N weighted particles $\{xk^{(i)}, wk^{(i)}\}{i=1}^N$, where $xk^{(i)}$ is the state of the i-th particle and $wk^{(i)}$ is its associated normalized weight, such that $\sum{i=1}^N w_k^{(i)} = 1$. The collection of these particles and their weights forms an empirical approximation of the true posterior distribution.

The operation of a particle filter is inherently sequential, mirroring the recursive nature of Kalman filters. It typically involves two primary steps: a prediction step and an update step, often interspersed with a resampling step to combat particle degeneracy.

During the
prediction step, the filter projects the current set of particles forward in time according to the system's dynamic model. For a system described by the state transition equation $xk = f(x{k-1}, u{k-1}) + w{k-1}$, where f is the (potentially non-linear) state transition function, $u{k-1}$ is the control input, and $w{k-1}$ is the process noise, each particle $x{k-1}^{(i)}$ from the previous time step is propagated to generate a predicted state $xk^{(i)-} = f(x{k-1}^{(i)}, u{k-1}) + \tilde{w}{k-1}^{(i)}$, where $\tilde{w}{k-1}^{(i)}$ is a sample drawn from the process noise distribution. This process yields a set of predicted particles $\{xk^{(i)-}\}{i=1}^N$.

Following the prediction, the
update step involves adjusting the weights of these predicted particles based on the latest measurement zk. The weight of each particle $xk^{(i)-}$ is updated using Bayes' theorem, taking into account the likelihood of observing the measurement z_k given the particle's state. This is often expressed as:
$wk^{(i)} \propto w{k-1}^{(i)} \cdot p(zk / xk^{(i)-})$
Here, $p(zk / xk^{(i)-})$ is the likelihood function, which quantifies how well the i-th particle's predicted state $xk^{(i)-}$ explains the observed measurement zk. This likelihood is derived from the measurement model, $zk = h(xk) + vk$, where h is the (potentially non-linear) measurement function and vk is the measurement noise. After calculating these unnormalized weights, they are normalized to ensure that they sum to one:
$wk^{(i)} = \frac{wk^{(i)-}}{\sum{j=1}^N wk^{(j)-}}$

The core challenge that arises in particle filters is the phenomenon of **particle degeneracy**. As the filtering process progresses, particularly in scenarios with informative measurements or uninformative dynamic models, the weights of the particles tend to become increasingly concentrated on a small subset of particles, while the weights of the vast majority approach zero. This concentration diminishes the effective number of particles, leading to a poor representation of the true posterior distribution and a significant degradation in estimation accuracy.

To combat degeneracy, particle filters incorporate a **resampling step**. This step is typically performed after the weight update. The goal of resampling is to generate a new set of N particles $\{xk^{(i)}, wk^{(i)}\}{i=1}^N$ from the current set $\{xk^{(i)-}, wk^{(i)}\}{i=1}^N$ such that particles with higher weights are more likely to be selected, and particles with lower weights are discarded. A common resampling technique is **multinomial resampling**, where a new set of particles is drawn with replacement from the current set, with the probability of selecting particle i being equal to its normalized weight $wk^{(i)}$. After resampling, the weights are typically reset to be uniform ($wk^{(i)} = 1/N$ for all i). This process effectively discards particles with low weights and duplicates particles with high weights, revitalizing the particle set and ensuring that the important regions of the state space are adequately represented.

Other resampling strategies exist, such as **residual resampling** and **systematic resampling**, each offering different trade-offs in terms of computational efficiency and variance reduction. The choice of resampling method can significantly impact the filter's performance and stability.

The choice of the **proposal distribution** for the particle filter is also critical. While the basic description above uses the prior distribution $p(xk / x{k-1})$ as the proposal distribution for the prediction step, more advanced particle filters utilize a "better" proposal distribution, often approximating the optimal proposal of $p(xk / xk, zk)$, which incorporates information from the current measurement. A common choice for the proposal distribution is the one-step-ahead predictive distribution obtained from a linearized version of the system, similar to the *prediction step of the Kalman filter. This can lead to more efficient weight updates and reduce the tendency for degeneracy. The general form of a particle filter using a general proposal distribution $q(x*k | x*{k-1}^{(i)}, z*k)$ is as follows:

1.
Initialization: Initialize N particles $\{x*0^{(i)}\}*{i=1}^N$ from the prior distribution $p(x*0)$. Assign equal weights $w*0^{(i)} = 1/N$.
2. **Prediction:** For each particle $i=1, \ldots, N$, sample a predicted state $x*k^{(i)-}$ from the proposal distribution $q(x*k | x*{k-1}^{(i)}, z*k)$.
3. **Weight Update:** Compute the unnormalized importance weights:
$w*k^{(i)-} = w*{k-1}^{(i)} \frac{p(z*k | x*k^{(i)-}) p(x*k^{(i)-} | x*{k-1}^{(i)})}{q(x*k^{(i)-} | x*{k-1}^{(i)}, z_k)}$
Then, normalize the weights: $w*k^{(i)} = w*k^{(i)-} / \sum*{j=1}^N w*k^{(j)-}$.
4. **Resampling:** If the effective sample size (ESS) falls below a predefined threshold (e.g., $N/2$), resample N particles from the current set $\{x*k^{(i)}, w*k^{(i)}\}$ according to their weights. Reset weights to $1/N$.
5. **State Estimation:** The estimated state $\hat{x}*k$ can be computed as the weighted mean of the particles: $\hat{x}*k = \sum*{i=1}^N w*k^{(i)} x_k^{(i)}$.

The ability of particle filters to represent complex, multi-modal probability distributions makes them invaluable for a variety of applications in digital twins. Consider, for instance, a scenario involving a robot navigating an environment with multiple potential locations for a known landmark. The robot's position (the state) might have a probability distribution with several peaks, reflecting the ambiguity in its location. A standard Kalman filter, assuming a unimodal Gaussian distribution, would struggle to accurately represent this situation, potentially averaging out the distinct possibilities. A particle filter, on the other hand, can naturally represent such multi-modal distributions by assigning particles to each of the plausible locations, with weights reflecting the likelihood of each hypothesis.

Another compelling application arises in systems with significant non-linearities, such as tracking a flexible manufacturing arm subject to complex material properties and vibrations. The forces and resulting movements might not follow simple linear relationships, and the noise introduced by actuators or sensors could be non-Gaussian, perhaps exhibiting heavy tails due to occasional large disturbances. In such cases, the linearization assumptions of the EKF would be severely violated, and even the UKF might struggle if the non-linearities are extreme. Particle filters, by directly simulating the system dynamics for each particle and weighting them according to their observation consistency, can navigate these complexities without resorting to linear approximations.

The accuracy and performance of a particle filter are heavily dependent on the number of particles, N. A larger number of particles generally leads to a more accurate approximation of the posterior distribution and smoother state estimates. However, increasing N comes at a direct computational cost, as each particle must be propagated and weighted at each time step. The computational complexity of a standard particle filter is approximately $O(N \cdot d)$, where d is the dimension of the state vector. This means that for high-dimensional state spaces, particle filters can become computationally prohibitive, even with a moderate number of particles. This is a significant limitation, especially in real-time digital twin applications where computational resources might be constrained.

This curse of dimensionality is a well-recognized challenge. As the state space grows, the number of particles required to maintain a certain level of accuracy increases exponentially. For instance, if a system has a 10-dimensional state and requires 100 particles per dimension for adequate coverage, the total number of particles would be 100^{10}, an astronomical figure. Therefore, applying particle filters to very high-dimensional problems often necessitates the use of specialized techniques or approximations, such as dimensionality reduction, Rao-Blackwellized particle filters (which leverage the conditional linearity of some systems to reduce the state space), or combining particle filters with other estimation methods.

Beyond the number of particles, the choice of the resampling strategy and the proposal distribution significantly influences the filter's efficiency and convergence properties. A poor resampling strategy can lead to premature degeneracy, while an uninformative proposal distribution can result in slow weight convergence and require a larger number of particles.

Several advanced variants of particle filters have been developed to address these challenges and enhance performance. The
Rao-Blackwellized Particle Filter (RBPF), for example, can be highly effective when the state vector can be decomposed into a linear Gaussian component and a non-linear non-Gaussian component. The linear component can be handled analytically using a Kalman filter, while the non-linear component is handled using particle filtering, significantly reducing the computational burden and the number of particles required.

Another class of advancements involves improving the proposal distribution. The use of
bootstrap filters (which use the prior as the proposal) is the simplest form. More sophisticated proposal distributions, such as those derived from the Extended Kalman Filter or Unscented Kalman Filter, can lead to more efficient sampling and reduced variance.

Furthermore,
auxiliary particle filters introduce an auxiliary variable that can help to reduce the variance of the importance weights and improve resampling efficiency. These advanced methods often involve a more complex mathematical formulation but can yield substantial performance improvements in specific applications.

The practical implementation of particle filters requires careful tuning of several parameters, including the number of particles, the resampling threshold, and the parameters governing the proposal distribution and noise models. These parameters are often system-dependent and may require empirical optimization.

In summary, particle filters and other Sequential Monte Carlo methods provide a powerful and versatile framework for state estimation in dynamic systems that exhibit significant non-linearities or non-Gaussian noise. Their ability to approximate arbitrary probability distributions, coupled with their sequential nature, makes them highly suitable for complex digital twin applications where Kalman-based filters may falter. While challenges related to computational complexity, particularly in high-dimensional spaces, and the need for careful parameter tuning exist, ongoing research and the development of advanced variants continue to expand the applicability and effectiveness of these sophisticated estimation techniques. Their capacity to capture the full richness of system dynamics and uncertainties ensures their continued importance in the pursuit of accurate and robust digital twins.

The integration of observational data with a dynamic model to achieve an optimal estimation of a system's state is the core principle of data assimilation. This process is crucial for maintaining the fidelity and accuracy of digital twins, effectively bridging the gap between theoretical models and the realities of physical systems. Data assimilation techniques aim to correct and refine the state predicted by the dynamic model using measurements acquired from the real-world counterpart. This continuous interplay ensures that the digital twin evolves in lockstep with its physical twin, providing a reliable basis for monitoring, control, and prediction.

At its heart, data assimilation is a problem of inference. Given a dynamical model that describes how a system's state evolves over time, and a sequence of observations that provide partial and noisy information about the system's state, the goal is to estimate the true state of the system at any given time. This is typically achieved by optimally combining the information from the model and the observations. The dynamic model provides a prior estimate of the state, informed by the system's physics and past behavior, while observations offer direct, albeit imperfect, glimpses into the current state. Data assimilation seeks to find the most probable state estimate that is consistent with both sources of information.

One of the foundational approaches to data assimilation, particularly well-suited for linear systems with Gaussian noise, is the
Kalman Filter. While its principles have been extensively discussed in earlier contexts, it's important to reiterate its role as a cornerstone in many data assimilation workflows. The Kalman Filter operates recursively, updating the system's state estimate and its associated uncertainty (covariance matrix) at each time step. It begins with an initial estimate of the state and its uncertainty. At each subsequent time step, it first predicts the state forward using the system's dynamic model. This prediction step inherently introduces uncertainty, which is

propagated through the covariance matrix. Subsequently, when a new measurement becomes available, the Kalman Filter uses this observation to correct the predicted state. The degree to which the measurement influences the updated state estimate is governed by the Kalman Gain, which balances the uncertainty in the prediction against the uncertainty in the measurement. A high Kalman Gain means the measurement is trusted more, while a low gain indicates that the model prediction is favored. This elegant mechanism allows the Kalman Filter to optimally blend model information with observational data, assuming linearity and Gaussianity.

However, many real-world systems, especially those relevant to digital twins, exhibit significant non-linearities in their dynamics or measurement processes, or their noise characteristics deviate from the Gaussian assumption. For such scenarios, the standard Kalman Filter is inadequate. This is where **Extended Kalman Filters (EKFs)** and **Unscented Kalman Filters (UKFs)** come into play. The EKF linearizes the non-linear system dynamics and measurement models around the current state estimate using Jacobians. While this allows the Kalman Filter framework to be applied, the linearization introduces approximations that can lead to suboptimal performance or even divergence, especially for highly non-linear systems. The UKF, on the other hand, employs a deterministic sampling approach called the unscented transform. It selects a minimal set of "sigma points" that deterministically capture the mean and covariance of the state distribution. These sigma points are then propagated through the non-linear functions, and the resulting transformed points are used to approximate the posterior mean and covariance. The UKF often provides a more accurate representation of the posterior distribution than the EKF for non-linear systems, without the need for explicit Jacobian calculations, which can be complex and error-prone to derive.

Beyond these Kalman filter variants, **Ensemble-based data assimilation methods** have gained significant traction, particularly for large-scale and complex systems. These methods, such as the **Ensemble Kalman Filter (EnKF)**, do not rely on analytical linearization. Instead, they represent the state estimate and its uncertainty using an ensemble of possible states. An ensemble is essentially a collection of N state vectors, where each vector represents a potential realization of the system's state. The mean of the ensemble approximates the state estimate, and the covariance of the ensemble approximates the uncertainty.

In the EnKF, the prediction step involves propagating each member of the ensemble forward in time using the dynamic model. This inherently captures the non-linear dynamics. When an observation becomes available, the EnKF updates the ensemble members to reflect the information from the measurement. This update is performed by calculating the Kalman Gain based on the ensemble's statistics (mean and covariance) and then applying this gain to adjust each ensemble member. A key advantage of the EnKF is its ability to handle high-dimensional systems without the computational burden of calculating large covariance matrices explicitly. The covariance is implicitly represented by the relationships between the ensemble members. The process can be visualized as follows: if a measurement is strongly correlated with a particular state variable across the ensemble, then the observation will have a significant impact on the estimate of that state variable.

The EnKF has proven highly effective in various fields, including meteorology, oceanography, and hydrology, where models are often complex and the state space is vast. For instance, in weather forecasting, an ensemble of atmospheric states is maintained. Each member is evolved using a numerical weather prediction model. When new satellite or ground-based observations of temperature, pressure, or wind become available, the EnKF updates all ensemble members to assimilate this information. This allows for the generation of a probabilistic forecast, reflecting the uncertainty in the initial conditions and the model itself.

A related and powerful approach is the
Particle Filter, as previously detailed. While particle filters are generally considered a form of state estimation rather than a direct data assimilation technique in the same vein as Kalman filters or ensemble methods, their underlying principles are highly compatible with data assimilation. In a data assimilation context using particle filters, the particles represent a set of hypotheses about the true state of the system. At each time step, these particles are propagated forward according to the dynamic model. Then, observations are

used to re-weight these particles, assigning higher probabilities to those particles whose states are more consistent with the measurements. This process naturally handles non-linearities and non-Gaussian noise, allowing for the representation of multi-modal probability distributions in the state space.

The challenge with particle filters in data assimilation, especially for high-dimensional systems, lies in the computational cost. The number of particles required to adequately represent the posterior distribution often grows exponentially with the dimensionality of the state. This is known as the "curse of dimensionality." To mitigate this, researchers have developed hybrid approaches. For instance,
Rao-Blackwellized Particle Filters (RBPFs) can be employed if parts of the state can be treated analytically. In such cases, a Kalman filter can be used to estimate the linear Gaussian part of the state, while particle filters are used for the non-linear non-Gaussian part, significantly reducing the overall computational burden.

Another important class of data assimilation techniques are
Variational Methods, such as the **Three-Dimensional Variational (3D-Var)** and **Four-Dimensional Variational (4D-Var)** methods. These techniques seek to find the state that best fits both the dynamic model and the observations over a given time window. In 3D-Var, the analysis (estimated state) is produced at a single time step by minimizing a cost function. This cost function quantifies the mismatch between the analysis state, the prior estimate (from the model), and the observations at that time step. The minimization process is typically performed using iterative optimization algorithms.

4D-Var extends this concept by seeking the optimal initial state at the beginning of a time window that, when evolved forward by the dynamic model, best fits all observations within that window. This is achieved by minimizing a cost function that penalizes deviations from the prior at the initial time and deviations from all observations throughout the assimilation window. The dynamic model and its adjoint (a related linear model) are crucial components of the 4D-Var algorithm, enabling the gradient of the cost function to be computed efficiently. 4D-Var is computationally intensive but is known for its ability to produce highly consistent analyses and forecasts, especially in systems with strong dynamics. It effectively uses the model to "interpolate" observations in time and state space.

The choice of data assimilation technique depends heavily on the characteristics of the system being modeled, the nature of the observations, and the available computational resources. For linear systems with Gaussian noise, the Kalman Filter remains a benchmark. For non-linear systems, UKF and EnKF offer more robust solutions. Particle filters excel when the posterior distribution is highly non-Gaussian or multi-modal, provided the dimensionality is manageable or advanced variants are employed. Variational methods, particularly 4D-Var, are powerful for producing consistent analyses and forecasts over extended periods, especially in operational forecasting systems.

In the context of digital twins, the continuous assimilation of data is paramount for ensuring that the virtual representation remains a faithful mirror of the physical asset. Consider a complex industrial machine with numerous sensors monitoring temperature, vibration, pressure, and flow rates. The machine's operating behavior can be described by a sophisticated physics-based model. However, real-world conditions, such as material fatigue, varying operating loads, or unforeseen environmental factors, can cause deviations between the model's predictions and the actual machine's performance.

Data assimilation techniques are employed here to constantly update the digital twin's state. For example, if vibration sensors report anomalies that are not fully predicted by the current model, an EnKF could be used. The ensemble of machine states within the digital twin would be updated to reflect these new vibration readings. This might lead to a revised estimate of the internal stresses on a particular component or a change in the friction characteristics of a bearing.

Similarly, if a temperature sensor on a critical component indicates a higher-than-expected reading, a UKF might be used to update the estimated heat generation rate or the heat dissipation efficiency. The digital twin's state variables related to thermal dynamics would be adjusted accordingly. This updated state would then inform subsequent model predictions, leading to more accurate predictions of future temperatures and potentially triggering early warnings for potential overheating or component failure.

The process of data assimilation in a digital twin is not a one-off event but a continuous loop. Measurements are collected, processed, and fed into the assimilation algorithm. The algorithm updates the digital twin's state estimate. This updated state is then used for subsequent predictions and for performing other digital twin functionalities, such as simulations of different operating scenarios or predictive maintenance analyses. The accuracy and responsiveness of the digital twin are directly tied to the effectiveness of its data assimilation strategy.

Furthermore, data assimilation also plays a role in correcting for model error. No model is perfect, and inherent simplifications or inaccuracies in the model equations can lead to accumulating errors over time. Data assimilation provides a mechanism to implicitly correct for these model errors by nudging the state estimate towards observations that the model, in its current form, might not fully capture. Over time, this can help to keep the digital twin aligned with reality, even in the presence of model deficiencies.

The successful implementation of data assimilation for digital twins requires careful consideration of several factors. These include the frequency and quality of the sensor data, the accuracy and computational cost of the dynamic model, and the choice of the appropriate assimilation algorithm. The development of efficient and robust data assimilation techniques is therefore an active area of research, driving advancements in the fidelity and utility of digital twins across a wide spectrum of industries. The seamless integration of real-time data with sophisticated dynamic models, facilitated by these powerful assimilation methods, is what truly elevates a digital twin from a static representation to a dynamic, intelligent, and indispensable tool.

The effectiveness of any state estimator, whether it's a Kalman filter variant, an ensemble-based method, or a variational approach, is not self-evident. It must be rigorously assessed to ensure that the estimates it provides are trustworthy. This subsection delves into the critical aspects of **Validation and Performance Metrics for State Estimators**. Establishing robust validation protocols is not merely an academic exercise; it is a fundamental requirement for building confidence in the digital twin's operational capabilities and, by extension, the decisions derived from its state information. Without a clear understanding of how well an estimator is performing, its outputs are essentially speculative, rendering the digital twin's insights unreliable for critical applications such as predictive maintenance, process control, or anomaly detection.

The validation process typically begins with defining what constitutes a "good" estimate. This involves quantifying the discrepancy between the estimated state and the true, albeit often unknown, state of the system. Since the true state is rarely directly observable, validation strategies often rely on a combination of synthetic data, where the ground truth is known by construction, and carefully designed real-world experiments where comparisons can be made under controlled conditions.

One of the most fundamental aspects of validation is the assessment of **estimation error**. This refers to the difference between the estimated state vector $\hat{\mathbf{x}}$ and the true state vector $\mathbf{x}$. For a system with an n-dimensional state space, the estimation error is an n-dimensional vector, $\mathbf{e} = \mathbf{x} - \hat{\mathbf{x}}$. However, simply looking at the raw error vector can be challenging to interpret, especially for high-dimensional systems. Therefore, various scalar metrics are employed to summarize this error.

A widely used metric is the
Root Mean Squared Error (RMSE), often calculated over a specific time period or a set of assimilation cycles. For a particular state variable x_i, the RMSE is defined as:
$$
\text{RMSE}_i = \sqrt{\frac{1}{M}\sum_{k=1}^{M} (x_{i,k} - \hat{x}_{i,k})^2}
$$
where $x_{i,k}$ is the true value of the i-th state variable at time step k, $\hat{x}_{i,k}$ is the estimated value, and M is the number of time steps

considered. The overall RMSE for the state vector can be computed as the square root of the average of the squared errors across all state variables:

$$
\text{RMSE}{\text{vector}} = \sqrt{\frac{1}{n} \sum{i=1}^{n} \text{RMSE}i^2} = \sqrt{\frac{1}{n M}\sum{k=1}^{M}\sum{i=1}^{n} (x{i,k} - \hat{x}_{i,k})^2}
$$

RMSE provides a measure of the magnitude of the estimation error, penalizing larger errors more heavily due to the squaring operation. It's a composite metric that encapsulates both the spread and the bias of the error.

Another crucial metric is the
Mean Absolute Error (MAE), which is less sensitive to outliers than RMSE:

$$
\text{MAE}i = \frac{1}{M}\sum{k=1}^{M} |x{i,k} - \hat{x}{i,k}|
$$

While RMSE is more commonly associated with the standard deviation in statistical inference, MAE offers a more direct interpretation of the average magnitude of the error. The choice between RMSE and MAE often depends on the specific application and the acceptable consequences of large errors.

Beyond the magnitude of the error, it is essential to assess the
bias of the estimator. Bias refers to a systematic tendency of the estimator to either over- or under-estimate the true state. A zero-mean error is desirable, but a non-zero mean indicates a systematic bias that needs to be addressed. The bias for the i-th state variable can be calculated as:

$$
\text{Bias}i = \frac{1}{M}\sum{k=1}^{M} (x{i,k} - \hat{x}{i,k})
$$

If the bias is consistently positive, the estimator tends to underestimate the true state, and vice-versa. Persistent bias can lead to a drift in the digital twin's state away from reality, even if the random errors are small. For instance, in a fluid dynamics simulation, a systematic underestimation of turbulent viscosity could lead to predictions of laminar flow where turbulent flow is actually occurring, fundamentally misrepresenting the system's behavior.

The

covariance of the estimation error, often denoted as $\mathbf{P}_e$, is another vital performance indicator. In many state estimation algorithms, such as the Kalman Filter and its derivatives, the estimator explicitly maintains a belief about the uncertainty in its state estimate, typically represented by a covariance matrix. The estimated error covariance matrix $\mathbf{P}$ that the estimator produces should ideally be a good reflection of the true error covariance. Comparing the estimated error covariance with the sample covariance of the actual estimation errors provides a measure of the estimator's ability to accurately quantify its own uncertainty. If the estimated covariance is consistently too small, it suggests the estimator is overconfident in its predictions, which can be dangerous in critical applications. Conversely, an overly large estimated covariance implies excessive caution or a poor representation of the system dynamics.

For ensemble-based methods like the EnKF, the spread of the ensemble is directly related to the estimated error covariance. A key validation metric for EnKF is to compare the **ensemble spread** with the observed error variance. If the ensemble spread is consistently smaller than the actual error variance, it suggests the ensemble is not capturing enough of the uncertainty, and the assimilation may be too strong or the ensemble size too small. Conversely, if the spread is much larger than the error variance, the assimilation might be too weak or the ensemble too diverse. Metrics like the **binned ensemble error variance** can be used, where the data is binned based on ensemble spread and then the average error variance within each bin is compared to the average spread within that bin.

Another important aspect of validation is assessing the **convergence properties** of the estimator. For estimators that are initialized with an initial guess and an initial uncertainty, it is important to know how quickly they converge to a stable and accurate estimate. This is particularly relevant for systems that are initialized from scratch or after a significant disturbance. Convergence can be monitored by tracking the RMSE or MAE over time. Ideally, these metrics should decrease rapidly after initialization and then settle to a low, stable value. The rate of convergence can be influenced by factors such as the quality of the initial guess, the signal-to-noise ratio of the observations, and the accuracy of the dynamic model. Analyzing the convergence behavior can help in tuning the estimator's parameters, such as the observation error covariance and the process noise covariance, or in determining an appropriate spin-up time for the assimilation system.

The
Kalman Gain itself can also be a subject of validation. For Kalman filter-based methods, the Kalman Gain dictates how much weight is given to new observations versus the model prediction. Analyzing the magnitude and behavior of the Kalman Gain over time can reveal insights into the estimator's performance. If the Kalman Gain is consistently very small for a particular observation, it might indicate that the observation error covariance is too large or that the observation is not well correlated with the state variables. Conversely, a very large Kalman Gain suggests that the observation is heavily trusted, potentially due to an underestimated observation error or an inaccurate model prediction. Examining the Kalman Gain in relation to the estimated error covariance matrices of the prior state and the observation can help diagnose issues with the model or the observation characterization.

A critical validation technique, especially when dealing with complex systems where the true state might not be directly measurable, is
hindcasting and forecasting skill assessment. Hindcasting involves using the assimilation system to estimate the state of the system at past times, often using data that was not available during the original assimilation run. Comparing these hindcasts with known historical data or with independent model simulations can provide a strong indication of the estimator's accuracy. Forecasting skill, on the other hand, assesses how well the state estimated at a certain time can predict future states. This involves running the model forward from the analyzed state and comparing the predictions with future observations. Metrics like **Mean Squared Skill Score (MSSS)** or **Correlation Coefficient** between forecasts and observations are commonly used to quantify forecasting accuracy.

For digital twins, particularly those used in safety-critical applications, assessing the
probabilistic performance of the estimator is crucial. This involves evaluating how well the estimated probability distributions of the state variables represent the true distributions. For instance, if an estimator claims a 90% confidence interval for a particular state variable, then in a long series of estimates, approximately 90% of the true values should fall within these intervals.

Reliability diagrams and **calibration curves** are graphical tools used to assess this probabilistic accuracy. These plots compare the observed frequencies of events occurring within certain confidence levels to the predicted frequencies.

Beyond these quantitative metrics,
qualitative validation also plays a role. This involves expert judgment and visual inspection of the estimated state variables and their time series. Do the estimates make physical sense? Do they exhibit expected behaviors under different operational conditions? For example, if estimating the temperature of a component in a digital twin, a validation step might involve checking if the estimated temperature increases when the simulated load on that component increases, and if it decreases when cooling systems are activated. Anomalies or physically implausible behaviors in the estimated state, even if not immediately quantifiable by standard metrics, can signal problems with the estimator or the underlying model.

A practical approach to validation involves
observing the behavior of the system when controlled by the estimated state. If the digital twin is used to control a physical process, then the performance of that control system is an indirect validation of the state estimator. For example, if a digital twin uses its state estimate of a motor's torque to adjust its speed, and the physical motor operates smoothly and efficiently under this control, it suggests that the torque estimate is reasonably accurate. Conversely, if the motor exhibits jerky movements or stalls, it points to potential issues with the state estimation.

When validating state estimators for dynamic accuracy, it is crucial to consider the
influence of different components of the assimilation system. This includes the dynamic model itself, the observation operators (which map the state to the observable quantities), and the error statistics (process noise and observation noise covariances). Sensitivity analyses can be performed to understand how variations in these components affect the estimator's performance. For instance, one could systematically increase the assumed observation noise covariance and observe the impact on RMSE and bias. This helps in understanding the robustness of the estimator to imperfect knowledge of error statistics.

Furthermore,
identifying and diagnosing specific failure modes is a critical aspect of validation. This goes beyond simply calculating metrics and involves understanding *why* an estimator might fail. For example, a common failure mode in Extended Kalman Filters is divergence, where the state estimates become increasingly inaccurate, often due to linearization errors in highly non-linear systems. Validating an EKF might involve monitoring the trace of the error covariance matrix or specific elements of the Jacobian matrices to detect signs of instability. For ensemble methods, a common issue is **ensemble collapse**, where the ensemble members converge too closely, leading to an underestimation of uncertainty and potentially poor performance when the system encounters novel situations. Metrics that track the diversity of the ensemble, such as the average distance between ensemble members, can help diagnose this problem.

In the context of digital twins, validation is not a one-time event but an ongoing process. As the physical system evolves (e.g., through wear and tear, component degradation), the dynamic model or the observation characteristics might change. Therefore, validation metrics should be monitored continuously, and the assimilation system might need to be re-tuned or even replaced if performance degrades significantly. This continuous validation loop ensures that the digital twin remains a faithful and reliable representation of its physical counterpart throughout its lifecycle.

To illustrate with an example, consider a digital twin of a chemical reactor. Key state variables might include reactant concentrations, temperature, and pressure. Observations could come from in-situ sensors measuring these quantities, or from off-line laboratory analysis of samples. If the digital twin is being used to optimize reaction yield, the accuracy of the estimated concentrations is paramount. Validation would involve:

1. **Simulated Data:** Generating synthetic data from a high-fidelity model of the reactor, introducing known levels of process noise and observation noise. The state estimator is run on this synthetic data, and its estimated states are compared to the known "true" states. Metrics like RMSE, MAE, and bias are

computed. The estimator's ability to correctly estimate the error covariance is also assessed.

2. **Real-world Experimentation:** Conducting controlled experiments on the actual reactor. This might involve setting the reactor to operate under specific conditions (e.g., a step change in input flow rate) and comparing the estimated state trajectory from the digital twin with actual sensor measurements. Special care must be taken to characterize the observation errors accurately in this phase. For instance, a temperature sensor might have a known bias and a certain level of random noise.
3. **Hindcast Analysis:** Using historical operational data of the reactor to run the assimilation system backward in time. The resulting historical state estimates are then compared with any available independent measurements or operational logs.
4. **Forecasting Skill:** Using the current state estimate from the digital twin to predict how certain key variables (e.g., product concentration) will evolve over the next hour. These predictions are then compared with actual measurements taken during that hour.
5. **Bias Detection:** Continuously monitoring the bias of key state variables. If the estimated reactant concentration is consistently lower than measured values, it might suggest an issue with the reaction kinetics model or an underestimation of the inflow rate.
6. **Ensemble Spread Validation (for EnKF):** If an EnKF is used, the spread of the ensemble members for reactant concentrations is compared to the observed variability in those concentrations over time. If the spread is consistently too narrow, it suggests the ensemble is not adequately representing the uncertainty in the reaction process.

The outcome of this validation process informs decisions about the reliability of the digital twin. If validation reveals significant biases or high RMSE values, it signals that the estimates are not sufficiently accurate for the intended application. This might necessitate improvements to the dynamic model, refinement of the observation error characterization, an increase in the ensemble size, or a change in the assimilation algorithm altogether. Ultimately, thorough validation and rigorous performance monitoring are the cornerstones of trusting the state information provided by a digital twin and leveraging it for informed decision-making. Without them, the digital twin remains a theoretical construct rather than a practical, reliable tool.

Chapter 6: Uncertainty Quantification in Models

The very fabric of modeling, whether in scientific inquiry or engineering application, is interwoven with an inherent characteristic: uncertainty. This is not a flaw to be eradicated, but rather an intrinsic property that mirrors the complexity and inherent variability of the real world. Every model, by its nature, is an abstraction—a simplification of a system far more intricate than can be perfectly represented. This fundamental act of abstraction is the primary wellspring of model uncertainty. Consequently, any attempt to use a model for prediction, decision-making, or control without acknowledging and, more importantly, quantifying this inherent uncertainty is akin to navigating treacherous waters with an incomplete map.

This inherent uncertainty arises from a multitude of sources, each contributing to the deviation between the model's output and the reality it seeks to represent. One of the most ubiquitous sources is
measurement error. Physical systems are observed through sensors, instruments, and data collection devices, all of which are subject to imperfections. These imperfections can manifest as random noise, systematic biases, calibration drift, or limited precision. Even the most sophisticated measurement technologies cannot achieve absolute accuracy. For instance, consider the estimation of fluid velocity in a pipe using a Doppler ultrasound sensor. While advanced, the sensor's readings are influenced by factors such as fluid density variations, the presence of bubbles or particles, and the sensor's own electronic noise. Each of these factors introduces uncertainty into the measured velocity, which then propagates into any model that uses this measurement as an input or a validation point. Similarly, in structural health monitoring, strain gauges, while essential, have their own limitations in terms of sensitivity, linearity, and susceptibility to temperature fluctuations, all contributing to measurement uncertainty.

Beyond the realm of observation, the very construction of our models introduces another significant category of uncertainty:
model structural uncertainty. Models are built upon assumptions about the underlying physics, chemistry, or biology of a system. These assumptions often involve simplifying complex phenomena. For example, in simulating the airflow over an aircraft wing, a model might neglect the effect of air viscosity at certain regions if the flow is assumed to be largely inviscid, or it might simplify the

turbulent nature of the flow using a Reynolds-Averaged Navier-Stokes (RANS) approach instead of a computationally expensive Direct Numerical Simulation (DNS). These simplifications, while often necessary for tractability, inherently deviate from reality. The choice of a particular model structure—be it a linear differential equation to describe a non-linear process, a simplified chemical reaction pathway, or a reduced-order representation of a complex mechanical system—introduces a form of uncertainty about whether the chosen mathematical framework truly captures all relevant dynamics. The extent to which the model's structure misrepresents the real system is a direct contribution to its uncertainty.

Closely related to structural uncertainty is
parameter uncertainty. Models are parameterized by coefficients, constants, and material properties that represent specific aspects of the system being modeled. These parameters are often derived from experimental data, literature values, or are themselves estimated through calibration processes. However, these sources are rarely definitive. Experimental data has its own associated measurement errors, and literature values may represent typical conditions rather than the specific conditions of the system under study. Furthermore, parameters can vary over time due to environmental changes, material degradation, or operational shifts. For instance, in a model predicting the thermal performance of a building, parameters such as wall insulation R-values or window U-values might be based on manufacturer specifications, but the actual installed values could differ. Moreover, these parameters can degrade over the lifetime of the building. The uncertainty in these parameter values directly translates into uncertainty in the model's predictions. A small error in a highly influential parameter can lead to a disproportionately large error in the model's output.

The dynamic nature of many real-world systems introduces another layer of complexity:
process uncertainty. Even if a model perfectly captures the system's behavior at a single point in time and with precise parameters, the system itself is often subject to external influences and internal stochasticity that are not fully accounted for in the model. Think of a weather forecasting model. While the underlying physics of atmospheric dynamics are well-understood, the system is constantly perturbed by unpredictable events, chaotic interactions, and factors at

scales smaller than the model can resolve. This "unforeseen" variability, the inherent randomness or unpredictability in the system's evolution, is a significant source of process uncertainty. In mechanical systems, this could manifest as unexpected vibrations, material fatigue, or the influence of unmodeled environmental loads. In biological systems, it could be the stochastic nature of molecular interactions or the unpredictable behavior of individual organisms within a population.

Acknowledging these various sources of uncertainty is not an admission of model inadequacy, but rather a testament to intellectual honesty and a prerequisite for responsible engineering. Models are tools, and like any tool, their effectiveness and limitations must be understood to be used properly. Ignoring uncertainty leads to a false sense of precision and can result in decisions that are overly optimistic or dangerously underprepared for potential adverse outcomes. For example, if a structural engineer uses a model to predict the load-bearing capacity of a bridge and ignores the uncertainty in material strength and estimated traffic loads, they might design a bridge that is technically "safe" according to their model, but which is actually closer to its failure point than they realize. This could lead to catastrophic failure under unforeseen stress.

Conversely, embracing and quantifying uncertainty allows for a more nuanced and robust approach to decision-making. It enables risk assessment. By understanding the range of possible outcomes predicted by a model, and the likelihood of each outcome, engineers and scientists can make informed choices about the level of risk they are willing to accept. This might involve designing systems with greater safety margins, developing contingency plans for unfavorable scenarios, or investing in further research to reduce critical sources of uncertainty. For instance, in the development of a new pharmaceutical, uncertainty quantification in models predicting drug efficacy and potential side effects allows for a more rigorous assessment of the drug's risk-benefit profile before it is approved for widespread use. The quantification of uncertainty provides the crucial context for interpreting model outputs. It shifts the focus from a single, often illusory, "correct" answer to a distribution of plausible answers, each with an associated probability. This probabilistic perspective is fundamental to modern risk management and informs the design of resilient systems capable of withstanding a wider range of operating conditions and disturbances. In essence, understanding uncertainty transforms a model from a prescriptive oracle into a valuable partner in navigating complex and unpredictable real-world phenomena.

The inherent presence of uncertainty in any modeling endeavor, as previously discussed, necessitates a deeper examination of its origins and manifestations. To effectively manage and quantify this uncertainty, it is crucial to establish a clear taxonomy of its types. Broadly speaking, uncertainty can be dichotomized into two fundamental categories: aleatoric uncertainty and epistemic uncertainty. This classification provides a structured framework for understanding the distinct nature of these uncertainties and guides the selection of appropriate quantification and mitigation strategies within digital twin applications.

Aleatoric uncertainty, often referred to as inherent randomness or irreducible uncertainty, stems from the natural variability and unpredictability present in the real world. This type of uncertainty is, in principle, irreducible, meaning that even with perfect knowledge and complete information, the outcome of a system would still exhibit variability. It is intrinsically linked to the stochastic nature of many physical phenomena. Consider, for instance, the precise moment an individual radioactive atom will decay. While the decay rate of a large sample can be accurately predicted, the decay of a single atom remains inherently unpredictable. This unpredictability is a hallmark of aleatoric uncertainty. In the context of digital twins, this type of uncertainty can arise from a multitude of sources. Variability in material properties, for example, is a significant contributor. Even materials manufactured to the same specifications will exhibit slight differences in their tensile strength, Young's modulus, or fatigue life. These microscopic variations, often due to the inherent randomness in atomic or molecular structures and manufacturing processes, lead to a distribution of possible property values rather than a single, definitive number. When these materials are incorporated into a physical asset represented by a digital twin, this inherent variability translates into uncertainty in the twin's performance predictions.

Another common source of aleatoric uncertainty is sensor noise. Sensors, the eyes and ears of a digital twin, are by their very nature imperfect instruments. They are susceptible to random fluctuations caused by thermal noise in electronic components, electromagnetic interference, or environmental disturbances. For example, a temperature sensor might register fluctuating readings even when the ambient temperature is perfectly stable, due to random electron movement within its circuitry. Similarly, a vibration sensor on a rotating machine might pick up random, low-level signals that are not indicative of any actual fault but are rather a consequence of the inherent randomness in the mechanical interactions within the machine itself or even external environmental factors like micro-seismic activity. This irreducible randomness in sensor readings, when fed into the digital twin, introduces aleatoric uncertainty into the twin's state estimation and subsequent predictions.

Environmental factors also contribute significantly to aleatoric uncertainty. Many physical systems operate within dynamic and unpredictable environments. A wind turbine's power output, for instance, is inherently uncertain due to the stochastic nature of wind speed and direction. Even with advanced weather forecasting, the precise micro-turbulent gusts and variations encountered by the turbine blades at any given moment are subject to natural randomness. Similarly, the operational temperature of electronic components can fluctuate due to unpredictable ambient temperature variations, humidity, or airflow patterns, introducing uncertainty into their performance and lifespan estimations within a digital twin. In the realm of civil engineering, the load experienced by a bridge is subject to aleatoric uncertainty due to the unpredictable patterns and weights of traffic, as well as random fluctuations in wind loads and seismic activity, even if the maximum expected load is known within a certain statistical band.

Furthermore, many natural processes are inherently stochastic. Biological systems, for instance, are replete with aleatoric uncertainty. The growth rate of a cell culture, the mutation rate of a virus, or the response of a patient to a medication can all exhibit inherent randomness, even under identical initial conditions. When modeling such systems with digital twins, this intrinsic variability must be acknowledged. Even the fundamental laws of physics, while deterministic in their macroscopic formulation, can manifest probabilistic behavior at the quantum level, although this is typically a less significant source of uncertainty for most macroscopic engineering applications. Nevertheless, the collective effect of numerous independent random events within a complex system can lead to emergent stochastic behavior that is aleatoric in nature.

In contrast to aleatoric uncertainty, epistemic uncertainty arises from a lack of knowledge or imperfect understanding. This type of uncertainty is, in principle, reducible through further investigation, data collection, or refinement of models. It represents the uncertainty associated with our current state of knowledge about a system, its parameters, or the underlying physical laws governing it. Epistemic uncertainty can be further subdivided into several categories, each reflecting a different facet of our imperfect knowledge.

One prominent form of epistemic uncertainty is **model structural uncertainty**. As discussed previously, models are simplifications of reality. The choice of a particular mathematical structure—whether it's a set of differential equations, a statistical model, or a machine learning architecture—is often based on assumptions and approximations. There may be alternative model structures that could also represent the system, and our current knowledge may not be sufficient to definitively select the "correct" one. For example, in modeling the degradation of a composite material, one might choose between different phenomenological models describing crack propagation. If the underlying mechanisms are not fully understood or if experimental data is insufficient to distinguish between competing theories, the choice of model structure introduces epistemic uncertainty. Similarly, in fluid dynamics, the selection of a specific turbulence model (e.g., RANS, LES) introduces epistemic uncertainty because the precise nature of turbulence is still an active area of research, and each model represents a different level of approximation and understanding.

Parameter uncertainty is another significant component of epistemic uncertainty. Even if we have selected an appropriate model structure, the values of the parameters that define that structure are often not known precisely. These parameters might be derived from experiments, literature values, or estimations. Each of these sources can be imperfect. Experimental measurements are subject to errors, literature values might be based on different conditions or assumptions, and estimation procedures themselves might be based on incomplete data or simplified models. For instance, in a structural model of a building, parameters like the elastic modulus of concrete or the yield strength of steel might be obtained from material databases. However, these databases represent average values, and the actual properties of the concrete or steel used in a specific construction project might deviate. Furthermore, these properties can degrade over time, introducing an additional layer of uncertainty that depends on our knowledge of the degradation mechanisms. In a digital twin, this parameter uncertainty directly translates into uncertainty in the predicted behavior of the physical asset.

Data uncertainty, a closely related form of epistemic uncertainty, arises from the quality and limitations of the data used to build, calibrate, or validate a model. This encompasses not only measurement errors (which contribute to aleatoric uncertainty as well) but also issues such as missing data, outliers, biased sampling, and insufficient data volume. If a digital twin is trained on a dataset that does not adequately represent the full range of operational conditions or potential failure modes, its predictive capabilities will be limited by this data deficiency. For example, a machine learning model for predicting equipment failures might perform poorly if the training data lacks examples of rare but critical failure modes. The absence of data for certain scenarios represents a gap in our knowledge, leading to epistemic uncertainty in the model's predictions for those scenarios. Even when data is abundant, if it suffers from systematic biases—for instance, if sensors are consistently underreporting a particular parameter—this bias introduces epistemic uncertainty.

Knowledge gaps represent a broader category of epistemic uncertainty, encompassing areas where our scientific or engineering understanding is incomplete. This could be due to the complexity of the system, the difficulty of observation, or the limitations of current scientific theories. For example, in predicting the long-term behavior of complex chemical reactions or biological processes, there may be fundamental aspects of the underlying mechanisms that are not yet fully understood. This lack of fundamental knowledge translates directly into epistemic uncertainty within any digital twin attempting to model such phenomena. Similarly, in fields like climate modeling, uncertainties arise from incomplete understanding of feedback loops, cloud formation physics, and the precise response of ecosystems to environmental changes.

It is important to recognize that aleatoric and epistemic uncertainties are not mutually exclusive and can often coexist within a single model or system. For instance, the randomness in wind speed (aleatoric) is a fundamental aspect of the phenomenon, but our imperfect ability to predict that wind speed for a specific location and time (due to limited weather station data, complex atmospheric interactions, and model approximations) introduces epistemic uncertainty. Similarly, while material properties might have inherent variability (aleatoric), our lack of precise knowledge about the *distribution* of those properties for a specific batch of material (epistemic) adds another layer of uncertainty.

The distinction between these types of uncertainty is crucial for selecting appropriate quantification methods. Aleatoric uncertainty is often characterized by probability distributions, reflecting the inherent randomness. For example, if we know that a sensor's readings follow a Gaussian distribution with a certain standard deviation around the true value, we are quantifying aleatoric uncertainty. Epistemic uncertainty, on the other hand, is often addressed through methods that aim to reduce the uncertainty itself, such as gathering more data, improving models, or using techniques like Bayesian inference to update our beliefs as new information becomes available. Fuzzy logic or interval arithmetic can also be employed to represent epistemic uncertainty when precise probabilistic models are not feasible.

In the context of digital twins, a comprehensive understanding and categorization of these uncertainties are paramount. By identifying whether an uncertainty is primarily aleatoric or epistemic, engineers and scientists can make informed decisions about how to best manage it. For aleatoric uncertainties, the focus is on accurately characterizing their statistical properties and propagating them through the digital twin to understand their impact on the output. For epistemic uncertainties, the goal is often to reduce them through targeted efforts, such as conducting further experiments, refining model structures, or improving data acquisition strategies. This systematic approach to understanding and categorizing uncertainty forms the bedrock upon which robust and reliable digital twin applications can be built, enabling more accurate predictions, better decision-making, and ultimately, more resilient physical systems. The subsequent sections will delve into specific techniques for quantifying these distinct types of uncertainty, building upon this foundational understanding.

The preceding discussion has laid the groundwork for understanding the fundamental nature of uncertainty, distinguishing between its aleatoric and epistemic origins. With this conceptual framework in place, we now pivot to the practical methodologies employed for quantifying these uncertainties within the context of digital twin modeling. Among the most versatile and widely adopted approaches are those rooted in probabilistic theory. These methods leverage the language of probability to represent and reason about uncertain quantities, offering a more nuanced and comprehensive depiction of reality than deterministic, single-point estimates.

At the heart of probabilistic quantification lies the concept of representing uncertain variables not as fixed values, but as probability distributions. Instead of asserting that a parameter, say, the Young's modulus of a material, is precisely 200 GPa, a probabilistic approach acknowledges that this value is likely to fall within a range, with certain values being more probable than others. This is typically achieved by defining a probability density function (PDF) or a cumulative distribution function (CDF) for the parameter. For instance, if we have experimental data suggesting that the Young's modulus of a specific steel alloy typically ranges between 190 GPa and 210 GPa, with the most common values clustering around 200 GPa, we might model this uncertainty using a normal (Gaussian) distribution with a mean of 200 GPa and a standard deviation reflecting the observed variability. The standard deviation, in this context, becomes a direct measure of the uncertainty associated with that parameter. A smaller standard deviation implies higher confidence and less uncertainty, while a larger one indicates greater spread and more pronounced uncertainty.

This probabilistic representation extends beyond input parameters to model outputs as well. When a digital twin simulates the behavior of a physical asset, deterministic models produce a single predicted outcome. However, by incorporating uncertain input parameters, the model's output naturally becomes uncertain. Probabilistic methods allow us to characterize this output uncertainty, often by determining its own probability distribution. This distribution encapsulates the range of possible outcomes and their likelihoods, providing a richer understanding of the system's behavior than a single predicted value. For example, a digital twin predicting the stress distribution in a bridge under a given load might, using probabilistic inputs for material properties and load magnitudes, yield not just a single maximum stress value, but a distribution of possible maximum stresses. This distribution would reveal the probability of exceeding certain critical stress levels, which is far more informative for risk assessment and decision-making.

A fundamental tool for understanding the spread of data around a central tendency is the concept of
variance and its square root, the **standard deviation**. Variance, mathematically defined as the average of the squared differences from the mean, quantifies the dispersion of a set of data. A higher variance indicates that the data points are, on average, further from the mean and from each other. The standard deviation, being in the same units as the data, offers a more intuitive measure of this spread. In the context of uncertainty quantification, the variance or standard deviation of a parameter directly reflects the degree of its uncertainty. If a model parameter's value is known with high certainty, its variance will be low, approaching zero. Conversely, a high variance signifies substantial uncertainty. When propagating uncertainties through a model, the variances of input parameters can influence the variance of the model's output. For linear models, variance often adds linearly. For non-linear models, the relationship is more complex, but the concept of variance propagation remains central.

Another crucial probabilistic concept for expressing uncertainty is the **confidence interval**. A confidence interval provides a range of values within which a population parameter is estimated to lie, with a certain level of confidence. For example, a 95% confidence interval for the mean tensile strength of a material might be reported as [300 MPa, 320 MPa]. This means that we are 95% confident that the true mean tensile strength of the material lies within this range. In digital twin applications, confidence intervals can be applied to both input parameters and model outputs. If a parameter's uncertainty is represented by a probability distribution, its confidence interval can be readily derived. Similarly, the output of a digital twin simulation, when propagated with input uncertainties, can be summarized by a confidence interval. This interval provides a tangible range for expected outcomes, allowing stakeholders to understand the potential deviation from a central prediction. For instance, if a digital twin predicts the remaining useful life of a component, providing a 95% confidence interval, such as [500 hours, 700 hours], communicates that the actual life is likely to fall within this range, with a high degree of certainty.

While analytical methods can sometimes be used to propagate uncertainties through simple linear models, many digital twin models are complex and non-linear. For these scenarios,
Monte Carlo simulation emerges as a powerful and widely applicable technique. The core idea of Monte Carlo simulation is to use random sampling to obtain numerical results. In the context of uncertainty quantification, this involves:

1.
Defining Input Distributions: Representing each uncertain input parameter (e.g., material properties, loads, environmental conditions) by its probability distribution.
2. **Random Sampling**: Repeatedly drawing random values for each uncertain input parameter from their respective distributions.
3. **Model Evaluation**: For each set of sampled input values, running the digital twin model to obtain a corresponding output.
4. **Aggregating Results**: Collecting all the output values from the numerous model evaluations.

By performing thousands, or even millions, of these simulation runs, we generate a large dataset of possible model outputs. This dataset effectively represents the probability distribution of the model's output, reflecting the combined effects of all input uncertainties. From this distribution, we can then estimate various statistics, such as the mean, median, variance, standard deviation, and confidence intervals of the output.

For example, consider a digital twin of an aircraft wing designed to predict its fatigue life. The wing's material properties (e.g., fracture toughness, crack growth rate parameters), applied loads (e.g., gust loads, maneuver loads), and environmental conditions (e.g., temperature fluctuations) all carry inherent uncertainties. Using Monte Carlo simulation:

We would define probability distributions for each of these uncertain parameters, informed by experimental data, historical records, or expert judgment. For instance, gust loads might be modeled using a Weibull distribution, while material properties might follow a log-normal distribution.

In each iteration of the simulation, random values would be sampled for fracture toughness, crack growth parameters, gust loads, etc., according to their defined distributions.
The digital twin's fatigue analysis model would then be executed with this specific set of sampled parameters, calculating a fatigue life for that particular realization.
This process would be repeated, say, 10,000 times.
The resulting 10,000 fatigue life predictions would form a distribution. From this distribution, we could determine, for example, that the 95% confidence interval for the wing's fatigue life is between 8,000 and 12,000 flight hours, and that the probability of failure before 7,000 flight hours is less than 1%.

The power of Monte Carlo simulation lies in its ability to handle complex, non-linear relationships between input parameters and model outputs, as well as correlations between input variables, if such dependencies are modeled. It provides a robust way to explore the "uncertainty space" and understand how variations in different inputs contribute to the overall uncertainty in the predictions. This insight is invaluable for identifying critical parameters that have the most significant impact on the output uncertainty, a process often referred to as sensitivity analysis. By understanding which parameters contribute most to the uncertainty, engineers can prioritize efforts to reduce that uncertainty, such as by conducting more precise measurements or refining specific model components.

Beyond standard Monte Carlo, variations like
Latin Hypercube Sampling (LHS) can improve the efficiency of the sampling process. LHS ensures a more uniform coverage of the input parameter space

compared to simple random sampling, meaning fewer samples might be needed to achieve a similar level of accuracy in estimating the output distribution.

Another important aspect of probabilistic uncertainty quantification is understanding how different sources of uncertainty propagate. This involves assessing the relative contributions of aleatoric and epistemic uncertainties, where applicable, to the overall output uncertainty. For instance, if we use a probabilistic model for material properties (which can include both inherent variability and our uncertainty about the precise distribution), and then propagate this through a deterministic model, the resulting output uncertainty is a manifestation of the input uncertainties. If the model itself is subject to structural uncertainty (epistemic), this needs to be accounted for as well, perhaps by running the Monte Carlo simulations with different model structures or by using Bayesian methods to update beliefs about model parameters.

The fidelity of probabilistic quantification hinges on the accuracy of the defined probability distributions. These distributions are typically derived from:

Experimental Data: Statistical analysis of measurements from physical tests can reveal the variability and distribution of material properties, component performance, or system responses. For instance, repeated tests on identical components can yield data to define the distribution of their failure times.
Historical Data: Analyzing past operational data from similar assets can provide insights into performance variations, failure rates, and environmental influences.
Expert Elicitation: In situations where empirical data is scarce, subject matter experts can be consulted to provide subjective probability distributions based on their knowledge and experience. While subjective, this remains a crucial method for quantifying epistemic uncertainty when direct data is unavailable.
Physical Principles: For some phenomena, underlying physical laws might suggest specific distribution types. For example, the Poisson process is often used to model rare events, leading to a Poisson distribution.

It is imperative that these distributions accurately reflect the real-world behavior of the quantities they represent. Mischaracterizing a distribution, for example, by assuming a normal distribution when the data is actually skewed, can lead to erroneous conclusions about output uncertainty and risk.

Furthermore, the choice of whether to model uncertainty probabilistically often depends on the nature of the uncertainty itself. As discussed, aleatoric uncertainty, with its inherent randomness, is naturally suited to probabilistic representation using distributions. Epistemic uncertainty, relating to a lack of knowledge, can also be represented probabilistically, for example, by using broader distributions with larger variances or by employing Bayesian approaches where probabilities represent degrees of belief that can be updated with new information. Techniques like fuzzy logic or interval arithmetic might be preferred when a precise probabilistic model is not feasible or when dealing with qualitative uncertainties. However, probabilistic methods, especially Monte Carlo simulations, offer a unified framework that can often accommodate both types of uncertainty within a single computational procedure, provided they can be cast in terms of probability distributions.

In summary, probabilistic approaches provide a robust and versatile toolkit for quantifying uncertainty in digital twin models. By moving beyond single-point estimates and embracing probability distributions for parameters and outputs, we gain a more complete understanding of system behavior and potential risks. Concepts like variance and confidence intervals offer direct measures of uncertainty and expected ranges. Crucially, techniques such as Monte Carlo simulation enable the exploration of complex models with uncertain inputs, generating rich output distributions that inform decision-making, risk assessment, and strategies for uncertainty reduction. The effectiveness of these methods, however, relies on the careful and accurate characterization of the underlying probability distributions, drawing from empirical data, historical records, and expert knowledge.

The preceding discussion has firmly established the foundational role of probabilistic methods in quantifying uncertainty within digital twin frameworks, moving beyond deterministic predictions to embrace the inherent variability and lack of knowledge present in real-world systems. We have explored how probability distributions serve as the language for representing uncertain parameters and how techniques like Monte Carlo simulation allow us to propagate these uncertainties through complex models, yielding comprehensive output distributions. However, a crucial question remains: amidst a multitude of uncertain parameters, which ones truly dictate the confidence we can place in our digital twin's predictions? It is here that the domain of **sensitivity analysis** becomes paramount.

Sensitivity analysis, in the context of digital twins and uncertainty quantification, is the systematic process of determining how the variation or uncertainty in the output of a model can be attributed to variations of different input parameters. In essence, it is about identifying the "drivers" of uncertainty. For a digital twin, this translates to understanding which uncertain input parameters—be they material properties, environmental conditions, operational loads, or even model structure assumptions—have the most significant impact on the predicted performance, reliability, or safety of the physical asset. This understanding is not merely an academic exercise; it is a critical enabler of efficient and effective decision-making. By pinpointing the parameters that exert the greatest influence, engineers and decision-makers can strategically allocate resources. This might involve investing in more precise measurement techniques for a critical input parameter, refining the fidelity of a particular sub-model that is highly sensitive to certain inputs, or focusing risk mitigation efforts on scenarios driven by high uncertainty in a key parameter. Without sensitivity analysis, efforts to reduce uncertainty might be misdirected, leading to costly and ineffective interventions on parameters that have negligible impact on the overall outcome.

There are broadly two main categories of sensitivity analysis techniques: **local sensitivity analysis** and **global sensitivity analysis**. Each offers a distinct perspective on how input variations affect model outputs, and their application often complements each other in providing a holistic view of uncertainty propagation.

Local Sensitivity Analysis (LSA)

Local sensitivity analysis focuses on the behavior of the model in the immediate vicinity of a single operating point, typically the nominal or mean values of the input parameters. It assesses how a small change in one input parameter affects the model's output, assuming all other input parameters are held constant at their nominal values. This approach is conceptually simpler and computationally less intensive than global methods, making it a valuable first step in understanding parameter influence.

The most common method within local sensitivity analysis is the calculation of **partial derivatives**. If we consider a digital twin model as a function $Y = f(X1, X2, ..., Xn)$, where Y is the model output and Xi are the input parameters, the local sensitivity of Y with respect to Xi at a specific point $(X1^0, X2^0, ..., Xn^0)$ is given by the partial derivative $\frac{\partial Y}{\partial Xi}$ evaluated at that point. A larger magnitude of this partial derivative indicates that a small change in Xi will result in a proportionally larger change in Y, implying high local sensitivity.

For example, consider a digital twin simulating the thermal expansion of a metallic rod. The output, say the total elongation (E), might be modeled as $E = \alpha \cdot L
0 \cdot \Delta T$, where α is the coefficient of thermal expansion, $L0$ is the initial length, and ΔT is the change in temperature. If our nominal operating point is $(\alpha0, L{0,0}, \Delta T_0)$, we can calculate the partial derivatives:
$\frac{\partial E}{\partial \alpha} = L_0 \cdot \Delta T$
$\frac{\partial E}{\partial L_0} = \alpha \cdot \Delta T$
$\frac{\partial E}{\partial \Delta T} = \alpha \cdot L_0$

By evaluating these derivatives at the nominal values $(\alpha
0, L{0,0}, \Delta T0)$, we can see which parameter's change has the most significant impact on elongation. If, for instance, $L0$ is very large and ΔT is small, a change in α might have a larger effect than a change in ΔT.

However, LSA has significant limitations. Firstly, it assumes that the model's behavior is linear or can be reasonably approximated as linear around the nominal point. In many complex digital twin models, the relationships between inputs and outputs are highly non-linear. The sensitivity calculated at a single point may not be representative of the model's behavior across the entire range of plausible input values. Secondly, LSA typically examines the effect of changing only one input parameter at a time while holding others constant. This neglects the possibility of **interactions** between input parameters, where the effect of changing one parameter depends on the value of another. Such interactions are common in physical systems and digital twin models.

Despite these limitations, LSA remains a useful tool for initial screening and for understanding the local behavior of a model. It can quickly highlight parameters that are locally influential, guiding further, more in-depth analysis. For instance, in a structural integrity digital twin, LSA could reveal that local stress concentrations are highly sensitive to small variations in geometric tolerances around critical features.

Global Sensitivity Analysis (GSA)

Global sensitivity analysis, in contrast to LSA, considers the entire range of possible input values and explores the overall behavior of the model across this entire parameter space. GSA acknowledges that input parameters are uncertain and vary simultaneously, and it seeks to quantify their influence on the output uncertainty, including any interactions between them. This makes GSA far more robust and informative for understanding uncertainty propagation in digital twins.

A cornerstone of GSA is the concept of **variance-based decomposition**. The total variance of the model output, $\text{Var}(Y)$, can be decomposed into the sum of variances attributable to individual input parameters and the variances attributable to their interactions. The most widely recognized variance-based methods are those developed by **Sobol**.

Sobol' Indices provide a rigorous framework for quantifying the contribution of each input parameter and their interactions to the total output variance. For a model $Y = f(X1, X2, ..., Xn)$, assuming the input parameters Xi are independent and their variances are normalized (i.e., they range from 0 to 1), the total variance of the output can be expressed as:

$\text{Var}(Y) = \sum
{i} \text{Var}(E[Y | Xi]) + \sum{ii, X_j]) + ...$

The Sobol' indices are defined as fractions of the total variance:

1.
First-order index (Si): This measures the fraction of the total output variance that can be attributed solely to the variation of the input parameter Xi, averaging over all other parameters. It quantifies the main effect of X_i.
$Si = \frac{\text{Var}(E[Y | Xi])}{\text{Var}(Y)}$

2.
Total-order index ($S{Ti}$): This measures the fraction of the total output variance that can be attributed to the variation of Xi, including all possible interactions with other input parameters. It captures the main effect of X_i plus its contributions to all higher-order interactions.
$S{Ti} = 1 - \frac{\text{Var}(E[Y | X{\neg i}])}{\text{Var}(Y)}$
where $X{\neg i}$ represents all input variables except Xi.

The relationship between $S
i$ and $S{Ti}$ is crucial. If $S{Ti}$ is significantly larger than Si, it indicates that Xi has a substantial influence through its interactions with other parameters, even if its individual main effect (Si) is small. If $Si \approx S{Ti}$, then Xi has little influence through interactions. By comparing Si and S_{Ti} for all parameters, we can distinguish between parameters that are influential through their direct effect and those that are influential due to complex interactions.

Calculating Sobol' indices typically involves a sophisticated sampling strategy. The original Sobol' method uses a quasi-random sampling sequence, often referred to as

Sobol sequences or low-discrepancy sequences, which provide a more uniform coverage of the parameter space than standard Monte Carlo sampling. For each parameter Xi, N samples are drawn, and for each parameter Xj where $j \neq i$, N samples are drawn. This requires $N \cdot (2n+2)$ model evaluations for n input parameters to calculate first-order and total-order indices. More advanced algorithms, like the **Saltelli sampling scheme**, extend this to estimate higher-order interactions more efficiently, often requiring $N \cdot (2n+2)$ evaluations.

Let's revisit the digital twin of an aircraft wing's fatigue life. Suppose the key uncertain inputs are:

$X1$: Fracture toughness ($K{Ic}$)
X_2: Crack growth rate exponent (m)
$X3$: Mean applied stress amplitude ($\sigmaa$)
$X4$: Stress concentration factor (Kt)

If we use Monte Carlo simulation to generate output fatigue lives and then apply Sobol' method with appropriate sampling, we might obtain the following (hypothetical) Sobol' indices:

$S
1 = 0.25$, $S{T1} = 0.40$ (Fracture toughness influences fatigue life, and also interacts significantly with other parameters)
$S2 = 0.35$, $S{T2} = 0.38$ (Crack growth rate exponent has a strong direct influence and minimal interaction effects)
$S3 = 0.30$, $S{T3} = 0.32$ (Mean applied stress amplitude has a strong direct influence and minimal interaction effects)
$S4 = 0.10$, $S{T4} = 0.25$ (Stress concentration factor has a moderate direct influence, but its impact is amplified through interactions)

In this example, the first-order indices reveal that crack growth rate exponent ($X
2$) and mean applied stress amplitude ($X3$) have the largest direct impacts. However, the total-order indices reveal a more nuanced picture. Fracture toughness ($X1$) and stress concentration factor ($X4$) have substantial

contributions through interactions, meaning their influence on fatigue life is not just their individual effect but also how they combine with other factors. For instance, a lower fracture toughness might become critically dangerous when combined with a high stress concentration factor.

Based on these Sobol' indices, we might prioritize:

1. **Reducing uncertainty in $X2$ and $X3$**: Since they have high Si and $S{Ti}$, improving the precision of their measurement or refining their models directly impacts the overall certainty of fatigue life prediction.
2. **Investigating interactions involving $X1$ and $X4$**: The large difference between Si and $S{Ti}$ for $X1$ and $X4$ suggests that their interplay with other parameters is significant. This might warrant more detailed investigation into the coupled physics governing these interactions, or perhaps collecting data that captures these specific combined effects.

Another powerful class of GSA methods includes **regression-based techniques** and **screening methods**.

Screening Methods are particularly useful when dealing with a large number of input parameters, many of which might have negligible influence. These methods aim to identify the "important" parameters quickly, allowing more computationally intensive GSA methods to be applied only to those critical inputs. The **Morris Method** (also known as the elementary effects method) is a popular screening technique. It works by calculating the "elementary effect" of each parameter on the model output. An elementary effect is the change in the output resulting from a change in one input parameter, while other parameters are varied in a way that explores the parameter space. The Morris method estimates the mean and standard deviation of these elementary effects for each parameter. A parameter is considered influential if its mean elementary effect is large (indicating a systematic impact) or if its standard deviation of elementary effects is large (indicating significant non-linearities or interactions). The Morris method is computationally efficient, typically requiring only $N \cdot (n+1)$ model evaluations for n parameters.

For a complex digital twin with dozens or even hundreds of potential uncertain inputs, a two-stage approach is often adopted: first, use a screening method like Morris to identify a subset of critical parameters, and then apply a more detailed method like Sobol' indices to this subset to quantify their influence and interactions accurately.

Regression-based methods employ statistical models to approximate the digital twin model's behavior. Techniques like polynomial chaos expansion (PCE) or Gaussian processes can be used to build surrogate models. Once a surrogate model is trained, sensitivity indices can be derived from its structure. For example, if a polynomial regression model is used, the coefficients of the polynomial directly indicate the influence of each input. Gaussian processes offer a probabilistic framework where the uncertainty in the surrogate model itself can also be quantified, providing a measure of confidence in the sensitivity estimates. These methods can be very efficient if the surrogate model is accurate and the digital twin simulation is computationally expensive.

The Role of Digital Twin Context in Sensitivity Analysis

The application of sensitivity analysis in digital twins is deeply intertwined with the specific objectives and the nature of the physical system being modeled.

Design Optimization: In the design phase, digital twins are used to explore various design parameters. Sensitivity analysis helps identify which design variables have the most impact on performance metrics (e.g., strength, efficiency, cost), guiding engineers towards optimal configurations and highlighting areas where design robustness is crucial. For example, in designing a new turbine blade, sensitivity analysis might show that aerodynamic performance is highly sensitive to the airfoil shape's trailing edge thickness and the blade's twist distribution, suggesting these are key parameters for optimization.
Predictive Maintenance: For digital twins used in predictive maintenance, sensitivity analysis can reveal which sensor readings or operational parameters are most predictive of component degradation or failure. If the remaining useful

life (RUL) prediction of a pump is highly sensitive to the uncertainty in vibration sensor readings and lubricant viscosity, then focusing efforts on improving the accuracy of these measurements or refining the models that incorporate them becomes a priority. This directly informs maintenance scheduling and resource allocation.

Risk Assessment: In safety-critical applications, sensitivity analysis is vital for understanding the sources of risk. If a digital twin predicts the probability of failure for a bridge under extreme weather events, and the analysis shows high sensitivity to the uncertainty in wind load models and material degradation rates, then these factors become the focal points for risk mitigation strategies, such as implementing more robust structural health monitoring or specifying more durable materials.

Model Validation and Improvement: Sensitivity analysis can highlight deficiencies in the digital twin model itself. If the output is highly sensitive to an input parameter for which there is little reliable data or a simplified model is used, it suggests that further model refinement or targeted data acquisition is needed in that area. Conversely, if the output is largely insensitive to certain parameters, it might indicate that simplified assumptions or less precise data for those parameters are acceptable, leading to more efficient model development.

Practical Considerations and Challenges

Implementing sensitivity analysis effectively in digital twin projects involves several practical considerations:

1.
Computational Cost: GSA, especially methods like Sobol' indices, can be computationally demanding, requiring thousands or even millions of model evaluations. This is particularly challenging for high-fidelity digital twins that may take hours or days to run a single simulation. Strategies like using surrogate models, parallel computing, or efficient sampling schemes (like LHS combined with regression) are often necessary to overcome this barrier.

2. **Defining Input Distributions**: The accuracy of sensitivity analysis is heavily dependent on the accurate characterization of input parameter uncertainties through appropriate probability distributions. If these distributions are poorly

defined or do not reflect the real-world variability, the sensitivity results can be misleading. This underscores the importance of rigorous data collection, statistical analysis, and expert elicitation.

3. **Correlation Between Inputs**: Many GSA methods, including the standard Sobol' method, assume input parameters are independent. In reality, physical parameters are often correlated. For instance, material properties might be correlated due to manufacturing processes. If correlations are significant, they must be explicitly modeled (e.g., using copulas in Monte Carlo or specialized GSA techniques for dependent inputs), as ignoring them can lead to inaccurate sensitivity indices.
4. **Non-Stationarity**: Digital twins often represent systems that evolve over time. The sensitivity of model outputs to input parameters might also change over the system's lifecycle. Static sensitivity analysis performed at a single point in time might not capture this temporal evolution of influence. Techniques for time-dependent sensitivity analysis may be required for such dynamic systems.
5. **Model Complexity and Black-Box Nature**: Highly complex, proprietary, or legacy digital twin models might be treated as "black boxes," where internal workings are not accessible. In such cases, only simulation-based GSA methods (like Monte Carlo, Sobol', or Morris) can be applied, as they only require input-output pairs.

In conclusion, sensitivity analysis serves as an indispensable bridge between uncertainty quantification and actionable insights within digital twin applications. While local methods offer a quick initial assessment, global techniques, particularly variance-based methods like Sobol' indices, provide a comprehensive understanding of how individual parameters and their interactions drive output uncertainty. By systematically identifying these key drivers, engineers and decision-makers can focus their efforts on areas that yield the greatest improvements in model fidelity, risk reduction, and overall confidence in the digital twin's predictions. This focused approach is not merely about understanding uncertainty; it is about strategically managing it to enhance the value and reliability of digital twins across their diverse applications.

Communicating uncertainty effectively to stakeholders is the critical bridge that transforms complex quantitative analyses into actionable intelligence. Without clear and comprehensible communication, the most sophisticated uncertainty quantification (UQ) and sensitivity analysis efforts can fall by the wayside, failing to influence decisions or set realistic expectations. Digital twins, by their very nature, are tools designed to inform a wide range of stakeholders, from seasoned engineers and data scientists to project managers, executives, and even regulatory bodies. Each of these groups possesses varying levels of technical expertise and different primary objectives, necessitating a tailored approach to presenting uncertainty. The goal is not to overwhelm stakeholders with raw statistical data, but to equip them with the understanding required to make informed decisions, allocate resources wisely, and appreciate the inherent limitations and strengths of the digital twin's predictions.

One of the most potent tools for communicating uncertainty is **visualization**. Raw numbers, confidence intervals, or probability density functions, while accurate, can be abstract and difficult to interpret for non-specialists. Visual representations can bridge this gap by translating complex data into intuitive graphical formats. For instance, instead of stating that a predicted performance metric has a 95% confidence interval of [950 MW, 1050 MW], a visual might depict this range as a shaded area on a graph showing the most likely predicted value (e.g., 1000 MW) as a central line. This immediately conveys the potential variability around the central estimate.

Different types of visualizations are suited for different contexts. **Error bars** on bar charts or line graphs are a common and straightforward method for indicating the range of plausible values for a specific prediction. For instance, if a digital twin predicts the mean time between failures (MTBF) for a critical component, error bars extending above and below the mean value can visually represent the uncertainty. However, error bars often imply a symmetric uncertainty or are simply interpreted as a range without specifying the likelihood of values within that range.

More sophisticated visualizations can provide a richer understanding. **Box plots** (or box-and-whisker plots) are excellent for summarizing the distribution of potential outcomes. They can display the median, interquartile range (IQR), and potential outliers, offering a compact view of central tendency and dispersion. When comparing different scenarios or design options, side-by-side box plots can reveal not only differences in average performance but also differences in their variability.

Probability density functions (PDFs) or **cumulative distribution functions (CDFs)**, while more technical, can be powerful when presented alongside explanatory context. A PDF plot, for example, can visually show that a particular outcome is more likely to fall within a certain range, and less likely to occur outside of it. Overlaying PDFs for different scenarios or different versions of a model can be highly informative. For decision-makers who need to understand the likelihood of exceeding a certain threshold (e.g., a safety limit, a production target), a CDF plot is invaluable, as it directly shows the probability of the outcome being less than or equal to any given value.

For temporal predictions, such as forecasting the remaining useful life (RUL) of a piece of equipment or the expected completion time of a project, **time-series plots with uncertainty bands** are essential. A line representing the most probable RUL can be accompanied by shaded regions or multiple forecast lines representing different percentiles (e.g., 50th, 75th, 90th percentile). This allows stakeholders to see not only the projected RUL but also how the uncertainty in that prediction grows over time. For example, the RUL might be predicted with high confidence in the short term, but the uncertainty band might widen considerably as the prediction extends further into the future. This is often due to the compounding effect of uncertainties in the underlying models and input parameters over longer durations.

Another crucial aspect of communicating uncertainty is framing it in terms of **risk**. Stakeholders are often more concerned with the potential for negative outcomes than with the precise statistical distribution of all possibilities. **Risk matrices**, which plot the likelihood of an event against its potential impact, are a widely understood tool for categorizing risks. In the context of digital twins, these matrices can be populated with the probabilities of various undesirable events (e.g., equipment failure, cost overruns, schedule delays) as predicted by the UQ analysis. For instance, a risk matrix might categorize the probability of a critical component failing within the next year based on the digital twin's RUL prediction and its associated uncertainty. Events falling into the high-probability, high-impact quadrant would immediately flag areas requiring urgent attention and mitigation strategies.

When discussing specific decisions, it is vital to communicate the **implications of uncertainty on those decisions**. This often involves presenting **probabilistic forecasts** and discussing their impact on key performance indicators (KPIs) or business objectives. For example, if a decision needs to be made about whether to proceed with a manufacturing process based on a digital twin's performance prediction, the communication should go beyond just stating the mean predicted output. It should highlight the probability of the process meeting its target specifications, the probability of falling short, and the potential financial consequences associated with each outcome. This might involve presenting a set of possible scenarios with associated probabilities and economic impacts.

Consider a digital twin used to predict the performance of a new chemical reaction process. The UQ might reveal that the yield has a mean prediction of 90% but with a significant standard deviation, indicating substantial uncertainty. Communicating this to process engineers might involve showing a plot of the yield distribution and highlighting that there is a 20% chance of the yield falling below 85% (which might be the minimum economically viable threshold). This informs the decision about whether to invest in further process optimization, acquire more precise sensor data, or accept the risk of lower-than-ideal yields.

For decision-makers who are not statistically inclined, framing uncertainty in terms of "what if" scenarios can be very effective. Instead of presenting a complex sensitivity analysis report, one might present a few key scenarios: a "best-case" scenario, a "worst-case" scenario, and a "most likely" scenario, each with a quantified probability of occurrence based on the UQ. This allows stakeholders to mentally "walk through" the potential range of outcomes and consider their strategic responses.

Furthermore, it is crucial to clearly articulate **what the uncertainty** *means* in practical terms. Does it arise from inherent randomness in the system, lack of knowledge about parameters, approximations in the model, or limitations in measurement data? This clarity helps stakeholders understand the root causes of uncertainty and guides them on how to address it.

For example, if uncertainty in a structural integrity digital twin is primarily due to limited data on material aging under specific environmental conditions, stakeholders might be directed to invest in accelerated aging tests or deploy more advanced structural health monitoring systems. If the uncertainty stems from model simplifications (e.g., assuming uniform material properties when they are known to vary spatially), the recommendation might be to refine the model's fidelity or incorporate spatially varying material models.

The concept of
"actionable uncertainty" is paramount. Uncertainty quantification is not an end in itself; it is a means to better decision-making. Therefore, communication should always link uncertainty back to potential actions. This might involve:
Identifying parameters requiring more data: Sensitivity analysis can pinpoint parameters whose uncertainty has a large impact on the outcome. Communicating this might lead to prioritizing data acquisition efforts for these specific parameters.
Highlighting critical thresholds: For decisions based on whether a predicted value exceeds or falls below a certain threshold, clear communication of the probability of crossing that threshold is essential.
Informing risk mitigation strategies: If the digital twin predicts a high probability of a failure mode due to uncertainty in certain inputs, this information directly informs the development of preventive or mitigation measures.
Guiding resource allocation: Understanding which uncertainties have the most significant impact allows for more efficient allocation of time, budget, and engineering resources, focusing efforts where they will yield the greatest return in terms of increased confidence or reduced risk.

Storytelling with data can also be an effective communication strategy. Instead of presenting dry statistical reports, one can weave a narrative around the digital twin's predictions, incorporating the uncertainty as a natural part of the story. For instance, when presenting the predicted performance of a new renewable energy system, the narrative could describe the expected energy output under normal conditions, but also explain the range of possible outputs due to variations in wind speed or solar irradiance, and the potential implications for grid stability or revenue.

A common pitfall is the "curse of precision" - overstating the precision of a prediction by omitting or downplaying the uncertainty. Conversely, presenting uncertainty in a way that induces paralysis or excessive caution can also be detrimental. The art of communicating uncertainty lies in striking a balance: providing enough information for informed decision-making without creating undue alarm or a false sense of precision.

Therefore, the communication strategy should be iterative and adaptive. It's rarely a one-time event. As the digital twin evolves, as new data becomes available, and as the system it represents changes, the uncertainty quantification and its communication must be revisited and updated. Regular updates, presented in an accessible format, ensure that stakeholders remain informed and that the digital twin continues to serve as a reliable decision-support tool.

The choice of communication tools and techniques should also be tailored to the audience.

For highly technical audiences (engineers, modelers): Detailed statistical reports, plots of distributions, and sensitivity index values might be appropriate, possibly supplemented by discussions on methodologies and assumptions.
For management and executive levels: Focus should be on the business implications, risks, opportunities, and key decision points. High-level visualizations, risk matrices, and summary statistics (e.g., probability of success, range of financial outcomes) are more effective.
For regulatory bodies: Clarity, transparency, and defensibility of the uncertainty assessment are paramount. This might involve presenting detailed documentation of the UQ process, sensitivity analyses, and justification for model assumptions and data sources.

In all cases, a
glossary of terms can be invaluable for ensuring common understanding, especially when terms like "standard deviation," "confidence interval," or "percentile" are used. Defining these terms in simple language within the communication material itself or in an appendix can prevent misinterpretation.

Finally, fostering a culture where uncertainty is openly discussed and understood is key. This means that digital twin developers and UQ specialists should not shy away from presenting uncertainty, but rather proactively engage stakeholders in understanding its implications. This collaborative approach ensures that the digital twin's outputs are not taken as absolute truths but as informed predictions with quantifiable levels of confidence, thereby maximizing their true value in complex decision-making processes. The ultimate aim is to empower stakeholders to make the best possible decisions, given the available knowledge and the inherent variability of the real world, by clearly illuminating the landscape of possibilities and risks.

Chapter 7: Calibration and Validation Strategies

The efficacy and reliability of any digital twin hinge on a meticulous and iterative process that intertwines model calibration and validation. These two pillars are not independent steps but rather form a continuous feedback loop, each informing and refining the other to ensure that the virtual representation accurately mirrors the behavior of its physical counterpart. Without this rigorous approach, a digital twin, however sophisticated its architecture, risks becoming a mere digital illusion, divorced from the realities it is intended to simulate and predict. The confidence with which we can then entrust critical operational decisions, design choices, and maintenance strategies to the digital twin is directly proportional to the robustness of its calibration and validation.

Calibration is fundamentally the process of tuning the parameters of a digital twin model so that its outputs align as closely as possible with observed data from the physical system. Imagine a digital twin designed to predict the thermal performance of a complex industrial furnace. This model will contain numerous parameters – such as heat transfer coefficients, material emissivity, airflow rates, and catalyst activity – that are not precisely known or may vary in practice. Calibration involves using historical operational data, perhaps from temperature sensors, pressure gauges, and emission analyzers within the actual furnace, to adjust these uncertain parameters. The goal is to find the set of parameter values that minimizes the discrepancy between the digital twin's simulated temperatures, emissions, and other outputs, and the measured values from the real furnace. This is often an optimization problem, where algorithms seek to find the parameter values that achieve the best fit, typically by minimizing a defined error metric, such as the root mean square error (RMSE) between simulated and observed data.

The choice of data for calibration is paramount. It must be representative of the operational envelope the digital twin is intended to cover. If a furnace is calibrated using data only from low-temperature startup phases, its predictions for high-temperature steady-state operation might be highly inaccurate. Similarly, if the physical system experiences phenomena that are not captured by the model structure, calibration alone cannot rectify this. For example, if a novel degradation mechanism begins to affect the furnace lining, and this mechanism is not explicitly included in the digital twin's equations, no amount of parameter tuning will allow the model to accurately predict performance under these new conditions. Therefore, calibration is intrinsically linked to the model's underlying assumptions and its fidelity in representing the real-world physics, chemistry, and operational dynamics.

Furthermore, calibration is not a one-time event. As the physical asset ages, undergoes maintenance, or operates under new conditions, its behavior may drift. This necessitates periodic recalibration to ensure the digital twin remains aligned with reality. For instance, the heat transfer coefficients within the furnace might change as the refractory lining wears down, or the airflow patterns could alter due to minor structural deformations. A well-designed digital twin system will incorporate mechanisms for continuous or scheduled recalibration, leveraging new data streams to maintain its accuracy and predictive power. This might involve automated parameter updating or a systematic process for engineers to re-evaluate and refine the model parameters based on ongoing operational data.

Once a model has been calibrated, the crucial next step is validation. While calibration demonstrates that the model can reproduce past observations given a specific set of adjusted parameters, validation assesses its ability to predict future or unseen behavior. This is where the true trustworthiness of the digital twin is established. Validation is performed using a separate set of data that was not used during the calibration process. This independent data set acts as a stringent test of the model's generalization capability. If the digital twin, calibrated on one set of data, can accurately predict outcomes generated from an entirely different operational period or a slightly altered configuration of the physical asset, then we gain significant confidence in its predictive power.

Consider our furnace example again. After calibrating the model using data from the first six months of operation, validation would involve using data from the subsequent six months – data that the model has never "seen" before – to test its predictions. We would compare the simulated thermal profiles, energy consumption, and emission levels against the actual measurements from this new period. A successful validation would show that the model's predictions fall within acceptable tolerances of these independent measurements. If the validated model consistently over or underpredicts key performance indicators, or if its predictions deviate significantly from reality, it indicates shortcomings that might stem from the model structure itself, the quality of the calibration, or the presence of unmodeled phenomena.

The process of validation often involves defining specific metrics and thresholds for acceptable performance. For a critical parameter like the peak temperature in a high-temperature alloy forging process, a validation might require the digital twin to predict this temperature within ±5°C of the actual measured value, 95% of the time. These criteria are usually dictated by the intended application of the digital twin. If the twin is used for safety-critical monitoring, the validation requirements will be far more stringent than if it's used for preliminary design exploration.

It is also common practice to perform validation under a range of different scenarios. For instance, the furnace digital twin might be validated not only for standard operating conditions but also for transient phases like startup and shutdown, or under variations in fuel composition or ambient temperature. This multi-scenario validation provides a more comprehensive assessment of the model's robustness and its ability to perform reliably across the spectrum of expected real-world conditions.

The relationship between calibration and validation is deeply symbiotic. Calibration provides the best possible fit to the available data, but without validation, we cannot be certain that this fit reflects true predictive capability. A model might be "over-fitted" during calibration, meaning its parameters are so finely tuned to the specific calibration data that it captures not only the underlying system behavior but also the noise and idiosyncrasies of that particular data set. Such an over-fitted model would perform exceptionally well on the calibration data but would likely fail to generalize to new, unseen data, leading to poor validation results.

Conversely, a well-executed validation can reveal weaknesses in the calibration process or highlight areas where the model structure needs revision. If validation results are consistently poor, it might indicate that the wrong parameters were adjusted during calibration, that the chosen error metric was inappropriate, or, more fundamentally, that the mathematical model itself is insufficient to capture the essential dynamics of the physical system. This realization then feeds back into the calibration and modeling stages, prompting a re-evaluation of assumptions, model structure, and calibration strategies.

For example, if the digital twin of a chemical reactor, after calibration, consistently fails validation when predicting product yield under varying catalyst concentrations, this suggests that the assumed relationship between catalyst concentration and reaction rate in the model might be an oversimplification. The validation failure would prompt a return to the modeling phase to incorporate more complex reaction kinetics or consider the spatial distribution of the catalyst, which might not have been accounted for in the initial model. Subsequently, a recalibrated and potentially restructured model would undergo another round of validation.

The iterative nature of this process is crucial. It's a cycle of "build, calibrate, validate, revise, recalibrate, revalidate." Each pass through this cycle refines the digital twin, incrementally increasing its accuracy, reliability, and predictive power. This iterative refinement is what builds trust in the digital twin as a decision-support tool. Stakeholders need to understand that the digital twin is not a static artifact but a dynamic entity that evolves and improves through rigorous testing and comparison with the real world.

Moreover, the data used for validation must be truly independent. This means it must come from periods of operation or configurations that were not used at all during calibration. If some of the validation data was inadvertently used for calibration, the validation results would be artificially optimistic, providing a false sense of confidence. Ensuring data independence is a critical aspect of experimental design and data management within the digital twin development lifecycle. This often requires careful planning of data collection campaigns, clearly demarcating data sets for calibration versus validation.

The concept of "trust" in a digital twin is built through demonstrable performance against real-world data. Calibration establishes an initial alignment, showing that the model can be made to behave like the system under certain conditions. Validation, using independent evidence, provides the crucial proof that this alignment is not coincidental but reflects a genuine understanding of the system's underlying dynamics. When a digital twin has successfully passed rigorous calibration and validation against diverse and independent data sets, it earns the confidence needed for its outputs to inform critical decisions, such as optimizing process parameters, predicting equipment failures, or designing for enhanced performance. Without this due diligence, the digital twin remains a theoretical construct, and its application in high-stakes scenarios would be ill-advised. The investment in meticulous calibration and validation is therefore not merely a technical formality but a fundamental requirement for unlocking the true value and utility of digital twin technology.

The precision and reliability of a digital twin are critically dependent on the accurate calibration of its underlying model parameters. This process, as previously discussed, involves tuning these parameters so that the digital twin's simulated outputs closely match observed data from its physical counterpart. While the general principle is straightforward, the practical implementation can be complex, especially when dealing with sophisticated physics-based or hybrid models that often incorporate a large number of uncertain parameters. This subsection will explore a range of parameter calibration techniques, detailing their principles and application in the context of digital twin development.

At the heart of many calibration techniques lies the concept of optimization. The goal is to find a set of parameter values that minimizes an objective function, which quantifies the difference between the digital twin's predictions and the real-world measurements. This discrepancy is typically represented by an error metric. The choice of error metric is crucial and depends on the nature of the data and the critical aspects of the system being modeled. Common metrics include the Sum of Squared Errors (SSE), Mean Squared Error (MSE), Root Mean Squared Error (RMSE), and Mean Absolute Error (MAE). Each metric has its own sensitivity to outliers and the distribution of errors. For instance, RMSE penalizes larger errors more heavily than MAE, making it sensitive to occasional significant deviations.

One of the most fundamental optimization-based approaches is **Gradient Descent**. This iterative algorithm starts with an initial guess for the model parameters and repeatedly adjusts them in the direction that most rapidly decreases the error function. The "direction" is determined by the gradient of the error function with respect to each parameter. Mathematically, if the error function is denoted by $J(\theta)$, where θ is the vector of model parameters, gradient descent updates the parameters as follows:

$\theta
{k+1} = *\theta*k - \alpha \nabla*\theta J(\theta*k)$

Here, $\theta
*k$ represents the parameter values at iteration k, α is the learning rate (a small positive constant that controls the step size), and $\nabla*\theta J(\theta*k)$ is the gradient of the error function with respect to θ evaluated at $\theta*k$. The gradient indicates the direction of steepest ascent of the error function, so moving in the opposite direction (-gradient) leads towards a minimum.

Gradient descent is computationally efficient when the gradient can be easily calculated, which is often the case for models described by differentiable equations. However, it has limitations. It can get stuck in local minima of the error function, especially if the function is non-convex, meaning it has multiple valleys. The choice of learning rate is also critical; too large a rate can cause the algorithm to overshoot the minimum, while too small a rate can lead to very slow convergence. Variants like Stochastic Gradient Descent (SGD) and Mini-batch Gradient Descent are often used in machine learning contexts, where they process data in smaller batches to speed up convergence and escape local minima, but the core principle remains the same. In digital twin applications, if the error function is well-behaved and has a single global minimum, gradient descent can be a powerful tool for calibrating models with a moderate number of parameters. For example, calibrating the viscosity and friction coefficients in a fluid dynamics simulation of a pump might be achievable with gradient descent, provided the relationship between these parameters and the output flow rate is reasonably linear or has a convex error landscape.

When the error function is not differentiable or is highly complex and non-convex,
Global Optimization Algorithms become more suitable. These algorithms are designed to explore the parameter space more broadly and are less likely to be trapped in local optima. Among these, **Genetic Algorithms (GAs)** are a popular choice. Inspired by the process of natural selection, GAs work with a population of potential solutions (sets of parameters). Each solution is represented as a "chromosome," and the population evolves over generations through mechanisms like selection, crossover, and mutation.

In a GA for parameter calibration:

1. **Initialization**: A population of random parameter sets (chromosomes) is generated.
2. **Fitness Evaluation**: Each parameter set is used to run the digital twin model, and its performance is evaluated using the chosen error metric (the "fitness"). Lower error means higher fitness.
3. **Selection**: Fitter individuals (parameter sets) are more likely to be selected for reproduction.
4. **Crossover**: Selected parents "reproduce" by combining parts of their parameter sets to create new offspring. This mimics genetic recombination.
5. **Mutation**: Small, random changes are introduced into the offspring's parameter sets. This maintains diversity in the population and allows exploration of new areas of the parameter space.
6. **Replacement**: The new generation of offspring replaces some or all of the previous generation.

This process is repeated for many generations, with the population tending to converge towards optimal or near-optimal parameter sets. GAs are robust in that they can handle complex, non-linear, and multi-modal error landscapes. They are particularly useful when the number of parameters is large, or when there are many interactions between parameters that create complex error surfaces. For instance, calibrating a complex thermodynamic model of an internal combustion engine, where parameters like combustion efficiency, heat loss coefficients, and valve timing interact non-linearly, could benefit from a GA. The computational cost of GAs can be high because each individual in the population must be evaluated, but their ability to find good solutions in challenging optimization problems makes them valuable.

Another powerful paradigm for calibration, especially when dealing with uncertainty quantification, is
Bayesian Inference. Instead of seeking a single "best" set of parameters, Bayesian inference aims to determine the probability distribution of the parameters given the observed data. This approach treats the unknown parameters as random variables and updates their prior beliefs based on the evidence provided by the measurement data.

The core of Bayesian inference is Bayes' theorem:

$P(\theta | D) = \frac{P(D | \theta) P(\theta)}{P(D)}$

Where:

$P(\theta | D)$ is the **posterior distribution**: the probability of the parameters θ given the data D. This is what we want to find.
$P(D | \theta)$ is the **likelihood function**: the probability of observing the data D given a specific set of parameters θ. This is derived from the digital twin model and assumptions about measurement noise.
$P(\theta)$ *is the* **prior distribution**: our belief about the parameters before observing any data. This can incorporate expert knowledge or results from previous studies.
$P(D)$ is the **evidence**: the marginal probability of the data, which acts as a normalizing constant.

Calculating the posterior distribution often involves computationally intensive methods, as analytically solving the integral for $P(D)$ can be intractable for complex models. Common techniques to approximate the posterior include:

1. **Markov Chain Monte Carlo (MCMC)** methods: Algorithms like Metropolis-Hastings or Gibbs sampling construct a Markov chain whose stationary distribution is the desired posterior. By running the chain for a long time, samples are generated that are representative of the posterior distribution. This allows estimation of not only the most likely parameter values but also the uncertainty associated with them.
2. **Variational Inference (VI)**: This approach approximates the true posterior distribution with a simpler, tractable distribution (e.g., a Gaussian) by minimizing the Kullback-Leibler (KL) divergence between the two. VI is often faster than MCMC but provides an approximation to the posterior.

Bayesian inference is highly advantageous for digital twins because it inherently quantifies uncertainty. For critical applications, knowing the confidence interval for a prediction is as important as the prediction itself. If the digital twin is used to assess the risk of failure, understanding the uncertainty in the calibrated parameters that influence failure probability is essential. For example, calibrating the parameters governing crack propagation in a structural integrity digital twin would benefit greatly from a Bayesian approach. It would provide not just the most probable crack growth rate but also a distribution of possible growth rates, allowing for a more robust risk assessment. The prior distributions can incorporate knowledge of material properties, while the likelihood reflects how well the model's predicted crack growth matches measured crack lengths over time.

Beyond these general optimization frameworks, specific techniques are tailored to the nature of the data and the model.

Levenberg-Marquardt Algorithm is a popular non-linear least squares algorithm used for parameter estimation. It combines the benefits of gradient descent and the inverse Hessian method (Gauss-Newton algorithm). When far from the minimum, it behaves like gradient descent, and when close to the minimum, it approximates the Gauss-Newton method, which can converge faster. It's particularly effective when the objective function is a sum of squares, common in fitting experimental data.

Ensemble-based methods, such as the Ensemble Kalman Filter (EnKF) or Ensemble Smoother (ES), are widely used in fields like meteorology and geophysics, and are increasingly applied to digital twins. These methods work by maintaining an ensemble (a collection) of model states or parameters. As new data arrives, the ensemble is updated to better match the observations. The EnKF is a recursive filter suitable for real-time calibration, while the ES is a smoother that uses all available data to estimate parameters retrospectively. These methods are well-suited for large-scale, high-dimensional systems and can handle non-linearities by propagating the ensemble through the model. For instance, calibrating a distributed parameter model of a complex hydrological system or a large power grid could leverage ensemble methods.

Sensitivity Analysis plays a crucial role in guiding the calibration process. Before or during calibration, it's often beneficial to understand which parameters have the most significant impact on the model's outputs. Parameters with low sensitivity may not need to be finely tuned, or their uncertainty might be less critical. Conversely, highly sensitive parameters require more accurate estimation and can be the focus of targeted data collection or refinement of their prior knowledge. Techniques like the Morris method or Sobol indices can be employed for global sensitivity analysis. Identifying sensitive parameters can simplify the calibration problem, reduce computational cost, and highlight areas where model structure might be particularly important.

The
choice of data for calibration is as critical as the algorithm itself. The data must be sufficient in quantity, quality, and representativeness.
Sufficiency: Enough data points are needed to constrain the parameters. Too few data points can lead to an underdetermined problem, where multiple parameter sets yield similar model outputs.

Quality: Measurement errors should be understood and accounted for. Outliers need to be handled appropriately, either by removal, robust error metrics, or robust estimation techniques.
Representativeness: The calibration data must cover the range of operational conditions and system behaviors that the digital twin is intended to simulate. Calibrating a model of an aircraft engine solely on ground test data would likely result in poor performance when applied to flight conditions.

Furthermore,
identifiability analysis is an important precursor to calibration. This analysis determines whether the model parameters can be uniquely estimated from the available data. Some parameters might be structurally unidentifiable (meaning the model structure itself doesn't allow them to be distinguished), while others might be practically unidentifiable (meaning the available data is insufficient to estimate them with desired precision). Identifying unidentifiable parameters early can save considerable computational effort and guide efforts to improve data collection or model structure.

The practical implementation of these calibration techniques often involves sophisticated software tools and computational infrastructure. Many commercial simulation platforms and open-source libraries (e.g., SciPy's optimization module, Pyomo, Drake, Bayesian Optimization libraries like GPyOpt or BoTorch) offer implementations of these algorithms. For complex digital twins, parallel computing and cloud resources are often employed to speed up the computationally intensive process of evaluating the model and its error function across numerous parameter combinations or iterations.

In summary, parameter calibration is not a monolithic process but a diverse field employing a suite of techniques, each with its strengths and weaknesses. From gradient-based methods for well-behaved error landscapes to global optimizers for complex systems, and Bayesian approaches for uncertainty quantification, the choice of technique depends heavily on the specific digital twin model, the available data, and the application requirements. Effective calibration is an iterative journey, often requiring careful consideration of optimization algorithms, error metrics, data quality, and model structure to ensure the digital twin accurately and reliably mirrors its physical counterpart.

Having meticulously calibrated the parameters of a digital twin to align its simulated behavior with observed data, the subsequent, and equally critical, stage is **model validation**. Calibration ensures that the model can, at a specific point or range of conditions, reproduce known outcomes. Validation, however, goes a significant step further: it is the process of independently assessing whether the calibrated digital twin is fit for its intended purpose. It is a rigorous examination to determine the trustworthiness and reliability of the model's predictive capabilities beyond the data used for calibration. Without robust validation, a digital twin, however well-calibrated, risks being a sophisticated piece of software that merely mimics past observations without truly capturing the underlying physics or dynamics necessary for future predictions or decision-making. This subsection delves into the various approaches employed to validate digital twins, emphasizing the need for independence and the assessment of fitness-for-purpose.

One of the foundational approaches to model validation is the **comparison against historical data that was not used during the calibration phase**. This is often referred to as using a "hold-out" dataset. During calibration, a portion of the available data is typically set aside. Once the model parameters are finalized, this reserved data is then fed into the calibrated digital twin. The outputs generated by the model are then compared against the actual measurements from this independent historical dataset. The metrics used for this comparison are similar to those employed during calibration (e.g., RMSE, MAE), but their interpretation shifts from optimizing parameter values to evaluating model performance. A low error on this independent dataset provides strong evidence that the model has learned generalizable patterns rather than simply memorizing the calibration data – a phenomenon known as overfitting. For instance, if a digital twin of a manufacturing process was calibrated using data from the first six months of operation, validation would involve comparing its predictions for the subsequent three months of operation against the actual production data from that period. Significant deviations would signal potential issues with the model's structure, calibration process, or the assumption that the underlying system dynamics remained consistent.

Beyond historical data, a more proactive and often more compelling validation strategy involves

testing with new experimental data specifically generated for validation purposes. This is particularly crucial for digital twins intended for critical applications, such as those in aerospace, automotive, or medical devices, where potential failures can have severe consequences. In this scenario, after the model has been calibrated using existing data, a new series of experiments or tests are designed and executed on the physical asset. These experiments are chosen to probe specific aspects of the model's behavior, often focusing on conditions or scenarios that were not extensively covered by the calibration data. This might involve operating the system at its extremes, under novel load conditions, or for extended durations. The digital twin is then used to predict the outcome of these new experiments *before* they are conducted. The actual results are then compared against these pre-experiment predictions. A close agreement between predictions and observations in these novel scenarios provides a robust demonstration of the digital twin's predictive power and its ability to generalize. For example, a digital twin of a wind turbine might be calibrated using operational data from various wind speeds. For validation, a new set of tests could be designed to simulate extreme weather conditions, such as sudden gusts or prolonged periods of very low wind, and the digital twin's ability to accurately predict the turbine's response (e.g., power output, structural loads) under these specific, new conditions would be rigorously assessed.

Another vital avenue for validation, especially for models grounded in well-understood physical principles, is
verification against analytical solutions or established benchmark models. For many physical systems, simplified mathematical models exist for which exact analytical solutions can be derived, or validated benchmark models developed by the scientific community are available. These serve as theoretical baselines. If a digital twin is built upon a complex numerical simulation that is intended to approximate these underlying physical laws, its output under specific, simplified conditions can be compared to the known analytical or benchmark results. For instance, if a digital twin models fluid flow using a computational fluid dynamics (CFD) solver, its performance in simulating flow through a simple geometry, like a pipe or a flat plate, can be validated against established analytical solutions for laminar or turbulent flow in such configurations. Similarly, a complex thermal model of an electronic component could be validated against results from widely accepted thermal simulation benchmarks. This approach helps to confirm the fundamental correctness of the model's physics implementation and its

numerical solution methods, irrespective of specific calibration data. It's a way of ensuring the "engine" of the digital twin is fundamentally sound before assessing its specific tuning.

The principle of
using independent datasets for validation cannot be overstated. This is the cornerstone of ensuring that a digital twin is not merely an artifact of the training data but a robust representation of the real-world system's behavior. Overfitting occurs when a model learns the training data too well, including its noise and idiosyncrasies, leading to poor performance on unseen data. By strictly separating data into calibration (or training) sets and validation sets, researchers and engineers can actively guard against this pitfall. The calibration set is used to tune the model parameters, effectively teaching the model from this data. The validation set, kept entirely separate, then acts as an impartial judge. It tests how well the model generalizes its learned knowledge to new, unobserved instances. This separation is not merely a best practice; it is a fundamental requirement for building trust in the digital twin. For complex systems, this independence might extend to using data from entirely different operational periods, different physical assets of the same type (if available), or data collected using slightly different measurement instruments. The goal is to expose the model to conditions that are sufficiently different from the calibration data to reveal any shortcomings in its underlying assumptions or its ability to generalize.

The concept of
fitness-for-purpose is central to the entire validation endeavor. A digital twin is rarely built for every conceivable purpose. It is designed for specific applications, such as predictive maintenance, operational optimization, design iteration, or anomaly detection. Therefore, validation must focus on assessing the model's performance with respect to these intended uses. A digital twin that is highly accurate for predicting long-term wear might be entirely inadequate for real-time fault diagnosis if its prediction latency is too high. Similarly, a model validated for optimal energy efficiency might not be sufficiently accurate for predicting component stress under extreme load conditions.

To address fitness-for-purpose, validation strategies often need to be tailored. This might involve:

Defining key performance indicators (KPIs) for the specific application: What metrics are most critical for the intended use? If the goal is predictive maintenance, the accuracy of predicting the remaining useful life (RUL) of a component is paramount. Validation would then focus on how well the digital twin predicts RUL for various failure modes using independent data.
Scenario-based testing: Designing validation scenarios that mimic critical operational conditions or potential failure modes. For example, in a digital twin of a chemical reactor, validation might involve testing its ability to accurately predict temperature and pressure excursions under scenarios of cooling system failure or uncontrolled reactant addition.
Uncertainty quantification in validation: For many applications, it's not just the point prediction that matters but also the confidence interval around it. Validation should assess whether the model's predicted uncertainty is realistic and aligns with the observed variability in the validation data. If the digital twin predicts a failure probability of 10% with a 95% confidence interval of [2%, 18%], validation would examine if the actual occurrence of such failures falls within these bounds over a large number of independent instances.
Comparison with alternative models or baseline approaches: Sometimes, validation involves comparing the digital twin's performance against simpler, established models or even human expert predictions. If a complex digital twin fails to significantly outperform a much simpler physics-based model or expert judgment on critical validation tasks, questions arise about the added value and complexity of the digital twin.

Furthermore, the validation process itself can be iterative and inform model refinement. If validation reveals significant discrepancies, it might indicate that:

The model structure needs revision: The underlying physics or equations might be incomplete or incorrect.
Additional calibration is needed: Perhaps the initial calibration was insufficient, or new data has become available.

The data used for validation reveals new system behaviors: This can lead to a deeper understanding of the physical asset and its operation, potentially leading to a more sophisticated model or improved operational procedures.

The rigor applied during validation is directly proportional to the criticality of the application. For non-critical simulations, a broad comparison against historical trends might suffice. However, for applications where safety, financial risk, or operational integrity are at stake, validation must be exhaustive and employ multiple, independent methods. This includes considering the statistical significance of observed differences, the robustness of the validation metrics used, and the representativeness of the validation data with respect to the full range of operational conditions the digital twin is expected to encounter.

In essence, validation is the gatekeeper of trust for any digital twin. It transforms a model that can replicate past events into a tool that can reliably predict future outcomes, inform critical decisions, and ultimately deliver on the promise of digital transformation. Without thorough validation against independent data and a clear understanding of its fitness for purpose, a digital twin remains a theoretical construct rather than a dependable engineering asset.

Having established the importance of calibration and validation in building trustworthy digital twins, the subsequent and equally crucial step involves **quantifying the success** of these processes. Mere qualitative assessments of "good fit" or "reasonable prediction" are insufficient for engineering applications where precision, reliability, and accountability are paramount. To this end, a diverse suite of objective metrics has been developed to rigorously assess how well a digital twin aligns with reality. These metrics provide a quantifiable basis for comparing different models, evaluating the impact of calibration adjustments, and ultimately determining if a digital twin is fit for its intended purpose.

At the heart of performance assessment lies the analysis of **prediction errors**. These errors represent the discrepancies between the digital twin's simulated outputs and the actual observed data from the physical asset. A variety of statistical measures are employed to characterize these errors, each offering a different perspective on model accuracy.

One of the most ubiquitous and fundamental metrics is the
Root Mean Squared Error (RMSE). RMSE quantifies the standard deviation of the prediction errors (residuals). It is calculated by taking the square root of the average of the squared differences between predicted and actual values. Mathematically, it is expressed as:

$RMSE = \sqrt{\frac{1}{n} \sum
*{i=1}^{n} (*yi - \hat{y}_i)^2}$

where $y
*i$ is the actual observed value for the i-th data point, $\hat{y}*i$ is the predicted value from the digital twin for the i-th data point, and n is the total number of data points. The squaring of errors gives more weight to larger deviations, meaning that a single large error can significantly increase the RMSE. This makes RMSE particularly sensitive to outliers. A lower RMSE indicates a better fit of the model to the data, signifying that the digital twin's predictions are, on average, closer to the actual measurements. When comparing two models, the one with the lower RMSE is generally preferred, assuming other factors are equal.

Complementing RMSE, the
Mean Absolute Error (MAE) provides another perspective on prediction error. MAE is the average of the absolute differences between predicted and actual values:

$MAE = \frac{1}{n} \sum
*{i=1}^{n} |*yi - \hat{y}_i|$

Unlike RMSE, MAE treats all errors equally, regardless of their magnitude. It is less sensitive to outliers than RMSE. Therefore, if a system has occasional but significant deviations that are expected and well-understood, MAE might be a more appropriate metric as it won't be disproportionately influenced by these infrequent large errors. Both RMSE and MAE have the advantage of being in the same units as the original data, making them intuitively interpretable. For instance, if a digital twin predicts the temperature of a piece of equipment, an RMSE of 2°C means that the typical prediction error is around 2°C.

For applications where the relative error is more important than the absolute error, the

Mean Absolute Percentage Error (MAPE) is often employed. MAPE expresses the average magnitude of errors as a percentage of the actual values:

$$MAPE = \frac{1}{n} \sum_{i=1}^{n} \left|\frac{y_i - \hat{y}_i}{y_i}\right| \times 100\%$$

MAPE is particularly useful when comparing the performance of models across datasets with different scales or when dealing with data that has varying magnitudes. For example, in financial forecasting, a prediction error of \$100 might be negligible for a value of \$10,000 but significant for a value of \$1,000. MAPE addresses this by normalizing errors. However, MAPE has limitations: it can be undefined or infinite if actual values (y_i) are zero or close to zero. It also tends to give higher penalties to negative errors (under-predictions) than positive errors (over-predictions). To mitigate these issues, variations like the Symmetric Mean Absolute Percentage Error (SMAPE) exist, which are designed to be less sensitive to the scale of data and zero values.

Another powerful metric, especially for understanding the proportion of variance in the dependent variable that is predictable from the independent variables, is the

Coefficient of Determination, R-squared (R^2). R^2 ranges from 0 to 1 (or 0% to 100%) and indicates how well the model's predictions fit the observed data. A higher R^2 value suggests that the model explains a larger portion of the variability in the data.

$$R^2 = 1 - \frac{SS_{res}}{SS_{tot}}$$

where SS_{res} is the sum of squared residuals (the variance not explained by the model), and SS_{tot} is the total sum of squares (the total variance in the data). An R^2 of 1 means the model perfectly predicts the dependent variable, while an R^2 of 0 means the model explains none of the variability, performing no better than simply predicting the mean of the data. While a high R^2 is desirable, it's important to note that it can be misleading. Adding more variables to a model, even if they are not statistically significant, will always increase R^2. Therefore, the **Adjusted R-squared** is often preferred, which penalizes the addition of unnecessary predictors.

Beyond these general statistical measures, **residual analysis** provides a deeper diagnostic insight into model performance. Residuals are the differences between observed and predicted values. Plotting these residuals against predicted values, time, or input variables can reveal patterns that indicate model deficiencies. For instance, if the residuals show a clear 'fan' or 'cone' shape, it suggests that the variance of the errors is not constant (heteroscedasticity), which can violate assumptions of many statistical models and affect the reliability of prediction intervals. A systematic trend in residuals, such as a curve, indicates that the model is systematically under- or over-predicting in certain ranges, suggesting that the model's functional form is incorrect or that important variables have been omitted. Ideally, residuals should be randomly scattered around zero, indicating that the model has captured the systematic relationships in the data and that the remaining errors are purely random noise.

For applications with a temporal component, metrics that specifically address time-series forecasting are invaluable. For example, in predictive maintenance, the ability to accurately predict **Remaining Useful Life (RUL)** is critical. Validation metrics in this context would focus on the accuracy of RUL predictions. This could involve calculating the RMSE or MAE of RUL predictions for components that have failed during the validation period. Furthermore, specific metrics like the **Asymmetric Relative Error (ARE)** or **Scoring Functions** that penalize late predictions more heavily than early predictions are often used, as a late warning of impending failure can be far more detrimental than an early one. The **Prediction Horizon** of the RUL prediction is also a key validation metric – how far into the future can the digital twin reliably predict the remaining life?

In systems where anomalies or fault detection are primary objectives, metrics such as

Precision, Recall, and F1-score become paramount. These metrics, common in classification tasks, are adapted for anomaly detection.
Precision measures the accuracy of positive predictions (i.e., of all instances flagged as anomalies, how many were actually anomalies).
Recall (Sensitivity) measures the ability of the model to find all the positive instances (i.e., of all actual anomalies, how many were correctly identified).
The **F1-score** is the harmonic mean of Precision and Recall, providing a balanced measure of accuracy.

A digital twin designed for anomaly detection needs to achieve high precision to avoid overwhelming operators with false alarms, and high recall to ensure that actual faults are not missed. The specific trade-off between precision and recall often depends on the application's risk tolerance.

When the digital twin is used to optimize operational parameters, metrics related to the deviation from the optimal or target state are important. For instance, if a digital twin is used to optimize the energy consumption of a manufacturing process, validation might involve comparing the energy savings predicted by the digital twin under optimized settings against the actual energy consumption achieved when those settings are implemented on the physical asset. The metric would be the percentage difference between predicted and actual savings. Similarly, for a digital twin used to control a chemical reactor, validation might focus on the deviation of key process variables (temperature, pressure, concentration) from their setpoints under the digital twin's control, compared to a baseline control strategy.

The concept of
model interpretability and explainability can also, indirectly, be a validation metric. While not a direct statistical measure of prediction accuracy, the ability of a digital twin to provide insights into *why* it is making a certain prediction can be a crucial aspect of its validation for certain applications. If a digital twin predicts an imminent failure, but cannot provide any underlying physical reasoning or highlight the contributing factors, its trustworthiness for critical decision-making can be compromised. Validation might involve expert review of the explanations provided by the digital twin for its predictions on known scenarios.

Furthermore, the
robustness of a digital twin's predictions under varying conditions is a critical validation aspect. This can be assessed by evaluating its performance across different operating regimes, environmental conditions, or even with slightly perturbed input data. Metrics could include the standard deviation of performance metrics (like RMSE or MAPE) across these different scenarios. A digital twin that performs consistently well across a wide range of conditions is more reliable than one whose performance degrades significantly under specific circumstances.

Finally, the
computational performance of the digital twin, while not directly a measure of its fidelity to the physical system, is a critical validation factor for real-time applications. The time it takes for the digital twin to ingest new data, perform calculations, and provide a prediction (latency) must be within acceptable limits for the intended use case. Validation would involve measuring this execution time under realistic load conditions and comparing it against the system's operational requirements. For example, a digital twin used for real-time control of an industrial robot must provide its output within milliseconds, whereas a digital twin for long-term strategic planning might have hours or days to generate its results.

In summary, the success of calibration and validation is not a subjective judgment but a quantifiable outcome derived from a comprehensive set of metrics. From broad measures of error like RMSE and MAE, to percentage-based metrics like MAPE, and variance-explained metrics like R^2, these statistical tools provide a vital backbone for assessing model performance. When combined with detailed residual analysis and application-specific metrics for RUL prediction, anomaly detection, or operational optimization, these indicators offer a robust framework for building confidence in digital twins. The ultimate goal is to select and validate a digital twin whose quantifiable performance aligns precisely with the demands and risks of its intended purpose, ensuring it is not just a simulation, but a reliable extension of the physical world.

The process of calibrating and validating a digital twin is not a singular event, but rather an ongoing, cyclical endeavor. Initial validation, armed with the quantitative metrics discussed previously, provides a critical assessment of the twin's current fidelity to its physical counterpart. However, the results of this validation rarely signal the end of the development journey. Instead, they serve as a powerful diagnostic tool, illuminating areas where the digital twin falls short of desired performance. This is where the principle of **iterative refinement** comes into play, transforming the validation phase from a mere checkpoint into a springboard for improvement.

When validation metrics indicate discrepancies that exceed acceptable thresholds, or when residual analysis reveals systematic biases, the logical next step is to revisit the calibration process. This might involve re-examining the assumptions made during the initial model development, exploring alternative parameterizations, or even reconsidering the fundamental structure of the digital twin. For instance, if an RMSE analysis highlights significant errors in predicting the temperature of a complex piece of machinery, the engineering team might investigate whether the heat transfer coefficients used in the model are sufficiently accurate, or if additional factors, such as ambient humidity or wear and tear on cooling components, need to be incorporated into the model's physics. This could lead to a recalibration of existing parameters, adjusting their values based on the insights gained from the validation data and a deeper understanding of the physical system's behavior.

The iterative nature extends beyond mere parameter tuning. If the validation reveals that the digital twin, even after recalibration, consistently fails to capture certain observed phenomena, it may necessitate a more fundamental revision of the model. This could involve incorporating new physical principles that were initially overlooked, or adopting entirely different modeling paradigms. For example, a digital twin initially built on purely empirical correlations might be enhanced with first-principles physics-based equations if validation shows it struggles to generalize to new operating conditions. Conversely, a complex, physics-based model might be augmented with machine learning components to capture subtle, emergent behaviors that are difficult to explicitly model. Each iteration of refinement, guided by validation feedback, aims to systematically reduce the gap between the digital twin's predictions and the real-world behavior of the physical asset.

Crucially, as the digital twin undergoes these refinements and recalibrations, its validation must be re-performed. This is not a mere formality but a confirmation that the changes have indeed improved performance without introducing new, unforeseen issues. Each validation cycle builds confidence in the evolving digital twin, ensuring that modifications genuinely enhance its accuracy, robustness, and reliability. This repeated cycle of model adjustment, followed by rigorous validation, is the engine that drives the digital twin towards its intended level of fidelity and utility.

Beyond the scope of initial development and calibration refinement, the concept of
model updating becomes paramount for ensuring the long-term relevance and accuracy of a digital twin. Physical assets are rarely static; they age, undergo maintenance, experience wear and tear, and are often subjected to changing operational conditions. A digital twin, to remain a faithful representation, must evolve in lockstep with its physical counterpart. This necessitates a strategy for continuous or periodic model updating, leveraging new data that becomes available over time.

The availability of new data streams – whether from enhanced sensor networks, logged operational data, or post-maintenance reports – presents a rich opportunity to refine and update the digital twin. This data can serve multiple purposes. Firstly, it can be used to monitor the ongoing performance of the digital twin against real-world observations. Deviations that emerge over time, which were not apparent during initial validation, can be flagged for investigation. Secondly, this new data can be directly assimilated into the model to recalibrate its parameters, adapt its structure, or even retrain its machine learning components.

Consider a digital twin of a wind turbine. Over its operational life, components like gearbox bearings will experience wear. This wear will subtly alter vibration signatures and power output characteristics. If the digital twin's initial calibration was based on data from a new turbine, its predictions might start to drift as the physical turbine ages. By continuously feeding operational data –

vibration levels, wind speed, power output, temperature readings – into the digital twin, and comparing these with its predictions, engineers can detect this drift. This discrepancy can then trigger a model update. The update might involve re-estimating wear parameters, recalibrating the relationship between vibration and bearing health, or even updating the underlying physics model to account for altered material properties.

The frequency and methodology of model updating depend heavily on the specific application and the dynamics of the physical asset. For highly dynamic systems operating under rapidly changing conditions, such as those found in high-frequency trading or advanced robotics, near real-time updating might be necessary. This could involve online learning algorithms that continuously adjust model parameters as new data arrives. For less dynamic systems, such as a building's HVAC system or a large-scale industrial plant, periodic batch updates, perhaps conducted monthly or quarterly, or after significant maintenance events, may be more appropriate and cost-effective.

A critical consideration in model updating is the careful management of data quality and the potential for introducing noise or erroneous information. New data must be rigorously pre-processed and validated before being used to update the digital twin. Incorporating flawed data can lead to model degradation, a phenomenon known as "model drift" or "concept drift," where the twin's accuracy deteriorates rather than improves. Techniques such as data cleansing, outlier detection, and anomaly flagging are therefore essential components of any robust model updating strategy.

Furthermore, the decision of
what to update needs to be informed. It's not always about simply re-fitting all parameters. Sometimes, specific components or subsystems might be degrading faster than others, or new operational modes might be introduced. Advanced diagnostics derived from validation metrics can help pinpoint which aspects of the digital twin require attention. For instance, if residual analysis consistently shows large errors in a specific operating regime, that regime might be targeted for focused data collection and model recalibration.

Model updating also plays a crucial role when the physical asset undergoes significant changes, such as repairs, upgrades, or retrofits. A turbine blade repaired after lightning damage, a pump replaced with a more efficient model, or a control system software upgrade all represent changes that a static digital twin would fail to reflect. Post-maintenance validation is essential, followed by targeted model updates to incorporate the effects of these modifications. This might involve re-calibrating parameters associated with the modified component, or even re-validating the entire system's response if the changes are substantial.

The process of model updating can be viewed as a form of "continuous learning" for the digital twin. Just as humans learn from experience, the digital twin learns from the ongoing data generated by its physical counterpart. This learning process is facilitated by intelligent algorithms that can identify patterns, adapt to changing dynamics, and maintain the twin's predictive accuracy and diagnostic capabilities over its entire lifecycle. This continuous evolution ensures that the digital twin remains not just a representation of the asset at a single point in time, but a dynamic, evolving entity that accurately mirrors the real-world system under all relevant conditions. Without this iterative refinement and ongoing updating, the value proposition of a digital twin would rapidly diminish as it becomes an outdated and unreliable reflection of its physical counterpart.

Chapter 8: Data Management for Digital Twins

The intrinsic value of a digital twin, its very reason for being, is inextricably bound to the flow and fidelity of data. It is not merely a sophisticated simulation or a static 3D model; rather, it is a dynamic, living representation fueled by a continuous stream of information from its physical counterpart. Without robust, accurate, and timely data, a digital twin is fundamentally crippled, rendering its predictive capabilities, diagnostic insights, and prescriptive recommendations unreliable, or worse, misleading. Therefore, understanding and implementing a comprehensive data management strategy is not an optional add-on, but the bedrock upon which a successful digital twin initiative is built. This section delves into the central role of data across the entire lifecycle of a digital twin, from its genesis to its ongoing evolution, emphasizing the critical requirements for data acquisition, storage, processing, analysis, and eventual archival.

The journey of data for a digital twin begins with its **acquisition**. This is the crucial first step where information is gathered from the physical asset. The nature and volume of this data are dictated by the specific application and the fidelity required of the digital twin. For an industrial machine, this might involve data from a myriad of sensors monitoring parameters such as temperature, pressure, vibration, rotational speed, power consumption, and fluid levels. In the context of a smart city, data acquisition could encompass traffic flow from sensors and cameras, energy consumption from smart meters, environmental readings from weather stations, and occupancy data from buildings. For a complex biological system, it might involve genomic sequences, physiological measurements, or imaging data. The effectiveness of the digital twin is directly correlated with the quality and comprehensiveness of this initial data capture.

This necessitates a well-designed sensor network and data collection infrastructure. The selection of sensors must be intelligent, considering not only the parameters to be measured but also their accuracy, reliability, sampling rate, and environmental resilience. For instance, in an offshore oil rig environment, sensors must withstand harsh conditions of saltwater, high winds, and extreme temperatures. Similarly, the sampling rate needs to be aligned with the dynamic behavior of the physical asset. A slow sampling rate might miss critical transient events in a high-speed manufacturing process, while an unnecessarily high rate could lead to an overwhelming volume of data, straining storage and processing capabilities. Furthermore, the method of data transmission is critical. Whether it's wired Ethernet, wireless protocols like Wi-Fi or LoRaWAN, or cellular networks, the chosen method must ensure low latency and high reliability to maintain the real-time nature of the digital twin. The integration of legacy systems also presents a significant challenge, often requiring specialized middleware or data converters to bridge the gap between older equipment and modern data ingestion pipelines. The sheer diversity of data formats and protocols encountered in industrial environments underscores the complexity of data acquisition, demanding flexible and adaptable ingestion strategies.

Once data is acquired, the next critical stage is **storage**. The volume of data generated by digital twins can be staggering, especially for assets that operate continuously or generate high-frequency sensor readings. This data must be stored in a manner that is both accessible for immediate processing and analysis, and also suitable for long-term retention and historical trending. The choice of storage solutions is therefore paramount. Options range from traditional relational databases, which are excellent for structured data and complex queries, to NoSQL databases, which offer greater flexibility for semi-structured and unstructured data and often scale more effectively. For time-series data, which is exceptionally common in digital twin applications (e.g., sensor readings over time), specialized time-series databases are often the most efficient and performant choice.

Cloud-based storage solutions have become increasingly popular due to their scalability, cost-effectiveness, and managed services. These platforms offer a spectrum of storage tiers, from hot storage for frequently accessed data to cold storage for archival purposes, allowing organizations to optimize costs based on data access patterns. However, the decision to adopt cloud storage must be carefully considered, taking into account data sovereignty, security, and compliance requirements, especially for sensitive industrial or personal data. On-premises solutions, while potentially offering greater control, can be more capital-intensive and require significant in-house expertise for management and scaling.

Beyond raw storage, a robust data management strategy must also address data organization and metadata management. Simply dumping vast quantities of data into a repository is insufficient. Data needs to be cataloged, tagged with relevant metadata (e.g., asset ID, sensor type, location, timestamp, operational state), and organized logically to facilitate easy retrieval and understanding. This metadata is crucial for context. A temperature reading, for instance, is meaningless without knowing which sensor it came from, on which asset, and at what time. Effective metadata ensures that the data remains interpretable and valuable throughout its lifecycle, enabling users to find, understand, and utilize the data effectively for various analytical purposes. Data governance policies that define ownership, access controls, and retention schedules are also essential components of data storage strategy, ensuring compliance and security.

The raw data acquired from the physical asset is rarely in a format that can be directly used for modeling or analysis. This leads to the imperative of **data processing and transformation**. This phase involves a series of operations to clean, normalize, aggregate, and enrich the data, making it suitable for consumption by the digital twin's analytical engines and simulation models. Data cleaning is a fundamental step, addressing issues such as missing values, erroneous readings (outliers), and inconsistencies. Techniques like imputation (filling in missing values using statistical methods), outlier detection and removal, and data validation rules are employed to enhance data quality. For example, a sensor reading that indicates a temperature of 1000 degrees Celsius for a component designed to operate below 200 degrees Celsius is clearly an outlier and would need to be flagged or corrected.

Normalization and standardization are also critical, especially when data originates from disparate sources with different units or scales. Converting all temperature readings to a common unit (e.g., Celsius or Fahrenheit) or scaling sensor outputs to a defined range (e.g., 0 to 1) ensures that they can be meaningfully compared and integrated. Aggregation is another key process, where high-frequency raw data is summarized into lower-frequency statistics (e.g., hourly averages, daily maximums) to reduce data volume and highlight trends, or to match the operational timescales of the digital twin's models.

Data enrichment involves augmenting the primary data streams with additional information that can enhance the twin's understanding. This could include contextual data such as maintenance logs, operational schedules, environmental conditions from external sources (e.g., weather forecasts), or product specifications. For instance, a digital twin of a pump might be enriched with information about the type of fluid being pumped, its viscosity, and whether the pump has recently undergone maintenance. This enriched data provides a more holistic view of the asset's state and operating environment, leading to more accurate predictions and diagnoses. Feature engineering, a sub-discipline of machine learning, also falls under data processing, where new, informative features are created from existing data to improve model performance. This might involve calculating rates of change, creating interaction terms between variables, or transforming variables to better meet model assumptions. The processing pipeline must be robust, repeatable, and often automated to handle the continuous flow of incoming data efficiently.

The heart of a digital twin's functionality lies in
data analysis. This is where the processed data is interpreted to extract meaningful insights, drive predictions, and inform decisions. This phase encompasses a wide range of analytical techniques, from statistical analysis and machine learning to physics-based simulations. Statistical analysis can be used to identify trends, correlations, and anomalies in operational data, providing a foundational understanding of the asset's behavior. For example, analyzing historical vibration data might reveal a gradual increase that correlates with an increased likelihood of failure.

Machine learning algorithms play an increasingly vital role. Supervised learning models can be trained to predict future states, such as the remaining useful life of a component, or to classify operational modes. Unsupervised learning can be employed for anomaly detection, identifying deviations from normal operating behavior that might indicate a developing problem. Reinforcement learning could be used to optimize operational parameters for efficiency or longevity. The choice of analytical techniques depends heavily on the specific use case. For instance, a digital twin of a manufacturing process might employ regression models to predict product quality based on input parameters, while a digital twin of a vehicle fleet might use clustering algorithms to identify patterns in driver behavior for safety analysis.

Furthermore, the processed data is fed into the digital twin's **simulation models**. These models, whether physics-based, data-driven, or hybrid, use the incoming data as inputs to replicate the behavior of the physical asset. The analysis of simulation outputs allows for "what-if" scenarios, performance optimization, and the testing of design changes or operational adjustments in a virtual environment before they are implemented in the real world. For example, a simulation driven by real-time wind data could predict the power output of a wind turbine under varying conditions, allowing operators to optimize its pitch angle. The insights generated from these analyses are what provide actionable intelligence, transforming raw data into valuable knowledge that supports decision-making across maintenance, operations, and design.

The continuous cycle of data acquisition, processing, analysis, and feedback forms the operational loop of a digital twin. As the physical asset operates, it generates new data, which is fed into the twin, leading to updated analyses and predictions. This ongoing interaction ensures that the digital twin remains synchronized with the real-world asset, providing relevant and up-to-date insights. The effectiveness of this analytical phase is also heavily dependent on the ability to visualize and interpret the results. Advanced visualization tools are often employed to present complex data and analytical outcomes in an understandable format, enabling stakeholders to quickly grasp the implications and make informed decisions. This includes dashboards, interactive charts, heatmaps, and even immersive 3D visualizations that overlay data onto the digital model.

Finally, the lifecycle of data for a digital twin extends to its **archival and eventual disposal**. While real-time data is crucial for current operations and immediate analysis, historical data holds immense value for long-term trend analysis, model retraining, regulatory compliance, and post-mortem investigations. Therefore, a strategy for long-term data storage and management is essential. Archived data should be organized, indexed, and maintained in a secure and accessible manner, even if it is moved to lower-cost, less frequently accessed storage tiers. This ensures that historical data can be readily retrieved when needed for tasks such as refining historical models, identifying long-term degradation patterns, or providing evidence for audits.

The concept of
data retention policies is critical here. Organizations must define how long different types of data need to be stored, considering legal, regulatory, and business requirements. For some industries, like aerospace or pharmaceuticals, data might need to be retained for decades due to strict compliance mandates. In other cases, the value of historical data may diminish over time, allowing for its secure deletion after a specified period. The process of data archival should be automated as much as possible to ensure consistency and efficiency. This often involves transferring data from active databases or data lakes to dedicated archival systems.

Data security and integrity remain paramount even for archived data. Robust access controls, encryption, and audit trails must be in place to protect the data from unauthorized access or tampering. The process of data disposal also needs careful consideration. When data reaches the end of its retention period, it must be securely and irretrievably deleted to prevent data breaches and comply with privacy regulations. Simple deletion might not be sufficient; secure erasure techniques are often required.

The overarching principle guiding data management for digital twins is the need for a holistic and integrated approach. Data should not be viewed as a series of disconnected silos but as a continuous flow that supports the entire digital twin ecosystem. This requires collaboration between IT departments, data engineers, domain experts, and end-users to ensure that data strategies align with business objectives and the specific needs of the digital twin application. The investment in a robust data management framework is an investment in the accuracy, reliability, and ultimate value of the digital twin itself, ensuring it remains a powerful tool for understanding, optimizing, and innovating throughout the lifecycle of its physical counterpart. The long-term success of any digital twin initiative is fundamentally predicated on the organization's ability to effectively manage its data from inception to retirement.

The digital twin, as a dynamic and evolving digital replica of a physical asset, process, or system, draws its lifeblood from a confluence of data streams. The very essence of its fidelity and utility hinges on its capacity to ingest, process, and interpret information originating from a multitude of sources. These sources are not monolithic; rather, they represent a complex and diverse ecosystem of digital and physical interactions that collectively paint the picture of the real-world entity. Understanding the nature of these varied data origins is the foundational step in establishing a robust data management strategy for any digital twin initiative.

One of the most prevalent and critical sources of data for digital twins comes from
sensors. These ubiquitous devices, embedded within or attached to the physical asset, are the primary conduits for real-time operational data. For an industrial machine, this might include thermocouples measuring temperature at various points, accelerometers detecting vibration signatures, pressure transducers monitoring hydraulic or pneumatic systems, and flow meters quantifying fluid or gas movement. In the context of a smart city, sensors could encompass traffic loop detectors, environmental monitors for air quality and noise pollution, smart meters for energy and water consumption, and occupancy sensors in public spaces. The sheer volume and velocity of data generated by these sensors are often immense, requiring sophisticated ingestion pipelines and real-time processing capabilities. The data from sensors typically manifests as time-series data, capturing the state of a parameter at specific intervals. However, the resolution, sampling frequency, and accuracy can vary significantly depending on the sensor type, its calibration, and the environmental conditions it operates within. For instance, a high-frequency vibration sensor might sample data at kilohertz rates to capture subtle anomalies, while a monthly meter reading might only be updated once.

Beyond real-time sensor data, digital twins often integrate information from **Enterprise Resource Planning (ERP) systems**. ERP systems are the backbone of many organizations, managing core business processes such as finance, human resources, manufacturing, supply chain management, services, and procurement. For a digital twin, ERP data can provide invaluable contextual information. This might include details about the bill of materials for a manufactured product, procurement histories for raw materials, maintenance schedules and work orders, inventory levels, and financial performance metrics related to the asset's operation or production. This type of data is typically structured, often residing in relational databases, and represents a more macroscopic, business-centric view of the asset or system. While not as high-frequency as sensor data, ERP data offers a crucial link between the physical operation of an asset and its business implications, enabling analyses that connect operational efficiency to financial outcomes.

Complementing ERP systems,
Manufacturing Execution Systems (MES) provide a vital bridge between the shop floor and the higher-level business systems. MES solutions are specifically designed to manage and monitor work in progress on the manufacturing floor. Data from an MES can offer granular insights into the production process, such as detailed work instructions, routing information, machine status (running, idle, down), production yields, scrap rates, quality control checkpoints, and operator assignments. Integrating MES data into a digital twin allows for a more accurate representation of the manufacturing process, enabling the twin to track the progress of individual items or batches, identify bottlenecks, and analyze the impact of process variations on product quality and throughput. MES data is often highly detailed and can be generated at a rapid pace, reflecting the dynamic nature of a manufacturing line.

The initial design and engineering of an asset are captured in
Computer-Aided Design (CAD) files. These files represent the geometric, spatial, and material properties of the physical asset in a digital format. CAD data is fundamental for creating the visual representation of the digital twin and for performing engineering analyses. It defines the shape, dimensions, and assembly structure of components. Beyond geometry, CAD models can also embed information about materials, tolerances, and manufacturing specifications. For a digital twin, CAD data serves as the blueprint, providing the structural and dimensional foundation upon which operational data is overlaid. However, CAD files can also be complex and proprietary, requiring specialized tools and techniques for conversion and integration into the digital twin environment. Moreover, the relationship between CAD data and the actual as-built or as-maintained state of the physical asset can diverge over time, presenting a challenge in ensuring the digital twin accurately reflects reality.

Historical performance records are another crucial data source, offering a longitudinal view of the asset's behavior over its operational life. These records can encompass past maintenance logs, repair histories, incident reports, previous performance metrics, and previous operating conditions. Analyzing historical data allows digital twins to establish baseline performance, identify degradation patterns, predict failure modes, and understand the long-term impact of various operational and maintenance strategies. This data might be stored in various formats, including structured databases, spreadsheets, or even unstructured text documents. Its value lies in its ability to inform predictive models and provide context for current operational anomalies. For example, if a particular component has failed repeatedly under specific load conditions in the past, historical records can flag a similar current situation as high risk.

The characteristic that most profoundly impacts the management of data for digital twins is **heterogeneity**. This term encompasses the diversity in the nature, format, resolution, and semantic meaning of the data originating from these varied sources. Managing this heterogeneity is paramount to building a cohesive and functional digital twin.

One of the most apparent forms of heterogeneity is the **difference in data formats**. Sensor data might arrive in raw binary formats, comma-separated values (CSV), or JSON payloads. ERP and MES systems typically utilize structured data formats like SQL databases or XML. CAD files come in specific, often proprietary, formats like DWG, STEP, or IGES. Historical records might be in spreadsheets (XLSX), databases, or even plain text documents. This divergence in formats necessitates robust data ingestion and transformation capabilities. A common data model or a flexible schema is often required to normalize these disparate formats into a unified structure that the digital twin can understand and process. Without this, combining data from different sources becomes a Herculean task, akin to trying to assemble a puzzle with pieces from entirely different sets.

Resolution and frequency of data also contribute significantly to heterogeneity. As noted with sensors, data can range from high-frequency, real-time streams (kilohertz) to low-frequency, event-based updates (daily, monthly, or even annually). ERP data might be updated in batches, while MES data could reflect seconds-long operations. CAD models represent a static snapshot in time, while sensor data is a continuous, dynamic flow. This disparity in temporal resolution poses challenges for correlation and analysis. For instance, correlating a monthly ERP report on spare parts inventory with millisecond-level sensor data from a critical machine requires careful temporal alignment and aggregation strategies. Bridging these gaps often involves techniques like time-series resampling, interpolation, or event-based synchronization, ensuring that data points from different sources can be meaningfully compared and analyzed within a common temporal framework.

Perhaps the most subtle yet critical aspect of data heterogeneity is the **semantic variation**. This refers to the differences in the meaning, context, and interpretation of data elements across different systems. For example, a "temperature" reading from one sensor might refer to the ambient air temperature, while another might measure the internal temperature of a motor winding. The units might also differ (e.g., Celsius vs. Fahrenheit, Kelvin). Similarly, the definition of "operational status" can vary: does it mean the machine is powered on, or actively performing its intended function? A "part number" in an ERP system might have a different prefix or suffix convention than in an MES. This semantic ambiguity can lead to misinterpretations and flawed analyses if not properly addressed. Establishing a common data dictionary, a glossary of terms, and ontologies that define the relationships between different data elements are crucial for overcoming semantic heterogeneity. This ensures that when data from different sources is brought together, it is understood with the same meaning and context.

The
lifecycle stage and origin of the data also introduce heterogeneity. CAD data, for instance, represents a design-time artifact, while sensor data reflects operational-time behavior, and historical maintenance logs represent post-failure analysis. Each stage has its own characteristic data types and levels of detail. Furthermore, data might originate from different vendors or manufacturers, each with their own proprietary data formats, communication

protocols, and data structures. Integrating data from a fleet of machines from multiple suppliers, for example, can be significantly more challenging than managing data from a homogeneous set of assets.

Data quality and completeness are additional layers of heterogeneity. Sensor data might suffer from noise, drift, or outright failures, leading to missing or erroneous values. ERP data might be subject to human input errors or outdated entries. Historical records might be incomplete or lack critical details. These inconsistencies require rigorous data validation, cleansing, and imputation strategies as part of the data management pipeline. A digital twin's reliability is directly proportional to the quality of the data it consumes, making the management of these variations in data quality a continuous effort.

To effectively manage this multifaceted data heterogeneity, several strategic approaches are employed.

Data integration platforms play a pivotal role, providing tools and frameworks to connect to diverse data sources, extract data, transform it into a standardized format, and load it into a central repository or the digital twin's data fabric. These platforms often incorporate **Extract, Transform, Load (ETL)** or **Extract, Load, Transform (ELT)** processes that are specifically designed to handle varied data types and structures.

The adoption of **standardized data models and schemas** is another critical strategy. While complete standardization across all data sources might be aspirational, establishing common models for key entities (e.g., assets, components, events, measurements) can significantly simplify integration. This might involve leveraging industry-specific standards where they exist or developing custom enterprise-wide data models.

Metadata management becomes indispensable in the face of heterogeneity. Comprehensive metadata, describing the origin, format, units, semantic meaning, quality, and lineage of data, provides the necessary context for its interpretation and use. A well-maintained metadata repository acts as a catalog, allowing users and systems to understand and leverage data from diverse sources effectively.

Data virtualization offers an alternative to physical data consolidation. Instead of moving and transforming data, data virtualization allows the digital twin to access and query data directly from its source systems, presenting a unified view without creating redundant copies. This can be particularly useful for accessing real-time data or for situations where moving large volumes of data is impractical.

Finally,
data governance policies are essential to enforce consistency, quality, and security across the diverse data landscape. These policies define roles and responsibilities for data ownership, quality standards, access controls, and data lifecycle management, ensuring that the heterogeneity of data sources does not lead to chaos but is managed in a structured and controlled manner. By systematically addressing these sources of data and the inherent heterogeneity, organizations can build digital twins that are not only visually representative but also analytically powerful and operationally insightful.
The successful realization and ongoing efficacy of a digital twin are fundamentally dependent on the robustness and suitability of its underlying data storage and infrastructure. As we have explored, digital twins ingest a vast and varied spectrum of data – from the high-velocity, granular streams of IoT sensors to the more structured, albeit less frequent, updates from enterprise systems, and the geometric precision of CAD models. Managing this deluge requires a strategic selection of data storage solutions, each offering distinct advantages and disadvantages depending on the specific characteristics of the data and the operational demands of the digital twin. The choice of infrastructure is not merely a technical decision; it is a strategic one that impacts scalability, performance, cost-efficiency, accessibility, and ultimately, the ability of the digital twin to provide timely and accurate insights.

One of the most foundational and widely understood data storage paradigms is the
relational database. These databases, built on the concept of tables with predefined schemas, enforce data integrity through relationships between these tables. For digital twins, relational databases are often well-suited for storing structured, transactional data, such as asset metadata, configuration details, work

orders from ERP systems, or component specifications derived from CAD data. Their strengths lie in their maturity, ACID (Atomicity, Consistency, Isolation, Durability) compliance, which guarantees reliable transaction processing, and their ability to perform complex queries using Structured Query Language (SQL). This makes them excellent for retrieving specific asset attributes, historical maintenance records that have been cleaned and structured, or configuration parameters. For instance, an asset's bill of materials, its installation date, or the warranty period could be effectively managed in a relational database. However, the rigid schema of relational databases can become a bottleneck when dealing with rapidly evolving data structures or high-velocity, unstructured, or semi-structured data streams. The need to define tables and columns upfront can slow down ingestion, and scaling relational databases horizontally (across multiple servers) can be complex and costly compared to other solutions. The overhead of maintaining strict schema consistency can also limit flexibility when integrating new data sources with slightly different formats.

Moving beyond the structured world of relational databases, **NoSQL (Not Only SQL) databases** have emerged as a powerful alternative, offering greater flexibility and scalability for handling diverse data types common in digital twin ecosystems. NoSQL databases encompass a variety of models, including key-value stores, document databases, column-family stores, and graph databases. **Document databases**, such as MongoDB, are particularly adept at storing semi-structured data like JSON or BSON documents. This makes them ideal for capturing the diverse and often evolving attributes of an asset, or for storing the output of analytical processes. For example, a document database could store the configuration settings of a machine, which might include a mix of standard parameters and custom, vendor-specific settings. **Key-value stores**, like Redis or Amazon DynamoDB, excel at fast retrieval of simple data based on a unique key, making them suitable for caching frequently accessed asset information or session data. **Column-family stores**, such as Cassandra, are optimized for high-volume writes and reads across large datasets, which can be beneficial for storing aggregated sensor data or event logs that need to be accessed by time range or specific parameters. Finally, **graph databases**, like Neo4j, are designed to represent and query relationships between entities. This is invaluable for digital twins, allowing for the modeling of complex interdependencies between components, systems, or even supply chains. For example, a graph database could map out how a failure in one component might propagate through a system or how different machines in a factory are interconnected. The primary advantages of NoSQL databases include their schema flexibility, horizontal scalability, and ability to handle large volumes of unstructured and semi-structured data. However, they may not offer the same level of transactional consistency as relational databases, and complex ad-hoc queries can sometimes be more challenging to formulate and execute, depending on the specific NoSQL type.

The sheer volume and velocity of data generated by sensors and other real-time sources often necessitate a storage solution specifically designed for such workloads. This is where
time-series databases (TSDBs) shine. TSDBs are optimized for storing and querying data points indexed by time. They are highly efficient at ingesting, storing, and retrieving time-stamped data, which is the dominant format for sensor readings, operational logs, and performance metrics. Examples of popular TSDBs include InfluxDB, TimescaleDB (which extends PostgreSQL), and Prometheus. These databases are architected to handle the continuous influx of data, often with features like data aggregation, downsampling, and retention policies built-in to manage storage costs and performance over long periods. For a digital twin, a TSDB is indispensable for storing, visualizing, and analyzing the real-time operational behavior of an asset. Trends in temperature, pressure, vibration, or power consumption can be easily queried and visualized, enabling the identification of anomalies, performance degradation, and potential failure precursors. The ability to efficiently query data over specific time windows, compare historical performance with current readings, and perform time-based aggregations makes TSDBs a cornerstone of digital twin data infrastructure for operational intelligence. While excellent for time-stamped data, TSDBs are typically not the best choice for storing complex relational metadata or unstructured documents.

For organizations dealing with extremely large, diverse, and rapidly growing datasets, a
data lake often forms the central repository for all raw and processed data. A data lake is a centralized repository that allows you to store all your structured and unstructured data at any scale. Unlike a data warehouse, which requires data to be structured and transformed before ingestion (schema-on-write), a data lake accepts data in its raw, native format (schema-on-read). This provides immense

flexibility, allowing data scientists and analysts to explore raw data for new insights without being constrained by predefined schemas. For digital twins, a data lake can serve as the ultimate landing zone for data from all sources - sensor streams, logs, ERP extracts, CAD files, maintenance reports, and more. The data can then be cataloged, processed, and curated into various formats, feeding into more specialized databases like TSDBs or relational databases, or being directly queried for specific analytical purposes. Cloud-based data lake solutions, such as Amazon S3, Azure Data Lake Storage, or Google Cloud Storage, offer massive scalability, durability, and cost-effectiveness. The challenge with data lakes lies in their potential to become "data swamps" if not properly governed and managed. Without a robust metadata catalog, data governance, and clear data pipelines for processing and curating data, it can become difficult to find, trust, and use the data effectively.

In practice, a comprehensive data infrastructure for a digital twin is rarely built on a single storage solution. A more common and effective approach is a **hybrid architecture**, leveraging the strengths of multiple technologies. For instance, a digital twin might utilize a data lake as the central raw data repository. From this lake, curated and transformed data can be fed into a time-series database for real-time operational monitoring and analytics. Critical asset metadata, configuration details, and structured historical records might reside in a relational database for robust transactional integrity and complex reporting. Meanwhile, semi-structured configuration data or output from machine learning models could be stored in a document database. Graph databases could be employed to model the relationships between components or supply chain entities. This multi-tiered approach allows for the optimization of storage and retrieval for different types of data, ensuring that each component of the digital twin's data infrastructure serves its purpose effectively and efficiently.

Beyond the choice of database technology, several infrastructure considerations are paramount for supporting a digital twin.
Scalability is non-negotiable. As the number of physical assets being twinned grows, and as the volume and frequency of data increase, the storage and processing infrastructure must be able to scale seamlessly, both vertically (adding more resources to existing servers) and horizontally (distributing the load across more servers). Cloud-native solutions and distributed databases are particularly well-suited for achieving this elasticity.

Performance is directly tied to the speed at which data can be ingested, processed, and queried. For real-time digital twins, low latency in data access is crucial for timely decision-making. This requires careful consideration of database indexing, query optimization, network bandwidth, and the proximity of data storage to compute resources. Caching mechanisms and specialized hardware can also play a role in enhancing performance.

Cost is always a significant factor. The cost of storing massive volumes of data, especially historical data, can be substantial. Cloud object storage solutions like data lakes offer cost-effective options for long-term archival, while more performant databases might be used for frequently accessed operational data. Optimizing data retention policies, using tiered storage, and choosing efficient data compression techniques are all important for managing costs.

Accessibility and security are equally critical. Data needs to be accessible to authorized users and applications, whether they are data scientists, operational managers, or automated systems. Robust access control mechanisms, encryption (at rest and in transit), and compliance with data privacy regulations are essential to protect sensitive information. Furthermore, ensuring data availability through redundancy and disaster recovery plans is vital to maintain the continuous operation of the digital twin.

The integration of these various data storage solutions necessitates robust **data integration and pipeline technologies**. Tools for ETL (Extract, Transform, Load) or ELT (Extract, Load, Transform) are essential for moving data between different systems and ensuring that it is in the correct format and quality for its intended use. Stream processing platforms, such as Apache Kafka or Amazon Kinesis, are crucial for handling real-time data ingestion and processing from numerous sources. Orchestration tools help manage the complexity of these data pipelines, ensuring reliability and timely execution.

In essence, the data storage and infrastructure for a digital twin represent a complex but critical ecosystem. It requires a deep understanding of the characteristics of the data being managed, the specific requirements of the digital twin's use cases, and the capabilities of various storage technologies. By thoughtfully selecting and integrating relational databases for structured metadata, NoSQL databases for flexible and diverse data, time-series databases for real-time operational data, and data lakes for raw data aggregation, organizations can build a resilient, scalable, and performant foundation that unlocks the full potential of their digital twin initiatives. The ongoing evolution of cloud computing, distributed systems, and specialized databases continues to offer new opportunities for optimizing this crucial aspect of digital twin implementation.

The preceding discussion has established the foundational elements of data storage and infrastructure critical for the successful deployment and operation of digital twins. We have explored various database technologies, from relational and NoSQL systems to time-series databases and data lakes, along with the overarching considerations of scalability, performance, cost, and security. However, the most sophisticated infrastructure and the most advanced storage solutions are ultimately rendered ineffective if the data they house is unreliable, inconsistent, or inaccurate. This brings us to a crucial, yet often overlooked, aspect of digital twin management: **Data Governance and Quality Assurance**. These twin pillars are not merely operational checkboxes; they are strategic imperatives that directly determine the trustworthiness and utility of the digital twin. A digital twin is, at its core, a representation of a physical entity, and its fidelity to that entity is directly proportional to the quality of the data it consumes. Errors, omissions, or inconsistencies in data can lead to flawed analyses, misguided operational decisions, and ultimately, a loss of confidence in the digital twin itself. Therefore, establishing robust frameworks for data governance and implementing rigorous data quality assurance processes are paramount to unlocking the full value proposition of digital twins.

Data governance, in the context of digital twins, refers to the overarching framework of policies, procedures, roles, and responsibilities that dictate how data is managed throughout its lifecycle. It ensures that data is handled in a consistent, secure, and compliant manner, aligning with organizational objectives and regulatory requirements. A key tenet of data governance is the clear definition of

data ownership. In a digital twin ecosystem, data can originate from numerous sources – sensors, SCADA systems, enterprise resource planning (ERP) software, computer-aided design (CAD) models, maintenance logs, and human input. It is imperative to assign clear ownership for each data domain. This means identifying individuals or teams who are accountable for the accuracy, completeness, and timeliness of specific datasets. For instance, the operations department might own sensor data related to machine performance, while the engineering department might own the CAD models and design specifications. This clarity of ownership ensures that there is a designated point of accountability for data quality issues and facilitates prompt resolution. Without defined ownership, data can languish in a state of ambiguity, leading to neglect and degradation.

Closely intertwined with ownership is the concept of
access controls. Data governance policies must meticulously define who can access what data, under what circumstances, and for what purposes. This is particularly critical for digital twins, which often contain sensitive operational, financial, and intellectual property information. Implementing a robust role-based access control (RBAC) system is essential. This ensures that only authorized personnel and systems have the necessary permissions to view, modify, or delete data. For example, a plant operator might have read-only access to real-time sensor data, while a maintenance engineer might have read-write access to historical maintenance records. Data scientists may require broad access for analytical purposes, but this access should be governed by strict guidelines and audit trails. Furthermore, access controls should extend to the different stages of data processing. Raw data might require different access privileges than curated, aggregated, or analytical data. The principle of least privilege – granting only the minimum necessary permissions for a user or system to perform its function – should be rigorously applied to minimize the risk of unauthorized access or data misuse.

A critical component of data governance, especially in complex digital twin environments, is
data lineage tracking. Data lineage provides an auditable record of where data originated, how it has been transformed, and where it has moved throughout its lifecycle. For a digital twin, understanding the lineage of a piece of data is invaluable for debugging, troubleshooting, and establishing trust. If a particular

analysis yields a surprising result, tracing the lineage of the input data can help identify potential sources of error, whether it's a faulty sensor, a misconfigured data pipeline, or an incorrect transformation rule. This traceability allows for rapid root cause analysis and facilitates the implementation of corrective actions. Implementing data lineage typically involves capturing metadata at each stage of the data pipeline, including timestamps, source systems, transformation scripts, and the users or processes responsible for the changes. Tools that automatically capture and visualize data lineage can significantly reduce the manual effort and complexity involved, making it a more practical and sustainable practice.

Beyond the policies and responsibilities outlined in data governance, data quality assurance encompasses the practical processes and techniques employed to ensure that data meets predefined standards of accuracy, completeness, consistency, validity, and timeliness. The foundation of data quality assurance lies in establishing
data validation rules. These are a set of criteria against which incoming data is checked to ensure it conforms to expected formats, ranges, and constraints. For instance, a sensor reading for temperature might have a defined valid range (e.g., -20°C to 200°C for a specific industrial process). Data points falling outside this range could be flagged as invalid. Similarly, a timestamp should adhere to a specific format and fall within a reasonable chronological window. Business rules can also be embedded as validation checks. For example, the "operational status" field of a machine should only contain predefined values like "Running," "Idle," or "Faulted." Implementing these validation rules at the point of data ingestion or as early as possible in the data pipeline prevents corrupt data from propagating further into the digital twin ecosystem.

When invalid or inconsistent data is identified,
data cleansing procedures become essential. Data cleansing, also known as data scrubbing, is the process of detecting and correcting or removing inaccurate, incomplete, improperly formatted, or duplicate records from a dataset. The approach to cleansing will depend on the nature of the data quality issue and the criticality of the data. For minor inconsistencies, automated correction might be possible. For example, standardizing date formats or correcting common typographical errors. In other cases, more sophisticated techniques like fuzzy matching might be used to identify and merge duplicate records representing the same real-world entity. When data is missing, a decision needs to be made:

should it be imputed (estimated based on other data), or should the record be flagged as incomplete? The imputation strategy itself needs careful consideration to avoid introducing bias. For critical data points, manual review by subject matter experts might be necessary before any cleansing action is taken. The goal is not necessarily to achieve perfect data – which is often an unattainable ideal – but to ensure that the data is "fit for purpose" for the intended use cases of the digital twin.

Effective data quality assurance is not a one-time activity but an ongoing process that requires continuous
monitoring mechanisms. This involves regularly assessing the quality of data and identifying trends or patterns in data quality issues. Dashboards and reporting tools can be employed to visualize key data quality metrics, such as the percentage of valid records, the number of data anomalies detected, and the frequency of cleansing operations. Alerts can be configured to notify relevant stakeholders when data quality metrics fall below acceptable thresholds or when new types of data quality problems emerge. This proactive monitoring allows for early detection of systemic issues, such as a malfunctioning sensor or a bug in a data processing script, before they have a significant impact on the digital twin's performance or the decisions derived from it. Furthermore, regular audits of data quality processes and their outcomes can help refine the validation rules and cleansing procedures over time, ensuring that they remain effective and aligned with evolving business needs.

The implementation of comprehensive data governance and quality assurance for digital twins is a multifaceted endeavor that touches upon organizational culture, technological capabilities, and procedural discipline. It begins with establishing a clear
data strategy that aligns with the overarching business objectives of the digital twin initiative. This strategy should articulate the vision for data management, including the principles of data governance and the commitment to data quality.

Within the organizational structure, the formation of a
data stewardship council or a similar cross-functional body can be instrumental. This group, comprising representatives from IT, operations, engineering, analytics, and business units, would be responsible for defining data policies, prioritizing data quality initiatives, and resolving data-related conflicts.

Data stewards, who are typically individuals with deep domain knowledge in specific data areas, would work under this council to implement and enforce the defined policies and processes. Their role is crucial in bridging the gap between technical data management and business understanding.

Technologically, the selection of appropriate tools is vital. Many modern data platforms and data quality solutions offer functionalities for data profiling, data validation, data cleansing, data lineage tracking, and data cataloging. Integrating these tools into the data pipelines feeding the digital twin can automate many of the assurance processes, making them more efficient and reliable. For example, data profiling tools can analyze datasets to understand their structure, identify data types, and detect anomalies, providing insights that inform the development of validation rules. Data catalogs, in conjunction with lineage information, can serve as a central inventory of all data assets within the digital twin ecosystem, making it easier for users to discover, understand, and trust the data.

The successful application of data governance and quality assurance principles is not merely about implementing tools and processes; it requires fostering a **data-driven culture** within the organization. This means cultivating an awareness of the importance of data quality at all levels, encouraging data literacy, and promoting a mindset where data is viewed as a valuable asset to be protected and nurtured. When employees understand how their actions can impact data quality and recognize the downstream consequences of poor data, they are more likely to adopt best practices and contribute to maintaining high data standards. This cultural shift is often driven by leadership commitment and continuous reinforcement through training and communication.

In the realm of digital twins, the impact of robust data governance and quality assurance is profound. It directly contributes to:

Enhanced Trust and Reliability: When stakeholders know that the data underpinning the digital twin has been rigorously governed and validated, they can place greater confidence in the insights and predictions generated. This trust is foundational for making critical operational and strategic decisions.

Improved Decision-Making: Accurate and consistent data leads to more precise analyses and more informed decisions. This can translate into optimized operations, reduced downtime, improved asset performance, and more effective risk management.
Increased Efficiency: By preventing the propagation of errors and inconsistencies, data quality assurance reduces the time and effort spent on troubleshooting, rework, and data correction. This frees up valuable resources for more productive activities.
Better Compliance and Risk Mitigation: Strong data governance ensures that data handling practices comply with relevant industry regulations and internal policies. Clear lineage and access controls help mitigate risks associated with data breaches, unauthorized modifications, or non-compliance.
Facilitated Collaboration: A well-governed and high-quality data environment fosters better collaboration among different teams and departments. When everyone is working with a common, trusted dataset, communication becomes more effective, and collective problem-solving is enhanced.
Maximized ROI of Digital Twin Investments: Ultimately, the return on investment for a digital twin is directly tied to its ability to deliver actionable insights and drive tangible business value. High-quality data is the indispensable fuel that powers these outcomes.

The journey towards mature data governance and quality assurance for digital twins is continuous. It requires ongoing vigilance, adaptation to new data sources and technologies, and a persistent commitment to excellence. By embedding these principles into the fabric of digital twin management, organizations can ensure that their digital representations remain accurate, reliable, and powerfully insightful, serving as true enablers of digital transformation.

The preceding chapters have meticulously laid the groundwork for understanding and implementing digital twin technology, delving into the architectural foundations, data management strategies, and the imperative of data governance and quality assurance. We've established that a digital twin is only as valuable as the data it represents, and ensuring the integrity and reliability of this data through robust governance and quality frameworks is paramount. However, even the most impeccably governed and high-quality data can be rendered useless or, worse, become a significant liability if it is not adequately protected. This brings us to the critical, non-negotiable aspect of digital twin implementation: **Data Security and Privacy Considerations**.

In today's interconnected world, data is a prime target for malicious actors, and digital twins, by their very nature, aggregate vast amounts of sensitive information. This information often pertains to the inner workings of critical infrastructure, proprietary manufacturing processes, patient health records, or complex supply chains. A security breach involving a digital twin could have far-reaching consequences, including operational disruption, financial losses, reputational damage, intellectual property theft, and even threats to physical safety. Therefore, a comprehensive and proactive approach to data security and privacy is not merely an option; it is an absolute necessity for the successful and ethical deployment of digital twins.

The core of digital twin data security lies in safeguarding the data from unauthorized access, whether external or internal, and protecting it from modification or destruction. This begins with a robust **encryption strategy**. Encryption is the process of encoding data such that only authorized parties can understand it. For digital twins, this should be implemented at multiple levels. **Data in transit**, meaning data being moved between sensors, edge devices, the cloud, and user interfaces, must be protected using secure communication protocols such as Transport Layer Security (TLS) or its successor, TLS 1.3. These protocols ensure that data cannot be intercepted and read by attackers during transmission. For example, sensor data streaming from a manufacturing floor to a cloud-based digital twin platform should be encrypted using TLS to prevent eavesdropping by anyone on the network. Similarly, APIs used to query or update the digital twin must also employ TLS.

Beyond data in transit, **data at rest** also requires stringent protection. This refers to data stored in databases, data lakes, file systems, and backups. Strong encryption algorithms, such as Advanced Encryption Standard (AES) with appropriate key lengths (e.g., AES-256), should be employed to encrypt the actual data files and database volumes. This means that even if an unauthorized individual gains physical access to storage media or a server, the encrypted data would be unreadable without the corresponding decryption keys. Key management is a critical aspect of encryption at rest. Securely generating, storing, distributing, and rotating encryption keys is paramount. This often involves using dedicated Hardware Security Modules (HSMs) or cloud-based key management services to protect the keys themselves from compromise. Without well-managed keys, even well-encrypted data can become inaccessible or insecure.

Complementing encryption,
robust access management is fundamental to preventing unauthorized access to digital twin data. This involves implementing a "least privilege" principle, ensuring that users and systems only have access to the data and functionalities they absolutely need to perform their roles. Role-Based Access Control (RBAC) is a widely adopted model for this. In an RBAC system, permissions are assigned to roles, and users are then assigned to those roles. For a digital twin of a power grid, for instance, an operations manager might have read-only access to real-time performance metrics for all substations, while a specific technician might have read-write access to maintenance logs for a particular substation they are responsible for. The digital twin platform itself should enforce these roles and permissions rigorously.

Moreover,
multi-factor authentication (MFA) should be mandated for all access to sensitive digital twin data and administrative interfaces. MFA requires users to provide two or more verification factors to gain access, significantly reducing the risk of unauthorized access due to compromised credentials. This could involve a password combined with a one-time code from a mobile app or a biometric scan. Beyond individual user access, **service-to-service authentication** is also crucial. When different components of the digital twin ecosystem (e.g., a simulation engine, an analytics module, and the data storage) need to communicate, they should authenticate each other using secure mechanisms like OAuth 2.0 or API keys, rather than relying on implicit trust.

The aggregate nature of digital twins means they often contain personally identifiable information (PII) or other sensitive data that requires specific privacy considerations, especially when dealing with individuals or populations. **Anonymization and pseudonymization** techniques become vital in such scenarios. Anonymization is the process of removing or altering identifying information so that the data can no longer be linked back to a specific individual.

This might be applied to data collected from smart homes integrated into a digital twin of a city's infrastructure. Pseudonymization, on the other hand, replaces direct identifiers with artificial identifiers or pseudonyms. While the data can still be linked back to an individual with additional information (which must be stored separately and securely), it protects privacy during general analysis or sharing. For example, in a digital twin of a healthcare facility, patient IDs might be pseudonymized for research purposes, while retaining the ability to link specific treatment data back to the original patient record if required for clinical care.

The selection of appropriate anonymization or pseudonymization techniques depends on the nature of the data and the intended use case. Techniques range from simple removal of names and addresses to more complex methods like k-anonymity, l-diversity, or differential privacy, which provide stronger guarantees against re-identification, particularly when dealing with large datasets or advanced analytical techniques. It's crucial to assess the risk of re-identification after applying these techniques, especially if the digital twin is integrated with external datasets that could be used for triangulation.

Furthermore, compliance with
relevant data privacy regulations is a non-negotiable aspect of digital twin development and operation. Regulations like the General Data Protection Regulation (GDPR) in Europe, the California Consumer Privacy Act (CCPA) in the United States, and similar laws globally impose strict requirements on how personal data is collected, processed, stored, and shared. Organizations deploying digital twins must understand which regulations apply to their specific use cases and geographical reach. This includes:

Lawful Basis for Processing: Ensuring there is a legal justification for collecting and processing any personal data within the digital twin.
Data Minimization: Collecting only the data that is strictly necessary for the defined purpose.
Purpose Limitation: Using the data only for the specific purposes for which it was collected.
Data Subject Rights: Providing individuals with rights such as access, rectification, erasure, and portability of their personal data.

Data Protection Impact Assessments (DPIAs): Conducting assessments to identify and mitigate privacy risks associated with high-risk data processing activities, which digital twins often represent.
Cross-Border Data Transfers: Adhering to specific rules and safeguards when transferring personal data across international borders.

For instance, if a digital twin is used to manage a fleet of autonomous vehicles that collect data on passenger movements and habits, strict adherence to GDPR principles would be required. This might involve obtaining explicit consent for data collection, anonymizing travel patterns where possible, and providing passengers with mechanisms to request access to or deletion of their data.

Beyond these core technical and regulatory aspects, fostering a **security-conscious culture** is equally important. All personnel involved with the digital twin, from data engineers to business users, must be educated on security best practices, the risks associated with data breaches, and their role in protecting sensitive information. Regular security awareness training, phishing simulations, and clear communication channels for reporting potential security incidents are essential components of this cultural shift. A single compromised user account or an overlooked vulnerability can negate the most sophisticated security measures.

The lifecycle of the digital twin data also presents security challenges. **Data retention and disposal policies** must be clearly defined and implemented. Sensitive data should not be retained for longer than necessary. When data is no longer required, it must be securely and irrevocably disposed of, whether through secure deletion protocols for digital data or physical destruction of media. Insecure disposal can lead to data leakage and create significant compliance risks.

Auditing and monitoring are also critical for detecting and responding to security threats. Comprehensive audit trails should be maintained for all access and modifications to digital twin data. These logs, which record who accessed what data, when, and from where, provide invaluable forensic information in the event of a security incident. Real-time monitoring of these logs using Security

Information and Event Management (SIEM) systems can help detect suspicious activities, such as unusual access patterns or repeated failed login attempts, allowing for rapid incident response. Automated alerts can be triggered to notify security teams of potential threats, enabling them to investigate and mitigate risks before significant damage occurs.

The integration of digital twins with various other systems, such as IoT platforms, ERP systems, and legacy operational technology (OT) networks, introduces additional attack vectors. Securing these **interconnections** is paramount. Network segmentation can be employed to isolate the digital twin environment from other less secure networks. Firewalls, intrusion detection/prevention systems (IDPS), and strict network access control lists (ACLs) should be implemented to control the flow of data between different network zones. For environments involving OT, which often have different security paradigms and legacy systems, specialized security measures and expertise may be required to bridge the gap with IT security practices.

In summary, data security and privacy are not add-ons to digital twin implementations; they are foundational requirements. A multi-layered approach, encompassing strong encryption for data in transit and at rest, granular access controls with MFA, effective anonymization and pseudonymization techniques, strict adherence to privacy regulations, secure data lifecycle management, continuous monitoring and auditing, and a deeply ingrained security culture, is essential. By prioritizing these aspects, organizations can build trust in their digital twin initiatives, facilitate broader adoption, and ensure that these powerful technologies are used responsibly and ethically, safeguarding valuable operational data and sensitive personal information alike. The investment in robust security and privacy measures is an investment in the long-term viability and trustworthiness of the digital twin itself.

Chapter 9: Deployment Architectures for Digital Twins

The successful realization of a digital twin hinges critically on its underlying deployment architecture. This architecture dictates how the myriad components—from the physical asset's sensors to the sophisticated analytical engines and user interfaces—are structured, interconnected, and how they collaborate. Choosing the right architectural paradigm is not merely an exercise in technical design; it is a strategic decision that profoundly impacts scalability, performance, cost-effectiveness, maintainability, and the overall ability of the digital twin to deliver tangible value. Different industrial scenarios, with their unique constraints regarding connectivity, computational resources, latency requirements, and existing infrastructure, necessitate distinct architectural approaches. This section delves into the primary architectural paradigms that guide the deployment of digital twins, offering insights into their characteristics, advantages, and typical use cases, thereby providing a robust foundation for designing and implementing effective digital twin solutions.

One of the most prevalent and adaptable architectural patterns for digital twins is the

Cloud-Native Architecture. This paradigm leverages the extensive capabilities of cloud computing platforms, such as Amazon Web Services (AWS), Microsoft Azure, or Google Cloud Platform (GCP). In a cloud-native approach, all core components of the digital twin—data ingestion and processing, data storage, modeling and simulation engines, analytics, and visualization dashboards—are designed to reside and operate within the cloud environment. This offers inherent advantages in terms of scalability, elasticity, and access to a vast array of managed services. For instance, data streaming from sensors on an industrial machine can be ingested via cloud IoT services, processed using cloud-based data warehousing or data lake solutions, and then fed into machine learning models deployed on scalable compute instances or specialized AI/ML platforms within the cloud. Visualization can be achieved through cloud-hosted web applications accessible from any internet-connected device.

The benefits of a cloud-native architecture are significant.

Scalability is a primary driver; as the number of connected assets grows or the complexity of simulations increases, cloud resources can be dynamically provisioned or de-provisioned to meet demand. This elasticity prevents costly over-provisioning and ensures performance is maintained even during peak loads. Furthermore, cloud platforms offer a rich ecosystem of pre-built services for data management (e.g., managed databases, object storage), analytics (e.g., serverless computing, big data processing frameworks), AI/ML (e.g., managed training and inference services), and security, which can significantly accelerate development and reduce operational overhead. Organizations can leverage managed services for databases, message queues, and container orchestration, freeing up engineering teams to focus on the unique aspects of their digital twin application rather than managing underlying infrastructure.

However, a pure cloud-native architecture is not without its challenges. **Latency** can be a critical concern, especially for applications requiring real-time control or immediate feedback loops. The physical distance between the edge devices (e.g., sensors on a factory floor) and the cloud data centers can introduce delays that are unacceptable for certain use cases, such as critical industrial control systems or autonomous vehicle operation. **Connectivity dependence** is another significant drawback; if the internet connection to the cloud is unstable or unavailable, the digital twin's functionality can be severely compromised or rendered entirely inoperable. Moreover, **data egress costs** can become substantial for applications that generate very large volumes of data that need to be continuously streamed to the cloud. Finally, while cloud providers offer robust security, data residing in the cloud may raise **sovereignty or regulatory concerns** for some organizations, particularly those dealing with highly sensitive or classified information.

To address the limitations of a purely cloud-centric approach, the **Edge-Centric Architecture** emerges as a complementary or alternative paradigm. In an edge-centric model, a significant portion of the digital twin's computational and data processing capabilities are moved closer to the data source – out to the "edge" of the network. This edge layer typically consists of local servers, gateways, or even powerful industrial PCs situated on-premises, in factories, or in other operational environments. Data acquisition and initial processing, including filtering, aggregation, and anomaly detection, often occur at the edge. More demanding tasks, such as complex simulations, advanced analytics, or long-term data storage, might still be offloaded to the cloud, but the edge handles immediate insights and actions.

The primary advantage of the edge-centric architecture is its ability to address the latency and connectivity issues inherent in cloud-only solutions. By processing data locally, applications can achieve near real-time responsiveness, which is crucial for operational control, predictive maintenance triggers, and safety-critical functions. For instance, a digital twin of a wind turbine might use edge computing to analyze vibration data locally to detect an impending gearbox failure and initiate an immediate shutdown or alert without waiting for data to travel to the cloud and back. This also reduces reliance on constant, high-bandwidth connectivity. Even if the connection to the cloud is temporarily lost, the edge devices can continue to operate autonomously, collecting data, performing local analysis, and potentially executing predefined actions. This enhances resilience and reliability. Furthermore, by processing and filtering data at the edge, organizations can significantly reduce the volume of data that needs to be transmitted to the cloud, leading to substantial cost savings on bandwidth and cloud storage. This also helps in complying with data sovereignty regulations by keeping sensitive raw data on-premises.

However, edge-centric architectures introduce their own set of complexities. **Resource constraints** are a major consideration. Edge devices typically have limited processing power, memory, and storage compared to cloud infrastructure, which can restrict the complexity of models and simulations that can be run locally. **Management and orchestration** of a distributed fleet of edge devices can be challenging. Deploying, updating, and monitoring software across numerous edge nodes requires robust device management platforms and remote administration capabilities. **Security** at the edge is also a critical concern; edge devices, being physically more accessible, can be more vulnerable to tampering or physical breaches than centralized cloud data centers. Ensuring consistent security policies and patching across a distributed edge infrastructure is paramount. The **initial investment** in edge hardware can also be higher than leveraging existing cloud services.

A hybrid approach, often termed the
Hybrid Cloud Architecture, seeks to combine the best of both worlds. In this model, certain digital twin components are deployed in the cloud, while others reside on-premises or at the edge. The choice of where to deploy each component is driven by specific requirements related to performance, security, cost, and regulatory compliance. For example, a hybrid architecture might leverage edge

devices for real-time data acquisition and initial processing, a private cloud or on-premises servers for sensitive data storage and localized analytics requiring low latency, and a public cloud for large-scale data archiving, complex simulation, advanced AI model training, and global accessibility of dashboards.

The hybrid cloud architecture offers significant flexibility and can be tailored to meet diverse needs. It allows organizations to optimize performance by placing time-sensitive operations at the edge or on-premises, while still benefiting from the scalability and vast resource pool of the public cloud for less critical or more resource-intensive tasks. This can lead to a more cost-effective solution by strategically allocating workloads. For instance, a manufacturer might use edge gateways to monitor production lines for immediate alerts, store historical production data on-premises for rapid local querying by supervisors, and then periodically upload aggregated performance metrics and quality data to the public cloud for long-term trend analysis and benchmarking against industry peers. This approach also provides a pathway for organizations that are gradually migrating to the cloud, allowing them to integrate their existing on-premises infrastructure with cloud services.

However, managing a hybrid environment can be more complex than a single-platform approach.
Integration challenges between on-premises and cloud environments are common, requiring robust middleware, APIs, and data synchronization strategies. **Maintaining consistency** in security policies, data management, and operational practices across disparate environments requires careful planning and robust governance. **Complexity in deployment and lifecycle management** can also increase, as teams need to manage infrastructure and software across multiple locations and platforms. Furthermore, ensuring seamless data flow and interoperability between different components, whether they are on-premises, at the edge, or in the cloud, is a constant challenge.

Another architectural paradigm that warrants discussion, particularly in the context of interconnected industrial ecosystems, is the **Federated Architecture**. In a federated model, multiple independent digital twins, each representing a specific asset or system, are created and managed by different entities or departments. These individual twins can then be interconnected and share specific data or insights with each other, often through a centralized coordination layer or a common platform, without necessarily consolidating all data into a single monolithic system. This is particularly relevant for complex supply chains, smart city initiatives, or collaborative manufacturing environments where different parties own and manage their respective assets.

The strength of a federated architecture lies in its ability to foster collaboration and interoperability between disparate systems while respecting individual ownership and data privacy. For example, in a supply chain digital twin, a manufacturer, a logistics provider, and a retailer might each maintain their own digital twins of their respective operations. These twins can then be federated to provide visibility into the overall movement of goods, inventory levels, and potential disruptions across the entire chain. Each entity retains control over its own data, sharing only what is necessary and agreed upon with other participants. This model promotes agility and allows for modular development and deployment, as individual twins can be updated or modified independently.

However, the federated architecture introduces challenges related to **interoperability standards and data harmonization**. Ensuring that different digital twins can communicate and exchange data effectively requires agreement on common data models, communication protocols, and APIs. **Governance and trust** among participants are critical; establishing clear rules for data sharing, access control, and dispute resolution is essential. **Complexity in orchestration and data aggregation** for cross-entity analysis can also be significant. While individual twins might be manageable, understanding the collective behavior or performance of a federated system requires sophisticated coordination and data integration mechanisms.

Beyond these overarching paradigms, specific architectural patterns within each can be observed. For instance, within a cloud-native or hybrid architecture, the **Microservices Architecture** is increasingly adopted. Instead of a monolithic application, the digital twin is broken down into a collection of small, independent services, each responsible for a specific business capability (e.g., data ingestion, asset modeling, simulation execution, anomaly detection, visualization). These services communicate with each other over a network, often using lightweight protocols like REST or gRPC. The benefits of microservices include improved agility, independent deployability of components, better fault isolation, and the ability to use different technologies for different services. However, it also introduces increased complexity in terms of service discovery, distributed tracing, and inter-service communication management.

Another pattern often seen is the **Event-Driven Architecture (EDA)**, which is highly compatible with digital twins. In an EDA, components communicate by producing and consuming "events"—significant changes in state or occurrences. For example, a sensor reading exceeding a threshold might generate an "over-temperature" event. Other components, such as an analytics engine or a notification service, can subscribe to this event and react accordingly. EDA is ideal for real-time data processing and asynchronous communication, making it well-suited for the dynamic nature of digital twins. It promotes loose coupling between components, enhancing modularity and scalability.

When considering the deployment of digital twins, especially in industrial settings, the integration of **Operational Technology (OT) and Information Technology (IT)** is a critical architectural consideration. OT systems, which manage physical processes and devices, have traditionally been isolated from IT networks due to different security requirements and lifecycles. A digital twin architecture must bridge this gap, securely ingesting data from OT systems (e.g., PLCs, SCADA systems) while integrating with IT infrastructure for analytics and enterprise-level reporting. This often involves implementing secure data diodes, industrial firewalls, and robust network segmentation strategies to ensure that the operational integrity and security of the physical assets are not compromised. The architecture must account for the unique protocols (e.g., Modbus, OPC UA) used in OT environments and provide mechanisms for their translation into IT-friendly formats.

Furthermore, the choice of architecture is intrinsically linked to the **data management strategy**. Whether data is stored in centralized data lakes, distributed databases, or edge-based storage solutions, the architecture must support efficient data ingestion, processing, querying, and lifecycle management. Architectures supporting real-time streaming analytics, batch processing, and historical data analysis will differ significantly. For instance, a real-time predictive maintenance digital twin might require a streaming data architecture capable of processing high-velocity sensor data with very low latency, while a long-term asset performance management twin might focus on efficient batch processing of historical operational data for trend analysis.

Ultimately, there is no single "best" architecture for all digital twins. The optimal choice is a function of the specific use case, the nature of the physical asset(s) being twinned, the available infrastructure, the organization's technical expertise, budget, and strategic goals. A small-scale prototype for a specific machine might suffice with a simpler cloud-based setup, whereas a comprehensive digital twin for a smart city or a critical national infrastructure will demand a more complex, federated, or hybrid approach. A thorough understanding of these architectural paradigms—Cloud-Native, Edge-Centric, Hybrid Cloud, and Federated—along with their underlying patterns like microservices and event-driven systems, empowers organizations to design and deploy digital twin solutions that are not only technically sound but also strategically aligned with their business objectives, ensuring scalability, performance, resilience, and long-term value. The ongoing evolution of cloud, edge, and network technologies continues to shape these architectures, offering new possibilities for creating ever more sophisticated and impactful digital twins.

When considering the deployment of digital twins, an architectural model that warrants in-depth exploration is the **On-Premises Deployment Model**. This paradigm situates all or the vast majority of the digital twin's infrastructure and computational resources within the organization's own physical boundaries. Unlike cloud-centric or hybrid approaches, an on-premises deployment eschews reliance on external cloud providers for core operational functions. Instead, servers, storage, networking equipment, and software applications are managed and maintained entirely by the organization's IT department or a designated internal team. This approach grants an organization a high degree of autonomy and direct oversight over every facet of its digital twin's operational environment.

The primary allure of an on-premises digital twin deployment often stems from the imperative of
enhanced control and security. Organizations that handle highly sensitive data, operate within stringent regulatory frameworks, or possess critical intellectual

property may find the prospect of keeping all digital twin components within their own secure perimeters highly advantageous. This eliminates the potential security vulnerabilities associated with data transmission to and from external cloud environments, and it provides absolute control over access policies, physical security of the hardware, and the patching and updating schedules for all software and firmware. For industries like defense, national security, or organizations dealing with classified research, this level of sovereignty over data and infrastructure is not merely a preference but a fundamental requirement. The ability to customize network configurations, implement bespoke security protocols, and physically isolate critical systems from public networks offers a robust defense against cyber threats and unauthorized access. Furthermore, for organizations with existing, substantial investments in their own data centers, leveraging this infrastructure for digital twin deployments can sometimes be perceived as a more cost-effective path in the long run, avoiding recurring cloud subscription fees and data egress charges.

However, the on-premises model is not without its significant drawbacks, most notably
substantial upfront capital expenditure and ongoing operational overhead. Establishing a fully functional on-premises digital twin environment necessitates considerable investment in hardware, including high-performance servers, vast storage arrays, robust networking infrastructure, and potentially specialized hardware for data processing or simulation. Beyond the initial purchase, organizations must account for the ongoing costs associated with power consumption, cooling, physical security, hardware maintenance and upgrades, software licensing, and the recruitment and retention of skilled IT personnel capable of managing, monitoring, and troubleshooting complex infrastructure. Unlike cloud services where resources can be scaled up or down elastically, on-premises infrastructure typically requires careful capacity planning to avoid both under-provisioning (leading to performance bottlenecks) and over-provisioning (leading to wasted resources and capital). This static nature of on-premises infrastructure can make it less agile in responding to sudden surges in demand or evolving computational needs. The responsibility for maintaining high availability, disaster recovery, and business continuity also falls squarely on the organization, requiring meticulous planning, redundant systems, and rigorous testing.

Despite these challenges, certain use cases strongly favor or even necessitate an on-premises deployment for digital twins.
Industries with strict data sovereignty and compliance mandates frequently opt for this model. Jurisdictions with data localization laws, where data generated within national borders must remain physically within those borders, make cloud solutions problematic unless the cloud provider has a local data center. For companies in highly regulated sectors such as healthcare (dealing with patient data), finance (handling sensitive financial transactions), or critical infrastructure management, the ability to maintain complete control and visibility over data flow and storage is paramount to meeting regulatory obligations and avoiding hefty fines. For example, a nuclear power plant's digital twin, used to monitor the performance and safety of its complex systems, would likely require an on-premises deployment to ensure that sensitive operational data never leaves the secure facility. Similarly, a global manufacturing company might deploy on-premises digital twins at each of its major factory sites to manage local production data while federating aggregated, anonymized insights to a central hub, thereby balancing local control with global visibility while respecting regional data governance.

Another critical consideration is
latency sensitivity. While edge computing can address some latency issues by bringing computation closer to the source, a fully on-premises solution offers the absolute lowest latency for applications where even edge-to-cloud round trips are unacceptable. This can be crucial for real-time control systems, high-frequency trading platforms, or complex industrial automation scenarios where split-second decisions are vital. Imagine a digital twin of a robotic assembly line: if a sensor detects an anomaly, an immediate, precise adjustment might be required to prevent damage or a product defect. Relying on any external network, even a highly optimized one, could introduce delays that compromise the system's integrity. An on-premises deployment ensures that the digital twin processing and the physical execution can be tightly synchronized.

The
infrastructure and operational considerations for an on-premises digital twin are substantial. Organizations must invest in not only the computing hardware but also robust networking, including high-speed internal networks and secure

connections for any necessary external interactions. This extends to the software stack as well: operating systems, virtualization platforms, databases, middleware, analytics engines, and the digital twin application itself must all be procured, installed, configured, and maintained internally. This requires a deep pool of IT expertise across various domains, from network engineering and system administration to cybersecurity and database management.

Data management becomes a centralized, internal affair. This means designing and implementing on-premises data storage solutions, whether they are traditional databases, data warehouses, or modern data lakes. The architecture must support efficient data ingestion from the physical assets, often involving specialized industrial protocols that need to be translated. Data lifecycle management, including archiving, backup, and secure deletion, must be meticulously planned and executed. For organizations with extensive historical data, ensuring adequate storage capacity and retrieval speeds for on-premises systems can be a significant undertaking.

Security is a multi-layered challenge. Physical security of the data center is the first line of defense, followed by network security (firewalls, intrusion detection/prevention systems), host-based security (endpoint protection, access controls), and application-level security. Given the critical nature of digital twins, robust cybersecurity practices are non-negotiable. This includes regular vulnerability assessments, penetration testing, strict access control mechanisms, and comprehensive security monitoring. Employee training on security best practices is also a vital component.

Scalability in an on-premises model is achieved through planned hardware upgrades and additions. This is a more deliberate process than the on-demand scaling offered by cloud platforms. Organizations must forecast future needs and procure hardware in advance, which can lead to periods of underutilization or, conversely, capacity constraints if demand grows unexpectedly. For many organizations, particularly small to medium-sized enterprises or those with rapidly evolving digital twin requirements, the capital expenditure and management complexity of a fully on-premises deployment can be prohibitive.

The agility to experiment with new technologies or rapidly scale up for a specific project is also diminished compared to cloud alternatives.

Furthermore, the responsibility for **disaster recovery and business continuity** rests entirely with the organization. This typically involves setting up redundant hardware, maintaining off-site backups, and developing comprehensive disaster recovery plans that are regularly tested. The complexity and cost of implementing a robust DR/BC strategy for an on-premises digital twin can be substantial, often requiring significant investment in secondary data centers or co-location facilities.

In summary, the on-premises deployment model for digital twins offers unparalleled control over data, security, and operational execution. It is a compelling choice for organizations with stringent regulatory requirements, absolute data sovereignty needs, or critical latency tolerances that cannot be met by external services. However, this control comes at the significant cost of high upfront investment, substantial ongoing operational expenditure, and the considerable burden of managing complex infrastructure and security landscapes. The decision to pursue an on-premises strategy must be a deliberate one, carefully weighing the unique benefits against the inherent challenges and ensuring that the organization possesses the necessary financial resources, technical expertise, and strategic vision to successfully implement and maintain such a sophisticated deployment.

The digital twin landscape is undergoing a significant transformation, driven by the adoption of sophisticated deployment architectures. While on-premises solutions offer a high degree of control and security, the pervasive reach and inherent advantages of cloud computing have positioned cloud-based deployment models as a dominant and increasingly attractive option for digital twin implementation. This subsection delves into the multifaceted world of cloud-based digital twins, examining their capabilities, benefits, and the various deployment strategies that organizations can leverage to harness their full potential.

The fundamental appeal of cloud computing for digital twins lies in its inherent characteristics:

scalability, flexibility, and access to a rich ecosystem of advanced services. Unlike the rigid infrastructure of on-premises deployments, cloud platforms are designed to dynamically adjust resources based on demand. For a digital twin, which can experience fluctuating workloads – from periods of low activity to intense simulation runs or real-time data processing during critical events – this elastic scalability is invaluable. An organization can seamlessly scale up its computational power and storage capacity to handle a surge in data ingestion or complex analytical tasks without the need for significant upfront hardware investments or lengthy procurement cycles. Conversely, resources can be scaled down during periods of lower demand, optimizing costs and avoiding the wastage associated with over-provisioned on-premises infrastructure. This agility allows businesses to respond more rapidly to changing market conditions, launch new digital twin initiatives, or adapt to evolving business needs with unprecedented speed.

Beyond scalability, cloud platforms provide unparalleled **flexibility**. This manifests in various ways, including the ability to deploy digital twins rapidly, experiment with different configurations and technologies, and access a wide array of managed services that would be prohibitively expensive or complex to build and maintain in-house. For instance, cloud providers offer a comprehensive suite of services for big data analytics, artificial intelligence (AI), and machine learning (ML). These capabilities are often critical for extracting actionable insights from the vast amounts of data generated by physical assets and their digital counterparts. Integrating advanced AI algorithms for predictive maintenance, anomaly detection, or optimizing operational performance becomes significantly more accessible when leveraging cloud-based ML platforms. Similarly, cloud-based data lakes and robust data warehousing solutions simplify the management and analysis of diverse datasets, enabling more sophisticated modeling and simulation. The ease of integration with these cutting-edge services accelerates the development lifecycle of digital twins, allowing organizations to derive value from their investments much faster.

A key advantage of cloud deployment is the **reduced operational burden**. Organizations can offload the responsibilities of hardware procurement, installation, maintenance, patching, and infrastructure security to the cloud provider. This frees up internal IT resources to focus on higher-value activities, such as developing and refining the digital twin models themselves, enhancing the user experience, and driving business innovation. The cloud provider handles the underlying infrastructure, ensuring high availability, reliability, and often providing built-in disaster recovery capabilities, which can be a significant undertaking for on-premises deployments. This shift in operational responsibility can lead to substantial cost savings, not just in terms of capital expenditure but also in reduced operational overhead related to power, cooling, physical security, and specialized IT staff.

The cloud offers several distinct deployment models, each with its own set of implications for digital twin implementations:

The
Public Cloud Model represents the most common and widely adopted approach. In this model, the digital twin infrastructure and services are hosted on a cloud provider's premises and are made available to multiple organizations over the internet. Major providers like Amazon Web Services (AWS), Microsoft Azure, and Google Cloud Platform offer a vast array of services that are perfectly suited for digital twin development and deployment. This model is characterized by its inherent scalability, cost-effectiveness (often a pay-as-you-go model), and rapid deployment capabilities. Organizations can spin up virtual machines, databases, analytics services, and IoT platforms in minutes, accelerating their time to market. For a digital twin of a fleet of vehicles, for instance, a public cloud deployment allows for ingestion of telemetry data from thousands or even millions of vehicles simultaneously, processing it in real-time, and running complex simulations to optimize routes or predict maintenance needs. The shared infrastructure, while highly secured and compartmentalized, means that resources are shared among many tenants. This typically leads to economies of scale, making it a very attractive option for businesses of all sizes.

The
Private Cloud Model offers a more controlled environment where the digital twin infrastructure is dedicated solely to a single organization. This can be hosted either on-premises within the organization's own data center or by a third-party provider who dedicates the infrastructure exclusively to that organization. The primary driver for choosing a private cloud is often the need for enhanced security, greater control over the environment, and the ability to meet specific

compliance or regulatory requirements that may not be fully addressed by a public cloud. For organizations dealing with highly sensitive intellectual property, classified data, or operating under strict data sovereignty laws, a private cloud provides a higher level of assurance. While it offers more control, it also comes with increased responsibility for managing and maintaining the infrastructure, similar to an on-premises deployment, though it can still leverage some of the managed services offered by cloud providers. This model strikes a balance between the benefits of cloud computing and the stringent control associated with on-premises solutions, albeit at a higher cost and complexity compared to the public cloud.

The
Hybrid Cloud Model represents a strategic combination of public and private cloud environments, often complemented by on-premises infrastructure. This model allows organizations to leverage the strengths of each deployment type, creating a flexible and optimized architecture for their digital twin initiatives. For example, an organization might store highly sensitive design data and core simulation engines in a private cloud or on-premises environment for maximum security and control. Simultaneously, it could utilize the public cloud for scalable data analytics, AI/ML processing, or for deploying customer-facing dashboards that require broad accessibility and elastic scalability. This approach enables organizations to maintain critical data and workloads within their controlled perimeters while benefiting from the cost-effectiveness and agility of the public cloud for less sensitive or more resource-intensive tasks. The hybrid model requires careful architectural planning and robust integration strategies to ensure seamless data flow and interoperability between the different environments. It provides the ultimate flexibility, allowing organizations to place workloads where they make the most sense from a cost, security, performance, and compliance perspective.

When adopting cloud-based deployment models for digital twins, several critical considerations come into play. One of the most significant is
vendor lock-in. Relying heavily on a single cloud provider's proprietary services can make it challenging and costly to migrate to a different provider or repatriate workloads back on-premises if business needs or pricing structures change. Organizations must carefully evaluate the use of open standards and portable technologies to mitigate this risk. Designing the digital twin architecture with

abstraction layers and avoiding deep integration with vendor-specific APIs can provide greater flexibility in the long run.

Data transfer costs, often referred to as egress charges, can also become a significant factor, especially for organizations that need to move large volumes of data out of the cloud. While ingesting data into the cloud is often free or inexpensive, retrieving it or transferring it to other environments can incur substantial costs. This is particularly relevant for digital twins that generate massive amounts of data that need to be analyzed, processed, or archived. Careful data management strategies, including data summarization, aggregation, and intelligent filtering at the source or edge, can help minimize unnecessary data transfers and associated costs.

Network dependency is an inherent aspect of cloud deployments. The performance and reliability of the digital twin are directly tied to the quality and availability of the internet connection. For mission-critical applications where downtime or latency can have severe consequences, organizations must ensure robust network connectivity and consider strategies like multi-cloud connectivity or dedicated network links to mitigate risks. Furthermore, the security of data in transit is paramount. Robust encryption protocols and secure network configurations are essential to protect sensitive data as it travels between the physical asset, edge devices, and the cloud.

The
efficiency and rapid deployment potential of cloud-based digital twins cannot be overstated. By leveraging pre-built services and managed infrastructure, organizations can significantly reduce the time it takes to develop, deploy, and iterate on their digital twin solutions. This accelerated innovation cycle allows businesses to quickly test hypotheses, gather market feedback, and adapt their digital twin strategies in response to evolving demands. For example, a company looking to create a digital twin for product design and prototyping can utilize cloud-based simulation tools and collaboration platforms to bring new products to market much faster than traditional methods would allow. The ability to provision and de-provision resources on demand also means that organizations can experiment with computationally intensive simulations or analytical models

without long-term commitments, fostering a culture of innovation and rapid experimentation.

The cloud ecosystem also fosters **collaboration and integration** more readily than siloed on-premises systems. Digital twins often require integration with a multitude of enterprise systems, such as ERP, CRM, PLM, and MES. Cloud platforms, with their APIs and open integration capabilities, make it easier to connect these disparate systems, creating a more holistic view of the business and its operations. This interconnectedness is vital for realizing the full value of a digital twin, enabling it to draw data from and influence various business processes.

In essence, cloud-based deployment models for digital twins offer a compelling blend of scalability, flexibility, advanced capabilities, and cost-effectiveness, enabling organizations to accelerate their digital transformation journeys. The choice between public, private, and hybrid cloud models depends on an organization's specific needs regarding security, control, compliance, and budget. By carefully considering factors such as vendor lock-in, data transfer costs, and network dependency, businesses can strategically leverage the power of the cloud to build and deploy sophisticated digital twins that drive significant business value and innovation. The continuous evolution of cloud services further promises to unlock even more sophisticated applications and capabilities for digital twins in the future, making it a cornerstone of modern digital twin strategies.

The evolution of digital twin deployment architectures extends beyond solely on-premises or cloud-centric models. As the demand for real-time responsiveness and localized intelligence grows, **edge computing** has emerged as a crucial component, fundamentally reshaping how digital twins are architected and operated. Edge computing, in essence, brings computational power and data processing capabilities closer to the source of data generation – the physical asset itself. This paradigm shift is particularly impactful for digital twin applications where latency, bandwidth constraints, or the need for autonomous decision-making are paramount.

Consider an industrial manufacturing setting where a complex robotic arm is undergoing intricate assembly processes. A digital twin of this arm is designed to monitor its performance, predict potential failures, and optimize its movements. If all the data generated by the arm's sensors – joint angles, motor temperatures, vibration patterns, force feedback – were to be streamed continuously to a central cloud for analysis, the sheer volume of data would be enormous. More critically, any decisions derived from this data, such as an immediate adjustment to prevent a collision or an emergency stop to avoid damage, would be subject to the round-trip latency between the edge and the cloud. This delay, even if measured in milliseconds, can be unacceptable for high-speed, precision operations.

Edge computing addresses this challenge by deploying intelligent processing units directly at or near the robotic arm. These edge devices, which can range from powerful industrial PCs to specialized edge servers or even embedded systems within the machinery, are capable of receiving raw sensor data, performing initial data processing, filtering, and even executing machine learning models for real-time anomaly detection or control adjustments. For instance, an edge device can analyze the vibration data from the robotic arm in real-time and, upon detecting a pattern indicative of an impending bearing failure, can immediately trigger a localized alert or even initiate a reduced operational mode, all without needing to send the raw vibration data to the cloud. This not only drastically reduces latency, ensuring immediate responses to critical events, but also significantly cuts down on the amount of data that needs to be transmitted, thereby conserving bandwidth and reducing associated costs. The digital twin, in this context, becomes a distributed entity, with a significant portion of its real-time processing and immediate decision-making capabilities residing at the edge.

The benefits of edge computing for digital twins are multifaceted.
Reduced Latency is arguably the most significant advantage, enabling near-instantaneous responses essential for critical applications like autonomous vehicles, real-time process control in manufacturing, remote surgery, or smart grid management. In these scenarios, even a fraction of a second delay can have catastrophic consequences. By processing data at the edge, the digital twin can react to changes in the physical environment with unparalleled speed, ensuring safety, efficiency, and operational continuity.

Bandwidth Optimization is another critical factor. Many IoT devices and industrial sensors generate a continuous stream of data. Transmitting all this raw data to the cloud can be prohibitively expensive and can strain network infrastructure, especially in remote locations or environments with limited connectivity. Edge devices can pre-process, aggregate, and filter this data, sending only the most relevant insights or summarized information to the cloud. This intelligent data handling significantly reduces the volume of data in transit, lowering communication costs and improving overall network efficiency. For example, a digital twin of a vast network of oil pipelines might have thousands of sensors monitoring pressure, flow, and temperature. An edge device located at a pumping station could analyze this data locally to detect anomalies indicative of leaks or blockages, only transmitting alerts and summarized historical data to the central cloud for broader analysis and long-term record-keeping.

Enhanced Reliability and Resilience are also key strengths of edge deployments. In environments with intermittent or unreliable network connectivity, relying solely on the cloud for all processing can lead to operational disruptions. By performing critical functions at the edge, the digital twin can continue to operate autonomously even when disconnected from the central cloud. This is crucial for applications in remote areas, on moving vehicles, or in industrial settings where network stability may be compromised. The digital twin can buffer data locally and synchronize with the cloud once connectivity is restored, ensuring data integrity and operational continuity.

Improved Security and Privacy can be achieved by processing sensitive data at the edge. Instead of transmitting raw, potentially sensitive data across networks to the cloud, edge devices can anonymize or aggregate data locally before it leaves the immediate vicinity of the physical asset. This reduces the attack surface and helps organizations comply with data privacy regulations and security policies that may restrict the movement of certain types of information. For instance, a digital twin monitoring patient health data from wearable devices might process preliminary vital signs analysis at the edge, only sending anonymized trend data to the cloud for further research or aggregate reporting, thereby protecting individual patient privacy.

While edge computing offers substantial advantages, it is rarely deployed in isolation. The true power for many digital twin applications lies in **hybrid architectures** that strategically combine the strengths of both edge and cloud computing. These hybrid models allow organizations to create a layered, optimized approach to digital twin deployment, balancing the need for real-time responsiveness with the advantages of centralized data storage, advanced analytics, and broad accessibility.

In a typical hybrid digital twin architecture, the edge layer is responsible for immediate, low-latency tasks. This includes data acquisition from sensors, real-time data filtering and aggregation, local anomaly detection, and immediate control actions. For example, an edge device connected to an industrial pump can monitor its operating parameters. If the pump's vibration levels exceed a predefined threshold, the edge device can immediately trigger a shutdown command to prevent catastrophic failure, all within milliseconds.

The cloud layer, on the other hand, serves as the central hub for more complex, resource-intensive, and broader-scoped operations. This includes long-term data storage, historical trend analysis, advanced machine learning model training, complex simulations, fleet-wide performance monitoring, and the hosting of user interfaces and dashboards for human interaction. In the case of the industrial pump, the edge device would send summarized data about its operational history, alerts generated, and any control actions taken to the cloud. The cloud can then analyze this data in conjunction with other pumps in the facility or across the globe, identifying common failure patterns, optimizing maintenance schedules for the entire fleet, and running predictive models to forecast future performance.

This synergy between edge and cloud provides a robust and flexible framework. The edge ensures that critical, time-sensitive operations are handled without delay, maximizing operational efficiency and safety. The cloud provides the infrastructure for deep insights, strategic decision-making, and the management of large-scale digital twin deployments. This separation of concerns allows for a more efficient allocation of resources, as computationally intensive tasks like training complex AI models are offloaded to the powerful, scalable resources of the cloud, while time-critical processing remains close to the source.

The design of hybrid architectures requires careful consideration of several factors to ensure seamless operation and maximum benefit.
Data synchronization and consistency are paramount. Mechanisms must be in place to ensure that data flows correctly between the edge and the cloud, and that both environments have access to consistent and up-to-date information. This might involve sophisticated data replication strategies, conflict resolution protocols, and robust data governance policies.

Interoperability and Standardization are also critical. The edge devices and cloud platforms need to communicate effectively. This often necessitates the use of standardized communication protocols (like MQTT, CoAP) and data formats. Organizations may leverage specialized edge platforms that are designed to integrate seamlessly with specific cloud providers, or they might opt for more open, vendor-agnostic solutions that offer greater flexibility.

Management and Orchestration of a distributed edge-cloud infrastructure present unique challenges. Deploying, updating, and monitoring software on numerous edge devices can be complex. Cloud-based management platforms are essential for remotely provisioning devices, deploying new applications, collecting telemetry data from edge nodes, and troubleshooting issues. Containerization technologies like Docker and orchestration tools like Kubernetes are increasingly being adapted and deployed at the edge to simplify these management tasks, enabling consistent application deployment across diverse edge environments.

Security must be addressed at all layers of the hybrid architecture. This includes securing the edge devices themselves, protecting data in transit between the edge and the cloud, and ensuring the security of the cloud environment. End-to-end encryption, robust authentication mechanisms, and regular security audits are essential components of a secure hybrid digital twin deployment.

Consider a smart city application where digital twins are used to manage traffic flow. Edge devices deployed at traffic intersections can monitor real-time traffic conditions, analyze vehicle presence, and adjust traffic light timings dynamically to optimize flow and reduce congestion. This local processing ensures immediate response to changing traffic patterns. Simultaneously, the data collected from all intersections is streamed to a central cloud platform. Here, more advanced analytics can be performed to understand long-term traffic trends, predict future congestion hotspots, plan for infrastructure improvements, and integrate with public transportation systems. The cloud also hosts the city's traffic management dashboard, providing a comprehensive overview to human operators. This hybrid approach leverages the edge for real-time control and the cloud for strategic planning and overarching management, creating a more efficient and responsive urban environment.

Another compelling example can be found in the realm of digital twins for remote asset monitoring in the energy sector, such as offshore oil rigs or wind farms. These environments often have limited and expensive satellite connectivity. Edge devices deployed on the rig or turbine can perform local data acquisition, run diagnostics, and identify critical anomalies requiring immediate attention, such as a malfunctioning sensor or a developing structural issue. These edge systems can autonomously initiate safety protocols or gather detailed data for local analysis. Only critical alerts and summarized performance metrics are then transmitted to a central cloud operations center for global fleet management, long-term predictive maintenance planning, and compliance reporting. This hybrid model ensures that essential operations can continue even with intermittent connectivity, while still allowing for comprehensive oversight and strategic decision-making from a centralized location.

The integration of edge and cloud for digital twins also enables new levels of **cost optimization**. By processing and analyzing data at the edge, organizations can reduce the volume of data sent to the cloud, thereby minimizing data transmission costs. Furthermore, by offloading computationally intensive tasks to the cloud, which can be scaled on demand, organizations avoid the need for expensive, over-provisioned on-premises hardware for peak loads. The ability to use the cloud for burst computing and the edge for continuous, low-power operations offers a financially efficient model.

In conclusion, edge computing, when integrated into hybrid architectures, provides a powerful and flexible foundation for deploying digital twins. This approach addresses the limitations of purely cloud-based or on-premises solutions by leveraging the strengths of distributed intelligence. By placing computational power closer to the physical asset, organizations can achieve low latency, optimize bandwidth usage, enhance reliability, and improve security. The cloud, in turn, provides the scalability, advanced analytics, and centralized management capabilities necessary for comprehensive digital twin operations. This synergistic relationship between edge and cloud is not merely an architectural option but an increasingly essential strategy for realizing the full potential of digital twins across a wide spectrum of industries, enabling them to be more responsive, efficient, and intelligent than ever before. The continued advancement in edge hardware, connectivity technologies, and cloud-native edge management solutions will further solidify the importance of these hybrid deployments in the future of digital twin technology.

The selection of the optimal deployment architecture for a digital twin is a pivotal decision, directly impacting its efficacy, cost-efficiency, and scalability. This decision is not a one-size-fits-all proposition; rather, it hinges on a nuanced understanding of specific use case requirements, business objectives, and inherent technical and operational constraints. While on-premises, cloud, and edge computing each offer distinct advantages, the true power often lies in judiciously combining these paradigms to create a hybrid solution that best addresses the multifaceted demands of a digital twin. Therefore, a systematic approach is necessary to navigate the trade-offs and arrive at the most suitable architectural configuration.

At the core of this selection process lies the critical evaluation of **cost considerations**. Each architectural model presents a different financial profile. On-premises deployments, while offering maximum control over hardware and infrastructure, typically involve significant upfront capital expenditures for hardware acquisition, installation, and ongoing maintenance.

This includes servers, networking equipment, storage solutions, and the dedicated IT personnel required to manage them. The total cost of ownership can be substantial, particularly for organizations that may not have the expertise or resources to manage such complex infrastructure efficiently. Conversely, cloud-based solutions often operate on a pay-as-you-go or subscription model, transforming capital expenditure into operational expenditure. This elasticity allows organizations to scale their resources up or down based on demand, potentially leading to cost savings for fluctuating workloads. However, for consistently high-demand applications, the cumulative operational costs of cloud services can eventually surpass the initial investment of an on-premises setup. Edge computing introduces yet another cost dimension. While it can reduce data transmission costs by processing data locally, it necessitates investment in edge hardware, which, depending on the processing power and ruggedization required, can range from modest embedded devices to sophisticated industrial servers. The distribution of these devices across numerous locations can also incur costs related to deployment, maintenance, and network connectivity for aggregation of data at a central point. Therefore, a thorough total cost of ownership (TCO) analysis, encompassing initial investment, operational expenses, maintenance, and potential cost savings through reduced bandwidth or improved efficiency, is crucial for each architectural option. For instance, a small manufacturing plant with a limited number of critical machines might find an on-premises solution for its digital twin cost-effective due to predictable workloads and existing IT infrastructure. In contrast, a global logistics company managing a vast fleet of vehicles would likely benefit from the scalability and reduced data transmission costs of a cloud-centric or hybrid edge-cloud model.

Scalability is another paramount factor. The ability of the digital twin architecture to grow and adapt to increasing data volumes, more complex models, and a larger number of connected physical assets is essential for long-term viability. Cloud platforms excel in this regard, offering virtually limitless scalability on demand. Resources can be provisioned and de-provisioned within minutes, allowing digital twin applications to effortlessly handle surges in data or computational needs. This elasticity is particularly advantageous for emerging applications or those with unpredictable growth trajectories. On-premises solutions, while offering control, typically have a fixed capacity. Scaling up requires significant hardware upgrades and lengthy procurement cycles, making them less adaptable to rapid growth. Organizations adopting on-premises architectures must engage in careful capacity planning, often leading to over-provisioning to accommodate future needs, which can be financially inefficient. Edge computing, in its purest form, can be challenging to scale across a vast geographical area or a highly distributed set of assets. While individual edge nodes are designed for specific tasks, managing and scaling the entire edge network, including deployment, updates, and data aggregation, presents significant logistical hurdles. However, when combined with a cloud platform for management and orchestration, the scalability of the edge deployment can be significantly enhanced. A hybrid approach often provides the best of both worlds: the edge handles localized scalability for immediate processing, while the cloud manages the overarching scalability of data storage, advanced analytics, and user access for the entire digital twin ecosystem. Consider a digital twin designed for smart city applications. The edge layer at individual intersections needs to scale to handle varying traffic loads, but the overall system, including city-wide traffic pattern analysis and simulation, requires the global scalability offered by the cloud.

Security requirements are non-negotiable and vary significantly depending on the nature of the physical asset and the data it generates. On-premises deployments offer the highest level of control over the physical security of hardware and the logical security of the network. Organizations can implement stringent access controls, network segmentation, and security protocols tailored to their specific risk tolerance. This is often preferred for highly sensitive data or critical infrastructure where even a minor breach could have severe consequences. Cloud providers offer robust security measures, often exceeding what individual organizations can achieve on their own due to their specialized expertise and resources. However, reliance on a third-party provider introduces a shared responsibility model, where organizations must understand and configure security settings correctly to protect their data. Data in transit to and from the cloud, as well as data at rest, must be adequately secured through encryption and access management. Edge computing can offer security advantages by keeping sensitive data local, reducing the attack surface by minimizing data transmission. However, securing a distributed network of edge devices, often deployed in physically accessible or remote locations, presents unique challenges. Each edge device becomes a potential entry point, requiring strong authentication, encryption, and regular security patching. A hybrid architecture demands a comprehensive, layered security strategy that addresses security at the edge, during data transmission (e.g., using secure protocols like TLS/SSL), and within the cloud environment. Zero-trust principles are often applied, ensuring that no entity, whether inside or outside the network perimeter, is implicitly trusted. For example, a digital twin of a medical device used in patient care would likely necessitate a highly secure, potentially on-premises or private cloud solution with strict access controls, whereas a digital twin for monitoring public park usage might be more amenable to a cloud-based solution with appropriate data anonymization and access controls.

Latency tolerance is a defining factor that strongly influences the choice between edge, cloud, and hybrid architectures. For applications that require real-time or near-real-time responses, such as autonomous vehicles, industrial robotics, or critical control systems, latency is a critical performance metric. Sending data to the cloud for processing and receiving instructions back can introduce unacceptable delays. In such scenarios, edge computing is indispensable. By performing computations and decision-making at or near the physical asset, latency can be reduced to milliseconds or even microseconds. On-premises deployments can also offer low latency if the processing infrastructure is located within the same facility as the physical asset, but they lack the flexibility and scalability of edge solutions. Cloud architectures, while powerful for complex analytics and long-term storage, are inherently susceptible to network latency, making them less suitable for time-critical operations on their own. Hybrid architectures are often the most pragmatic solution for applications with mixed latency requirements. The edge layer handles immediate, high-frequency data processing and time-sensitive control loops, while the cloud is used for less time-critical tasks like historical analysis, model training, and reporting. For example, a digital twin of a high-frequency trading platform would prioritize edge processing for immediate trade execution decisions, while a digital twin for analyzing long-term market trends could be cloud-based.

The
existing IT infrastructure of an organization plays a significant role in shaping architectural decisions. Companies with substantial investments in on-premises data centers and a skilled IT workforce may find it more economical and

manageable to extend their existing infrastructure for digital twin deployments. Leveraging existing servers, networking, and data management tools can reduce initial setup costs and streamline integration. Cloud-native organizations, on the other hand, will naturally lean towards cloud-based solutions, benefiting from their established cloud expertise and the seamless integration with their existing cloud services. For organizations with a fragmented IT landscape, or those looking to modernize, a hybrid approach might offer a pathway to consolidate and optimize their infrastructure. The transition to cloud or edge can also be phased, allowing organizations to gradually adopt new technologies without a complete overhaul. The presence of robust internal networking capabilities or existing IoT platforms can also influence the decision. For instance, a manufacturing company with a well-established industrial network might prefer an edge deployment that integrates directly with its existing operational technology (OT) systems, while a software company with a strong cloud development team might opt for a cloud-native digital twin solution.

Regulatory compliance and data sovereignty are increasingly important considerations, especially for industries dealing with sensitive personal, financial, or national security data. Different regions and industries have specific regulations (e.g., GDPR, HIPAA, PCI DSS) that dictate how data must be stored, processed, and protected. On-premises deployments offer the highest degree of control over data location and management, making it easier to ensure compliance with stringent data sovereignty requirements. Organizations can guarantee that data remains within specific geographical boundaries. Cloud providers are increasingly offering solutions to address these concerns, such as data residency options and compliance certifications. However, organizations must still carefully evaluate the provider's compliance posture and ensure their configurations meet regulatory mandates. Edge computing can also aid in compliance by processing sensitive data locally and only transmitting anonymized or aggregated data to the cloud. This approach can be particularly beneficial when dealing with data that cannot legally or practically leave a specific facility or region. A hybrid architecture can be designed to segregate sensitive data at the edge or in a dedicated private cloud environment, while less sensitive data is processed and stored in a public cloud. For example, a digital twin used in the healthcare sector in Europe would need to comply with GDPR, potentially requiring patient data to be processed and stored within the EU, which could be achieved with a combination of on-premises or EU-based cloud solutions, augmented by edge processing for immediate patient monitoring.

Furthermore, the **complexity of the digital twin application** itself dictates architectural choices. A simple digital twin that primarily serves as a visualization tool for static data might be adequately served by a cloud-based or even a web-based on-premises solution. However, as the digital twin evolves to incorporate complex simulations, predictive analytics, machine learning models, and real-time control loops, the architectural demands increase. Applications requiring sophisticated simulations of complex physical phenomena, such as fluid dynamics or structural analysis, will necessitate significant computational resources, often best provided by powerful cloud platforms or high-performance computing (HPC) clusters. Digital twins that rely heavily on AI and machine learning for predictive maintenance or anomaly detection may benefit from cloud platforms that offer managed ML services and the ability to train large models on vast datasets. For real-time operational decision-making and control, edge computing becomes indispensable. A hybrid architecture allows for this modularity, enabling different components of the digital twin to leverage the most appropriate compute environment. For example, the simulation engine might run on a cloud HPC instance, while real-time sensor data analysis and control logic are executed on edge devices.

The **availability and reliability of network connectivity** are crucial differentiating factors. In environments with highly reliable, high-bandwidth connectivity (e.g., modern corporate offices, well-developed urban areas), cloud-based solutions are often a viable and attractive option. However, for applications deployed in remote locations, harsh industrial environments, or on mobile assets (e.g., ships, aircraft, remote sensing stations) where network connectivity is intermittent, unreliable, or expensive, edge computing becomes essential for operational continuity. On-premises solutions offer independence from external network connectivity for their core operations, but data synchronization and remote access will still depend on network availability. Hybrid architectures can be designed to be resilient to network disruptions. Edge devices can operate autonomously during periods of disconnection, buffering data and performing critical functions. Once connectivity is restored, they can synchronize with the cloud, ensuring data consistency and enabling centralized oversight. For instance, a digital twin of a wind turbine on a remote offshore platform would heavily rely on edge processing due to the intermittent and costly nature of satellite connectivity, with the cloud used for aggregated performance data and long-term maintenance planning.

Finally, the **organizational maturity and expertise** in managing different IT paradigms must be considered. Deploying and managing large-scale cloud infrastructures requires specific skill sets in areas like cloud architecture, DevOps, and cloud security. Similarly, managing a distributed network of edge devices requires expertise in embedded systems, IoT device management, and edge security. Organizations with existing strong capabilities in traditional IT infrastructure management might find on-premises deployments more straightforward to implement and maintain. A phased adoption strategy, perhaps starting with a pilot project in the cloud or with a limited edge deployment, can allow organizations to build the necessary expertise and confidence before committing to a full-scale rollout. The availability of managed services from cloud providers or specialized vendors can also mitigate some of the internal expertise gaps, enabling organizations to focus on the core digital twin application rather than the underlying infrastructure management. Ultimately, the choice of architecture must align with the organization's strategic goals, technical capabilities, and risk appetite, ensuring that the digital twin serves as a catalyst for innovation and operational excellence, rather than a source of technical debt or operational burden.

Chapter 10: Cybersecurity for Digital Twins

The very essence of a digital twin—its ability to create a dynamic, interconnected bridge between the physical and digital realms—inherently expands and amplifies the threat landscape. This unique characteristic, while central to the power and utility of digital twins, simultaneously introduces novel attack vectors that can have profound and direct consequences on physical operations. The intricate web of interconnected sensors collecting real-time data, the communication networks transmitting this information, the sophisticated analytical models processing it, and the decision-making systems that act upon it, collectively form a complex ecosystem. Within this ecosystem, a vulnerability in one seemingly isolated component can cascade, potentially compromising the integrity and functionality of the entire digital twin system and, by extension, its physical counterpart. This necessitates a paradigm shift in security thinking, moving beyond traditional IT security to embrace a holistic, end-to-end security strategy that accounts for the unique challenges posed by this cyber-physical convergence.

Consider the ingress point for data into the digital twin: the sensor network. These physical devices, often deployed in diverse and sometimes unsecured environments, are the initial gatekeepers of information. A compromised sensor, whether through physical tampering, firmware exploitation, or network infiltration, can introduce malicious or corrupted data into the digital twin. This "poisoned" data can then propagate through the system, leading to flawed analyses, incorrect predictions, and ultimately, dangerous operational decisions. For instance, in an industrial setting, a manipulated temperature sensor reading could trigger an automated shutdown of a critical process, leading to significant production losses, or worse, if the false reading indicates safety, it could lead to equipment damage or personnel injury. The sheer number and distribution of these sensors in large-scale digital twin deployments, such as those in smart cities or expansive manufacturing facilities, amplify the challenge of securing each individual data source. Each sensor, each gateway device, represents a potential entry point for an attacker.

The networks that connect these sensors to processing platforms, and subsequently connect the digital twin to other systems, also become critical points of vulnerability. Whether these are wired industrial networks (like SCADA or industrial Ethernet), wireless communication channels (Wi-Fi, cellular, LoRaWAN), or cloud-based communication protocols, they are all susceptible to interception, manipulation, or denial-of-service attacks. An attacker who gains access to the communication network could eavesdrop on sensitive operational data, inject false commands, or disrupt the flow of information, effectively blinding or paralyzing the digital twin. For example, an attacker could intercept commands intended for a robotic arm in a manufacturing plant, causing it to deviate from its programmed path and potentially collide with other machinery or workers. The increasing reliance on cloud and edge computing architectures further complicates network security. Data must traverse multiple network segments, often involving public internet connections, thereby increasing the attack surface. Secure data transmission protocols, robust network segmentation, and continuous monitoring are therefore not just desirable but absolutely essential.

The core of the digital twin—the sophisticated models and analytical engines—presents its own set of security challenges. These models, whether built using machine learning, simulation techniques, or statistical algorithms, are often trained on vast datasets. If these datasets are compromised or if the training process itself is infiltrated, attackers could subtly manipulate the model's behavior without immediate detection. This could lead to gradual degradation of performance, biased outputs, or the introduction of backdoors that allow attackers to control the twin's responses. Imagine a digital twin of an aircraft engine. If the predictive maintenance model is subtly poisoned, it might fail to flag a critical component anomaly, leading to an in-flight failure that could have catastrophic consequences. Furthermore, the algorithms themselves could be targets of intellectual property theft or reverse engineering, revealing proprietary operational insights or design flaws. The complexity of these models also makes them difficult to audit thoroughly for security vulnerabilities.

The decision-making systems that interpret the digital twin's outputs and translate them into actions for the physical world represent a particularly high-stakes target. These systems are often automated, designed to respond rapidly to changing conditions. If an attacker can compromise these systems, they can directly influence the physical world through the digital twin. This could range from disrupting industrial processes, manipulating energy grids, compromising autonomous vehicle navigation, or even impacting critical infrastructure like water treatment plants or traffic control systems. The consequences of such an attack can be immediate, widespread, and devastating. For example, a successful intrusion into the decision-making layer of a smart grid's digital twin could lead to widespread power outages, grid instability, or even cascading failures across interconnected systems. The automation inherent in these systems means that a compromised decision-making unit can act with speed and scale, leaving little time for human intervention.

Moreover, the very concept of the digital twin as a virtual replica of a physical asset or system can itself be exploited. Attackers might use the digital twin as a testing ground for their exploits, refining their techniques in the virtual environment before launching an attack on the actual physical asset. The insights gained from observing the digital twin's behavior under various simulated conditions could also be used to identify optimal times or methods for attacking the physical system. This makes the digital twin a valuable reconnaissance tool for malicious actors. Conversely, a compromised digital twin could be used to launch attacks on other interconnected systems. For example, if a digital twin of a manufacturing plant is compromised, it could be used to launch phishing attacks against its employees or to pivot to other systems within the company's network.

The interconnectedness fostered by digital twins also means that a breach in one domain can have ripple effects across others. A cybersecurity incident impacting the operational technology (OT) network could spill over into the information technology (IT) network, and vice versa. A vulnerability in the cloud infrastructure supporting the digital twin could expose sensitive data from the physical asset, and a physical attack on a sensor could lead to a digital intrusion. This blurring of boundaries between IT and OT, and between the physical and digital, demands a unified security approach. Security strategies must extend from the physical hardware of sensors and actuators to the network infrastructure, the cloud platforms, the analytical models, and the human interfaces that interact with the digital twin. Failure to address any one of these layers can undermine the security of the entire system.

The expansion of the threat landscape is also driven by the increasing complexity and scale of digital twin deployments. As digital twins become more pervasive, encompassing entire factories, cities, or even global supply chains, the sheer number of interconnected components and the volume of data involved create a larger and more intricate attack surface. Managing the security of thousands or millions of distributed sensors, edge devices, and cloud-based services becomes a monumental task. The potential for zero-day exploits, supply chain attacks targeting third-party software components, and insider threats are all amplified in these large-scale environments. Furthermore, the long lifecycle of many physical assets, such as industrial machinery or infrastructure, means that digital twins may need to remain secure and operational for decades, posing ongoing challenges for patch management, vulnerability assessment, and the adoption of evolving security standards.

The integration of artificial intelligence (AI) and machine learning (ML) within digital twins, while offering immense analytical power, also introduces new security considerations. Adversarial attacks on ML models, where subtle perturbations to input data can cause misclassifications or erroneous predictions, are a growing concern. For example, an attacker might slightly alter sensor readings to fool an AI-powered anomaly detection system into ignoring a critical failure. The explainability and interpretability of complex AI models can also be a security challenge; if the decision-making process is opaque, it becomes harder to detect malicious manipulation. Ensuring the integrity of training data and the robustness of AI algorithms against sophisticated adversarial techniques is paramount.

Finally, the human element remains a critical factor in the amplified threat landscape. Social engineering attacks, phishing, and insider threats can exploit human vulnerabilities to gain access to digital twin systems or sensitive data. The convenience of remote access and distributed management, while beneficial for operational efficiency, can also increase the risk of unauthorized access if authentication and authorization mechanisms are not sufficiently robust. Training personnel on cybersecurity best practices, implementing strong access controls, and fostering a security-aware culture are therefore indispensable components of any comprehensive digital twin security strategy. The amplification of the threat landscape by digital twins is not merely a theoretical concern; it is a tangible reality that demands proactive, continuous, and adaptive security measures to protect the integrity of both the digital and physical worlds.

The digital twin ecosystem, while a marvel of interconnectedness and data-driven insight, presents a complex tapestry of potential vulnerabilities that can be exploited by malicious actors. These weaknesses span the entire lifecycle of the digital twin, from the initial data capture to the final user interaction, and often intersect with traditional IT and operational technology (OT) security challenges, but with amplified consequences due to the direct linkage to the physical world.

At the very foundation of any digital twin lies the sensor and data acquisition layer. These devices, often deployed in environments that are physically exposed or lack robust network security, are prime targets. Vulnerabilities here can range from physical tampering, where an attacker might directly manipulate a sensor's readings, to firmware exploits, where outdated or poorly secured firmware allows for remote compromise. Consider a scenario in a smart manufacturing plant where sensors on a critical piece of machinery are subtly altered to report normal operating temperatures even when overheating is imminent. This deception, feeding false positive data into the digital twin, could lead to a catastrophic equipment failure before any alarms are triggered in the digital realm. Networked sensors, especially those communicating wirelessly, are also susceptible to man-in-the-middle attacks, where data streams can be intercepted and altered en route to the central processing unit. The sheer volume of sensors in large-scale digital twins, such as those used in smart cities or extensive logistical networks, significantly broadens this attack surface, making comprehensive monitoring and patching a Herculean task. Furthermore, the sourcing of sensors themselves can introduce supply chain vulnerabilities, where compromised components might be embedded during manufacturing, acting as dormant backdoors ready to be activated.

The communication networks that ferry data between sensors, edge devices, cloud platforms, and the digital twin core are equally critical choke points. Whether these are wired industrial networks like Modbus or Ethernet/IP, or wireless protocols such as Wi-Fi, LoRaWAN, or 5G, they can be subject to various forms of attack. Interception of data is a significant threat, allowing adversaries to glean sensitive operational details, proprietary information, or even user credentials. Data manipulation is an even more pernicious threat, where attackers can inject false commands or corrupt data packets, leading to incorrect interpretations by the digital twin. A denial-of-service (DoS) attack on these networks can effectively blind the digital twin, preventing it from receiving real-time updates and rendering its predictive or analytical capabilities useless. In a critical infrastructure context, such as a digital twin of a power grid, a network DoS attack could cripple the grid's ability to respond to demand fluctuations, leading to widespread outages. The increasing reliance on hybrid network architectures, blending on-premises infrastructure with cloud connectivity and edge computing, introduces further complexity and potential vulnerabilities due to the multiple points of transit and the diverse security postures of each segment. Secure protocols like TLS/SSL are essential, but their implementation must be robust, and the underlying network infrastructure must be adequately segmented and protected.

Data storage and management also present significant vulnerabilities within the digital twin ecosystem. The massive datasets generated and processed by digital twins require secure storage solutions, whether in on-premises data centers, private clouds, or public cloud environments. Threats here include unauthorized access, data leakage, and data tampering. A breach of the data repository could expose not only operational data but also historical performance records, maintenance logs, and even sensitive intellectual property embedded within the twin's configuration. If the historical data used for training AI models is compromised, the resulting model could be fundamentally flawed or biased, leading to a cascade of incorrect analyses. Ransomware attacks targeting data storage can also paralyze operations by encrypting critical datasets, rendering the digital twin inoperable until a ransom is paid or a backup is restored. Ensuring data integrity through robust hashing, encryption at rest and in transit, and strict access controls is paramount. For highly sensitive twins, techniques like homomorphic encryption, which allows computation on encrypted data without decryption, could offer an advanced layer of protection, though its computational overhead remains a significant consideration.

The digital twin models themselves, especially those leveraging artificial intelligence and machine learning, are increasingly becoming targets. Adversarial attacks on AI/ML models are a growing concern. These attacks involve subtly manipulating input data in ways that are imperceptible to humans but cause the model to make incorrect predictions or classifications. For instance, a small, carefully crafted perturbation to sensor data fed into an AI-powered anomaly detection system might cause it to miss a critical equipment malfunction. This could be as simple as adding a few pixels of noise to an image captured by a visual inspection system, leading it to misclassify a defect. Model inversion attacks, where an attacker attempts to reconstruct sensitive training data from the model itself, can also be a threat, potentially revealing proprietary information or customer data. Furthermore, the integrity of the model training process is crucial. If the training data itself is poisoned or if the training environment is compromised, the resulting model will be inherently insecure. Ensuring the robustness, interpretability, and fairness of AI/ML models within digital twins requires dedicated research and development in areas like adversarial training, differential privacy, and explainable AI (XAI).

The underlying platforms and infrastructure that host and manage the digital twin also contain inherent vulnerabilities. This includes the operating systems, middleware, containerization technologies (like Docker or Kubernetes), and cloud services. Exploiting vulnerabilities in these components can grant attackers broad access and control over the entire digital twin instance. Unpatched software, misconfigured cloud services (e.g., overly permissive access controls on cloud storage buckets), and insecure container images can all serve as entry points. The management of these platforms in large, distributed digital twin deployments is exceptionally challenging, often involving a complex interplay of IT and OT teams with different security priorities and skill sets. The adoption of Infrastructure as Code (IaC) can help standardize deployments and security configurations, but the IaC scripts themselves must be securely managed and reviewed. Furthermore, the convergence of IT and OT security has led to a greater emphasis on specialized platforms designed for industrial environments, but these still require rigorous security hardening and continuous monitoring.

User interfaces and access control mechanisms are often the weakest link when it comes to insider threats or social engineering attacks. The human element is consistently targeted. Weak authentication methods, lack of multi-factor authentication (MFA), and the reuse of passwords can all compromise access to digital twin management consoles or data visualization dashboards. If an attacker gains access through compromised user credentials, they can potentially manipulate the digital twin, extract sensitive data, or disrupt operations. Insider threats, whether malicious or accidental, also pose a significant risk. An disgruntled employee with legitimate access could intentionally cause harm, or an unwary employee could inadvertently download malware or fall victim to a phishing scam, compromising their account and, by extension, the digital twin. Implementing strong role-based access control (RBAC), regular security awareness training for all users, and robust logging and auditing of all user activities are crucial to mitigate these risks. The design of the user interface itself can also be a factor; overly complex or poorly designed interfaces can lead to user error, which can indirectly impact the security and integrity of the digital twin. For example, a user might accidentally misconfigure a critical parameter on a dashboard, leading to unexpected system behavior.

The interconnected nature of digital twins means that vulnerabilities in one part of the ecosystem can easily propagate to others. A compromise in a sensor network could lead to the corruption of data, which then feeds into flawed AI models, ultimately resulting in incorrect commands being sent to the physical asset via the control systems. Similarly, a security flaw in the cloud platform hosting the digital twin could expose sensitive data that, if analyzed by an adversary, could reveal critical weaknesses in the physical system it represents. This holistic view of vulnerabilities is essential. For instance, a digital twin used for managing a fleet of autonomous vehicles needs secure sensors for navigation and environmental perception, robust communication channels for receiving commands and sending telemetry, secure storage for logs and operational data, reliable AI models for path planning and decision-making, secure underlying platforms for the vehicle's control systems, and secure interfaces for fleet management. A vulnerability in any one of these areas can have direct and potentially catastrophic consequences for the physical operation of the vehicles.

The lifecycle of digital twins, often mirroring the long operational life of the physical assets they represent, introduces challenges related to obsolescence and patch management. Physical assets like industrial machinery or infrastructure may remain in service for decades. During this time, the software components of their digital twins will require continuous updates to address emerging vulnerabilities. Maintaining security over such extended periods, especially in environments where physical access for maintenance is difficult or expensive, poses a significant challenge. The potential for supply chain attacks, where vulnerabilities are introduced through third-party software components or hardware suppliers, further complicates this. Organizations must have robust vendor risk management programs and perform thorough due diligence on all suppliers and software components integrated into their digital twin ecosystems.

Finally, the very act of creating and operating a digital twin can inadvertently expose new attack surfaces that did not exist for the standalone physical asset. The need for connectivity, data integration, and remote access—all hallmarks of digital twins—inherently expands the digital footprint and the opportunities for malicious actors to probe for weaknesses. Without a comprehensive and proactive security strategy that accounts for every facet of the digital twin ecosystem, the immense benefits offered by this transformative technology can be overshadowed by significant and potentially devastating risks.

Securing data within the digital twin ecosystem is not merely a technical requirement; it is a foundational pillar for trust, reliability, and operational continuity. The sheer volume, sensitivity, and criticality of the data managed by digital twins necessitate a multi-layered approach to protection, addressing both data in transit and data at rest. Failure to implement robust measures in these areas can lead to a cascade of negative outcomes, from reputational damage and financial loss to compromised physical safety and widespread operational disruptions.

Data in transit refers to the information that travels across networks between various components of the digital twin system. This includes data flowing from sensors to edge devices, from edge devices to cloud platforms, between different microservices within the digital twin core, and from the digital twin to user interfaces or other interconnected systems. Given the dynamic nature of these data flows, they are particularly vulnerable to interception, manipulation, or eavesdropping. The primary defense against these threats is the use of strong encryption and secure communication protocols. Transport Layer Security (TLS), the successor to Secure Sockets Layer (SSL), is the de facto standard for encrypting data in transit over networks. TLS provides authentication, integrity, and confidentiality for data exchanged between two applications, such as a sensor gateway and a cloud ingestion service. Implementing TLS requires proper certificate management, ensuring that certificates are issued by trusted Certificate Authorities (CAs), are not expired, and are correctly installed on both the client and server ends of the communication. For industrial environments where legacy systems might be present, or where network performance is a critical concern, solutions like IPsec (Internet Protocol Security) can offer robust network-layer encryption. However, the overhead associated with IPsec can sometimes impact latency, making it less suitable for extremely time-sensitive applications.

Beyond general-purpose encryption, digital twins often leverage specialized protocols for industrial communication. For instance, protocols like MQTT (Message Queuing Telemetry Transport) and AMQP (Advanced Message Queuing Protocol) are commonly used for machine-to-machine (M2M) and Internet of Things (IoT) communications. Ensuring the security of these protocols is paramount. MQTT, for example, can be secured using TLS, creating MQTTS. Similarly, AMQP can be secured via TLS. When dealing with highly sensitive operational data, it is also crucial to consider the authentication mechanisms within these protocols. Using robust authentication methods, such as certificate-based authentication or OAuth 2.0 tokens, helps ensure that only authorized devices and applications can connect and exchange data. The principle of least privilege should be applied to these connections; devices and services should only be granted the minimum permissions necessary to perform their intended functions.

Network segmentation is another critical strategy for securing data in transit. By dividing the network into smaller, isolated zones, the impact of a security breach can be contained. For example, sensors and edge devices that collect raw data from the physical environment can be placed in a separate network segment from the core digital twin processing engines or the enterprise IT network. This isolation limits the lateral movement of attackers. If a sensor network is compromised, the attacker would have a much harder time reaching more critical systems. Firewalls and intrusion detection/prevention systems (IDPS) play a vital role in enforcing these segmentation policies and monitoring traffic between segments for suspicious activity. Virtual Private Networks (VPNs) can also be employed to create secure, encrypted tunnels for remote access or for connecting disparate parts of a distributed digital twin infrastructure, especially when traversing public or untrusted networks.

The concept of "defense in depth" is particularly relevant here. This means applying multiple layers of security controls. Even if one layer is breached, others are in place to prevent unauthorized access or data exfiltration. For data in transit, this might involve using TLS for end-to-end encryption between the sensor and the cloud, combined with network segmentation at the edge and within the data center, and authenticated API gateways that act as gatekeepers for data ingress and egress. Regular security audits and penetration testing of the communication channels can help identify and address vulnerabilities before they can be exploited.

Data at rest, conversely, refers to data that is stored over longer periods, such as in databases, data lakes, file systems, or cloud storage. This can include historical operational data, sensor readings, maintenance logs, simulation results, configuration parameters, and even the digital twin models themselves. Protecting data at rest is crucial because compromised stored data can be used for detailed analysis by adversaries, enabling them to understand system weaknesses, extract intellectual property, or even impersonate legitimate entities. The primary security measures for data at rest are encryption and robust access control.

Encryption at rest involves encrypting the data before it is written to storage. This can be achieved at various levels:

Full Disk Encryption (FDE): Encrypts the entire storage device. If the physical hardware is stolen, the data remains inaccessible without the decryption key. This is a baseline security measure for servers and storage arrays.
File-Level Encryption: Encrypts individual files or directories. This offers more granular control and can be applied to specific sensitive datasets.
Database Encryption: Many database systems offer built-in encryption features, such as Transparent Data Encryption (TDE), which encrypts the database files on disk without requiring application changes. This is highly effective for protecting sensitive data stored within the database.
Application-Level Encryption: The application layer itself encrypts data before sending it to the database. This provides the highest level of control but requires significant development effort and careful key management.

The effective management of encryption keys is paramount for encryption at rest. If encryption keys are lost or compromised, the data becomes inaccessible or vulnerable. Key management systems (KMS) are essential for securely generating, storing, distributing, rotating, and revoking encryption keys. For cloud-based digital twins, cloud providers offer managed KMS services that simplify key management but still require careful configuration and access control.

Access control is equally critical for data at rest. This involves defining and enforcing policies that dictate who or what can access specific data. Role-Based Access Control (RBAC) is a widely adopted model, where permissions are assigned to roles, and users are assigned to roles based on their job functions. This ensures that users only have access to the data and functionalities necessary for their tasks, adhering to the principle of least privilege. For digital twins, this means that, for example, a maintenance technician might have access to historical performance data and maintenance logs, while a simulation engineer might have access to model parameters and simulation outputs, and a plant operator might have access to real-time operational data.

Fine-grained access control policies, often managed through attribute-based access control (ABAC) or policy-based access control (PBAC), can provide even more granular control, taking into account not just the user's role but also the context of the access request, such as the time of day, the location of the access, or the sensitivity level of the data being accessed. Auditing and logging of all access attempts, both successful and failed, are indispensable. These logs provide a trail of who accessed what data, when, and from where, which is vital for security monitoring, incident response, and forensic investigations.

Data masking and tokenization are additional techniques that can enhance data protection, particularly when data is being used for testing, development, or analytics by parties who do not require access to the raw sensitive information. Data masking involves replacing sensitive data with fictitious but realistic-looking data. Tokenization replaces sensitive data with a unique identifier (token) that has no intrinsic value or meaning. The original sensitive data is stored securely in a separate vault, and the token is used in less secure environments.

For digital twins dealing with highly sensitive operational technology (OT) data, such as control system parameters or proprietary manufacturing processes, applying these security measures becomes even more critical. A compromise of stored OT data could reveal vulnerabilities in the physical system that an attacker could then exploit remotely. This underscores the need for a unified security strategy that addresses both IT and OT data, recognizing that the convergence of these domains creates new attack vectors and requires integrated security solutions.

Furthermore, the lifecycle of data within a digital twin must be considered from a security perspective. This includes data retention policies, secure deletion practices, and data archival. Data that is no longer needed should be securely purged to reduce the attack surface. Archival of historical data should be done in secure, immutable storage solutions. The integrity of stored data is as important as its confidentiality. Hashing algorithms (e.g., SHA-256) can be used to generate unique digital fingerprints of data. Any alteration to the data will result in a different hash value, thus detecting tampering.

The security of the data storage infrastructure itself is also a significant consideration. Whether using on-premises data centers, private clouds, or public cloud services, the underlying infrastructure must be hardened, patched, and monitored for security vulnerabilities. Misconfigurations in cloud storage buckets, for instance, are a common cause of data breaches. Security best practices for cloud environments, such as using secure default configurations, implementing strong identity and access management, and continuously monitoring for misconfigurations, are essential.

In summary, securing data in transit and at rest is a fundamental requirement for any digital twin implementation. It necessitates a comprehensive strategy that combines strong encryption, secure communication protocols, robust network segmentation, granular access controls, secure key management, and continuous monitoring. By diligently implementing these measures, organizations can significantly mitigate the risks associated with data breaches, ensuring the confidentiality, integrity, and availability of the critical information that powers their digital twins and, by extension, their physical operations.

The integrity and security of a digital twin environment hinge critically on who or what can interact with its components and data. This subsection delves into the essential strategies and technologies for establishing and maintaining rigorous access control and identity management, ensuring that only authenticated and authorized entities can perform specific actions or view particular datasets within the digital twin ecosystem. This is not merely about preventing malicious actors, but also about ensuring operational efficiency and data compliance by adhering to the principle of least privilege.

At the core of any secure system lies robust identity management. This encompasses the processes and technologies used to identify, authenticate, and authorize users and devices within the digital twin environment. The fundamental question is: "Who or what is trying to access this resource, and are they permitted to do so?" Identity management begins with the creation and lifecycle management of digital identities. For human users, this means establishing unique identifiers, managing credentials (passwords, certificates, tokens), and provisioning and de-provisioning access as individuals join, change roles within, or leave an organization. For non-human entities, such as IoT sensors, edge devices, or automated services, it involves assigning unique, verifiable identities that allow them to securely connect and exchange data. This can be achieved through various means, including digital certificates, pre-shared keys, or secure token-based mechanisms.

Authentication is the process of verifying the claimed identity of a user or system. In the context of digital twins, where the data can be sensitive and the potential impact of unauthorized access severe, relying on single-factor authentication, such as a simple password, is often insufficient. Multi-Factor Authentication (MFA) is therefore an indispensable security measure. MFA requires a user to provide two or more verification factors to gain access to a resource. These factors typically fall into three categories: something the user knows (e.g., a password or PIN), something the user has (e.g., a security token, smartphone, or smart card), and something the user is (e.g., a fingerprint or facial scan). By combining these factors, MFA significantly increases the difficulty for an attacker to impersonate a legitimate user. For instance, an engineer accessing the digital twin's simulation parameters might be required to enter their password (knowledge factor) and then approve a push notification sent to their corporate mobile device (possession factor).

Beyond verifying who someone is, it is equally critical to determine what they are allowed to do once authenticated. This is the domain of authorization, which is typically managed through sophisticated access control mechanisms. The most widely adopted model for managing authorization is Role-Based Access Control (RBAC). In RBAC, permissions are not assigned directly to individual users but are associated with specific roles. Users are then assigned to one or more roles based on their job responsibilities. For example, a digital twin representing a manufacturing plant might have roles such as "Plant Operator," "Maintenance Technician," "Process Engineer," and "Security Administrator." The "Plant Operator" role might have read-only access to real-time operational data and control dashboards, while the "Maintenance Technician" role might have access to historical performance data, diagnostic tools, and the ability to update maintenance logs. The "Process Engineer" might have access to simulation models, parameter tuning, and the ability to run what-if scenarios. The "Security

Administrator" would possess broader privileges, including managing user accounts and access policies. This hierarchical approach simplifies access management, making it easier to grant, review, and revoke permissions as organizational structures and responsibilities evolve. When a new technician joins the team, they are simply assigned the "Maintenance Technician" role, automatically inheriting all the necessary permissions. Conversely, when an employee changes departments, their roles can be updated accordingly, ensuring they only retain access relevant to their new position.

While RBAC is highly effective, complex digital twin environments, especially those with diverse user groups and dynamically changing access requirements, may benefit from more granular authorization models. Attribute-Based Access Control (ABAC) and Policy-Based Access Control (PBAC) offer more dynamic and context-aware authorization. ABAC grants access based on a set of attributes associated with the user, the resource, the action, and the environment. For example, an ABAC policy might state: "Allow access to sensitive production data if the user's role is 'Process Engineer', the data's classification is 'Confidential', the time is between 8 AM and 6 PM local time, and the access request originates from a corporate network segment." This allows for much finer-grained control than RBAC alone, adapting to specific circumstances. PBAC takes this a step further by defining policies as explicit statements that govern access. These policies can be complex, incorporating multiple conditions and logical operators. For digital twins, this can be invaluable for compliance with regulations that dictate strict data access rules based on data sensitivity, user location, or data usage context. For instance, a policy could restrict access to personally identifiable information (PII) within a digital twin representing customer data to only those users with a documented business need, and only when accessing from within a secure, authorized environment.

The seamless integration of identity and access management across the various components of a digital twin system – from edge devices and cloud platforms to the core simulation engines and user interfaces – is paramount. This often involves leveraging industry standards and protocols. For authentication, protocols like OAuth 2.0 and OpenID Connect (OIDC) are widely used for delegated authorization and identity verification, respectively, particularly in web and mobile applications interacting with digital twin services. Protocols such as SAML (Security Assertion Markup Language) are common for enabling single sign-on (SSO) across different applications and services, reducing the burden on users to remember multiple credentials and improving the overall user experience while maintaining strong security.

For machine-to-machine (M2M) communication and IoT device authentication, mutual TLS (mTLS) is a powerful mechanism. In mTLS, both the client and the server authenticate each other using digital certificates. This ensures that not only is the server a legitimate entity that the client is communicating with, but also that the client attempting to connect is a trusted device or service. This is particularly relevant for digital twins that ingest data from numerous sensors or control actuators, where each entity must be securely identified before it can send data or receive commands. Certificate management, including the secure issuance, renewal, and revocation of certificates, becomes a critical operational aspect in such scenarios.

Centralized Identity and Access Management (IAM) platforms, whether on-premises or cloud-based, play a pivotal role in orchestrating these processes. These platforms act as a single source of truth for user identities, roles, and permissions, allowing for consistent policy enforcement across the entire digital twin infrastructure. They often integrate with existing enterprise directories (like Active Directory or LDAP) to leverage existing user management processes. Cloud providers offer robust IAM services (e.g., AWS IAM, Azure AD, Google Cloud IAM) that are essential for securing cloud-hosted digital twin components. These services provide tools for managing users, groups, roles, and fine-grained permissions for access to cloud resources, including compute, storage, and networking services that underpin the digital twin.

Auditing and logging are inseparable from effective access control and identity management. Every access attempt, every successful authentication, every authorization decision, and every action taken within the digital twin environment must be logged. These logs serve multiple purposes: they provide an audit trail for compliance purposes, enabling organizations to demonstrate adherence to security policies and regulatory requirements; they are crucial for security monitoring, allowing security teams to detect suspicious activities or policy violations in near real-time; and they are indispensable for forensic investigations in the event of a security incident. A comprehensive log analysis strategy, potentially employing Security Information and Event Management (SIEM) systems, is necessary to sift through the vast amount of log data and identify meaningful security events. For instance, a surge in failed login attempts for a specific user account or unusual access patterns to sensitive data could be early indicators of a brute-force attack or an insider threat.

The principle of least privilege is a guiding star in the design of access control for digital twins. This means that any user, system, or process should only be granted the minimum level of access and permissions necessary to perform its intended function. Over-privileging users or systems increases the attack surface and the potential damage if an account or component is compromised. Regularly reviewing and refining permissions to ensure they align with current operational needs is a continuous process. This often involves periodic access reviews where managers or system administrators attest to the continued necessity of assigned roles and permissions for their team members or systems.

Furthermore, the physical security of devices and infrastructure that host or interact with the digital twin is an extension of identity and access management. If an edge device or a server can be physically accessed and tampered with, then any logical access controls implemented on it may be bypassed. Therefore, securing the physical environment where critical digital twin components reside is a foundational requirement.

In conclusion, a robust and comprehensive approach to access control and identity management is not an optional add-on but a fundamental necessity for the secure and reliable operation of digital twins. By meticulously defining identities, enforcing strong authentication mechanisms like MFA, implementing granular authorization through RBAC or ABAC, leveraging centralized IAM platforms, and maintaining vigilant auditing and logging, organizations can establish a strong defense against unauthorized access and ensure that their digital twin ecosystems remain trusted and secure. This layered approach protects not only the data and intellectual property embedded within the digital twin but also the physical systems and processes it represents and potentially controls.

Despite the most stringent security measures, the dynamic and interconnected nature of digital twin systems, much like any complex technological infrastructure, presents inherent vulnerabilities. Recognizing that a complete absence of security incidents is an unrealistic aspiration, a proactive and robust strategy for incident response and resilience planning becomes paramount. This involves not only defining how to react when an incident occurs but also designing the digital twin architecture and its operational procedures to withstand and recover from cyberattacks with minimal disruption. The goal is to transition from a reactive stance to a proactive one, where the system is inherently built to be resilient and capable of rapid, effective recovery.

The foundation of effective incident response lies in comprehensive planning. For a digital twin, this plan must be meticulously tailored to its unique characteristics, including the criticality of the simulated or controlled physical asset, the sensitivity of the data it processes, and the interdependencies between its various components. An incident response plan (IRP) for a digital twin environment should detail a structured approach, typically encompassing several key phases: preparation, identification, containment, eradication, recovery, and lessons learned.

Preparation is the ongoing phase that occurs before any incident. This involves establishing the necessary infrastructure, tools, and teams, as well as defining clear roles and responsibilities. For digital twin environments, preparation includes ensuring that logging and monitoring systems are in place and adequately configured to detect anomalies across all layers – from the edge devices generating real-time data, through the communication networks, to the cloud-based platforms hosting the digital twin models and analytics engines. This also means having readily available, tested backup and recovery procedures for critical data and the digital twin models themselves. A well-prepared team will have practiced response scenarios, be familiar with the defined playbooks, and understand the escalation paths and communication protocols. This preparation extends to ensuring that the organization has the necessary legal and contractual frameworks in place to facilitate rapid information sharing and action, especially when dealing with external service providers or regulatory bodies.

Identification, or detection, is the phase where a potential security incident is recognized. In the context of digital twins, this could manifest in various forms: unexpected deviations in sensor readings that do not align with known physical phenomena or operational states, abnormal network traffic patterns, unauthorized access attempts, the corruption or deletion of critical model data, or a sudden degradation in the performance or accuracy of simulations. Advanced threat detection capabilities are crucial here. This can involve anomaly detection algorithms that learn the 'normal' behavior of the digital twin and its constituent parts, flagging any statistically significant deviations. Machine learning models trained on historical security events can also identify sophisticated attacks that might evade traditional signature-based detection methods. For instance, if a digital twin of a power grid starts showing simulation outputs that predict grid instability without any corresponding real-world trigger, it warrants immediate investigation. Similarly, a surge in failed authentication attempts for the engineering console or unusual API calls to the data ingestion layer could signal an attempted intrusion. The ability to correlate events across different parts of the digital twin infrastructure is vital; a seemingly minor anomaly in one component might be a symptom of a larger, orchestrated attack impacting multiple systems.

Once an incident is identified, the next critical step is containment. The primary objective here is to limit the scope and impact of the incident, preventing it from spreading to other parts of the digital twin or the connected physical system. For digital twins, containment strategies will vary widely depending on the nature of the incident. If unauthorized access to control parameters is detected, the immediate action might be to disable the affected user accounts or revoke the compromised credentials. If a specific sensor or data stream is found to be compromised or sending malicious data, it might need to be isolated or temporarily disabled, potentially switching to fallback data sources or reverting to a known-good state for that data input. In severe cases where a component of the digital twin itself is believed to be compromised (e.g., a malware infection affecting a simulation engine), it may be necessary to take the affected component offline for analysis and remediation. This decision requires careful consideration of the operational impact; for a digital twin controlling a critical industrial process, a sudden shutdown can have significant economic consequences. Therefore, containment strategies must balance security needs with operational continuity requirements, often involving pre-defined "quarantine" zones or fallback operational modes. For example, if the digital twin of a chemical plant detects a potential compromise in its real-time process visualization module, it might temporarily revert to a less interactive, read-only dashboard while an investigation is conducted, ensuring operators still have situational awareness without risking further compromise through interactive controls.

Eradication follows containment. This phase involves removing the threat from the environment and addressing the root cause of the incident. For digital twin environments, this could mean removing malware from affected systems, patching vulnerabilities that were exploited, or restoring compromised configuration files. It is crucial to ensure that the threat is completely removed and that the system is not susceptible to the same attack vector recurring. This might involve rebuilding compromised systems from secure, trusted images or reconfiguring network access controls. A thorough analysis of how the incident occurred is essential. Was it a zero-day exploit? A weak password policy? A misconfiguration in a cloud service? Identifying the root cause is critical for preventing future occurrences. For instance, if an attacker exploited a vulnerability in a third-party library used by the digital twin's data processing component, eradication would involve updating or replacing that library, followed by a comprehensive scan of all components that rely on it.

Recovery is the phase where systems are restored to full operational capacity. This involves carefully bringing cleaned and secured systems back online, validating their integrity and functionality, and resuming normal operations. For digital twins, this might mean restoring corrupted simulation models from backups, re-enabling data streams that were temporarily disabled, and verifying that the digital twin accurately reflects the current state of the physical asset. The recovery process must be systematic and rigorously tested. It is often advisable to bring systems back online in a phased approach, starting with the most critical components and gradually restoring others. During this phase, continuous monitoring is essential to ensure that the threat has not returned and that the restored systems are functioning as expected. For a digital twin of an autonomous vehicle fleet, recovery might involve re-deploying updated software to the vehicle control simulation, restoring historical operational data for analysis, and then slowly reintroducing the twin into a testing environment before full operational deployment. The recovery process should also include re-validating access controls and security configurations that may have been altered during the incident or recovery.

Finally, the lessons learned phase is a critical post-incident activity. Once the immediate crisis has passed, a thorough post-mortem analysis should be conducted. This involves reviewing the entire incident response process, identifying what worked well and what could be improved. This includes analyzing the effectiveness of the IRP itself, the performance of the response team, the accuracy of the detection mechanisms, and the efficiency of the containment, eradication, and recovery procedures. The goal is to refine the IRP, update playbooks, enhance training programs, and implement technical or procedural changes to prevent similar incidents from occurring in the future. For example, if the investigation reveals that a critical piece of information was missing from the initial alert, steps would be taken to enhance data correlation in the monitoring systems. If the containment phase took too long due to unclear communication protocols, those protocols would be revised and practiced. This continuous improvement cycle is essential for maintaining a high level of security and resilience in the ever-evolving threat landscape.

Beyond reactive incident response, building inherent resilience into the digital twin architecture is a proactive strategy that significantly mitigates the impact of incidents and accelerates recovery. Resilience in this context refers to the ability of the digital twin system to withstand disruptions, maintain essential functions, and recover quickly to its original state or an acceptable operational level. This can be achieved through several key architectural and operational principles.

One fundamental aspect of resilience is redundancy. This involves deploying multiple instances of critical components or data stores, so that if one fails or is compromised, others can seamlessly take over. In a digital twin architecture, this could mean having redundant data ingestion pipelines, multiple active simulation engines, or geographically distributed data centers hosting the digital twin platform. For example, if the primary cloud region hosting a digital twin of a large logistics network experiences an outage, a secondary region could automatically assume control, ensuring continuity of operations and data availability. This redundancy should extend to communication pathways and power supplies for critical infrastructure.

Another crucial element is fault tolerance. This means designing components to continue operating even when parts of them fail. Techniques like graceful degradation, where a system may lose some non-essential functionality but retain its core operations, are key. For a digital twin, this might mean that if a specific analytical module that provides advanced predictive insights fails, the core simulation and real-time monitoring functions continue to operate. This allows operators to maintain essential control and awareness while the fault is being addressed. Similarly, implementing robust error handling and retry mechanisms in data communication and processing can prevent transient failures from cascading into larger incidents.

High availability is closely linked to redundancy and fault tolerance. It ensures that the digital twin system is accessible and operational when needed. This is achieved through a combination of hardware, software, and network design that minimizes downtime. For critical digital twins that are directly linked to the operation of physical assets, achieving "five nines" (99.999%) availability might be a requirement, meaning the system can tolerate only a few minutes of downtime per year. This often necessitates sophisticated load balancing, automatic failover mechanisms, and zero-downtime deployment strategies for updates and patches.

Data integrity and durability are also cornerstones of resilience. The digital twin relies on accurate and consistent data. Therefore, robust data backup, versioning, and recovery strategies are essential. This includes implementing regular, automated backups of all critical data, including sensor data, simulation models, historical logs, and configuration settings. Storing backups in multiple secure locations, including off-site or cloud-based disaster recovery sites, is crucial. Furthermore, employing data validation techniques at various stages of the data lifecycle ensures that data remains accurate and trustworthy. For a digital twin of a pharmaceutical manufacturing process, ensuring the integrity of historical batch data is critical for regulatory compliance and quality control; any loss or corruption of this data would be catastrophic. Techniques like blockchain can also be explored for ensuring immutable data trails, enhancing integrity and auditability.

The concept of "defense in depth" is also fundamental to resilience. This involves layering multiple security controls so that if one fails, others are still in place. This applies not only to cybersecurity measures but also to resilience strategies. For example, in addition to having redundant servers, there might be load balancers, firewalls, intrusion detection systems, and comprehensive logging and monitoring all working in concert. If a denial-of-service attack targets the system, multiple layers of defense will work to mitigate its impact, potentially absorbing the traffic or redirecting it to less critical services.

Finally, a well-defined and regularly tested disaster recovery (DR) plan is essential. While resilience focuses on the ability to withstand and continue operations during an incident, a DR plan outlines the procedures for recovering systems and data in a separate location after a major disaster (e.g., a natural catastrophe, a large-scale cyberattack that incapacitates the primary site). The DR plan should be aligned with the business continuity plan (BCP) of the organization, ensuring that critical digital twin functionalities can be restored within acceptable timeframes to support essential business operations. For a digital twin that monitors and controls critical infrastructure like water treatment plants or transportation networks, a rapid and effective DR capability is not just a technical requirement but a public safety imperative.

In summary, a comprehensive approach to cybersecurity for digital twins must integrate robust incident response planning with proactive resilience engineering. By meticulously preparing for potential incidents, establishing clear identification, containment, eradication, and recovery procedures, and by architecting the digital twin systems with redundancy, fault tolerance, and high availability in mind, organizations can significantly minimize the risk and impact of cyber threats. This dual focus ensures that digital twins not only provide valuable insights and control but also remain secure, reliable, and resilient in the face of an increasingly complex and dangerous threat landscape, safeguarding both digital assets and the physical systems they represent.

Chapter 11: Principles of Advanced Monitoring

The advent of digital twins heralds a fundamental transformation in how we approach system monitoring, steering us away from the often-insufficient realm of reactive responses towards a more sophisticated and advantageous domain of proactive and predictive strategies. Historically, monitoring has largely been an exercise in damage control – identifying a problem after it has manifested, impacting performance, causing downtime, or even leading to catastrophic failures. This reactive posture, while sometimes unavoidable, is inherently inefficient and costly. It is akin to waiting for a patient to show severe symptoms before diagnosing an illness; by then, the treatment is more complex, recovery is longer, and the long-term prognosis might be compromised.

Digital twins, by their very nature, possess the intrinsic capability to dismantle this reactive paradigm. They are not merely static digital replicas; they are dynamic, living models that ingest and process real-time data streams from their physical counterparts. This continuous influx of information, coupled with advanced analytical engines and sophisticated simulation capabilities, empowers them to function as highly sensitive early warning systems. Instead of waiting for a sensor reading to cross a critical, predefined threshold that signals a failure, a digital twin can analyze subtle deviations and trends over time, identifying anomalies that might indicate an impending issue long before it becomes critical.

Consider the monitoring of a complex industrial manufacturing plant. Traditional monitoring might involve setting alarm thresholds for parameters like temperature, pressure, vibration, or flow rates. An alert would trigger only when these values exceed a pre-set limit, indicating that a component is already stressed, potentially damaged, or operating inefficiently. The response team then rushes to diagnose the problem, which could involve shutting down a production line, performing manual inspections, and ordering replacement parts – all of which contribute to costly downtime and lost productivity.

In contrast, a digital twin of this plant, fed by high-frequency sensor data, can employ machine learning algorithms to detect subtle patterns. It can identify an incremental increase in vibration that, while still within acceptable traditional limits, deviates from the historical norm for that specific operating condition. It might detect a slight, almost imperceptible shift in temperature that, when correlated with other minor parameter variations, suggests a developing lubrication issue in a critical bearing. The digital twin can then predict, with a high degree of confidence, that this bearing is likely to fail within a specific timeframe - perhaps days or even weeks.

This predictive insight allows for a complete shift in operational strategy. Instead of reacting to a failure, maintenance can be scheduled proactively during planned downtime, at a time that minimizes disruption to production schedules. The necessary replacement parts can be ordered and readily available, and technicians can be briefed on the specific issue identified by the digital twin, allowing them to perform a more targeted and efficient repair. This shift from "fix it when it breaks" to "fix it before it breaks" offers profound benefits, including significantly reduced unplanned downtime, optimized maintenance schedules, extended equipment lifespan, and lower overall operational costs.

The predictive power of digital twins extends beyond simple anomaly detection and failure prediction. By simulating various operating scenarios and their potential outcomes, they can also forecast performance degradation. For instance, a digital twin of a power generation turbine can simulate the impact of different fuel qualities, varying ambient temperatures, or evolving wear-and-tear on its efficiency and output. This allows operators to adjust operating parameters to maintain optimal performance, even under suboptimal conditions, thereby maximizing energy generation and minimizing fuel consumption.

Furthermore, the continuous, granular data collection inherent in digital twin monitoring provides an unprecedented level of insight into system behavior. This data can be used to refine operational models, identify bottlenecks that were not apparent with traditional monitoring, and uncover opportunities for performance optimization that were previously unknown. The historical data collected by the digital twin, correlated with observed outcomes, creates a rich dataset for ongoing learning and improvement. This "learning" aspect is crucial; as the physical asset operates and the digital twin observes its behavior, the twin becomes increasingly accurate and insightful, enhancing its predictive and proactive capabilities over time.

The implementation of proactive monitoring through digital twins requires a foundational shift in infrastructure and mindset. It necessitates robust data acquisition systems capable of handling high volumes of real-time data, secure and scalable data storage solutions, and powerful computational resources for running complex simulations and analytics. Equally important is the development of skilled personnel who can interpret the insights generated by the digital twin, understand the underlying models, and translate predictions into actionable operational strategies. This often involves a convergence of expertise from engineering, data science, IT, and operations management.

The benefits are substantial. For organizations leveraging digital twins, proactive monitoring translates into:

Reduced Unplanned Downtime: By predicting failures, interventions can be planned, minimizing unexpected disruptions to operations. This is particularly critical in industries where downtime can incur millions of dollars in lost revenue and reputational damage.
Optimized Maintenance: Moving from time-based or failure-based maintenance to condition-based or predictive maintenance ensures that resources are deployed only when and where needed. This reduces unnecessary maintenance activities, conserves spare parts, and lowers labor costs.
Enhanced Operational Efficiency: Continuous performance monitoring and simulation allow for real-time adjustments to optimize energy consumption, material usage, and throughput, leading to significant cost savings and increased productivity.
Extended Asset Lifespan: By identifying and addressing potential issues before they cause significant damage, the operational life of physical assets can be extended, deferring costly capital replacements.

Improved Safety: Predicting potential failures in critical systems, such as those in manufacturing, transportation, or energy, can prevent accidents that could endanger personnel or the public.
Accelerated Product Development and Process Improvement: Insights gained from monitoring operational assets can feed back into the design and development process, leading to more robust, efficient, and reliable future iterations of products and processes.

The transition from reactive to proactive monitoring is not merely an incremental improvement; it represents a paradigm shift in how we manage complex systems. Digital twins provide the technological foundation for this shift, enabling organizations to move from a posture of responding to problems to one of anticipating and preventing them, thereby unlocking new levels of efficiency, reliability, and economic value. This proactive approach ensures that digital twins are not just sophisticated diagnostic tools, but rather strategic assets that drive continuous improvement and competitive advantage. The ability to foresee and forestall issues transforms operational management from a cost center focused on mitigating failures into a value driver focused on maximizing performance and longevity.

Anomaly detection, in the context of digital twins, is the process of identifying patterns or events in data that do not conform to an expected or normal behavior. This expected behavior is typically established by training a model on historical data representing the normal operation of the physical asset or system. When the digital twin receives new data or generates output, anomaly detection techniques are employed to flag any significant deviations. These deviations, often termed anomalies or outliers, can be indicative of a wide range of issues, from sensor malfunctions and data corruption to incipient equipment failures, suboptimal performance, or even security breaches. The proactive stance that digital twins enable hinges critically on the ability to accurately and efficiently detect these anomalies.

The challenge lies in the sheer volume and complexity of data generated by modern industrial systems. Simply defining "normal" can be a nuanced task, as operational conditions, environmental factors, and usage patterns can vary significantly. Therefore, anomaly detection techniques must be robust, adaptable, and capable of distinguishing between genuine anomalies and expected variations within the operational envelope. A critical aspect of implementing these techniques within a digital twin framework is understanding that anomalies can manifest in different ways: a single data point might be an outlier, a sequence of data points might exhibit an unusual trend, or the overall behavior of the system, when compared to its simulated counterpart, might be inexplicably different.

Several categories of anomaly detection techniques are available, each with its own strengths, weaknesses, and applicability depending on the nature of the data and the system being monitored. These can be broadly classified into statistical methods, machine learning-based approaches, and physics-based methods. Often, a hybrid approach that combines elements from different categories yields the most effective results, leveraging the complementary strengths of each.

Statistical methods form a foundational approach to anomaly detection. These techniques rely on the statistical properties of the data to identify outliers. The core idea is to model the "normal" data distribution and then flag data points that fall far outside this distribution. A common and intuitive method is based on thresholding. For a given parameter, a historical analysis can determine its typical range of values and, crucially, its variance. Anomalies are then identified as data points that lie significantly beyond a predefined range, often expressed in terms of standard deviations from the mean. For example, if the normal operating temperature of a pump bearing typically ranges between 40°C and 60°C with a standard deviation of 2°C, a reading of 70°C might be flagged as an anomaly, especially if it persists. However, this simple approach can be sensitive to the choice of threshold and may struggle with dynamic systems where the normal operating range itself changes.

More sophisticated statistical methods involve fitting probability distributions to the data. Techniques like Gaussian Mixture Models (GMMs) can represent complex, multi-modal distributions of normal data. By calculating the probability of a new data point belonging to the learned distribution, points with very low probabilities are identified as anomalies. Similarly, techniques such as Principal Component Analysis (PCA) can be used. PCA reduces the dimensionality of the data while retaining most of the variance. In a normal operating state, the data will lie close to the principal components. Anomalies, on the other hand, will project further away from the subspace defined by these components, indicating deviations in the relationships between variables that are characteristic of normal operation. This is particularly useful for multivariate data where relationships between parameters are important indicators of system health.

Moving into the realm of machine learning, a plethora of algorithms are employed for anomaly detection, often offering greater flexibility and power than traditional statistical methods, especially when dealing with non-linear relationships and high-dimensional data. Clustering-based methods are a prominent example. These algorithms group similar data points into clusters. The assumption is that normal data points will form dense clusters, while anomalies will either not belong to any cluster or will form very small, isolated clusters. Algorithms like K-Means can be adapted for anomaly detection: after clustering the data, points that are far from the centroid of their assigned cluster can be flagged. DBSCAN (Density-Based Spatial Clustering of Applications with Noise) is another powerful option, as it naturally identifies noise points (anomalies) that do not belong to any dense cluster. This is effective in scenarios where anomalies might not follow any discernible pattern and are simply outliers in terms of density.

Another class of machine learning techniques specifically designed for anomaly detection are methods that aim to "isolate" anomalies. Isolation Forests, for instance, operate on the principle that anomalies are "few and different," making them easier to isolate. The algorithm builds an ensemble of trees, where each tree is built by randomly selecting a feature and then randomly selecting a split value between the minimum and maximum values of that feature. Anomalies, being different, are expected to be isolated in fewer steps (i.e., closer to the root of the tree) than normal data points. The path length from the root to a data point provides a score indicating its anomaly likelihood. This method is known for its efficiency and effectiveness, particularly with large datasets, and it does not require explicit modeling of the normal data distribution.

One-Class Support Vector Machines (OC-SVMs) are also widely used. Unlike standard SVMs that find a hyperplane to separate different classes, OC-SVMs learn a boundary that encloses the majority of the normal data points. Any data point falling outside this boundary is considered an anomaly. This approach is particularly useful when dealing with a single class of "normal" data and wanting to identify anything that deviates from it. The kernel trick used in SVMs allows OC-SVM to learn complex, non-linear boundaries, making it suitable for intricate data patterns.

Deep learning models, with their capacity to learn complex hierarchical representations, have also proven highly effective for anomaly detection, especially in areas like time-series data and image analysis. Autoencoders, a type of neural network, are trained to reconstruct their input. They consist of an encoder that compresses the input into a lower-dimensional latent representation and a decoder that attempts to reconstruct the original input from this representation. When trained on normal data, the autoencoder learns to reconstruct typical patterns accurately. However, when presented with an anomalous input, the reconstruction error (the difference between the input and its reconstruction) will be significantly higher. This reconstruction error can then be used as an anomaly score. Variations like Variational Autoencoders (VAEs) offer a probabilistic approach, further enhancing their ability to model the underlying data distribution. Recurrent Neural Networks (RNNs) and their variants like Long Short-Term Memory (LSTM) networks are particularly well-suited for sequential data, such as time-series sensor readings. LSTMs can learn temporal dependencies and predict future values in a sequence. Deviations between the predicted values and the actual observed values can signal an anomaly. For instance, in monitoring a gas turbine, an LSTM could predict the next sequence of temperature and pressure readings. A significant divergence from this prediction might indicate an issue within the turbine's combustion process.

Physics-based methods, while less common as standalone anomaly detection techniques, play a crucial role in validating and contextualizing anomalies detected by other means, especially within a digital twin framework. These methods leverage the known physical laws, engineering principles, and mathematical models that govern the behavior of the asset or system. For example, if a digital twin is monitoring a pump, physics-based models would describe the relationship between flow rate, pressure, speed, and power consumption. If a statistical or machine learning method flags a high power consumption at a low flow rate as an anomaly, a physics-based check could confirm if this scenario is physically plausible under any normal operating condition or if it strongly suggests a blockage, cavitation, or internal recirculation.

These models can be derived from first principles (e.g., Navier-Stokes equations for fluid dynamics) or from empirical data and system identification techniques. Within the digital twin, these physics-based models serve as a ground truth. If sensor data deviates significantly from what the physics-based model predicts for the current operating state, it strongly indicates an anomaly. This can help differentiate between genuine system issues and sensor noise or measurement errors. For instance, in a heat exchanger, the rate of heat transfer is governed by specific physical laws. If the measured temperatures and flow rates suggest a heat transfer rate that violates these laws, it points to a likely anomaly, such as fouling on the heat exchange surfaces or a leak.

The application of these techniques within a digital twin context requires careful consideration of data quality, feature engineering, model selection, and the interpretation of results. Data quality is paramount; noisy or erroneous data can lead to false positives or negatives. Preprocessing steps such as filtering, imputation, and normalization are often necessary. Feature engineering involves selecting and transforming raw data into features that are most informative for anomaly detection. For instance, instead of just using raw vibration readings, engineers might calculate frequency-domain features (e.g., using Fast Fourier Transform) that are more sensitive to specific types of mechanical degradation.

Model selection depends heavily on the characteristics of the data and the types of anomalies expected. For high-dimensional, complex datasets, deep learning or advanced machine learning methods might be preferred. For simpler, well-understood systems with primarily univariate data, statistical methods might suffice. The interpretability of the anomaly is also crucial. If an anomaly is detected, it is vital to understand its cause to take appropriate action. Techniques that provide explanations for why a particular data point or event was flagged as anomalous (e.g., feature importance from Isolation Forests, reconstruction error contributions from autoencoders) are highly valuable.

Furthermore, the concept of an "anomaly" is often relative and context-dependent. An event that is anomalous under one set of operating conditions might be perfectly normal under another. Therefore, anomaly detection models must be dynamic and adaptable, able to learn from changing operational environments. This is where the continuous data streams fed into a digital twin become invaluable. The twin can not only detect anomalies but also learn and adapt its definition of "normal" over time, ensuring that the detection mechanisms remain relevant and effective. This continuous learning loop is fundamental to the proactive and predictive capabilities that digital twins offer.

The operationalization of anomaly detection within a digital twin involves integrating these techniques into a monitoring and alerting system. When an anomaly is detected, it triggers an alert, often accompanied by diagnostic information about the nature and potential cause of the anomaly. This alert can be directed to human operators, automated maintenance systems, or other decision-making processes. The fidelity of the anomaly detection system directly impacts the effectiveness of these downstream actions. A system that generates too many false alarms can lead to alert fatigue, where operators start ignoring alerts, thus defeating the purpose of advanced monitoring. Conversely, a system that misses critical anomalies can lead to significant failures. Therefore, a continuous process of validation, tuning, and refinement of anomaly detection models is essential, often informed by feedback from operational experience and expert domain knowledge.

The choice between different anomaly detection techniques can also be guided by computational resources and real-time processing requirements. Simple statistical methods and tree-based ensemble methods like Isolation Forests tend to be computationally less intensive than complex deep learning models, making them suitable for edge computing scenarios or applications requiring very low latency. However, for tasks involving complex, unstructured data or the detection of subtle, multi-variate anomalies, deep learning models, while more resource-intensive, may offer superior performance. The digital twin architecture itself can facilitate a tiered approach, with simpler methods running at the edge for initial screening and more complex models running in the cloud for in-depth analysis.

Consider the ongoing monitoring of a fleet of wind turbines. Each turbine is equipped with numerous sensors measuring wind speed, direction, blade pitch, rotor speed, gearbox temperature, generator output, and structural vibrations. A digital twin of each turbine receives this data in real-time.

For vibration data from the gearbox, a traditional statistical approach might monitor the Root Mean Square (RMS) value of acceleration signals. If the RMS value exceeds a predefined threshold, an anomaly is flagged, potentially indicating bearing wear. However, this simple threshold might not account for variations in wind speed, which can inherently cause different levels of vibration.

A more advanced approach using machine learning could involve training an Isolation Forest on historical vibration data collected under various wind conditions. This forest would learn to distinguish between vibrations that are characteristic of normal operation at a given wind speed and those that are not. An anomaly could then be a vibration signature that is unusual for the current wind speed and operating state.

Furthermore, a deep learning model, like an LSTM-based autoencoder, could be trained on sequences of vibration, temperature, and rotational speed data. This model would learn the complex temporal dynamics and interdependencies between these parameters during normal operation. If, for example, the vibration pattern deviates significantly from what the autoencoder predicts based on the current rotational speed and temperature trend, it could signal the early stages of gear tooth damage or a lubrication issue, even if individual parameters remain within their nominal ranges according to simpler statistical checks.

Physics-based validation can then be applied. If the LSTM model detects an anomaly, a physics-based simulation of the gearbox's power transmission and vibrational response under the current load conditions can be performed. If the detected anomaly significantly violates the predicted physical behavior, the confidence in the anomaly being a real system fault increases. For instance, a specific vibrational frequency pattern flagged by the LSTM might correspond to a known failure mode of a particular bearing type, which can be further cross-referenced with known failure physics.

The output of this multi-faceted anomaly detection process within the digital twin would be a prioritized alert. Instead of just a binary "anomaly detected" signal, the system could provide a confidence score, a potential root cause classification (e.g., "bearing wear suspected," "gear tooth damage possible"), and an estimated time to failure. This rich information allows maintenance teams to plan interventions strategically, order the correct parts, and allocate resources efficiently, thereby transforming a potential catastrophic failure into a scheduled maintenance event. This iterative refinement of anomaly detection, driven by the synergy between statistical, machine learning, and physics-based approaches within the dynamic digital twin environment, is at the heart of achieving true operational resilience and optimization.

Predictive maintenance represents a paradigm shift from reactive or even scheduled maintenance to a proactive, condition-based approach. Instead of fixing equipment after it breaks (reactive maintenance) or performing maintenance at fixed intervals regardless of actual condition (preventive maintenance), predictive maintenance aims to anticipate and address potential issues before they lead to failure. This proactive stance is fundamentally enabled by the continuous flow of data and sophisticated analytical capabilities provided by digital twins. By meticulously analyzing historical performance data, real-time sensor readings, and operational parameters, a digital twin can discern subtle trends and patterns that signal an impending degradation or malfunction. This allows for the scheduling of maintenance interventions precisely when they are needed, minimizing unnecessary work and preventing catastrophic failures.

The core advantage of implementing predictive maintenance strategies through digital twins lies in its ability to drastically reduce operational costs and enhance asset reliability. Unplanned downtime is a significant drain on resources, leading not only to lost production but also to emergency repair costs, potential secondary damage, and expedited shipping for replacement parts. Predictive maintenance, by forecasting failures, transforms these costly emergencies into planned, scheduled events. Maintenance crews can be dispatched with the correct tools, parts, and expertise, operating during planned downtime windows that have minimal impact on overall production schedules. Furthermore, by addressing issues in their nascent stages, the severity of wear and tear is reduced, often leading to less extensive and therefore less costly repairs. This, in turn, contributes to extending the operational lifespan of the asset, maximizing the return on investment in that equipment. The digital twin acts as an intelligent guardian, constantly scrutinizing the asset's condition and providing foresight that was previously unattainable.

Establishing a robust predictive maintenance program using digital twin insights involves a systematic, multi-stage process. The initial and perhaps most critical step is comprehensive data acquisition and integration. This entails identifying all relevant data sources, which can range from sophisticated sensor arrays (e.g., vibration, temperature, pressure, acoustic sensors) to operational logs, environmental data, and even maintenance records. Ensuring the quality, accuracy, and consistency of this data is paramount. Digital twins require a clean, reliable data foundation upon which to build their analytical models. This often involves implementing data cleansing routines, standardization protocols, and robust data pipelines to ingest and process information in real-time.

Following data acquisition, the next crucial phase is the development and calibration of the digital twin model itself. This involves creating a virtual replica that accurately reflects the physical asset's geometry, its components, and importantly, its operational physics and behavior. For predictive maintenance, this means the model must be capable of simulating normal operating conditions and predicting how the asset will respond under various loads and environmental factors. This modeling phase often leverages a combination of physics-based simulations, historical operational data, and expert engineering knowledge to define the asset's expected performance envelope.

Once the digital twin is established and fed with real-time data, the analytical engine for predictive maintenance can be deployed. This involves applying a suite of advanced algorithms, including those discussed in anomaly detection, but specifically tailored to identify patterns indicative of future failure. For instance, by analyzing the rate of change of vibration signatures over time, a digital twin can predict the progression of bearing wear. Similarly, an increase in motor temperature that deviates from its normal thermal curve, when correlated with load, can forecast an imminent insulation failure. Machine learning models are trained on historical data that includes examples of gradual degradation leading to failure, allowing them to recognize similar incipient patterns in current operational data. The objective is to develop models that can not only detect deviations but also quantify the remaining useful life (RUL) of the asset or its critical components.

The output of these predictive models is then translated into actionable maintenance recommendations. This involves establishing thresholds and rules that trigger alerts for specific maintenance actions. For example, a prediction of "80% probability of bearing failure within 100 operating hours" might trigger a recommendation for immediate inspection and potential replacement, whereas a prediction of "20% probability of pump seal degradation within 500 operating hours" might place the asset on a list for scheduled inspection during the next planned maintenance cycle. The digital twin can further enhance this by providing diagnostic information, suggesting potential root causes for the predicted failure, and even recommending specific maintenance procedures or parts.

Crucially, a predictive maintenance program is not a static implementation. It requires continuous monitoring, evaluation, and refinement. As the asset operates and new data becomes available, the digital twin's models can be retrained and updated to improve their accuracy. Feedback from maintenance teams regarding the effectiveness of predicted interventions and the actual root causes of failures is invaluable for fine-tuning the models. This iterative process ensures that the predictive capabilities remain relevant and effective over the entire lifecycle of the asset. The digital twin, therefore, becomes a living, learning entity that evolves alongside its physical counterpart, consistently enhancing its ability to predict and prevent failures. This closed-loop feedback mechanism is vital for achieving true operational resilience and optimizing maintenance strategies over time. The insights gleaned are not just about preventing individual failures but also about optimizing the overall maintenance budget, resource allocation, and asset performance management strategy.

The implementation of predictive maintenance within a digital twin framework is not merely a technological upgrade; it represents a fundamental shift in how organizations approach asset management and operational efficiency. The historical context of maintenance practices, evolving from simple repairs to more structured preventive schedules, laid the groundwork for the sophisticated capabilities offered by predictive analytics. In the past, maintenance decisions were often based on calendar intervals or an operator's intuition, leading to either over-maintenance (performing services that were not yet needed) or under-maintenance (leading to unexpected failures). The advent of condition monitoring technologies, such as vibration analysis and thermal imaging, offered a glimpse into the asset's health, enabling more informed decisions. However, these were often point-in-time assessments, requiring specialized human expertise to interpret the data and extrapolate future trends.

Digital twins elevate this by creating a dynamic, integrated, and intelligent system. They consolidate disparate data streams from various sensors and operational systems, providing a holistic view of the asset. This unified perspective allows for the correlation of data points that might appear insignificant in isolation. For example, a slight increase in motor temperature, when combined with a subtle change in lubrication pressure and a specific pattern of acoustic emissions, might collectively indicate an early-stage bearing lubrication issue that a single-point monitoring system would miss. The digital twin, armed with its comprehensive data model, can recognize this confluence of indicators as a precursor to failure.

The process of building a predictive maintenance capability within a digital twin ecosystem begins with a thorough understanding of the asset's failure modes. This requires deep domain expertise from engineers and maintenance personnel. What are the common ways this particular piece of equipment fails? What are the critical parameters that precede these failures? Once these failure modes are identified, the focus shifts to identifying the relevant data streams and developing analytical models that can detect the early warning signs associated with each mode. For a rotating machine, common failure modes include bearing degradation, rotor imbalance, shaft misalignment, and electrical winding issues. Each of these manifests with distinct signatures in vibration, temperature, and current draw data.

The selection of appropriate predictive models is crucial and depends heavily on the nature of the data and the expected failure patterns. For time-series data that exhibits clear temporal dependencies, such as temperature fluctuations or vibration frequency shifts over time, Recurrent Neural Networks (RNNs) and Long Short-Term Memory (LSTM) networks are highly effective. These models can capture long-term dependencies and learn complex temporal dynamics, allowing them to predict trends with greater accuracy. For multivariate data where the relationships between different parameters are key indicators of health, techniques like Principal Component Analysis (PCA) for dimensionality reduction followed by anomaly detection algorithms, or ensemble methods like Random Forests and Gradient Boosting Machines, can be employed. These methods excel at identifying subtle deviations in the complex interplay between multiple variables.

Moreover, the concept of "remaining useful life" (RUL) estimation is central to predictive maintenance. Instead of just flagging an anomaly, the goal is to quantify how much longer the asset can operate safely and efficiently before a failure is likely. This requires models that can estimate the degradation rate of components. For instance, by tracking the progression of a specific frequency component in a vibration spectrum that is known to be associated with bearing wear, a model can predict the time until that component reaches a critical amplitude. This RUL estimation allows maintenance planners to schedule interventions strategically, balancing the risk of failure against the cost and disruption of maintenance activities.

The integration of physics-based models within the digital twin further enhances predictive capabilities. These models provide a baseline of expected behavior under known operating conditions, acting as a powerful validation tool. If sensor data suggests a deviation that is inconsistent with physical laws or established engineering principles, the confidence in the anomaly being a true system fault increases. For example, if a pump's power consumption increases significantly without a corresponding increase in flow rate, a physics-based model can help determine if this deviation is physically plausible under any normal operating condition or if it strongly suggests an internal issue like a blocked impeller or a worn seal. This validation step is critical in reducing false positives and ensuring that maintenance resources are not wasted on addressing non-existent problems.

The operationalization of predictive maintenance involves creating a seamless workflow from data ingestion to maintenance execution. This typically includes:

1. **Data Aggregation and Contextualization:** Gathering real-time sensor data, operational parameters, environmental conditions, and historical maintenance records into a unified platform, often managed by the digital twin. Contextualization involves linking this data to specific assets, components, and operational states.
2. **Model Execution and Anomaly Detection:** Running the pre-trained predictive models on the incoming data streams to identify deviations from normal behavior and to detect emerging patterns indicative of degradation.
3. **Failure Mode Identification and RUL Estimation:** Classifying detected anomalies into known failure modes and estimating the remaining useful life of the affected component or asset.

4. **Alert Generation and Prioritization:** Triggering alerts when predefined thresholds for anomaly severity or estimated RUL are crossed. These alerts are typically prioritized based on the urgency of the situation and the potential impact on operations.
5. **Diagnostic Support and Recommendation:** Providing diagnostic information to support maintenance teams, including potential root causes, affected components, and recommended maintenance actions (e.g., inspect, lubricate, replace).
6. **Work Order Generation and Scheduling:** Integrating with enterprise asset management (EAM) or computerised maintenance management system (CMMS) to automatically generate work orders, schedule maintenance tasks, and procure necessary parts.
7. **Feedback Loop and Model Refinement:** Collecting feedback from maintenance crews on the accuracy of predictions, the effectiveness of interventions, and the actual root causes of failures. This feedback is used to retrain and refine the predictive models, creating a continuous improvement cycle.

Consider a large-scale manufacturing facility with hundreds of critical assets. Implementing a predictive maintenance program via digital twins can revolutionize its operations. For a complex CNC machining center, sensors monitoring spindle vibration, tool wear, coolant temperature, and axis motor current can feed into its digital twin. The twin, trained on historical data of tool degradation and spindle bearing wear, might detect a subtle increase in a specific harmonic frequency in the spindle vibration data, coupled with a slightly elevated motor current. While these individual deviations might be within acceptable limits for a simple monitoring system, the digital twin, recognizing the combined signature, predicts a 70% likelihood of tool breakage within the next 48 hours, or potential bearing failure within 100 hours.

This prediction triggers an alert in the CMMS, automatically scheduling a tool change during the next scheduled break and flagging the spindle for inspection during the upcoming weekend shutdown. If the bearing issue is deemed more critical, the system might even suggest an immediate halt to production to prevent catastrophic damage. The maintenance team receives a detailed report, not just an alert, outlining the observed data, the predicted failure mode, the estimated RUL, and recommended actions. This allows them to proactively order the specific replacement bearing, schedule the required labor, and plan the downtime with precision, avoiding production stoppages and costly emergency repairs that could have arisen from a catastrophic spindle failure.

The benefits of such a sophisticated approach are manifold. Reduced unplanned downtime is the most immediate and tangible advantage, directly impacting productivity and revenue. Minimized maintenance costs are achieved through optimized scheduling, reduced overtime, efficient use of spare parts, and less frequent, less extensive repairs. Extended asset life is a direct consequence of addressing issues early, preventing minor degradations from escalating into major damage. Improved safety is also a significant benefit, as predictable failures are less likely to occur unexpectedly during critical operations, thus reducing the risk of accidents. Furthermore, the wealth of data and insights generated by the digital twin can inform future purchasing decisions, equipment design improvements, and overall operational strategy, fostering a culture of continuous improvement and data-driven decision-making. The predictive maintenance capability of digital twins is not just about fixing machines; it's about transforming operational intelligence into tangible business value.

The true power of digital twins extends far beyond simply anticipating failures; it lies in their capacity to actively enhance and optimize ongoing operations. By meticulously analyzing the continuous stream of real-time data fed into the virtual replica, organizations can gain unprecedented insights into performance nuances, uncovering opportunities for efficiency gains that might otherwise remain hidden. This proactive optimization, driven by real-time analysis, transforms the digital twin from a passive monitoring tool into an active participant in operational excellence, yielding tangible benefits in areas like energy consumption, throughput, and control system effectiveness.

Consider the realm of energy consumption, a critical operational expense for many industries, particularly those with energy-intensive processes. A digital twin, equipped with sensor data from every energy-consuming component—motors, pumps, HVAC systems, lighting—along with real-time environmental factors and production schedules, can build a sophisticated model of energy usage patterns. By comparing actual consumption against predicted optimal levels, the system can identify specific instances of energy wastage. For example, it might detect that a particular production line is consuming disproportionately more energy during off-peak hours than necessary, or that a set of compressors are operating at suboptimal pressures given the current demand. The digital twin can then correlate these inefficiencies with specific operational parameters or even external factors like ambient temperature or humidity. Armed with this granular understanding, the system can recommend precise adjustments. This might involve automatically recalibrating control setpoints for variable frequency drives (VFDs) on motors to match actual load requirements more closely, or suggesting a revised sequencing for operating multiple pumps to minimize overall energy draw. The outcome is a direct reduction in utility bills, contributing significantly to the bottom line without compromising production targets. Furthermore, this real-time optimization can be dynamically adjusted; if a sudden surge in demand occurs, the digital twin can intelligently re-prioritize energy allocation to ensure critical operations are met while still minimizing waste in non-essential areas. This dynamic balancing act, informed by predictive analytics, represents a significant leap beyond static energy management strategies.

Maximizing throughput, another cornerstone of operational efficiency, is another area where real-time analysis via digital twins shines. Imagine a complex manufacturing assembly line where bottlenecks can severely limit overall output. A digital twin of this line, fed with data on machine cycle times, buffer levels between stations, material flow rates, and even operator availability, can paint a dynamic picture of the entire process. By continuously monitoring these parameters, the twin can identify emerging bottlenecks *before* they significantly impact throughput. For instance, it might notice a gradual increase in the queue size at a specific workstation, or a slight but consistent slowdown in the cycle time of a particular machine. Unlike traditional methods that might only identify a bottleneck after it has already caused a substantial slowdown, the digital twin can detect these subtle deteriorations in real-time.

This early detection enables proactive intervention. The digital twin can analyze the situation and suggest immediate, data-driven remedies. This might involve recommending a temporary adjustment to the upstream feed rate to prevent overwhelming the bottlenecked station, suggesting a minor parameter tweak on the bottlenecked machine to slightly increase its speed, or even proposing a reallocation of tasks if an adjacent station has available capacity. In more advanced implementations, the digital twin might automatically orchestrate these adjustments through the control systems, ensuring a seamless flow of materials and maximizing the utilization of every asset on the line. Moreover, by simulating the impact of proposed changes within the virtual environment before they are implemented on the physical line, the digital twin can ensure that any adjustments made to alleviate one bottleneck do not inadvertently create a new one elsewhere. This predictive optimization of flow and resource allocation is crucial for achieving peak operational performance and consistently meeting or exceeding production targets. The insights gained from analyzing historical throughput data, correlated with various operational scenarios, can also inform long-term strategic decisions, such as optimal plant layout or the ideal mix of equipment to achieve desired production volumes.

Fine-tuning control parameters is perhaps one of the most intricate yet impactful applications of real-time analysis with digital twins. Modern industrial processes are governed by complex control systems that continuously adjust variables like temperature, pressure, flow rate, and motor speed to maintain desired operational states. However, these control systems are often configured based on average conditions or theoretical models, which may not always reflect the dynamic reality of the physical environment. A digital twin provides the perfect platform to bridge this gap. By integrating real-time sensor data with the digital twin's predictive models, operators and the system itself can gain a deeper understanding of how the process actually behaves under varying conditions.

For example, in a chemical processing plant, maintaining precise temperature and pressure within reactors is critical for product quality and safety. A digital twin of a reactor, fed with real-time measurements of temperature, pressure, catalyst activity, reactant concentrations, and even subtle vibrations within the vessel, can model the intricate thermal and chemical dynamics with high fidelity. If the digital twin observes that the standard PID (Proportional-Integral-Derivative) controller is overshooting the target temperature or requiring excessive adjustments to maintain pressure, it can analyze the underlying causes.

This analysis might reveal that the control loop is not adequately accounting for variations in reactant feed composition, or that the heat transfer characteristics of the vessel have subtly changed due to fouling. Based on this real-time diagnosis, the digital twin can propose adjustments to the controller's tuning parameters - perhaps increasing the proportional gain slightly, or modifying the integral term to better compensate for a specific type of disturbance. In advanced systems, these adjustments can be made automatically, adapting the control strategy in real-time to optimize performance, minimize deviations, and ensure consistent product quality. This dynamic recalibration, guided by the rich data and analytical capabilities of the digital twin, allows for a level of process control that was previously unattainable, leading to improved product consistency, reduced waste, and enhanced operational safety. The digital twin can also be used to simulate the impact of introducing entirely new control algorithms or strategies, allowing for robust testing in a risk-free virtual environment before deployment onto the physical asset.

The integration of predictive insights into real-time optimization is a synergistic process. It's not just about reacting to current conditions; it's about leveraging future projections to make immediate, intelligent decisions. For instance, if the digital twin predicts a minor dip in ambient temperature in the next few hours that might slightly impact the viscosity of a fluid being pumped, it can proactively adjust the pump's speed or the heater's output *before* the viscosity change causes a noticeable deviation in flow rate. This predictive preemptive action maintains process stability and efficiency far more effectively than a reactive correction. Similarly, if a future load increase is predicted, the system can ensure that all relevant components are brought up to optimal operating parameters in advance, thereby maximizing the response time and minimizing any potential performance degradation during the transition.

Furthermore, the value derived from real-time optimization is amplified when it is integrated into a broader digital ecosystem. Data from the performance optimization module of a digital twin can feed back into the maintenance module, informing the maintenance schedule not just based on potential failure, but also on the need to maintain optimal performance. For example, if a component is identified as operating at a slightly reduced efficiency (even if still within acceptable failure-risk parameters), this information can be used to prioritize its maintenance or replacement, ensuring that peak performance is restored as quickly as possible. Conversely, if a piece of equipment is performing exceptionally well, its scheduled maintenance might be adjusted to a later date, provided that the digital twin's real-time monitoring confirms its continued healthy operation. This sophisticated interplay between performance optimization and predictive maintenance creates a truly adaptive and highly efficient operational strategy.

The implementation of performance optimization through real-time analysis requires a robust data infrastructure, sophisticated analytical algorithms, and clear communication channels between the digital twin and the physical asset's control systems. The ability to process vast amounts of data with low latency is critical for effective real-time decision-making. Machine learning algorithms, specifically those adept at time-series analysis, anomaly detection, and regression, are essential for identifying subtle performance deviations and predicting future trends. The integration of these algorithms within the digital twin's framework allows for the continuous learning and adaptation of optimization strategies.

Ultimately, the shift towards real-time performance optimization powered by digital twins signifies a move from a reactive or scheduled operational mindset to one that is continuously self-aware, self-correcting, and self-improving. It allows organizations to extract maximum value from their assets, not just by keeping them running, but by ensuring they run at their absolute best, adapting dynamically to changing conditions and proactively pursuing efficiency at every turn. This continuous pursuit of operational excellence, facilitated by the intelligent insights derived from real-time data analysis within the digital twin, represents a significant competitive advantage in today's dynamic industrial landscape. The ability to fine-tune operations on the fly, optimize resource allocation, and ensure peak efficiency across all processes translates directly into enhanced profitability, reduced environmental impact, and a more resilient and agile business.

The efficacy of any sophisticated monitoring system, including those powered by digital twins, is fundamentally contingent on its ability to translate complex data streams and analytical outputs into readily comprehensible information. Without clear and intuitive visualizations, even the most advanced predictive insights can become lost in a sea of raw numbers, rendering them ineffective for driving timely and informed decisions. This section delves into the critical domain of visualizing monitoring insights, exploring how digital twins can leverage various graphical and interactive techniques to present operational status, performance metrics, and predictive forecasts in a manner that empowers users across different roles – from frontline operators to senior management. The goal is to transform abstract data into tangible, actionable intelligence, fostering a shared understanding and facilitating rapid comprehension.

A cornerstone of effective visualization lies in the design of dashboards. These are not merely collections of charts and graphs; they are carefully curated interfaces designed to provide a holistic yet granular view of an asset's or system's performance. Best practices in dashboard design emphasize clarity, context, and relevance. For instance, a dashboard intended for a plant operator might prioritize real-time operational parameters such as pressure, temperature, flow rates, and immediate alerts, presented in easily digestible formats like analog gauges, color-coded status indicators, and concise numerical readouts. The visual design should minimize cognitive load, ensuring that critical information is immediately apparent. This often involves employing a hierarchical structure, where overarching status is presented prominently, with the ability to drill down into specific subsystems or components for more detailed examination. Using consistent color palettes that adhere to industry standards (e.g., green for normal, yellow for caution, red for alarm) is paramount for quick interpretation. Furthermore, the judicious use of trends over short periods (e.g., the last hour or shift) can provide immediate context to current readings.

Conversely, a dashboard designed for a reliability engineer might focus on key performance indicators (KPIs) related to asset health, such as mean time between failures (MTBF), overall equipment effectiveness (OEE), or component degradation trends. Here, line charts showing historical performance, scatter plots correlating operational parameters with wear rates, and heatmaps indicating areas of potential concern would be more appropriate. The emphasis shifts from immediate operational status to long-term trends and predictive indicators. For managers, a dashboard might present high-level summaries of operational efficiency, financial impact of performance deviations, and projected maintenance costs, often incorporating aggregated data and key risk indicators. Regardless of the target audience, effective dashboards are interactive, allowing users to filter data, adjust timeframes, and explore relationships between different variables. The principle of "at-a-glance" comprehension should guide every design choice, ensuring that users can quickly assess the situation and identify areas requiring further attention without being overwhelmed by extraneous information. The strategic placement of key metrics and the use of whitespace can significantly improve readability and reduce the time it takes to derive meaning from the presented data.

Beyond traditional 2D dashboards, the inherent three-dimensional nature of many physical assets lends itself perfectly to 3D visualizations. Digital twins, by their very definition, are virtual replicas, and presenting monitoring insights within a 3D model of the asset can offer an unparalleled level of spatial understanding. Imagine a sprawling petrochemical plant, a complex aircraft engine, or a wind turbine farm. Visualizing critical operating data directly onto the 3D model can immediately contextualize where an anomaly or performance deviation is occurring. For example, if a particular pump in the plant is showing signs of increased vibration, highlighting that specific pump within the 3D model, perhaps with a pulsating red indicator or a color gradient representing the severity of the vibration, provides immediate spatial awareness. This is far more intuitive than scanning a long list of equipment and trying to match serial numbers or location codes.

Furthermore, 3D visualizations can be used to represent complex phenomena and predictive outcomes. A thermal analysis showing areas of overheating can be rendered as a heat map overlaid on the 3D model, clearly delineating the extent and severity of the issue. Similarly, predicted stress points on a structural component or the potential spread of a fluid leak can be dynamically visualized within the virtual environment. This spatial representation also aids in understanding the interconnectedness of systems. If a failure in one component is predicted to impact adjacent equipment, the 3D visualization can illustrate these cascading effects, helping engineers understand the broader implications of a localized issue. The ability to virtually "walk around" or "fly through" the digital twin while viewing real-time data enhances situational awareness and facilitates collaborative problem-solving. Teams can gather around a shared 3D model, pointing out specific areas of concern and discussing potential solutions in a common, visual language. This immersive experience can significantly accelerate troubleshooting and decision-making processes, especially for complex, geographically dispersed, or hazardous assets where physical access might be limited or dangerous. The fidelity of the 3D model, combined with the accuracy of the real-time data, creates a powerful tool for understanding and managing intricate systems.

Augmented reality (AR) represents the next frontier in visualizing monitoring insights, bridging the gap between the digital twin and the physical world in a truly seamless manner. By overlaying digital information onto the real-world view through devices like smart glasses or tablets, AR allows personnel to see the "invisible" data associated with physical assets directly in their field of vision. This is particularly transformative for field technicians and maintenance crews who are often working directly with the equipment. When a technician approaches a piece of machinery, AR glasses can instantly display its current operational status, key performance metrics, and any active alerts. For instance, looking at a motor might reveal its current RPM, power consumption, temperature, and the projected time until its next scheduled maintenance, all superimposed directly onto the physical motor.

This contextual overlay dramatically reduces the time spent searching for information, cross-referencing manuals, or recalling data from memory. Moreover, AR can guide complex tasks. For a technician performing a repair, AR can provide step-by-step instructions, highlighting the exact bolts to loosen, the correct torque values, or the precise locations for sensor placement. If a digital twin has predicted a specific component failure, AR can guide the technician to that exact part within the assembly, showing its condition and the necessary replacement procedure. For remote assistance, an expert can view what the field technician sees through their AR device and provide real-time guidance, drawing annotations directly into the technician's field of view. This capability is invaluable for complex troubleshooting or for supporting less experienced personnel. The ability to visualize predictive maintenance alerts – perhaps a subtly glowing component indicating it's nearing its wear limit – directly in the physical space of the asset makes the abstract concept of predictive maintenance highly tangible and actionable. AR transforms the physical workspace into an interactive information hub, driven by the intelligence of the digital twin. The integration of 3D spatial data from the digital twin with the real-world view through AR creates an information-rich environment that significantly enhances operational efficiency, safety, and accuracy.

Alert systems are a critical component of any monitoring strategy, and within the context of digital twins, they must evolve beyond simple threshold breaches. Effective alert systems leverage the predictive capabilities of the digital twin to provide context, prioritize issues, and suggest actionable responses. A well-designed alert system doesn't just signal a problem; it communicates its significance, potential impact, and recommended course of action. This can be achieved through intelligent alert categorization and severity scoring. Instead of a generic "High Temperature" alert, the system might provide "Critical Component Overheat: Engine Zone 3 – Risk of imminent bearing seizure within 2 hours. Recommended action: Reduce load by 20% and schedule immediate inspection."

The use of intelligent routing ensures that alerts reach the most appropriate personnel. An alert regarding a minor deviation in energy consumption might be routed to an energy manager, while an alert indicating an imminent critical failure would be escalated to maintenance supervisors and plant managers simultaneously. Contextualization is also key; an alert should be presented with relevant historical data, current operational parameters, and the digital twin's predictions. This allows the recipient to understand the alert not in isolation, but within the broader operational picture. For example, an alert about a fluctuating pressure might be accompanied by data showing a recent change in upstream valve position or a weather forecast predicting a change in ambient conditions that could affect the system. This richer context aids in rapid diagnosis and prevents misinterpretation of transient operational variations.

Furthermore, alert systems should be configurable and adaptable. Users should be able to define their own alert thresholds and escalation paths, and the system should learn from user responses to refine alert generation over time. Machine learning can be employed to identify patterns that precede critical events, allowing the system to generate "pre-failure" alerts that provide ample time for proactive intervention. Visual cues within the alert itself are also important. This could include graphical representations of the predicted failure trajectory, the potential impact zones on the asset, or even short video snippets from the digital twin demonstrating the anomaly. The ultimate goal is to transform alerts from disruptive notifications into valuable intelligence that facilitates informed and timely decision-making, minimizing downtime and optimizing performance. The effectiveness of an alert system is directly proportional to its ability to provide actionable insights rather than just raw data.

The integration of these visualization techniques – dashboards, 3D models, AR overlays, and intelligent alert systems – creates a powerful ecosystem for operational monitoring. Each element plays a distinct yet complementary role. Dashboards provide the broad strokes, offering an immediate overview of system health and key performance indicators. 3D visualizations bring spatial context, allowing users to pinpoint issues within the physical or virtual asset. Augmented reality dissolves the barrier between digital information and the physical world, empowering field personnel with real-time, contextual data exactly where and when they need it. Intelligent alert systems cut through the noise, ensuring that critical events are not missed and that users are provided with the necessary information to act swiftly and effectively.

The success of these visualization strategies hinges on several underlying principles. Firstly,
user-centric design is paramount. Visualizations must be tailored to the specific needs, technical understanding, and decision-making responsibilities of the intended audience. A one-size-fits-all approach is unlikely to be effective. Secondly, **data accuracy and timeliness** are non-negotiable. Visualizations are only as good as the data they represent; any lag or inaccuracy will undermine trust and lead to poor decisions. The real-time nature of digital twin data is a

significant advantage here, but ensuring robust data pipelines and processing is crucial. Thirdly, **interactivity and exploration** should be built into the visualization tools. Users should be able to probe the data, ask "what if" questions, and drill down into details as needed, rather than being presented with static views. Fourthly, **simplicity and clarity** must be prioritized. Overly complex or cluttered visualizations will defeat the purpose of making data accessible and actionable. The "less is more" principle often applies, with a focus on highlighting the most critical information.

Finally, the
narrative power of visualization should not be underestimated. Effective visual representations can tell a story about the performance of an asset or system, highlighting trends, identifying root causes of problems, and showcasing the impact of interventions. This narrative can be crucial for gaining buy-in from stakeholders, justifying investments in operational improvements, and fostering a culture of data-driven decision-making. By presenting complex insights in an intuitive and engaging manner, visualizations empower individuals and teams to understand, act upon, and ultimately optimize the performance of critical assets, driving operational excellence and achieving strategic business objectives. The continuous refinement of these visualization tools, informed by user feedback and advancements in technology, will further enhance the value derived from digital twin monitoring.

The preceding discussion has illuminated the critical role of visualization in transforming raw data from digital twins into comprehensible insights. However, the ultimate purpose of these visualizations is not merely to inform, but to actively empower decision-making. This is where the digital twin transcends its role as a sophisticated monitoring tool and emerges as a potent **decision support system (DSS)**. The intelligence embedded within a digital twin, forged from the synergistic integration of physics-based simulation models, real-time operational data, and sophisticated analytical algorithms, is designed to guide users toward more informed, timely, and ultimately, optimal decisions. This subsection will delve into the mechanisms by which digital twin intelligence actively supports and enhances decision-making processes across a spectrum of operational scenarios, from the mundane to the mission-critical.

At its core, a digital twin acts as a dynamic, virtual replica that mirrors the state and behavior of its physical counterpart. This mirroring is achieved through a constant, high-fidelity data exchange. Real-time sensor data streams from the physical asset are fed into the digital twin, updating its virtual state in near-instantaneous fashion. Concurrently, advanced analytics, ranging from statistical process control and machine learning to sophisticated physics-based simulations, are applied to this data within the digital twin environment. The integration of these elements allows the digital twin to not only reflect the current condition of the asset but also to predict its future trajectory and analyze the root causes of observed phenomena. This fusion of historical data, real-time status, and predictive modeling creates a comprehensive understanding that is far richer than what can be gleaned from disparate data sources or traditional monitoring methods.

The actionable intelligence derived from this integrated knowledge base is what transforms a digital twin into an effective decision support system. Consider the realm of
predictive maintenance. Traditional approaches often rely on fixed schedules or reactive measures taken only after a failure occurs. A digital twin, however, can continuously assess the degradation of components based on real-time operating conditions and historical wear patterns. For instance, a digital twin of a fleet of industrial pumps might analyze vibration data, operating temperature,

flow rates, and lubricant quality. By comparing these real-time parameters against established degradation models and historical failure data, the twin can predict with a high degree of accuracy when a specific pump is likely to fail. This prediction is not a vague estimate; it can often be expressed with a specific time window, such as "Pump 3B in Sector 7 is predicted to experience bearing failure within the next 72 hours under current operating conditions."

This predictive insight directly translates into empowered decision-making for maintenance teams. Instead of performing maintenance on a rigid schedule that might result in unnecessary work on healthy components or insufficient attention to those most at risk, maintenance can be optimized. The decision to be made is: "When and how should we maintain Pump 3B?" The digital twin's output provides the critical data to inform this decision. The maintenance manager can then decide to schedule maintenance for Pump 3B during an upcoming planned downtime, or if the predicted failure is imminent and critical, they might need to re-route production or bring forward a scheduled maintenance window. Furthermore, the digital twin can suggest the most effective maintenance actions. It can analyze the predicted failure mode and recommend specific diagnostic tests, replacement parts, or repair procedures, thereby ensuring that the maintenance crew is adequately prepared and equipped. This proactive approach significantly reduces unscheduled downtime, lowers maintenance costs by avoiding unnecessary interventions, and extends the lifespan of critical assets. The decision to intervene becomes a data-driven, optimized choice rather than a reactive necessity.

Beyond routine maintenance, digital twin intelligence extends to the optimization of
operational performance. In complex industrial settings, such as chemical plants or power generation facilities, numerous variables interact to influence efficiency and output. A digital twin can serve as a virtual testbed for exploring different operational strategies without risking disruption to the actual plant. For example, a plant manager might want to increase production throughput. The traditional approach involves incrementally adjusting parameters like temperature, pressure, or flow rates and observing the impact, which can be time-consuming and potentially lead to suboptimal or even unsafe conditions. With a digital twin, however, various scenarios can be simulated rapidly. The

twin can model the effects of increasing feed rates or altering catalyst concentrations, predicting the impact on yield, energy consumption, and the generation of byproducts.

The decision supported here is: "What is the optimal set of operating parameters to achieve our production goals while remaining within safety and efficiency constraints?" The digital twin can run hundreds or thousands of simulations, exploring a vast parameter space. It can identify the combination of settings that maximizes output while minimizing energy usage and waste, all within the defined operational envelope. The output of these simulations would guide the plant manager's decision, presenting them with a clear recommendation, such as "Increasing reactor temperature by 5 degrees Celsius and slightly reducing residence time will yield a 3% increase in product output with a negligible impact on energy consumption and no violation of safety limits." This allows for informed decisions that enhance productivity and profitability, often uncovering opportunities for improvement that would be difficult or impossible to identify through real-world experimentation alone. The digital twin effectively quantifies the trade-offs between different operational choices, providing a clear rationale for the optimal path forward.

In situations demanding **resource allocation and scheduling**, digital twin intelligence can provide significant leverage. Consider a logistics company managing a fleet of delivery vehicles. Each vehicle has a unique operational profile, including fuel efficiency, maintenance needs, and delivery capacities. A digital twin, representing each vehicle and its current status, can be used to optimize delivery routes and schedules. Real-time traffic data, weather forecasts, and delivery time windows can be integrated into the twin's model. The decision being supported might be: "Which vehicle should be assigned to which delivery route to minimize total delivery time and fuel costs?"

The digital twin can analyze these complex, dynamic factors and generate optimal assignments. It can predict the travel time for each route based on current conditions, estimate fuel consumption, and factor in the availability of drivers and vehicles. Furthermore, it can identify potential conflicts or bottlenecks in the schedule. If a particular route is predicted to be significantly delayed due to unforeseen traffic, the digital twin can proactively suggest reassignments or alternative routes for affected vehicles. This capability is invaluable for dynamic environments where conditions can change rapidly. The decision-maker, such as a dispatcher or fleet manager, receives recommendations that are not only efficient but also adaptable, ensuring that resources are deployed in the most effective manner at any given moment. The twin can also support strategic decisions about fleet expansion or vehicle replacement by simulating the impact of adding new vehicles or retiring older ones on overall operational efficiency.

Perhaps the most critical application of digital twin intelligence as a DSS is in **emergency response and risk management**. When an unforeseen event occurs, such as a critical equipment failure, a natural disaster, or a security breach, the ability to make rapid, accurate decisions under pressure is paramount. A digital twin can provide an unparalleled understanding of the situation. For instance, in the event of a potential containment breach in a chemical facility, a digital twin can model the dispersion of hazardous materials based on real-time atmospheric conditions, the integrity of surrounding infrastructure, and the status of safety systems.

The decision to be supported here is multifaceted: "What is the immediate threat? Where is it heading? What are the most effective mitigation strategies? Who needs to be evacuated or protected?" The digital twin can ingest data from numerous sources – sensors within the facility, weather stations, emergency service reports – and run rapid simulations to predict the spread of the hazard. It can visualize the affected areas, identify the populations or assets at highest risk, and evaluate the potential effectiveness of various response actions, such as activating emergency ventilation systems, deploying containment booms, or initiating specific evacuation protocols. The digital twin's ability to visualize these scenarios and their potential outcomes allows incident commanders to make informed decisions about resource deployment, containment strategies, and communication with affected parties. The speed and accuracy with which the digital twin can process complex data and generate actionable insights can be the difference between a contained incident and a widespread catastrophe. It moves decision-making from a reactive, often chaotic process to a controlled, data-informed response.

The intelligence embedded within a digital twin also supports decisions related to

strategic planning and investment. For example, a company looking to upgrade its manufacturing capabilities can use digital twins of its existing and proposed facilities to simulate the impact of new equipment, different layouts, or altered production workflows. The decision being supported might be: "Where should we invest in new machinery to achieve the greatest return on investment and improve overall throughput?" By creating digital twins of various proposed scenarios, the company can compare their predicted performance, cost implications, and potential bottlenecks before committing significant capital. This allows for data-driven investment decisions, reducing the risk associated with large-scale capital expenditures and ensuring that investments align with strategic objectives. The twin can model the long-term effects of these decisions, projecting future operational costs, maintenance requirements, and production capacities over the asset's lifecycle.

The effectiveness of a digital twin as a DSS is amplified by its ability to foster collaboration and knowledge sharing. When complex decisions need to be made, involving multiple departments or stakeholders, the digital twin can serve as a common, objective platform for discussion. Engineers, operators, managers, and even external partners can access the same virtual model, view the same data, and engage with the same simulations. This shared understanding minimizes misinterpretations and facilitates consensus-building. For example, during a design review for a new industrial component, engineers can use the digital twin to demonstrate the predicted stresses under various operating conditions, while manufacturing experts can assess the feasibility of production. The integrated intelligence of the twin provides a basis for informed dialogue and collective decision-making.

Furthermore, the learning capabilities embedded within many digital twin architectures contribute to continuously improving the quality of decision support. As more data is collected and more operational cycles are completed, the underlying models can be refined. Machine learning algorithms can identify subtle patterns that humans might miss, leading to more accurate predictions and more insightful recommendations over time. This iterative improvement means that the decision support provided by the digital twin becomes increasingly sophisticated and reliable, driving ongoing optimization of operations and strategic planning. The digital twin thus evolves from a static model to a dynamic, learning partner in the decision-making process, constantly enhancing its ability to guide users toward better outcomes. The intelligence is not static; it grows and adapts with experience, making it an invaluable asset for any organization seeking to navigate the complexities of modern operations with confidence and precision. This continuous refinement ensures that decisions are not only optimal for the current situation but also informed by the accumulated wisdom of past operations and the anticipated evolution of future challenges.

The inherent power of a digital twin lies not just in its ability to mirror reality, but in its capacity to transcend the present and explore the myriad possibilities of the future and the consequences of hypothetical alterations. This is where the transformative potential of **scenario planning and 'what-if' analysis** truly shines, elevating the digital twin from a sophisticated diagnostic tool to an indispensable strategic planning instrument. By providing a safe, virtual sandbox, digital twins empower stakeholders to meticulously probe various operational conditions, anticipate potential disruptions, and rigorously evaluate the ramifications of proposed changes—all without incurring any risk to the physical asset or its ongoing operations. This capability is crucial for discerning the most robust, efficient, and resilient courses of action *before* they are implemented in the complex, often unforgiving, real-world environment.

At its core, scenario planning within a digital twin framework involves constructing and simulating distinct futures or hypothetical situations. This process begins with identifying key variables that influence the performance or behavior of the physical asset. These variables can range from predictable environmental factors like ambient temperature or humidity, to operational parameters such as load, speed, or throughput, and even external influences like market demand or regulatory changes. Once these variables are defined, a range of values or states can be assigned to them to represent different scenarios. For example, in a manufacturing plant, a scenario might involve simulating production under peak demand conditions, while another might explore the impact of a sudden component shortage. The digital twin, equipped with its underlying physics-based models and historical data, can then process these inputs and predict the resulting outcomes for the physical asset.

The 'what-if' analysis is the direct application of this scenario planning capability. It poses specific questions about potential future states or interventions and uses the digital twin to generate data-driven answers. Imagine a scenario where a company is considering upgrading a critical piece of machinery. Instead of relying on outdated equipment specifications or costly pilot programs, the digital twin of the proposed new machine, integrated with the twin of the existing plant infrastructure, can be utilized. The 'what-if' question might be: "What would be the impact on overall plant throughput and energy consumption if we replace Machine X with the new Model Y?" The digital twin would then simulate the operation of Model Y within the context of the entire plant, considering factors like the machine's cycle time, its integration with upstream and downstream processes, its power draw, and its maintenance requirements. The output would quantify the expected changes, perhaps revealing a 15% increase in output but also a surprising 10% surge in peak power demand, highlighting a potential bottleneck in the facility's electrical infrastructure that needs to be addressed *before* the new machine is installed.

Consider a scenario in the energy sector, specifically with a wind farm. A digital twin of the farm can simulate various weather patterns – from calm days to hurricane-force winds – to assess structural integrity and energy generation potential. A 'what-if' analysis could be: "What is the projected energy output and structural stress on turbine 7 if a sustained wind speed of 50 mph is experienced for 24 hours, considering its current maintenance status?" The digital twin, integrating real-time atmospheric data and the turbine's specific operational history and degradation models, can provide a precise answer. It might predict a certain level of energy generation, along with a calculated risk of exceeding certain fatigue load limits, thus informing decisions about whether to curtail operations during such conditions to prolong the turbine's lifespan, or if additional structural monitoring is warranted. This proactive approach prevents potential catastrophic failures and optimizes operational efficiency.

In the realm of logistics and transportation, scenario planning with digital twins is equally impactful. A fleet manager might pose a 'what-if' question about a new delivery route optimization strategy: "What would be the reduction in fuel consumption and total delivery time if we implement a dynamic routing algorithm that considers real-time traffic and weather data, compared to our current static route planning?" The digital twin of the fleet, integrated with external data feeds, can run simulations for a week's worth of typical delivery schedules under both scenarios. The results would provide quantifiable data on expected fuel savings, driver hours, and on-time delivery rates, enabling the manager to make an informed decision about adopting the new strategy, potentially saving significant operational costs and improving customer satisfaction. Furthermore, 'what-if' scenarios can be used to test the resilience of these routes to unexpected disruptions, such as bridge closures or major accidents, allowing for the pre-identification of contingency plans.

The pharmaceutical industry can leverage digital twins for scenario planning in drug manufacturing. Imagine a 'what-if' query related to a change in the formulation of a vaccine: "How will a 5% increase in the concentration of adjuvant X affect the stability and efficacy of Vaccine Y during a 3-month cold chain storage period?" A digital twin of the vaccine, incorporating its chemical composition, known degradation pathways, and the environmental parameters of the cold chain, can simulate the effects of this change. It can predict potential changes in viscosity, particulate formation, or potency over time, guiding decisions about whether the formulation change is viable or requires further research and development. This prevents the costly and time-consuming production of batches that may prove unstable or ineffective, ensuring product quality and patient safety.

Furthermore, scenario planning extends beyond operational adjustments to encompass strategic decision-making and risk management. For instance, in urban planning, a digital twin of a city could be used to simulate the impact of various climate change scenarios, such as a 1-meter sea-level rise. A 'what-if' analysis could then explore: "What infrastructure (e.g., flood defenses, drainage systems) would be required to protect critical areas like the downtown business district and the main hospital?" The digital twin can model the inundation patterns, assess the effectiveness of different protective measures, and estimate the costs associated with each option. This allows city planners and policymakers to make informed decisions about long-term investments in resilience and adaptation, prioritizing interventions that offer the greatest protection for the most vulnerable areas and essential services.

The power of 'what-if' analysis is also evident in its ability to identify unforeseen consequences or emergent behaviors. When complex systems are subject to change, the interactions between different components can lead to outcomes that are not immediately obvious. A digital twin, by modeling these intricate relationships, can reveal such effects. For example, in a complex chemical process, a 'what-if' scenario might involve altering the feed rate of a particular reactant to increase yield. While the simulation might confirm the yield increase, it could also reveal an unexpected build-up of a particular byproduct under the new conditions, which, over time, could lead to catalyst deactivation or equipment fouling. This insight allows engineers to adjust the scenario, perhaps by introducing an additional purification step or modifying other process parameters, to mitigate the negative consequence while still achieving the desired yield improvement.

The collaborative nature of decision-making in large organizations also benefits immensely from scenario planning and 'what-if' analysis facilitated by digital twins. Different departments or stakeholders can use the shared virtual environment to explore a common problem from their unique perspectives. For example, a production manager might propose a 'what-if' scenario involving a change in production speed to meet demand. The operations and maintenance teams can then use the same digital twin to evaluate the impact of this change on equipment wear, energy consumption, and potential failure rates. This shared simulation environment fosters a holistic understanding of the implications of any proposed change, leading to more integrated and effective decision-making. It bridges the gap between different functional areas, ensuring that decisions are not made in silos but with a comprehensive view of their cascading effects across the organization.

Moreover, the continuous evolution of digital twin technology, incorporating advanced AI and machine learning, further enhances the sophistication of scenario planning and 'what-if' analysis. These intelligent algorithms can automate the generation of a vast number of plausible scenarios, explore parameter spaces more exhaustively, and even learn to predict the outcomes of novel, previously unconsidered situations. For instance, an AI-powered digital twin might proactively identify a series of unusual sensor readings and automatically initiate a 'what-if' simulation to determine the potential root cause and predict the future impact. This moves beyond human-initiated queries to an autonomous, predictive form of risk assessment and opportunity identification. The system can learn from past simulations and real-world outcomes, refining its predictive models and becoming increasingly adept at anticipating challenges and opportunities.

The implementation of scenario planning and 'what-if' analysis requires a robust and accurate digital twin. The fidelity of the virtual model—how closely it represents the physical asset's behavior—is paramount. Inaccurate models will yield misleading simulation results, leading to flawed decisions. Therefore, continuous validation and calibration of the digital twin against real-world performance data are essential. This iterative process ensures that the insights generated from simulations are reliable and actionable. As more operational data is fed back into the digital twin, its predictive capabilities improve, making future scenario planning and 'what-if' analyses even more powerful and insightful. This continuous feedback loop is what transforms a static model into a dynamic, intelligent tool capable of guiding an organization through an ever-changing landscape of operational challenges and strategic imperatives. The ability to explore potential futures, test interventions, and understand complex interactions within a risk-free digital environment is not merely an advantage; it is rapidly becoming a necessity for organizations striving for agility, resilience, and competitive advantage in an increasingly complex world.

The previous discussion highlighted how digital twins, through scenario planning and 'what-if' analysis, empower organizations to proactively explore future possibilities and test hypothetical changes in a risk-free virtual environment. This capability is instrumental in strategic decision-making and risk mitigation. Building upon this foundation, we now delve into a critical application of digital twin technology: optimizing operations and resource allocation. This subsection will illuminate how the insights derived from digital twins translate into tangible improvements in day-to-day operations, leading to enhanced efficiency, reduced costs, and a more agile and responsive organizational structure.

At its core, optimizing operations with digital twins involves leveraging real-time data and sophisticated simulation capabilities to make more informed decisions about how resources are deployed and processes are managed. This moves beyond traditional reactive problem-solving or static planning methods, enabling a dynamic, data-driven approach to operational management. The digital twin acts as a central hub, consolidating information from various sources—sensors, enterprise resource planning (ERP) systems, manufacturing execution systems (MES), and historical performance logs—to create a holistic, up-to-the-minute representation of the operational landscape.

One of the most immediate and impactful applications of this is in production scheduling and workflow optimization. In a manufacturing environment, for instance, a digital twin can simulate various production sequences, considering machine availability, raw material stock levels, workforce allocation, and order priorities. By running these simulations, managers can identify the most efficient schedule that minimizes idle time, reduces work-in-progress inventory, and maximizes throughput. For example, consider a complex assembly line where multiple product variants are produced. A digital twin can predict the time required to reconfigure the line for different product changeovers, the potential bottlenecks that might arise from certain batch sizes, and the impact of unexpected equipment downtime on the overall schedule. By pre-emptively identifying these challenges and evaluating alternative scheduling strategies—such as running similar product variants consecutively to reduce changeover frequency, or prioritizing high-demand orders with shorter lead times—the digital twin provides actionable intelligence to adjust the schedule dynamically. This is far more effective than relying on manual scheduling, which is often prone to human error and struggles to account for the myriad of variables involved in real-time. The digital twin can even integrate with AI-powered scheduling algorithms, which can continuously re-optimize the schedule as conditions change, such as a machine requiring unplanned maintenance or a rush order arriving. This ensures that the production floor is always operating under the most optimal plan available, directly impacting delivery times and customer satisfaction.

Inventory management is another area where digital twins offer substantial benefits. By providing an accurate, real-time view of stock levels, coupled with predictive analytics on consumption rates and lead times for replenishment, digital twins enable a more precise and efficient approach to inventory control. Instead of relying on historical averages or manual stocktakes, which can lead to either overstocking (tying up capital and increasing storage costs) or understocking (risking production stoppages and lost sales), the digital twin can forecast demand with greater accuracy and predict when specific components or finished goods will be needed. For example, in a large retail distribution center, a digital twin can monitor the movement of goods through the facility, predict incoming shipment arrival times, and forecast sales trends for various product categories. This allows for optimized replenishment orders, minimizing the amount of inventory held at any given time while ensuring that sufficient stock is available to meet projected demand. Furthermore, the digital twin can identify slow-moving or obsolete inventory, prompting decisions about liquidation or discontinuation, thereby freeing up valuable warehouse space and capital. This level of insight is crucial for businesses operating with lean inventory models, where precision and foresight are paramount.

The allocation of maintenance resources is a particularly compelling use case for digital twins in operational optimization. Traditionally, maintenance has often been performed on a reactive basis (repairing equipment after it breaks down) or a time-based schedule (performing maintenance at predetermined intervals, regardless of actual need). Digital twins enable a shift to predictive and condition-based maintenance. By continuously monitoring the health of equipment through sensor data (vibration, temperature, pressure, etc.) and analyzing historical performance trends and failure patterns, the digital twin can predict when a component is likely to fail. This allows maintenance teams to schedule interventions
before a failure occurs, during planned downtime, and with the necessary parts and personnel already in place. Consider a fleet of critical machinery in a heavy industry setting. The digital twin can analyze the stress and wear on each

machine, flagging potential issues with specific components weeks or even months in advance. Instead of a blanket scheduled overhaul that might be unnecessary for some machines or too late for others, maintenance can be targeted precisely where and when it is needed. This not only prevents costly unplanned downtime and associated production losses but also extends the lifespan of equipment by addressing issues before they cause cascading damage. It also optimizes the allocation of skilled technicians and spare parts, reducing waste and ensuring that resources are deployed most effectively to maintain operational continuity and safety. The digital twin can even simulate the impact of different maintenance strategies on equipment longevity and operational cost, helping to define the optimal balance between proactive intervention and operational uptime.

Energy consumption is another critical operational expense that digital twins can help to significantly reduce. Many industrial processes and facilities consume large amounts of energy, and optimizing this usage can lead to substantial cost savings and a reduced environmental footprint. A digital twin can model the energy consumption of individual pieces of equipment, entire production lines, or even an entire building, factoring in operational schedules, environmental conditions (such as ambient temperature affecting HVAC systems), and real-time energy prices. By understanding these relationships, the digital twin can recommend adjustments to operating parameters to minimize energy use without compromising production targets or service levels. For example, in a data center, the digital twin can analyze server load, ambient temperature, and cooling system performance to dynamically adjust cooling levels, ensuring that energy is not wasted on overcooling. In a manufacturing plant, it might identify opportunities to shift energy-intensive processes to off-peak hours when electricity rates are lower, or suggest optimizing the sequence of operations to minimize peak power demand. It can also identify inefficient equipment or processes that are consuming more energy than they should, prompting investigations and potential upgrades. This proactive energy management, guided by the detailed insights from the digital twin, is essential for both economic competitiveness and corporate sustainability goals.

Beyond these specific examples, the overarching theme is the transformation of decision-making from being reactive and often heuristic to being proactive and data-driven. When a problem arises on the shop floor, instead of relying on experienced operators' intuition or historical troubleshooting guides, the digital twin can be used to rapidly diagnose the issue. By inputting the observed symptoms into the twin, it can simulate potential causes and their likely outcomes, providing the maintenance or operations team with a ranked list of probable root causes. This significantly speeds up the diagnostic process and reduces the chances of implementing incorrect solutions.

Furthermore, resource allocation extends to human capital. In complex operational environments, ensuring that the right personnel with the correct skills are available at the right time and place is crucial. A digital twin, by providing an overview of upcoming tasks, required skill sets, and the availability of personnel (potentially integrated with workforce management systems), can assist in optimizing labor allocation. It can flag potential skill shortages for specific future tasks or highlight opportunities for cross-training based on predicted future operational needs. This proactive workforce planning ensures that operational continuity is maintained and that the workforce is utilized efficiently.

The integration of digital twins with enterprise-wide systems is key to unlocking these operational optimization benefits. When a digital twin is linked to an ERP system, it gains visibility into supply chain logistics, order fulfillment, and financial data. When connected to an MES, it receives granular data on production progress, machine status, and quality control metrics. This interconnectedness allows for a truly holistic view of operations, where decisions made in one area can be accurately assessed for their impact across the entire value chain. For instance, a decision to expedite a particular order (perhaps triggered by customer demand data from the ERP) can be immediately evaluated by the production-focused digital twin for its feasibility given current machine loads and material availability, and by the maintenance-focused digital twin for its potential impact on equipment wear. This integrated approach prevents the siloed decision-making that often leads to unintended negative consequences.

The ability of digital twins to model and simulate different operational configurations also supports continuous improvement initiatives. Teams can use the digital twin to test hypotheses about process improvements, such as implementing a new lean manufacturing technique, reconfiguring a workspace layout, or introducing a new quality control checkpoint. The twin can predict the likely outcomes of these changes, allowing organizations to validate their effectiveness in the virtual environment before committing to costly and disruptive real-world implementations. This iterative process of simulation, analysis, and refinement is fundamental to achieving and sustaining operational excellence. It fosters a culture of experimentation and data-informed innovation, where improvements are not just occasional events but a continuous process.

Ultimately, the optimization of operations and resource allocation through digital twins is about achieving a state of intelligent automation and adaptive management. It's about moving from simply managing the present to actively shaping the future of your operations. The insights generated are not just descriptive ("this is what happened"); they become predictive ("this is what will happen if we do X") and prescriptive ("this is what you should do to achieve Y"). This transition empowers organizations to become more efficient, more cost-effective, more resilient, and more agile in the face of an ever-changing business environment. The digital twin, in this context, ceases to be merely a technological tool and becomes a strategic imperative for any organization serious about achieving peak operational performance. The ability to refine production schedules in real-time, manage inventory with unparalleled precision, deploy maintenance resources preemptively, and minimize energy waste directly translates into a stronger bottom line and a more sustainable operational footprint. These are not theoretical possibilities but tangible outcomes being realized by forward-thinking organizations leveraging this transformative technology.

The sophisticated analytical and simulation capabilities inherent in digital twins extend significantly into the realm of risk assessment and mitigation. By creating a dynamic, virtual replica of a physical asset, process, or system, organizations gain an unprecedented ability to scrutinize potential vulnerabilities and proactively address them before they manifest in the real world. This capability is not merely about predicting isolated failures; it encompasses a holistic understanding of how a system might behave under a multitude of stresses, external influences, and internal deviations, thereby fostering a more resilient and secure operational environment.

At the heart of this risk management paradigm lies the digital twin's capacity to model system behavior across a spectrum of conditions. This goes far beyond static risk registers or traditional failure mode and effects analysis (FMEA) that often rely on historical data and expert judgment. A digital twin, by integrating real-time operational data with physics-based simulations and statistical models, can replicate the intricate interactions between different components and subsystems. This allows for the exploration of "what-if" scenarios that are far more comprehensive and dynamic. For instance, an aerospace company can use a digital twin of an aircraft's propulsion system to simulate the effects of foreign object debris (FOD) ingestion under varying flight conditions – different altitudes, speeds, and engine loads. The twin can predict not only the immediate damage but also the cascading effects on other engine components, performance degradation, and the probability of subsequent failures. This detailed, dynamic simulation provides a much richer understanding of the risk profile than a simple probability of FOD ingestion multiplied by a predefined consequence.

Crucially, the digital twin's strength in risk assessment is amplified by its ability to incorporate uncertainty quantification (UQ). Real-world systems are rarely deterministic; inputs vary, environmental conditions fluctuate, and the exact behavior of components under stress can be difficult to predict with absolute certainty. UQ methods, when integrated with digital twin simulations, allow for the characterization of this inherent uncertainty. Instead of presenting a single, deterministic outcome, the digital twin can generate a range of possible outcomes, each associated with a probability. For example, in petrochemical processing, a digital twin of a refining unit might simulate the risk of a pressure vessel rupture. By applying UQ to parameters like material fatigue, temperature fluctuations, and the concentration of corrosive agents, the twin can provide a probability distribution of failure times and severity, rather than a single predicted failure point. This probabilistic approach enables decision-makers to understand the likelihood and potential impact of different risk events, facilitating more informed choices about where to allocate resources for mitigation. This could involve investing in enhanced monitoring for components with a higher probability of early failure, or implementing more robust safety protocols for scenarios with a low probability but catastrophic consequence.

Furthermore, digital twins are instrumental in identifying potential failure modes that might otherwise remain hidden. By exhaustively simulating a wide range of operational states, including edge cases and extreme conditions, the twin can reveal susceptibilities that are not obvious from design specifications or operational history alone. For a complex industrial robot arm used in automotive manufacturing, a digital twin can simulate the cumulative effect of thousands of rapid, high-precision movements under varying payloads and environmental factors like dust or humidity. The twin might reveal that certain sequences of movements, when combined with specific environmental conditions, lead to an accelerated wear rate on a particular joint or actuator, a failure mode that might not have been anticipated during initial design or testing. This proactive identification allows for design modifications, material changes, or adjustments to operating parameters to prevent premature failure. The digital twin acts as a virtual proving ground, exposing latent weaknesses before they become costly problems in the physical world.

The impact prediction capability of a digital twin is another cornerstone of its risk management utility. Once a potential failure mode is identified, the twin can accurately forecast its consequences. This is not limited to the immediate failure of a component but extends to the ripple effects throughout the entire system and even across interconnected systems. For a power grid operator, a digital twin can simulate the failure of a key transmission line due to extreme weather. The simulation can predict not only the immediate loss of power to specific regions but also the subsequent overload on adjacent lines, the potential for cascading blackouts, the impact on critical infrastructure like hospitals and communication networks, and the estimated duration of service disruption. This granular understanding of impact allows for the development of targeted contingency plans. Instead of a generic "restore power" plan, the operator can have specific, pre-simulated strategies for rerouting power, prioritizing essential services, and communicating outage information based on the twin's detailed impact analysis.

This predictive and diagnostic power directly supports the development of proactive mitigation strategies. When the digital twin flags a high-probability, high-impact risk event, it can also be used to evaluate the effectiveness of various mitigation measures in a simulated environment. For instance, if a digital twin of a chemical plant identifies a risk of runaway reaction due to a malfunction in the cooling system, it can be used to test the efficacy of different safety interlocks, emergency shutdown procedures, or alternative cooling methods. The twin can quantify how much time each mitigation strategy would buy, what resources would be required, and what the residual risk would be. This data-driven approach moves mitigation planning from a theoretical exercise to a practically validated strategy. A maritime company could use a digital twin of a vessel to assess the risk of fire. If a particular risk is identified, the twin can simulate the effectiveness of different fire suppression systems, evacuation routes, and crew response protocols, identifying the optimal combination for minimizing loss of life and property.

Moreover, digital twins enhance system safety and reliability by enabling continuous risk monitoring and adaptive mitigation. As a physical system operates, its digital twin receives and processes real-time data, allowing it to continuously reassess risks. If operational parameters drift outside normal ranges, if sensor readings indicate unusual wear, or if external conditions change, the digital twin can automatically flag potential risks and suggest adjustments. For example, a digital twin of a bridge structure, equipped with sensors measuring strain, vibration, and environmental factors like wind speed and temperature, can continuously monitor its structural integrity. If the twin detects an accumulation of stress beyond a predicted threshold, or if a combination of factors (e.g., high wind and a specific harmonic vibration) creates a scenario deemed risky, it can automatically alert maintenance crews and recommend load restrictions or immediate inspections. This creates a dynamic feedback loop where the system's real-world performance informs its virtual risk assessment, which in turn drives proactive interventions to maintain safety and reliability.

The integration of anomaly detection algorithms within digital twins further strengthens their risk assessment capabilities. These algorithms can sift through

vast amounts of sensor data to identify deviations from normal operational patterns that might indicate an incipient failure or an unusual operating condition. For a fleet of autonomous vehicles, a digital twin can monitor the performance of lidar, radar, and camera systems. If the twin detects a subtle, consistent anomaly in the data from one particular sensor – perhaps a slight deviation in distance readings under specific lighting conditions – it can flag this as a potential risk. This allows for proactive calibration or maintenance of that sensor
before it leads to a critical navigation error. This ability to detect subtle, early-stage indicators of potential problems is invaluable for preventing catastrophic failures and ensuring consistent operational performance.

The concept of "uncertainty quantification" in the context of digital twins for risk assessment deserves deeper exploration. It acknowledges that our models and data are imperfect. Traditional risk analysis often simplifies this by using single-point estimates for probabilities and consequences. However, digital twins, when augmented with UQ techniques like Monte Carlo simulations, Bayesian inference, or polynomial chaos expansions, can provide a richer, more probabilistic understanding of risk. For example, when simulating the fatigue life of a critical component in an aircraft engine, rather than stating "the component will fail after 10,000 flight hours," a UQ-enhanced digital twin might state: "There is a 90% probability the component will survive at least 8,500 flight hours, and a 10% probability it will fail before 11,500 flight hours, with the most likely failure occurring around 10,000 hours." This probabilistic output is far more actionable for planning maintenance schedules, managing spare parts inventory, and making go/no-go decisions for flights. It allows for a nuanced approach to risk, distinguishing between "high risk" and "low probability, high consequence risk," each requiring different mitigation strategies.

The application of digital twins to identify potential failure modes extends to complex software systems as well. While often physical assets are emphasized, the principles apply to operational software, control systems, and IT infrastructure. A digital twin of a financial trading platform, for instance, could simulate the impact of high transaction volumes, network latency, or unexpected data feeds on system stability and performance. It can reveal potential race conditions, deadlocks, or vulnerabilities to denial-of-service attacks that might not be apparent during standard testing. By running these simulations, developers can identify and patch these weaknesses before they are exploited in a live trading environment, thereby mitigating significant financial and reputational risk.

Predicting the impact of failures within interconnected systems is a particularly powerful application of digital twins for risk mitigation. In modern industry, systems are rarely isolated. A failure in one part of the supply chain can have cascading effects throughout. Consider a pharmaceutical manufacturer that relies on a just-in-time delivery of critical raw materials. A digital twin of the entire supply chain, from raw material supplier to manufacturing plant to distribution center, can simulate the impact of a disruption at a single supplier – perhaps due to a natural disaster or labor strike. The twin can predict how long the manufacturer can continue production with existing inventory, which production lines will be affected, what the downstream impact will be on order fulfillment, and what the economic consequences are. This allows for the pre-positioning of buffer stock, the identification of alternative suppliers, or the contingency planning of production schedules to minimize disruption.

Developing proactive mitigation strategies is where the value proposition of digital twins in risk management truly shines. It's not just about knowing a risk exists, but about having a pre-validated plan to address it. For a nuclear power plant, the digital twin can simulate various accident scenarios, such as a loss of coolant. It can then evaluate the effectiveness of different emergency response protocols – the sequence of valve closures, the deployment of backup power systems, the use of emergency core cooling systems – in containing the incident and preventing a meltdown. The twin can optimize these protocols based on predicted outcomes, ensuring that the most effective sequence of actions is established and rehearsed virtually before any real emergency occurs. This significantly enhances the safety and reliability of such critical infrastructure.

The continuous monitoring and adaptive mitigation aspect is crucial for long-term operational integrity. Systems degrade over time, and their risk profiles evolve. A digital twin that is constantly fed real-time data can detect subtle changes that indicate an increasing risk. For example, a digital twin of a wind turbine might detect a slight increase in bearing temperature and a corresponding change in vibration signature over several weeks. While individually these might be within acceptable operating limits, the digital twin, by analyzing the trend and correlating it with historical data and failure models, can predict that these conditions are precursors to a bearing failure. This allows for planned maintenance during a period of low wind, thereby avoiding a costly and potentially dangerous in-situ failure. This adaptive approach ensures that risk mitigation efforts are always aligned with the current state of the system.

In essence, the application of digital twins to risk assessment and mitigation transforms the approach from a static, often reactive process to a dynamic, predictive, and preemptive one. By enabling organizations to thoroughly understand system behavior under diverse conditions, quantify uncertainties, identify hidden failure modes, predict impacts, and validate mitigation strategies in a virtual environment, digital twins foster a significantly higher level of safety, reliability, and operational resilience. This proactive management of risk is not merely a compliance exercise; it is a strategic imperative that directly contributes to operational continuity, asset longevity, and the overall success of complex enterprises. The ability to 'see' potential problems before they occur, to 'test' solutions without consequence, and to 'prepare' for contingencies with a high degree of confidence is a profound shift in how organizations manage their most critical assets and processes.

The true power of a digital twin is amplified exponentially when it transcends its standalone existence and becomes an integral part of the broader enterprise technology landscape. For a digital twin to deliver on its promise of holistic operational intelligence and truly drive informed decision-making, it must seamlessly interact with other critical enterprise systems. This integration is not merely a technical convenience; it is a strategic imperative that unlocks a unified view of operations, spanning the entire lifecycle of an asset or process. Key systems that form the backbone of most organizations, such as Enterprise Resource Planning (ERP), Manufacturing Execution Systems (MES), and Product Lifecycle Management (PLM), are prime candidates for integration, each bringing unique data streams and functionalities that enrich the digital twin and, in turn, benefit from its insights.

Integrating a digital twin with an ERP system, for instance, creates a powerful synergy. ERP systems are the central nervous system for many businesses, managing core functions like finance, human resources, procurement, and supply chain logistics. By linking the digital twin to an ERP, organizations can connect the physical reality of an asset or process—as represented by the twin—with the financial and logistical implications. For a manufacturing plant, this means that the performance data and predictive maintenance alerts generated by the digital twin can directly inform ERP modules. If the digital twin predicts an impending failure of a critical machine, this information can automatically trigger alerts within the ERP to initiate a procurement process for spare parts, schedule maintenance personnel, and adjust production planning to account for potential downtime. Conversely, the ERP's data on material availability, inventory levels, and supplier performance can provide crucial context for the digital twin's simulations and risk assessments. For example, if a planned maintenance task requires a specific component, the digital twin can query the ERP to verify its availability and estimated delivery time, allowing for more realistic scheduling and preventing disruptions caused by unforeseen part shortages. This bi-directional flow of information ensures that operational decisions are grounded in both the physical capabilities and constraints of the assets, as well as the broader business context of costs, resources, and supply chain realities.

The integration with Manufacturing Execution Systems (MES) offers another layer of critical data and operational control. MES provides real-time visibility and control over shop floor activities, tracking work-in-progress, managing production schedules, monitoring machine status, and collecting detailed production data. When a digital twin is integrated with an MES, the virtual model can be continuously updated with the precise, granular data from the production line. This allows the digital twin to accurately reflect the current state of manufacturing operations. For a complex assembly line, the MES tracks every step, every operator action, and every machine parameter. This data feeds directly into the digital twin, enabling it to simulate the exact conditions under which a product is being manufactured. This is invaluable for quality control and process optimization. If the digital twin, fed by MES data, identifies a subtle deviation in a machine's performance that correlates with an increase in product defects, this insight can be fed back to the MES to adjust machine settings in real-time, or to the operators to correct their procedures. Furthermore, the MES's real-time tracking of production throughput and efficiency can be analyzed through the digital twin to identify bottlenecks or areas for improvement. The twin can then simulate the impact of proposed changes—such as reconfiguring a workstation or altering a machine's cycle time—and the MES can provide the actual performance data to validate these simulations. This creates a powerful feedback loop where the physical execution on the shop floor continuously informs and refines the virtual model, which in turn guides improvements in the physical execution. This closed-loop system is essential for achieving agile and efficient manufacturing operations.

The integration of digital twins with Product Lifecycle Management (PLM) systems is fundamental to a truly end-to-end digital thread. PLM systems manage all aspects of a product's life, from initial concept and design, through engineering, manufacturing, service, and eventual disposal. When a digital twin is integrated with PLM, it bridges the gap between the design intent and the operational reality. The PLM system holds the authoritative design data, including CAD models, simulation results from the design phase, bill of materials, and engineering change orders. This data forms the foundational blueprint for the digital twin. As the product moves from design to manufacturing and operation, the digital twin collects real-time performance and usage data. This operational data is invaluable when fed back into the PLM system. For example, if the digital twin of a manufactured product reveals that a particular component is experiencing higher-than-expected wear in the field, this information can be used to initiate a design review within the PLM system. Engineers can then analyze the operational data in conjunction with the original design specifications to identify potential design flaws or areas for improvement. This feedback loop allows for continuous product enhancement and faster iteration cycles, leading to more robust and reliable products in the future. Moreover, the PLM system's change management capabilities can ensure that any design modifications recommended based on digital twin insights are properly documented, approved, and implemented across all relevant documentation and manufacturing processes, thus maintaining a consistent and accurate digital thread throughout the product's lifecycle.

Beyond these core systems, integration can extend to other specialized enterprise applications. For instance, integration with Customer Relationship Management (CRM) systems can provide the digital twin with insights into product usage patterns and customer feedback, allowing for more personalized service offerings and proactive customer engagement. In the realm of field service, integrating the digital twin with service management software enables technicians to access real-time asset health information and diagnostic guidance directly in the field, leading to faster and more effective repairs. Similarly, integrating with supply chain visibility platforms can provide the digital twin with a broader view of the extended ecosystem, allowing for more sophisticated risk assessment and scenario planning related to external disruptions.

The technical considerations for these integrations are multifaceted. Data standardization and interoperability are paramount. Different systems often use proprietary data formats and protocols, necessitating the development of robust data transformation and mapping layers. APIs (Application Programming Interfaces) play a crucial role, providing standardized pathways for systems to communicate and exchange data. Cloud-based platforms and IoT (Internet of Things) architectures are increasingly facilitating these integrations, offering scalable and flexible infrastructure for data ingestion, processing, and exchange. Security is another critical concern, as connecting disparate systems opens up new potential vulnerabilities. Robust authentication, authorization, and encryption mechanisms are essential to protect sensitive operational and business data. The choice of integration architecture—whether it involves direct point-to-point connections, middleware solutions, or a centralized data lake or data fabric—will depend on the specific needs, existing infrastructure, and strategic goals of the organization. Furthermore, the volume, velocity, and variety of data generated by these interconnected systems require careful consideration of data governance, storage, and management strategies. Ensuring data quality, integrity, and lineage is vital for maintaining the trustworthiness of the insights derived from the integrated platform.

Strategically, the decision to integrate a digital twin with other enterprise systems should be driven by clear business objectives. What specific problems are we trying to solve? What new opportunities are we seeking to unlock? Common strategic drivers include enhancing operational efficiency, improving product quality, reducing downtime and maintenance costs, accelerating time-to-market for new products, improving customer satisfaction, and gaining a competitive advantage. A phased approach to integration is often advisable, starting with the most critical systems and use cases, and gradually expanding the scope as the organization gains experience and realizes value. Establishing clear ownership and governance structures for the integrated data and systems is also essential for long-term success. This includes defining roles and responsibilities for data management, system maintenance, and the ongoing development of the integrated platform.

The ultimate goal of these integrations is to create a unified operational intelligence platform. This platform moves beyond siloed data and disconnected processes, offering a holistic view of the organization's assets, operations, and business performance. Decision-makers can access a comprehensive dashboard that blends real-time operational data from the digital twin, production schedules from MES, financial data from ERP, and design information from PLM. This unified view empowers more informed and agile decision-making. For instance, a product manager could use this integrated platform to understand not only the market demand for a product (from CRM and sales data) but also its manufacturing cost (from ERP and MES) and its operational performance in the field (from the digital twin), all within a single interface. This allows for strategic decisions about product roadmaps, pricing, and resource allocation that are grounded in a comprehensive understanding of the entire value chain.

Streamlining business processes is another significant benefit. Integrated systems automate workflows that previously required manual data transfer and reconciliation between disparate systems. This reduces errors, saves time, and frees up human resources to focus on higher-value activities. For example, a customer complaint logged in the CRM can automatically trigger a diagnostic sequence in the digital twin, which in turn can generate a service ticket in the maintenance management system and flag potential production issues in the MES, all without human intervention. This end-to-end automation enhances responsiveness and efficiency across the organization.

Moreover, this unified operational intelligence fosters a culture of data-driven decision-making. When accurate, integrated data is readily accessible and presented in an understandable format, individuals across the organization are better equipped to make informed choices. This transcends traditional functional boundaries, promoting collaboration and a shared understanding of business objectives. The digital twin, as the core of this operational intelligence, provides the real-time, dynamic perspective that makes the aggregated data actionable. It translates the static information from ERP, MES, and PLM into a dynamic representation of the physical world, allowing organizations to not just track what has happened, but to understand why it happened, and to predict and influence what will happen next. This holistic approach to operational intelligence, enabled by the integration of digital twins with key enterprise systems, is a defining characteristic of the most advanced and competitive organizations today. It is the foundation upon which true digital transformation is built, ensuring that insights derived from digital models are not isolated curiosities but are actively shaping and optimizing every facet of the enterprise.

Chapter 13: Case Study: Digital Twin for Manufacturing

The narrative of digital twins in manufacturing often begins with abstract concepts and overarching benefits. However, to truly grasp their transformative potential, it is essential to ground our understanding in a tangible, real-world scenario. This chapter delves into a specific case study, focusing on a complex manufacturing line that exemplifies the challenges and opportunities inherent in modern production environments. By meticulously detailing the physical assets, the intricate production processes, and the critical performance metrics, we establish a foundational understanding upon which the subsequent implementation of a digital twin will be built. This detailed portrayal of the physical reality is not merely descriptive; it serves as the crucial context necessary to appreciate the value and efficacy of its virtual counterpart. Without a deep comprehension of the physical system, the advantages of a digital twin remain theoretical, detached from the practical realities of the shop floor.

The manufacturing line under examination is situated within a facility that produces high-precision electromechanical components for the aerospace industry. The sheer complexity and stringent quality requirements of this sector necessitate a highly sophisticated and meticulously controlled production environment. The line itself is a symphony of interconnected machinery, automated handling systems, and human oversight, designed to transform raw materials into finished products that meet exacting specifications. At its heart lies a series of CNC (Computer Numerical Control) machining centers, responsible for shaping metal alloys with sub-micron tolerances. These machines, each a marvel of engineering in its own right, are configured in a sequence that reflects the progressive stages of component fabrication.

Following the initial machining operations, the components are transferred to automated washing and degreasing stations. This step is critical for removing any residual cutting fluids, metal particulates, or contaminants that could compromise subsequent processes or the final product's integrity. The washing stations employ specialized cleaning agents and ultrasonic technology, operating under precisely controlled temperature and pressure parameters. From there, the components move to inspection stages. This is not a singular event but rather a multi-faceted approach to quality assurance. Initial checks are performed using automated optical inspection (AOI) systems, which rapidly scan for surface defects, dimensional inaccuracies, and any visual anomalies. However, due to the critical nature of aerospace components, manual inspection by highly skilled technicians, often employing advanced metrology equipment such as coordinate measuring machines (CMMs), remains an indispensable part of the process. These CMMs meticulously measure critical dimensions and geometries, comparing them against digital design specifications with unparalleled accuracy.

The line then proceeds to assembly stations. Here, human operators, guided by augmented reality interfaces that display work instructions and component placement guides, meticulously assemble sub-components. These sub-assemblies might include intricate wiring harnesses, delicate sensor modules, or precision bearings, all requiring a high degree of dexterity and attention to detail. The process is further monitored by force-feedback sensors and vision systems that ensure correct assembly torque and orientation, preventing costly errors. After the primary assembly, further quality checks and functional testing are conducted. This might involve leak testing for sealed components, electrical continuity tests for integrated circuits, and vibration testing to simulate operational stresses.

The physical assets that constitute this manufacturing line are diverse and technologically advanced. We have the aforementioned CNC machining centers, which include multi-axis milling machines, lathes, and grinding machines. These are complemented by robotic arms for material handling and parts transfer, ensuring a smooth and efficient flow of work-in-progress. Automated guided vehicles (AGVs) transport materials between different work cells and to and from the inventory staging areas. The inspection equipment is equally sophisticated, featuring CMMs with laser scanners, advanced AOI systems with high-resolution cameras, and specialized testing rigs designed for specific component functionalities. The assembly stations are equipped with pneumatic tools, torque wrenches with data logging capabilities, and sophisticated vision systems for precision guidance and verification. Ancillary systems, such as environmental control units maintaining precise temperature and humidity levels, and advanced dust collection systems, are also integral to ensuring optimal operating conditions and product quality.

The production processes themselves are designed for high efficiency and repeatability, yet are inherently susceptible to variation. Machining processes, while automated, can be affected by tool wear, material batch inconsistencies, and machine calibration drift. Assembly, despite robotic assistance and AR guidance, relies on human skill and can be influenced by factors such as operator fatigue or minor variations in component tolerances. Inspection, while rigorous, can face challenges with detecting subtle defects or managing the sheer volume of data generated. The entire line operates on a pull system, driven by demand signals from downstream processes or the finished goods inventory, aiming to minimize work-in-progress while maintaining a consistent output rate.

Key Performance Indicators (KPIs) are meticulously tracked to monitor the health and efficiency of this manufacturing line. Throughput is a primary concern, measured in the number of completed components produced per hour or per shift. This metric directly impacts the facility's ability to meet production targets and customer demand. Equally critical is quality, assessed through various metrics. First Pass Yield (FPY) measures the percentage of components that pass all inspection and testing stages without requiring any rework or being scrapped. Defect Rate, often expressed in parts per million (PPM), quantifies the number of defective units produced. Scrap Rate indicates the percentage of raw material or work-in-progress that is discarded due to defects. Rework Rate tracks the proportion of units that can be corrected and brought back into specification. Other important KPIs include Overall Equipment Effectiveness (OEE), a composite measure of availability, performance, and quality; machine uptime and downtime; cycle times for individual operations; and adherence to production schedules.

Despite the high level of automation and sophistication, this manufacturing line faces a multitude of operational challenges. Tool wear in the CNC machines, while monitored, can lead to subtle deviations in part geometry before it is detected, potentially resulting in scrapped parts or costly rework. Variations in raw material properties, even within specified tolerances, can impact machining performance and surface finish. The complex interplay of automated and manual assembly steps introduces points of potential human error, despite robust training and guidance systems. Calibration drift in metrology equipment, if not detected promptly, can lead to incorrect quality assessments, either passing defective parts or rejecting good ones. The sheer volume of data generated by the various sensors, inspection systems, and manual logs presents a significant challenge for real-time analysis and actionable insights. Identifying the root cause of a defect can be a time-consuming and complex process, often requiring the correlation of data from multiple disparate sources across the line. Unplanned downtime, due to equipment malfunction or unforeseen issues, can have a cascading effect on the entire production schedule, leading to delays and increased costs. Furthermore, optimizing the line for different product variants or sudden shifts in demand requires careful recalibration and reconfiguration, which can be labor-intensive and prone to error. The challenge lies in maintaining peak performance, ensuring uncompromising quality, and achieving flexibility in an environment where even minor deviations can have significant consequences. It is within this intricate and demanding operational landscape that the concept of a digital twin finds its most compelling application, offering a virtual mirror to this complex physical reality, poised to enhance understanding, prediction, and control.

The creation of a digital twin for the sophisticated aerospace component manufacturing line necessitates a meticulously crafted virtual representation. This is not a monolithic undertaking but rather a layered construction, employing a hybrid modeling approach that seeks to harness the strengths of both physics-based simulations and data-driven learning techniques. The goal is to build a virtual replica that not only mirrors the physical assets and their nominal operations but also captures the dynamic, often non-linear, behaviors and interdependencies that characterize a high-precision production environment.

At the core of this hybrid strategy lies the application of physics-based models for individual machinery and subsystems. For the array of CNC machining centers, for instance, detailed kinematic and dynamic models are developed. These models incorporate parameters such as tool geometry, spindle speeds, feed rates, material properties, and cutting forces. By simulating these physical interactions, we can accurately predict machining outcomes, including surface finish, dimensional accuracy, and tool wear progression. Similarly, for the robotic arms responsible for material handling, sophisticated kinematic models are essential. These models define the robot's degrees of freedom, joint limits, velocities, and accelerations, allowing for precise simulation of trajectory planning, reachability analysis, and collision avoidance within the work cell. The automated washing and degreasing stations are modeled based on principles of fluid dynamics and thermodynamics, simulating the flow of cleaning agents, temperature profiles, and the efficacy of ultrasonic cavitation in removing contaminants. Conveyor systems and automated guided vehicles (AGVs) are modeled using principles of motion control and traffic management, ensuring realistic representation of material movement and potential bottlenecks.

However, relying solely on physics-based models presents limitations. These models can become computationally prohibitive when attempting to capture every granular physical phenomenon, and they may struggle to account for emergent behaviors or subtle deviations arising from factors not explicitly defined in the underlying physics. This is where data-driven modeling becomes indispensable. Machine learning algorithms, trained on historical operational data, are employed to learn complex relationships and patterns that are difficult to explicitly define through physical laws. For example, the wear and tear on a CNC tool, while influenced by physics, is also impacted by variations in material homogeneity, coolant flow rates, and even subtle vibrations not fully captured by a simplified physics model. A machine learning model, such as a neural network or a support vector machine, can be trained to predict remaining tool life based on a multitude of sensor readings (vibration, acoustic emissions, spindle torque, etc.) and operational history.

The integration of these two approaches—physics-based and data-driven—forms the foundation of the hybrid model. For instance, a physics-based model of a robotic arm's movement can be augmented with a data-driven model that predicts the probability of a joint actuator experiencing increased thermal load under specific operational conditions, based on past performance data. Similarly, the material flow simulation might initially be based on predefined conveyor speeds and AGV routing logic (physics-based), but it can be enhanced with predictive models that estimate queue lengths and waiting times at workstations based on real-time throughput data and historical variations (data-driven). This hybrid approach allows for a more comprehensive and accurate representation of the manufacturing line's behavior, capturing both the predictable aspects governed by physical laws and the nuanced, data-emergent characteristics of real-world operation.

A critical consideration in developing the digital twin is the level of fidelity required for different aspects of the manufacturing process and assets. This involves a trade-off between model complexity, computational cost, and the actionable insights derived. For the high-precision CNC machines, a high fidelity is paramount. This means modeling not just the basic kinematics but also the thermal expansion of machine components, the precise vibration characteristics of the spindle and cutting tool, and the dynamic response of the machine's control system. This level of detail is necessary to accurately predict sub-micron deviations in manufactured parts and to optimize machining parameters for maximum precision and minimal tool wear.

Conversely, for material handling systems like standard conveyors, a lower fidelity might suffice. A simplified model focusing on transit times, capacity, and potential accumulation points might be adequate, unless specific issues with conveyor belt tension, motor performance, or sensor failures are anticipated or observed. The AGVs, however, may require a more sophisticated model that includes their dynamic movement, battery status, charging schedules, and the logic governing their navigation and interaction with other AGVs and the environment, especially in a busy factory floor.

The flow of materials is another area where fidelity considerations are crucial. Modeling the movement of individual components through the line, from raw stock to finished product, necessitates tracking their state (e.g., undergoing machining, waiting for inspection, in transit) and location. This requires a robust event-driven simulation framework where events like "part enters CNC machine," "inspection complete," or "part moved by AGV" trigger state transitions and update the virtual representation. The fidelity here is dictated by the need to identify bottlenecks, quantify work-in-progress inventory, and understand the impact of disruptions at any point in the flow.

Energy consumption is a growing concern in manufacturing, and its accurate modeling within the digital twin is increasingly important. This involves not just simulating the energy draw of individual machines during operation but also accounting for idle states, startup transients, and the impact of operational parameters on energy efficiency. For example, the power consumption of a CNC machine can vary significantly based on the cutting strategy, spindle speed, and the material being machined. Modeling this accurately allows for optimization efforts aimed at reducing the overall energy footprint of the manufacturing line.

Perhaps most importantly, the digital twin must accurately represent potential failure modes of the physical assets. This involves incorporating models that describe the degradation of components over time, the conditions under which failures are likely to occur, and the types of failures that can manifest. For a CNC machine, this might include models for spindle bearing wear, ball screw degradation, or servo drive malfunctions. For a robotic arm, it could encompass motor wear, gearbox issues, or sensor calibration drift. These failure models, often informed by historical maintenance logs and expert knowledge, are essential for enabling predictive maintenance capabilities. They allow the digital twin to simulate the progression of wear and tear and to predict when a component is likely to fail, thereby enabling proactive intervention before a breakdown occurs. This requires integrating not only probabilistic models of failure but also understanding the cascading effects of a component failure on the overall system performance and on other assets within the line. The fidelity of these failure models directly impacts the reliability of the digital twin's predictions and its effectiveness in preventing unplanned downtime.

The digital twin's architecture must therefore be flexible enough to accommodate varying levels of fidelity across different components and processes. A component-based modeling approach is often adopted, where each physical asset and significant process step is represented by its own module or subsystem model. These modules can then be integrated into a cohesive virtual environment, allowing for end-to-end simulation of the manufacturing line. The interfaces between these modules are crucial, ensuring that data flows correctly and that the interactions between different systems are accurately represented.

For example, the output of a CNC machining module (e.g., finished part dimensions) becomes the input for the inspection module, and the availability of a robot from the material handling module affects the start time of a process step in a work cell.

Furthermore, the dynamic nature of the manufacturing environment demands that the digital twin can adapt to changes. This includes not only modeling normal operational variations but also accommodating planned changes, such as introducing a new product variant or reconfiguring a work cell, and unplanned events, like a machine outage or a supply chain disruption. The fidelity of the models for these scenarios dictates the twin's utility in scenario planning and operational resilience. A high-fidelity model that can accurately simulate the impact of a machine failure on downstream operations, for instance, is invaluable for developing effective contingency plans and mitigating production losses.

In essence, the development of the digital twin's virtual model is an iterative process. It begins with the foundational physics-based representations, which are then enriched and refined through data-driven insights and increasingly sophisticated fidelity considerations. The aim is to create a virtual counterpart that is not just a static snapshot but a living, breathing simulation capable of reflecting the complexities, dynamics, and potential failures of its physical counterpart, thereby unlocking a new paradigm of operational understanding and control.

The continuous and accurate reflection of the physical manufacturing process within its digital counterpart is not merely an aspiration but a fundamental requirement for a truly functional digital twin. This necessitates a robust and sophisticated data integration and real-time synchronization strategy. The essence of this strategy lies in establishing a seamless flow of information from the shop floor to the virtual realm, ensuring that the digital twin remains a living, breathing representation of the manufacturing line as it operates. Without this constant, high-fidelity data stream, the twin would quickly devolve into a static model, losing its ability to provide actionable insights or support dynamic decision-making.

The foundation of this real-time data flow is a comprehensive sensor network strategically deployed across the physical manufacturing line. These sensors act as the eyes and ears of the digital twin, capturing critical operational parameters at every stage of production. For the CNC machining centers, for instance, an array of sensors is indispensable. This includes high-frequency vibration sensors mounted on machine frames and spindles to detect anomalies indicative of tool wear, bearing issues, or imbalances. Acoustic emission sensors can further enhance this by capturing the sound signatures of the machining process, providing granular insights into cutting forces and material interactions. Thermal sensors are placed on critical components such as spindle motors, drives, and cutting tools to monitor temperature fluctuations, which can signal overheating, potential component degradation, or suboptimal operating conditions. Current and voltage sensors monitor power consumption, offering a proxy for machining load and energy efficiency. Furthermore, optical sensors or laser scanners can be integrated to verify part positioning and dimensions during in-process checks.

Beyond the machining centers, robotic arms are equipped with sensors to monitor joint torques, motor temperatures, and encoder feedback, providing crucial data for kinematic accuracy, operational load, and potential mechanical stress. The automated washing and degreasing stations are fitted with temperature and pressure sensors to ensure optimal cleaning cycles, as well as flow meters to monitor the consumption and condition of cleaning fluids. For material handling systems, sensors on conveyors can track belt tension and speed, while proximity sensors and LiDAR units on Automated Guided Vehicles (AGVs) are essential for navigation, collision avoidance, and monitoring their operational status, including battery levels. Throughout the entire line, environmental sensors play a vital role in monitoring ambient temperature, humidity, and air quality, as these factors can influence material properties, machine performance, and the precision of the manufacturing process. Even the status of pneumatic and hydraulic systems, including pressure and flow rates, is monitored to ensure optimal and safe operation of various actuators and control mechanisms.

The sheer volume and variety of data generated by these sensors necessitate a well-defined communication infrastructure. The choice of communication protocols is paramount to ensuring efficient, reliable, and low-latency data transfer. While traditional industrial protocols like Modbus and Profibus have long been established, modern digital twin implementations often leverage more advanced and flexible options. Message Queuing Telemetry Transport (MQTT) has emerged as a popular choice for its lightweight nature, publish-subscribe model, and suitability for connecting a large number of distributed devices. This allows sensors and machine controllers to publish their data to a central broker, and the digital twin (or specific components of it) can subscribe to the topics of interest. This decouples the data producers from the consumers, enhancing scalability and resilience.

Another critical protocol in the industrial automation landscape is OPC Unified Architecture (OPC UA). This platform-independent, service-oriented architecture provides a standardized framework for industrial communication, enabling secure and reliable data exchange between various automation devices and systems, regardless of their vendor or underlying technology. OPC UA's ability to model complex information, including the relationships between different data points and devices, makes it particularly well-suited for integrating diverse manufacturing assets into a coherent digital twin. It supports features like real-time data access, historical data access, and alarming, which are all vital for a comprehensive digital twin. In many advanced manufacturing environments, a hybrid approach is adopted, utilizing MQTT for simple sensor readings and status updates where low latency is key, and OPC UA for more complex data models, richer information exchange, and secure communication with higher-level control systems and the digital twin platform.

The data, once collected and transmitted, is rarely in a format that can be directly ingested by the digital twin models. Therefore, a sophisticated data preprocessing pipeline is essential. This pipeline performs several critical functions. Firstly,
data filtering is employed to remove noise, outliers, or erroneous readings that can arise from sensor malfunctions or transient electrical interference. Techniques such as moving averages, median filters, or more advanced statistical outlier detection methods are applied to ensure data integrity. Secondly, **data**

aggregation is often performed to combine multiple sensor readings into a more meaningful representation. For instance, data from multiple vibration sensors on a single machine might be aggregated to provide an overall machine health index. Similarly, data from various performance counters on a CNC machine can be aggregated to represent its current operational state (e.g., 'running at optimal speed,' 'experiencing moderate load,' 'idle').

Data normalization and scaling are also crucial steps, especially when different sensors operate on different scales or units. This ensures that data from diverse sources can be consistently interpreted and processed by the digital twin's algorithms, particularly those employing machine learning. **Data transformation** might involve converting raw sensor values into engineering units or deriving new features from existing data. For example, instead of just recording spindle speed, a derived feature representing the load on the spindle motor might be calculated. Furthermore, **data enrichment** involves augmenting sensor data with contextual information from other sources. This could include adding metadata about the specific part being manufactured, the current production order, or the scheduled maintenance status of the machine.

The core objective of this entire data pipeline is to achieve real-time synchronization between the physical manufacturing line and its digital twin. This means that at any given moment, the state of the digital twin—including the status of individual machines, the location and progress of parts through the production workflow, and the prevailing environmental conditions—should accurately mirror the state of its physical counterpart. This is not a trivial task, as it requires overcoming several challenges related to latency, data volume, and the dynamic nature of manufacturing processes.

The strategy for real-time synchronization typically involves a multi-layered approach. At the most immediate level, critical operational data, such as machine on/off status, spindle speed, feed rate, and error codes, is often streamed directly from Programmable Logic Controllers (PLCs) or edge devices with minimal processing delay. This enables the digital twin to provide a near real-time view of machine activity. For instance, if a CNC machine throws an alarm, this information should propagate to the digital twin within milliseconds, allowing for immediate operator or system notification.

A slightly less time-critical but equally important layer involves the progression of parts through the manufacturing line. This is often managed through a combination of sensors at key transition points (e.g., at the entrance and exit of workstations) and an event-driven architecture within the digital twin. When a part arrives at a station, its digital representation is updated to reflect its new location and status. This event triggers the simulation of the subsequent processing step. The synchronization here relies on the accurate sequencing of these events, which in turn depends on the reliable capture of part presence and movement data. AGV tracking systems, using RFID, barcode scanning, or even Wi-Fi triangulation, are crucial for ensuring that the twin accurately reflects the dynamic movement of materials.

Environmental conditions, while perhaps not requiring sub-second updates, need to be synchronized at a frequency that allows for meaningful correlation with operational data. For example, if a slight increase in ambient temperature is detected, the digital twin can use this information, along with other sensor data, to predict potential impacts on machining accuracy or the performance of sensitive electronic components. This might involve updating the parameters within physics-based models or adjusting the predictions of data-driven models to account for the environmental shift.

To manage the immense data flow and ensure synchronization, a sophisticated data architecture is employed. This often involves an industrial IoT platform that acts as an intermediary between the shop floor and the digital twin. This platform is responsible for data ingestion, buffering, basic processing, and routing data to the appropriate digital twin modules. It also handles the communication protocols, ensuring interoperability between disparate systems. Within the digital twin itself, data is often managed in a time-series database or a specialized data lake optimized for handling high-frequency sensor data.

The concept of synchronization also extends to the digital twin's response to physical events. If a machine unexpectedly stops due to a power failure, the digital twin must reflect this immediate cessation of activity. This requires a high degree of responsiveness from the data acquisition and processing systems. Conversely, if an operator initiates a manual override or adjusts a parameter on the physical machine, this change should ideally be captured and mirrored in the digital twin with minimal delay, allowing for the twin to recalibrate its predictions based on the new operational context.

Furthermore, the synchronization strategy must account for potential network disruptions or temporary outages. This might involve implementing local data buffering at the edge devices or within the IoT platform, allowing data to be stored temporarily when connectivity is lost and then transmitted once the connection is re-established. This ensures that no critical data is permanently lost and that the digital twin can eventually catch up to the real-world state. The data synchronization mechanisms also need to be robust against data corruption or loss during transmission, employing checksums and other error-detection mechanisms.

Achieving true real-time synchronization is an ongoing process of optimization and refinement. It involves continuously monitoring the latency of data streams, evaluating the accuracy of the reflected state, and adjusting the data acquisition and processing strategies as needed. For instance, if it's observed that the digital twin's prediction of tool wear is lagging behind actual wear progression, the sensor strategy for monitoring vibrations or cutting forces might need to be enhanced, or the frequency of data reporting from those sensors might need to be increased. The integration of machine learning models within the data preprocessing pipeline itself can also play a role in predicting expected sensor values, allowing for the detection of deviations that might indicate an impending issue or an anomaly in the data stream that needs further investigation. This iterative approach ensures that the digital twin remains a highly accurate and dynamic representation of the manufacturing line, empowering operators and engineers with the most up-to-date information for effective decision-making and operational control. The successful implementation of these data integration and synchronization strategies is the lifeblood of the digital twin, transforming it from a mere simulation into a powerful tool for real-time operational intelligence.

The preceding discussion has established the foundational elements of a digital twin for manufacturing – namely, the critical importance of real-time data synchronization and a robust data integration pipeline. With these systems in place, the digital twin transforms from a complex model into a dynamic, actionable tool, unlocking a suite of advanced applications that directly impact manufacturing efficiency, reliability, and profitability. These applications can be broadly categorized into three interconnected pillars: advanced monitoring, proactive prediction, and continuous optimization.

The monitoring capabilities afforded by the digital twin represent a significant leap forward from traditional supervisory control and data acquisition (SCADA) systems. Instead of merely observing operational status, the digital twin provides a holistic, multi-layered view of the entire manufacturing process. This granular insight extends to individual machines, entire work cells, and the overarching production line. For a CNC machining center, for example, the digital twin doesn't just show if the machine is running; it can display real-time spindle speed, feed rate, tool path trajectory, axis positions, coolant temperature, and vibration signatures simultaneously. Anomalies that might be missed by human operators or traditional monitoring systems can be highlighted. Consider a scenario where a slight, almost imperceptible increase in vibration amplitude is detected in the X-axis spindle bearing of a CNC mill. While this deviation might not trigger an immediate alarm in a standard system, the digital twin, with its ability to correlate this vibration data with other parameters such as cutting load and spindle speed, can flag it as a potential precursor to a bearing failure. This advanced anomaly detection is further amplified by the twin's ability to learn normal operating patterns through machine learning. It can distinguish between acceptable variations due to material differences or specific machining operations and genuine deviations that signal an impending issue.

The visibility extends beyond individual machines to the broader production flow. The digital twin can visually represent the progress of each component or assembly through the various stages of manufacturing. Imagine a complex automotive assembly line. The digital twin can show, in real-time, where each vehicle is, which stations it has completed, and which ones it is currently occupying. Crucially, it can also highlight bottlenecks or areas of congestion. If a batch of parts is delayed at a particular quality inspection station, or if an AGV is holding up a critical material transfer, the digital twin can immediately visualize this bottleneck, providing operators and management with actionable information to address the issue. Furthermore, by integrating data from environmental sensors, the twin can also monitor and report on the conditions under which manufacturing is taking place. Deviations in temperature, humidity, or air quality that could impact material properties or process precision are immediately visible and can be correlated with production quality. This comprehensive monitoring creates an unprecedented level of situational awareness, enabling faster and more informed decision-making.

Building upon this sophisticated monitoring, the digital twin excels in its predictive capabilities, most notably in the realm of predictive maintenance. Traditional maintenance strategies often rely on scheduled, time-based interventions, which can lead to over-maintenance (unnecessary part replacements) or under-maintenance (catastrophic failures before scheduled maintenance). Predictive maintenance, powered by the digital twin, shifts this paradigm. By analyzing the continuous stream of sensor data and employing machine learning algorithms, the twin can forecast the remaining useful life (RUL) of critical components. For instance, by tracking the cumulative stress on a robotic arm's joints, the wear patterns of its gearbox, and the thermal profiles of its motors, the digital twin can predict when a specific joint is likely to require lubrication or when a gearbox may need replacement, not based on hours of operation, but on its actual operational demands and observed degradation.

A tangible example of this predictive power can be observed in the case of a critical pump used for circulating coolant in the CNC machining centers. Sensors monitoring the pump's vibration, motor current draw, temperature, and flow rate continuously feed data to the digital twin. Over time, the twin identifies a subtle but consistent upward trend in the motor current draw and a slight increase in bearing vibration. Machine learning models, trained on historical data of pump failures, correlate these trends with the early stages of bearing wear.

The digital twin then issues a predictive maintenance alert, specifying the likely failure mode (bearing degradation) and recommending a maintenance window within the next two weeks. This allows the maintenance team to schedule the replacement during a planned downtime, avoiding an unscheduled stoppage that would disrupt production and incur significant costs.

Beyond component wear, predictive capabilities extend to process-related failures. For example, the digital twin can monitor the pressure and flow rate of the hydraulic system powering a stamping press. A gradual decrease in pressure, coupled with erratic flow patterns, could indicate a developing leak or a failing valve. The twin can predict a potential system failure within a defined timeframe, allowing for proactive repair and preventing damage to the press or the dies. Similarly, for the automated washing stations, the twin can predict when the cleaning fluid concentration might drop below optimal levels or when filters might become clogged, based on flow rates, pressure drops, and the history of fluid replenishment and filter changes. This predictive power not only minimizes unplanned downtime but also optimizes maintenance schedules and spare parts inventory.

The third, and arguably most impactful, application of the digital twin lies in its ability to drive real-time optimization of the manufacturing process. This is where the twin moves beyond merely reflecting and predicting to actively guiding improvements. By simulating different operational scenarios and evaluating their outcomes against defined Key Performance Indicators (KPIs), the digital twin can recommend adjustments to production parameters to enhance efficiency, reduce waste, and improve quality.

Consider the CNC machining operations. The digital twin can be used to virtually experiment with different cutting speeds, feed rates, and tool engagement strategies for a specific part. By running simulations that incorporate the real-time data of the machine's thermal state, vibration levels, and cutting forces, the twin can identify the optimal combination of parameters that minimizes cycle time while maintaining surface finish and tool life within acceptable limits. If the twin detects that a particular machining operation is consistently generating excess heat, leading to potential thermal distortion or reduced tool life, it can suggest adjustments to the coolant flow rate, spindle speed, or even the cutting tool geometry itself.

A compelling example of optimization can be seen in the material handling system. AGVs are crucial for transporting raw materials and finished goods. The digital twin, by monitoring the real-time location and status of all AGVs, as well as the demands from various workstations, can optimize their routes and task assignments dynamically. If a bottleneck is detected at a particular unloading station, the twin can reroute available AGVs to assist or prioritize their tasks to clear the backlog. It can also optimize charging schedules for AGVs, ensuring that they are charged during periods of low demand or during planned downtime, thereby maximizing their operational availability. Furthermore, by analyzing the energy consumption patterns of the AGVs, the twin can identify opportunities for energy savings, such as optimizing acceleration and deceleration profiles.

Another area ripe for optimization is the scheduling and sequencing of production orders. The digital twin can incorporate real-time data on machine availability, current production status, and incoming order priorities to create and dynamically adjust production schedules. If a machine unexpectedly goes offline for maintenance, the twin can immediately re-evaluate the schedule, reallocate tasks to other available machines, and provide updated estimated completion times for all affected orders. This agility in scheduling minimizes disruptions and ensures that production remains as efficient as possible.

The optimization extends to energy consumption. By monitoring the energy usage of individual machines and processes in real-time, and correlating this with production output, the digital twin can identify areas of significant energy waste. For instance, it might reveal that certain machines are consuming substantial power even when idle, or that specific processes are inherently energy-intensive and could be re-engineered. Based on this data, the twin can recommend actions such as implementing smart power management strategies (e.g., automatically powering down idle machines) or suggesting modifications to process parameters that reduce energy requirements without compromising quality or throughput.

The tangible benefits realized from these applications are substantial. In one instance, a manufacturer utilizing a digital twin for their CNC machining department experienced a 15% reduction in unplanned downtime due to predictive maintenance alerts identifying bearing failures several weeks in advance. This allowed for planned replacements, preventing costly production stoppages. Concurrently, by leveraging the twin's simulation capabilities to optimize cutting parameters, they achieved a 10% increase in throughput for a critical product line, alongside a reduction in tool wear, leading to further cost savings.

In another case study, a complex assembly line implemented the digital twin for real-time monitoring of the production flow. The twin identified recurring delays at a specific manual assembly station caused by inconsistent part presentation. By visualizing this bottleneck and correlating it with the AGV activity, the operations team was able to implement a revised AGV dispatch strategy, significantly improving the buffer management at the station. This resulted in a 5% improvement in overall line efficiency and a reduction in work-in-progress inventory.

Furthermore, the optimization of energy consumption through the digital twin led to a 7% decrease in the plant's overall electricity bill. By identifying and addressing idle power consumption of non-critical machinery and by fine-tuning the operating parameters of high-energy-demand processes, significant cost savings were realized. These examples underscore the transformative power of digital twin technology, moving beyond theoretical concepts to deliver concrete, measurable improvements in manufacturing operations. The continuous feedback loop between monitoring, prediction, and optimization ensures that the digital twin remains a powerful catalyst for ongoing operational excellence.

The implementation of a digital twin within the described manufacturing environment has yielded a demonstrable array of quantifiable improvements, directly impacting critical Key Performance Indicators (KPIs) and showcasing the tangible value of this advanced technological adoption. One of the most significant achievements has been the substantial reduction in unplanned downtime. By leveraging the predictive maintenance capabilities, which accurately forecast component failures based on real-time operational data and advanced algorithms, the manufacturing line experienced a remarkable decrease of approximately 18% in unscheduled stoppages over a twelve-month period. This reduction is not merely a statistic; it translates directly into increased production uptime, allowing for more consistent and reliable output. For instance, a critical injection molding machine, previously prone to unexpected hydraulic system failures, now benefits from early warnings generated by its digital twin regarding degrading valve seals. This foresight has enabled maintenance teams to schedule replacements during planned minor maintenance windows, effectively eliminating the disruptive, costly breakdowns that were once a frequent occurrence.

Further contributing to this enhanced operational efficiency is the significant uplift in Overall Equipment Effectiveness (OEE). The combined impact of reduced downtime, improved performance (achieved through real-time process optimization), and enhanced quality (resulting from proactive issue identification) has led to an average OEE increase of 12% across the monitored production lines. This means that the equipment is not only running more frequently but is also operating closer to its theoretical maximum capacity and producing a higher proportion of good quality parts. For the automated assembly stations, the digital twin's ability to dynamically reroute autonomous mobile robots (AMRs) in response to real-time production flow changes has smoothed out bottlenecks, ensuring a consistent and optimal pace of assembly. This has directly contributed to the performance aspect of OEE by minimizing minor stops and ensuring machines are running at their optimal speed.

Product quality has also seen a notable enhancement, with a measured reduction of 7% in scrap and rework rates. The granular monitoring and predictive analytics provided by the digital twin allow for the early detection of subtle deviations in process parameters that could compromise product integrity. For example, in the painting and coating process, the digital twin monitors not only temperature and humidity but also the precise viscosity of the coating material and the spray pattern consistency. If any of these parameters drift beyond optimal thresholds, even by a minute margin, the system alerts operators, enabling immediate adjustments. This proactive approach to quality control prevents entire batches of products from being manufactured with defects, thereby reducing material waste and the labor costs associated with rework. The continuous feedback loop ensures that any identified quality issues are addressed before they propagate through the production system.

The financial implications of these operational improvements are equally compelling. Cost savings have been realized across multiple fronts. The reduction in unplanned downtime has directly translated into decreased costs associated with emergency repairs, overtime labor for unscheduled maintenance, and the expensive expediting of replacement parts. Furthermore, the optimization of processes, such as the reduction in cycle times for certain machining operations and the minimization of material waste through improved quality control, has led to significant reductions in the cost of goods sold. Energy consumption has also been a focus area for optimization. By analyzing the energy usage patterns of individual machines and entire production lines, and by implementing smart power management strategies recommended by the digital twin (e.g., optimizing the sequencing of high-demand equipment to avoid peak load charges), the facility has achieved an estimated 9% reduction in its overall energy expenditure. The enhanced predictive maintenance, by allowing for the procurement of spare parts based on anticipated need rather than immediate emergency, has also contributed to better inventory management and reduced holding costs.

Beyond these quantifiable results, the journey of implementing and operating the digital twin has been rich with invaluable lessons learned. One of the most critical lessons is the absolute necessity of a robust and reliable data infrastructure. The digital twin is only as good as the data it receives. Early in the deployment, challenges were encountered due to intermittent data flow from certain legacy sensors and inconsistencies in data formatting from various sources. This highlighted the importance of investing not only in the digital twin software itself but also in the underlying network, sensor technology, and data integration platforms. Establishing clear data governance policies, ensuring data accuracy, and implementing redundancy measures for critical data streams are paramount to the success and trustworthiness of the digital twin. A dedicated effort to standardize data protocols and implement data cleansing routines was essential to overcome these initial hurdles and build confidence in the twin's outputs.

Another significant learning pertains to the crucial role of change management and user adoption. Introducing a sophisticated tool like a digital twin into a long-established manufacturing workflow requires more than just technical implementation; it demands a fundamental shift in how personnel at all levels perceive and interact with their work. Initial resistance from some operators and supervisors, who were accustomed to traditional methods, was observed. Overcoming this required a concerted effort to demonstrate the benefits of the digital twin through clear communication, hands-on training, and by actively involving end-users in the design and refinement process. Highlighting how the twin augments, rather than replaces, human expertise, and showing how it can make their jobs easier and more effective, was key to fostering buy-in. Creating champions within the operational teams who could advocate for the technology and provide peer-to-peer support proved to be an exceptionally effective strategy.

The process also underscored the importance of starting with a clearly defined scope and prioritizing specific use cases. Attempting to model and monitor every single aspect of the manufacturing process from day one would have been overwhelming and likely led to project fatigue. Instead, focusing initially on high-impact areas such as predictive maintenance for critical machinery and real-time monitoring of bottlenecked workstations allowed for demonstrable successes early on. These early wins built momentum and provided a solid foundation for expanding the digital twin's capabilities to other areas of the plant. Iterative development, where functionality is added and refined in phases based on feedback and observed value, is a far more sustainable and effective approach than a monolithic, all-or-nothing deployment.

Furthermore, the experience reinforced the understanding that a digital twin is not a static entity but a continuously evolving platform. The manufacturing environment itself is dynamic, with changes in product lines, materials, and operational strategies. The digital twin must be capable of adapting to these changes. This involves ongoing calibration of models, retraining of machine learning algorithms with new data, and updating simulation parameters as operational conditions evolve. A dedicated team or resource responsible for the ongoing maintenance, monitoring, and evolution of the digital twin is essential to ensure its continued relevance and effectiveness. This includes regularly reviewing the performance of the twin against its objectives and identifying new opportunities for optimization and prediction.

The integration of domain expertise with data science and IT capabilities emerged as another critical success factor. While data scientists can build sophisticated algorithms, they may lack the deep understanding of the physical processes and machinery that experienced manufacturing engineers and operators possess. Conversely, domain experts may not have the data analysis skills to interpret complex patterns or build predictive models. A collaborative approach, where cross-functional teams work together, ensures that the digital twin is both technically sound and practically relevant. This synergy allows for the creation of models that accurately reflect the physical reality and for the interpretation of results in a way that leads to actionable insights.

Finally, the importance of cybersecurity cannot be overstated. As the digital twin becomes increasingly integrated with operational technology (OT) systems and handles sensitive production data, it becomes a potential target for cyber threats. Robust security protocols, regular vulnerability assessments, and strict access controls are non-negotiable requirements. Ensuring the integrity and confidentiality of the data flowing into and out of the digital twin is paramount to maintaining trust in the system and protecting the manufacturing operations from malicious interference or data breaches. The lessons learned highlight that while the pursuit of technological advancement is exciting, it must be balanced with a pragmatic, phased approach, a strong emphasis on people and process, and an unwavering commitment to data integrity and security.

Chapter 14: Future Trends and Innovations

The journey of digital twins, as evidenced by their successful implementation in enhancing manufacturing operations, is far from over. Instead, what we are witnessing is the dawn of an ever-more sophisticated and pervasive era for these virtual replicas. The foundational capabilities of monitoring, simulation, and prediction, which have already delivered significant value, are now being augmented by a suite of emerging technologies and conceptual shifts. This evolution is pushing digital twins beyond static representations to become dynamic, intelligent, and deeply integrated components of a broader digital fabric that permeates industries.

One of the most significant trajectories for digital twins is their increasing autonomy and intelligence. While current twins often rely on human operators to interpret data and initiate actions, future iterations will be endowed with a greater capacity for self-awareness and self-governance. This is being driven by advancements in artificial intelligence (AI) and machine learning (ML), particularly in areas like deep learning and reinforcement learning. Imagine a digital twin not merely flagging a potential anomaly in a turbine's vibration patterns but, based on its learned understanding of optimal operating parameters and the potential consequences of failure, autonomously adjusting the turbine's speed or load to mitigate the risk, all while notifying maintenance personnel of the proactive intervention. This shift from reactive alerts to proactive, automated adjustments represents a paradigm leap, moving the digital twin from a sophisticated diagnostic tool to an active participant in operational management. The ability of AI algorithms to process vast amounts of real-time sensor data, correlate it with historical performance, and predict future states with increasing accuracy allows the twin to "learn" the optimal behaviors of its physical counterpart under various conditions. This learning extends to understanding complex interactions between different components and systems, enabling more nuanced and effective autonomous decision-making. For instance, in a complex chemical process plant, an AI-powered digital twin could learn to fine-tune the flow rates and temperatures of multiple reactors simultaneously to maximize yield while minimizing energy consumption and ensuring safety, without direct human intervention for every minor adjustment.

Furthermore, the integration of digital twins with the Internet of Things (IoT) is becoming increasingly seamless and sophisticated. While current implementations often involve connecting sensors to a digital twin, the future will see a more pervasive network of interconnected digital twins, each representing a component, a system, or even an entire environment. This creates a hierarchical and interconnected web of virtual representations that can interact with each other. A digital twin of a single machine might contribute its operational data to the digital twin of an entire production line, which in turn feeds into the digital twin of a factory, and subsequently into a digital twin of a supply chain. This layered approach enables holistic simulation and optimization across vastly different scales. Consider a city's infrastructure: digital twins of individual traffic lights could feed into a city-wide traffic management digital twin, which could then interact with digital twins of public transport vehicles and smart grids to optimize the flow of people and energy. This interoperability is critical for tackling complex, multi-domain challenges. The concept of "systems of systems" where digital twins of individual assets collaborate and exchange information is a key area of development. For example, the digital twin of an autonomous vehicle could communicate with the digital twin of the road infrastructure it is traversing, allowing for dynamic route planning that accounts for real-time traffic, road conditions, and even the predicted behavior of other connected vehicles. This level of interconnectedness opens up unprecedented possibilities for coordinated optimization and intelligent automation.

The concept of "federated digital twins" is also gaining traction. Instead of a single, monolithic digital twin that encompasses every aspect of a physical asset or system, federated twins allow for distributed ownership and management of twin components. Different stakeholders – perhaps a manufacturer, a maintenance provider, and an end-user – could each maintain and contribute to different aspects of a shared digital twin. This approach addresses data sovereignty concerns and allows for more modular and scalable twin development. For instance, a wind turbine manufacturer might own the digital twin of the turbine's core mechanics, while the energy utility operating it might manage the twin's power generation performance module, and a specialized maintenance firm could oversee the predictive maintenance component. These federated twins would then communicate and collaborate to provide a comprehensive view and manage the asset's lifecycle. This distributed model is particularly relevant for complex ecosystems involving multiple organizations, such as smart cities or large-scale industrial complexes, where no single entity has complete oversight or control over all components.

Another significant evolution is the increasing use of digital twins for "what-if" scenario planning and foresight beyond simple predictive maintenance. While current simulations are powerful, future twins will be capable of more complex, long-term predictive modeling. This includes simulating the impact of market shifts, regulatory changes, or even climate events on an asset or system. For example, a logistics company could use its digital twin to simulate the impact of a sudden fuel price surge on its delivery routes and costs, allowing it to proactively adjust its fleet management strategies or explore alternative fuel options. Similarly, urban planners could use digital twins of cities to simulate the long-term effects of new building developments on traffic congestion, air quality, and energy demand, enabling more informed decision-making. This capability extends to "digital twins of the future," where simulations explore potential future states of physical assets or environments based on current trends and planned interventions. This allows for proactive design and adaptation rather than reactive problem-solving. The ability to run these simulations at scale, potentially leveraging distributed computing and cloud resources, will be crucial for tackling the complexity of these future-oriented scenarios.

The convergence of digital twins with technologies like Augmented Reality (AR) and Virtual Reality (VR) is also a key trend, blurring the lines between the physical and digital worlds. Imagine technicians wearing AR glasses that overlay real-time diagnostic data from a digital twin directly onto the physical equipment they are servicing. This allows for intuitive, hands-free troubleshooting and maintenance. VR can be used for immersive training environments, allowing engineers to interact with a virtual replica of a complex piece of machinery before ever touching the real thing, or to experience the simulated consequences of operational errors in a safe, controlled setting. The integration of haptic feedback can further enhance the realism of these experiences, making the digital twin feel almost tangible. This fusion of digital twins with immersive technologies enhances human interaction with complex systems, leading to improved understanding, faster problem-solving, and more effective training. For complex assembly tasks, AR can provide step-by-step visual guidance projected onto the workspace, synchronized with the digital twin's precise instructions. For emergency response, VR simulations powered by digital twins can train personnel to handle scenarios like fires or chemical spills in a highly realistic and safe manner.

The concept of "digital threads" is intrinsically linked to the future of digital twins. A digital thread is the communication pathway that connects all the data related to a product or system throughout its lifecycle, from design and manufacturing to operation and disposal. Digital twins act as living repositories and enablers of these digital threads, providing a contextualized, real-time view of the physical asset as it moves along its lifecycle. This ensures that design intent is maintained through manufacturing and operation, and that lessons learned in the field can be fed back into future designs. For example, a digital thread for an aircraft engine could link its original design specifications, manufacturing records, maintenance history, and real-time performance data, all accessible through its digital twin. This comprehensive traceability and connectivity is essential for product lifecycle management, regulatory compliance, and continuous improvement. The ability to weave together data from disparate sources – CAD models, simulation results, manufacturing execution systems (MES), enterprise resource planning (ERP) systems, and sensor data – into a coherent digital thread, anchored by the digital twin, is a key objective for many industries.

The application of digital twins is also expanding beyond traditional industrial sectors into areas like healthcare, urban planning, and environmental management. In healthcare, digital twins of patients could be created to simulate the effects of different treatments, personalize medicine, and monitor chronic conditions remotely. Digital twins of hospitals could optimize patient flow, resource allocation, and equipment utilization. In urban planning, digital twins of cities can help model the impact of new infrastructure, simulate disaster responses, and improve sustainability. Environmental digital twins can monitor pollution levels, predict the impact of climate change, and optimize resource management. The potential for digital twins to address some of the world's most pressing challenges is immense. For example, a digital twin of a coral reef ecosystem could integrate data on water temperature, acidity, and pollution to predict the impact of climate change and inform conservation efforts. A digital twin of a critical water management system could simulate drought scenarios and optimize water allocation to different regions.

Moreover, the development of "digital twins of the digital twins" is emerging as a meta-concept, where sophisticated AI models are used to represent and optimize the behavior and performance of the digital twin systems themselves. This is particularly relevant as digital twins become more complex and interconnected, requiring advanced methods for managing, updating, and ensuring the integrity of the twin models and their underlying data. This recursive aspect allows for continuous improvement of the digital twin technology itself, ensuring that it remains an effective and efficient tool for mirroring and managing the physical world. For instance, an AI could monitor the performance of a fleet of digital twins, identifying inefficiencies in data processing or simulation execution, and then propose optimizations to the underlying twin architecture or algorithms.

The future of digital twins is also intertwined with the concept of "digital continuums," a framework that emphasizes the seamless flow of data and intelligence between the physical and digital worlds across various dimensions, including space, time, and abstraction levels. Digital twins are a key component of this continuum, acting as the bridge between physical assets and the digital intelligence that governs them. This holistic vision sees digital twins as integral parts of a vast, interconnected network that drives innovation and efficiency across all sectors of the economy and society. The pursuit of this continuum will necessitate continued advancements in areas such as edge computing, 5G connectivity, cybersecurity, and data standardization to enable the real-time, secure, and reliable exchange of information across increasingly complex digital ecosystems. The ability to manage and leverage this data effectively will define the success of future digital twin applications.

The maturation of digital twin technology will also necessitate robust standards and interoperability protocols. As more organizations adopt and develop digital twins, the ability for these twins to communicate and collaborate with one another will become paramount. Industry-wide standards for data formats, communication protocols, and model definitions will be crucial to unlock the full potential of interconnected digital twins and prevent the proliferation of isolated, proprietary systems. Initiatives to define these standards are underway, aiming to foster an ecosystem where digital twins can be easily integrated and leveraged across different platforms and applications. Without such standardization, the vision of a truly interconnected digital world, powered by a network of digital twins, will remain a distant aspiration. This includes developing common languages for describing physical assets, their behaviors, and their relationships within larger systems, allowing for seamless data exchange and functional interoperability between twins created by different vendors or organizations.

The evolution of digital twins is not merely about technological advancement; it is also about a fundamental shift in how we design, build, operate, and maintain the physical world. As these virtual counterparts become more intelligent, autonomous, and interconnected, they will transform industries, drive innovation, and enable us to tackle complex challenges with unprecedented insight and efficiency. The journey from simple data mirrors to sophisticated, AI-driven orchestrators is well underway, promising a future where the digital and physical realms are inextricably linked, working in concert to create a more optimized, resilient, and sustainable world. The ongoing research and development in areas like AI, IoT, edge computing, and advanced simulation techniques will continue to push the boundaries of what digital twins can achieve, cementing their role as a cornerstone of the digital transformation across virtually every sector.

The relentless march of Artificial Intelligence (AI) and Machine Learning (ML) is not merely augmenting existing digital twin capabilities; it is fundamentally reshaping their very nature. As these intelligent systems mature, their integration with digital twins is unlocking unprecedented levels of predictive accuracy, fostering sophisticated autonomous decision-making, and injecting a profound sense of realism into simulations. This symbiotic relationship promises to elevate digital twins from powerful analytical tools to proactive, self-optimizing entities capable of navigating complex operational landscapes with remarkable autonomy.

One of the most transformative AI advancements is the rapid development and application of
deep learning. Unlike traditional ML algorithms that often require extensive feature engineering, deep learning models, particularly neural networks with multiple layers, can automatically learn hierarchical representations of data. For digital twins, this translates into a significantly enhanced ability to discern subtle patterns and correlations within vast streams of sensor data. Imagine a complex industrial machine, such as a gas turbine. A deep learning model integrated into its digital twin can analyze terabytes of operational data – vibration frequencies, temperature gradients, fuel flow rates, and acoustic signatures – to identify precursors to failure that might be imperceptible to human analysts or simpler algorithms. These models can learn to distinguish between normal operational noise and genuine anomalies, even in the presence of significant environmental variability or component degradation over time. This capability moves beyond mere anomaly detection to sophisticated fault diagnosis and prognostics, enabling the digital twin to not only predict *that* a failure might occur but also to pinpoint *why* and *how* it is likely to manifest. For instance, in the petrochemical industry, deep learning-powered digital twins of reactors can analyze intricate chemical process data, identifying complex interactions between reaction kinetics, catalyst performance, and feedstock variations to predict optimal operating parameters for maximizing yield and minimizing impurity formation. The ability of deep neural networks to process sequential data, such as time-series sensor readings, is also crucial for understanding the dynamic evolution of system states, allowing for more accurate predictions of remaining useful life (RUL) for critical components. This is achieved by training models on historical data that captures the degradation patterns leading up to failure, enabling the twin to extrapolate these trends into the future with greater confidence.

Closely related is the advancement in
reinforcement learning (RL), a paradigm where an AI agent learns to make decisions by interacting with an environment and receiving feedback in the form of rewards or penalties. When applied to digital twins, RL allows the virtual replica to learn optimal control strategies through trial and error in a simulated environment, without risking damage to the physical asset. Consider a robotic arm in a manufacturing assembly line. Its digital twin, equipped with an RL agent, can explore millions of possible movement sequences, learning to perform

intricate tasks with maximum speed and precision while minimizing energy consumption and wear on the physical arm. The reward function could be designed to incentivize task completion within a time limit, adherence to safety constraints, and minimal deviation from ideal trajectory. This is particularly powerful for dynamic environments where conditions can change rapidly. For example, an RL-powered digital twin of a fleet of autonomous delivery drones could learn to navigate complex urban airspace, optimizing routes in real-time to avoid obstacles, manage battery life, and respond to changing weather conditions, all based on simulated interactions and learned optimal behaviors. This goes beyond pre-programmed responses, enabling true adaptive control. In the realm of energy grids, RL agents within digital twins of substations can learn to dynamically balance supply and demand, optimize energy storage, and respond to grid disturbances, contributing to a more resilient and efficient power infrastructure. The ability of RL to learn from delayed rewards is crucial for systems where the consequences of a decision may not be immediately apparent, such as optimizing the long-term operational efficiency of a complex manufacturing process or managing the lifecycle of a renewable energy asset.

The emergence of
generative AI, exemplified by models like Generative Adversarial Networks (GANs) and Variational Autoencoders (VAEs), is opening up new frontiers for digital twin simulations. These models excel at creating novel, realistic data that mimics the characteristics of existing data. For digital twins, this means the ability to generate synthetic yet highly plausible scenarios that may be rare, expensive, or impossible to replicate in the physical world. Imagine needing to train maintenance personnel on how to handle an extremely rare equipment malfunction. A generative AI model integrated with the digital twin can create a multitude of hyper-realistic simulations of this malfunction, complete with subtle variations in symptoms and progression. This allows for extensive, risk-free training and preparedness. Furthermore, generative AI can be used to augment existing datasets, filling in gaps or creating more diverse training data for other ML models within the digital twin. For instance, in the automotive industry, GANs can generate synthetic sensor data representing various road conditions, lighting scenarios, and pedestrian behaviors to train the perception systems of autonomous vehicles within their digital twins, thereby accelerating the development and validation process. In product design, generative AI can explore a vast design space, proposing novel configurations or material combinations for

a product based on performance requirements defined in its digital twin, leading to innovative and optimized designs. The ability to generate variations of digital twin models themselves, perhaps exploring slightly different physical properties or operational characteristics, can also aid in robust design and risk assessment. This capability is invaluable for exploring the "unknown unknowns" - scenarios that were not explicitly considered during the initial design phase.

Beyond these specific AI techniques, the overarching trend is the development of **more sophisticated and context-aware AI models** for digital twins. This includes advancements in areas like explainable AI (XAI), which aims to make the decision-making processes of AI models more transparent and understandable. For digital twins, XAI is crucial for building trust and enabling human operators to validate the insights and recommendations provided by the AI. If an AI-powered digital twin suggests a radical operational change, XAI can provide the rationale behind that suggestion, allowing engineers to assess its feasibility and risks more effectively. Techniques like LIME (Local Interpretable Model-agnostic Explanations) or SHAP (SHapley Additive exPlanations) can help identify which input features or historical data points contributed most significantly to a particular prediction or decision, fostering confidence in the AI's output.

Furthermore, the integration of **physics-informed neural networks (PINNs)** represents a powerful synergy between AI and the fundamental physical laws governing the asset. PINNs incorporate physical principles, such as differential equations, directly into the neural network's loss function. This means that even with limited training data, the digital twin can generate physically plausible simulations and predictions. For complex systems where empirical data is scarce or expensive to obtain, such as novel materials or advanced aerospace components, PINNs enable digital twins to maintain a strong grounding in physical reality. For example, a PINN-powered digital twin of a new composite material could predict its stress-strain behavior under various loads, even before extensive physical testing, by encoding the relevant elasticity equations into the learning process. This dramatically reduces the need for costly and time-consuming experimentation and allows for more accurate early-stage design validation.

The application of AI within digital twins is also driving the evolution towards

autonomous digital twins. These are twins that can not only predict and simulate but also autonomously take corrective actions within predefined operational boundaries. This moves the digital twin from a passive observer and advisor to an active manager of the physical asset. For example, in a smart manufacturing facility, an AI-driven digital twin of a production line could detect an impending bottleneck caused by a machine slowdown. Instead of merely alerting an operator, it could autonomously adjust the speeds of upstream machines to buffer production, re-route work orders, or even initiate a self-diagnostic routine for the underperforming machine, all while providing a real-time status update to human supervisors. This level of autonomy is particularly valuable in high-speed, complex environments where human reaction times may be insufficient to prevent operational disruptions or capitalize on fleeting optimization opportunities. This also extends to supply chain management, where AI-powered digital twins can dynamically reconfigure logistics networks in response to real-time events like port congestion, natural disasters, or sudden shifts in demand, ensuring continuity and efficiency.

The potential for AI to unlock new levels of insight and automation through digital twins is truly profound. As AI algorithms become more capable of understanding context, learning from experience, and interacting with the physical world through their digital counterparts, we are witnessing a paradigm shift. The future digital twin will be a continuously learning, self-optimizing entity, capable of managing complex systems with an intelligence that rivals, and in many cases surpasses, human capabilities. This will lead to unprecedented gains in efficiency, reliability, sustainability, and innovation across a vast array of industries. The ability to forecast, simulate, and act with such precision and autonomy, powered by cutting-edge AI, positions digital twins as a cornerstone of the next industrial revolution.

The integration of Extended Reality (XR) – a spectrum encompassing Virtual Reality (VR) and Augmented Reality (AR) – with digital twins marks a pivotal evolution in how we perceive, interact with, and leverage these sophisticated virtual replicas. XR technologies are not merely enhancing the visualization capabilities of digital twins; they are fundamentally transforming the user experience, making complex data and simulations intuitively accessible and actionable for human operators. This synergy creates immersive environments where the abstract world of digital twins becomes tangible, enabling a deeper understanding and more effective engagement with the physical assets they represent.

Virtual Reality, in its purest form, allows users to be fully immersed in a completely digital environment. When applied to digital twins, this means stepping
into the virtual model. Imagine a complex manufacturing plant, with all its machinery, workflows, and operational data represented in a highly detailed VR simulation. An engineer could don a VR headset and virtually walk through the plant floor, observing machinery in operation, identifying potential bottlenecks, or even simulating different production scenarios from a first-person perspective. This immersive quality is particularly invaluable for training purposes. Instead of relying on static manuals or limited physical demonstrations, trainees can experience real-world operational conditions in a safe, controlled virtual space. For example, new technicians learning to operate and maintain intricate machinery like a CNC milling machine or a chemical reactor can be exposed to a wide range of operational states, including emergency procedures and fault conditions, without any risk to themselves or the actual equipment. They can manipulate virtual controls, diagnose simulated issues, and practice repair sequences, building muscle memory and procedural knowledge in a highly effective manner. This deep level of engagement fosters a much stronger grasp of complex systems compared to traditional training methods. Furthermore, VR can be used for collaborative design reviews and factory layout planning. Multiple stakeholders, geographically dispersed, can meet within a shared virtual space to inspect a digital twin of a proposed facility, providing feedback and making design adjustments in real-time. This collaborative potential dramatically accelerates the design iteration process and reduces costly errors that might only be discovered late in the physical construction phase. The ability to experience the scale and spatial relationships of a new facility or a redesigned product within VR offers an unparalleled advantage in grasping the holistic impact of design decisions. Beyond industrial applications, architects can use VR to walk clients through virtual models of buildings, allowing them to experience the design and flow of spaces before construction begins, leading to more informed decisions and increased client satisfaction.

Augmented Reality, on the other hand, overlays digital information onto the user's view of the real world. This creates a powerful bridge between the physical asset and its digital twin, providing context-sensitive information and interactive capabilities directly in the user's line of sight. For field service technicians, AR can be a game-changer. Armed with an AR-enabled device – such as smart glasses or a tablet – a technician approaching a piece of equipment can see overlaid digital twin data directly on the physical machine. This might include real-time sensor readings, operational status indicators, maintenance histories, or step-by-step repair instructions. For instance, when diagnosing an issue with a complex HVAC system, AR could highlight the specific components that are reporting errors, display their current operating parameters, and guide the technician through the diagnostic process by overlaying visual cues and instructions. This drastically reduces the time spent searching for information, cross-referencing manuals, or making educated guesses. The ability to see the "digital twin" of the component or system in situ, with its live data, empowers the technician to make faster, more accurate decisions. Beyond maintenance, AR applications extend to assembly processes. In manufacturing, AR can guide assembly line workers by projecting instructions, component placements, and quality checks directly onto the work area, ensuring accuracy and consistency, especially for complex or novel assemblies. This not only improves efficiency but also reduces the likelihood of human error. Furthermore, AR can provide enhanced operational interfaces. Imagine a pilot viewing flight instrument data not just on a dashboard but also projected onto the cockpit windows via an AR heads-up display, with critical information seamlessly integrated into their forward view. Similarly, surgeons can benefit from AR overlays during complex procedures, visualizing patient anatomy, medical imaging data, or surgical plans directly onto the patient's body, enhancing precision and safety. The potential for AR to contextualize digital twin information within the physical environment makes it an incredibly powerful tool for operational efficiency and safety across a multitude of domains.

The combination of VR and AR, often referred to as Mixed Reality (MR), further expands the possibilities by allowing virtual objects to interact with the real world and vice versa. This means that a digital twin can not only be visualized within a real environment but can also respond to and influence that environment in a more dynamic way. For example, in a factory setting, an AR system could allow a worker to "place" a virtual component into a real assembly station, and the digital twin would then update its simulation based on this interaction, perhaps triggering an alert if the placement is incorrect or suboptimal. This blend of physical and digital interaction provides a richer, more intuitive way to work with digital twins.

One of the most significant impacts of XR integration is in the realm of **remote assistance and collaboration**. When a problem arises with a physical asset, an expert located anywhere in the world can virtually join the on-site technician. Using AR, the expert can see what the technician sees, and then overlay annotations, drawings, or instructions directly onto the technician's view of the equipment. This allows for real-time guidance and problem-solving, minimizing downtime and travel costs. The digital twin itself can serve as the shared context for this interaction, providing the expert with the complete virtual model and all its associated data to diagnose the issue effectively. This capability is particularly vital in industries with remote operations, such as offshore oil rigs, mining sites, or expansive agricultural lands, where getting expert personnel on-site can be time-consuming and expensive. This technology effectively democratizes access to expertise, making it available wherever and whenever it is needed. The digital twin acts as the common ground upon which the remote expert and the on-site operator can collaborate, sharing insights derived from both the physical reality and the virtual replica.

XR also enhances the **comprehensibility and discoverability of digital twin data**. Traditional interfaces for interacting with digital twins often involve complex dashboards, charts, and tables, which can be overwhelming and difficult to interpret for non-technical users. XR transforms this data into intuitive visual representations. Instead of looking at a graph of temperature fluctuations, a user in VR might see a heat map overlaid onto a 3D model of a machine, with vibrant colors indicating areas of high temperature. Similarly, in AR, a complex flow diagram can be visualized spatially, allowing users to trace the path of materials or energy through a system with greater ease. This visual and spatial approach to data makes it more accessible, leading to quicker identification of trends, anomalies, and opportunities for improvement. The cognitive load associated with data interpretation is significantly reduced, empowering a wider range of personnel to engage with and benefit from the insights provided by digital twins. For example, a plant manager who may not be an engineer could easily understand the operational status of their facility by simply looking at an AR-enhanced overview, where color-coded indicators on machinery suggest performance levels.

The applications of XR-integrated digital twins span across numerous sectors. In **healthcare**, VR is used for surgical planning, where surgeons can practice complex procedures on a patient's digital twin before entering the operating room. AR can then provide real-time guidance during the actual surgery. In **architecture, engineering, and construction (AEC)**, VR allows for immersive walkthroughs of building designs, enabling stakeholders to visualize the finished product and identify potential design flaws early in the process. AR can then be used on-site to overlay construction plans onto the physical site, ensuring accurate placement of structures and utilities. In the **automotive industry**, XR is used for vehicle design and prototyping, allowing engineers to interact with and evaluate virtual car models. It also plays a crucial role in training mechanics to service complex vehicles and in providing drivers with enhanced navigation and information systems.

The development of user interfaces for XR-enabled digital twins is a critical area of ongoing innovation. Natural language processing and gestural controls are becoming increasingly sophisticated, allowing users to interact with digital twins in a more intuitive and less hardware-dependent manner. Imagine being able to ask a virtual assistant within a digital twin about the status of a specific component, or to manipulate a virtual object simply by pointing and speaking. This moves towards a more seamless and human-centric interaction model. As XR hardware becomes more advanced – lighter, more comfortable headsets, higher resolution displays, and more precise tracking – the immersion and utility of these applications will continue to grow. The convergence of AI, digital twins, and XR technologies is not just about creating more sophisticated simulations; it's about fundamentally changing the human-machine interface, making complex systems more understandable, manageable, and efficient than ever before. This creates a powerful feedback loop where human intuition and experience, augmented by the precision and data-rich environment of XR-powered digital twins, can lead to breakthroughs in operational performance, innovation, and problem-solving. The future of digital twins is inextricably linked with the immersive and interactive capabilities offered by Extended Reality, promising a more intuitive, insightful, and actionable digital future.

The evolution of digital twins is moving beyond individual asset representations towards the creation of interconnected, collaborative ecosystems. This paradigm shift is giving rise to the concepts of "federated digital twins" and "systems of systems of digital twins." Imagine a scenario where not just a single machine, but an entire factory, and not just a factory, but a network of factories, a city's infrastructure, or even a global supply chain, is represented by a constellation of interlinked digital twins. This is the essence of federated digital twins: a framework where multiple, often independently developed and managed, digital twins can communicate, share data, and collaborate to provide a holistic view of a larger, more complex system.

The need for such federated structures arises from the inherent complexity of modern enterprises and societal infrastructures. No single digital twin can capture the entirety of a smart city's operations, from traffic flow and energy grids to waste management and public safety. Similarly, a global supply chain involves myriad entities - manufacturers, logistics providers, retailers, and regulatory bodies - each with their own operational data and potentially their own digital twin implementations. Forcing all this data into a single, monolithic digital twin would be logistically impossible, computationally prohibitive, and fundamentally unmanageable. Federated digital twins offer a distributed, scalable, and more practical approach.

At its core, a federated digital twin system relies on interoperability. This means establishing standardized protocols, data formats, and communication interfaces that allow disparate digital twins to understand and interact with each other. It's akin to creating a common language that different components of a complex system can use to exchange information. For instance, a digital twin of a particular manufacturing plant might need to communicate its production output to a digital twin representing a logistics company responsible for its distribution. This communication could involve sharing real-time production schedules, inventory levels, and shipment readiness. The logistics digital twin, in turn, would interact with a digital twin of a port or a fleet of trucks, sharing expected arrival times and cargo manifests. This seamless flow of information, enabled by interoperability standards, is critical for optimizing the entire supply chain, reducing lead times, and mitigating disruptions.

The concept extends further into building "systems of systems" where the collective behavior and emergent properties of interconnected digital twins are of paramount importance. A system of systems is more than just a collection of individual systems; it is a collection of systems that are purposefully designed to work together to achieve a common goal, often exhibiting capabilities that the individual systems do not possess on their own. In the context of digital twins, this means creating dynamic, adaptive models of complex environments like smart cities. The digital twin of a city might comprise federated digital twins for its transportation network, energy grid, water supply, emergency services, and environmental monitoring. When an event occurs, such as a major traffic accident or a power outage, the relevant digital twins would share information. The transportation digital twin would update traffic flow simulations, potentially rerouting vehicles. The energy grid digital twin might adjust power distribution to mitigate overload. Emergency services digital twins would receive real-time situational awareness, enabling faster and more targeted responses. The "system of systems" aspect comes into play as these individual digital twins react and interact, creating a dynamic, city-wide simulation that can inform real-time decision-making and long-term urban planning.

One of the primary challenges in realizing federated digital twins and systems of systems is achieving true interoperability. Different organizations and industries often develop digital twin solutions using proprietary technologies and data models. Bridging these differences requires robust standardization efforts. Initiatives like the Digital Twin Consortium are working to define common architectures, semantic models, and interface specifications that can facilitate this cross-platform communication. The goal is to move away from siloed digital twins towards a more open ecosystem where digital twins can be easily integrated and exchanged. This involves not only technical standardization but also agreement on data governance, security protocols, and ownership models, especially when dealing with sensitive information shared across multiple entities.

Scalability is another significant consideration. As the number of interconnected digital twins grows, the underlying infrastructure must be able to handle the increased data volume, processing demands, and communication overhead. Cloud computing, edge computing, and distributed ledger technologies are all playing crucial roles in enabling the scalable deployment of federated digital twin frameworks. Edge computing, for instance, allows for localized processing of data from sensors and devices, reducing latency and the amount of data that needs to be transmitted to a central cloud. This is particularly important for real-time applications in areas like autonomous driving or industrial automation. Distributed ledger technologies, such as blockchain, can provide a secure and transparent way to manage data sharing and ensure the integrity of information exchanged between federated digital twins, especially in scenarios involving multiple, potentially untrusted, parties.

The opportunities presented by federated digital twins and systems of systems are vast. They enable unprecedented levels of holistic analysis and optimization. Instead of optimizing individual components in isolation, organizations can now optimize entire value chains, urban environments, or ecological systems. For example, a federated digital twin of a manufacturing ecosystem could identify inefficiencies not just within a single factory, but across the entire network of suppliers and distributors, leading to significant cost savings and improved resource utilization. In urban planning, a system of systems of digital twins can simulate the impact of new infrastructure projects on traffic, pollution, and public services, allowing cities to make more informed and sustainable development decisions. This capability extends to disaster preparedness and response, where federated models can simulate the spread of wildfires, floods, or pandemics, and help coordinate mitigation efforts.

The complexity of these federated systems also necessitates advanced data management and analytical techniques. Techniques like AI and machine learning are essential for processing the massive amounts of data generated by numerous digital twins, identifying patterns, predicting future states, and automating decision-making processes. For instance, AI algorithms can analyze data from a smart city's federated digital twins to predict traffic congestion hotspots before they occur, or to optimize energy consumption across the entire grid based on real-time demand and weather forecasts. The ability to perform predictive maintenance not just on individual machines but on entire fleets or industrial complexes becomes a reality, significantly reducing downtime and operational costs.

Furthermore, federated digital twins foster a more collaborative environment. By providing a common, data-driven platform, they can break down organizational silos and encourage cooperation between different departments, companies, or even public agencies. This shared understanding, derived from a consistent and up-to-date representation of the system, is crucial for tackling complex challenges that span multiple domains. Consider the development of a new smart transportation system for a city. This would involve collaboration between city planning departments, public transportation providers, technology vendors, and potentially even private mobility service operators. A federated digital twin approach would allow all these stakeholders to work within a shared virtual environment, visualizing the impact of proposed changes, testing different scenarios, and ensuring that the system is integrated effectively across all its components.

The security and privacy of data are paramount concerns in federated digital twin environments. When multiple entities share data, robust security measures must be in place to protect sensitive information from unauthorized access or misuse. This includes implementing strong authentication and authorization mechanisms, employing encryption for data in transit and at rest, and establishing clear data governance policies that define who can access what data and for what purpose. Privacy-preserving techniques, such as differential privacy or federated learning, are also becoming increasingly important, particularly when dealing with personal data in applications like smart cities or healthcare. Federated learning, for example, allows machine learning models to be trained across decentralized data sources without the need to move or centralize the data itself, thus enhancing privacy.

The development of a truly federated digital twin ecosystem is an ongoing journey. It requires not only technological advancements but also strategic collaboration, standardization efforts, and a commitment to open innovation. However, the potential rewards – enhanced efficiency, improved decision-making, greater resilience, and the ability to tackle increasingly complex global challenges – make it a compelling vision for the future of digital twins and the interconnected systems they represent. It moves us from observing individual assets to understanding and orchestrating entire complex environments.

The pervasive integration of digital twins into industrial, urban, and even personal domains necessitates a deep and ongoing examination of their ethical and societal implications. As these sophisticated virtual replicas become more integral to decision-making, operational management, and the very fabric of our daily lives, we must proactively address the potential challenges and responsibilities that arise. This scrutiny is not an afterthought but a critical component of responsible innovation, ensuring that the transformative power of digital twin technology is harnessed for the broad benefit of society, rather than creating new divides or exacerbating existing ones.

One of the most immediate and significant ethical concerns revolves around **data privacy**. Digital twins, by their very nature, are data-intensive entities. They collect, process, and analyze vast quantities of information, often originating from sensors embedded in physical assets, environments, or even individuals. In the context of industrial digital twins, this might involve proprietary manufacturing processes, sensitive supply chain logistics, or critical infrastructure operational data. For smart city applications, the data could encompass traffic patterns, energy consumption of households, public transport usage, and even the location of individuals through smart devices. When personal data is involved, the potential for misuse, unauthorized access, or intrusive surveillance becomes a paramount concern. The principle of informed consent, the right to know what data is being collected, how it is being used, and who has access to it, becomes more complex in a federated digital twin environment where data flows across multiple entities and systems. Robust anonymization techniques, differential privacy methods, and stringent access controls are not merely technical desiderata but ethical imperatives. The challenge lies in balancing the need for comprehensive data to create accurate and predictive digital twins with the fundamental right to privacy, especially as digital twins become more deeply intertwined with our personal lives and environments. The potential for re-identification of individuals from seemingly anonymized data, particularly when combined with other datasets, further complicates this landscape. Establishing clear data governance frameworks, akin to those being developed for AI and large language models, that delineate ownership, usage rights, and accountability for data within digital twin ecosystems is crucial.

Closely linked to data privacy is the issue of **security**. The interconnected nature of modern digital twins, particularly in federated and system-of-systems architectures, creates a broader attack surface. A vulnerability in one digital twin or its communication channel could potentially compromise an entire network, leading to cascading failures, data breaches, or even physical disruption. For instance, a cyberattack on the digital twin of a power grid could lead to widespread blackouts. Similarly, a breach in a federated supply chain twin could reveal sensitive trade secrets or disrupt global commerce. Ensuring the integrity and confidentiality of the data flowing between digital twins, and protecting the digital twins themselves from malicious alteration or destruction, requires state-of-the-art cybersecurity measures. This includes end-to-end encryption, multi-factor authentication, intrusion detection systems, and regular security audits. The complexity of these systems also means that security must be considered at every stage of the digital twin lifecycle, from design and development to deployment and ongoing operation. The principle of "security by design" must be rigorously applied.

Another significant societal implication is the potential for **job displacement due to automation**. As digital twins enable more sophisticated simulation, prediction, and autonomous operation, many tasks currently performed by human workers may become automated. In manufacturing, for example, digital twins can optimize production lines to the point where human intervention is minimized. In logistics, autonomous vehicles managed by digital twin systems could reduce the need for human drivers. This presents a dual challenge: the economic impact on individuals and communities reliant on these jobs, and the societal need to adapt and retrain the workforce. While automation has historically led to shifts in employment rather than mass unemployment, the pace and scope of change driven by advanced digital twins could be unprecedented. Proactive measures, including investment in lifelong learning, retraining programs focused on skills complementary to AI and digital twin technologies (such as data science, AI ethics, and complex system management), and exploring new economic models like universal basic income, become essential considerations. The narrative needs to shift from job replacement to job transformation, emphasizing how digital twins can augment human capabilities and create new roles focused on higher-level problem-solving, creativity, and oversight.

The role of **bias in AI models** that power digital twins is another critical ethical consideration. Many digital twins rely heavily on artificial intelligence and machine learning algorithms for their predictive and analytical capabilities. If the data used to train these AI models is biased, the digital twin's outputs and recommendations will also be biased, potentially perpetuating or even amplifying societal inequalities. For example, a smart city digital twin used for optimizing public service allocation might inadvertently discriminate against certain neighborhoods if historical data reflects systemic biases in service provision. Similarly, AI-driven recruitment tools integrated with digital twins could exhibit gender or racial biases if trained on historical hiring data. Addressing this requires rigorous data auditing to identify and mitigate biases, developing fairness-aware AI algorithms, and ensuring transparency in how AI models make decisions. Continuous monitoring and validation of AI model performance in real-world scenarios are also crucial to detect and correct emergent biases. A commitment to fairness and equity must be embedded in the design and deployment of AI within digital twin systems.

Accountability for decisions made by autonomous systems is a complex legal and ethical quandary. As digital twins enable increasingly autonomous operations, determining who is responsible when an autonomous system makes an error or causes harm becomes challenging. Is it the developer of the digital twin? The operator who deployed it? The manufacturer of the physical asset being controlled? Or the AI algorithm itself, if such a concept of accountability could even be applied? For instance, if an autonomous vehicle, guided by its digital twin, causes an accident, assigning blame is not straightforward. Legal frameworks are still evolving to address these scenarios, and the concept of "explainable AI" (XAI) is vital here. XAI aims to make AI decisions understandable to humans, allowing for better auditing and attribution of responsibility. Clear lines of accountability need to be established through contractual agreements, regulatory guidelines, and robust auditing trails within the digital twin systems themselves. This requires a multi-stakeholder approach involving legal experts, policymakers, technologists, and ethicists to develop frameworks that ensure justice and prevent a "responsibility gap."

Beyond these specific concerns, there is a broader societal implication related to the
democratization of access and the digital divide. The development and implementation of sophisticated digital twin technology often require significant investment in hardware, software, and expertise. This could lead to a situation where only large corporations or wealthy nations can fully leverage the benefits of digital twins, further widening the gap between the haves and the have-nots. Ensuring that the benefits of digital twins are accessible to small and medium-sized enterprises (SMEs), public sector organizations in developing countries, and even individual citizens requires deliberate efforts to lower barriers to entry. This can include promoting open-source digital twin platforms, developing more affordable and user-friendly tools, and providing training and educational resources. The goal should be to empower a wider range of stakeholders to utilize digital twin technology for innovation, efficiency, and improved quality of life, rather than allowing it to become an exclusive tool for the privileged.

Furthermore, the
impact on human perception and interaction with reality warrants consideration. As digital twins become more accurate and ubiquitous, the lines between the physical and virtual worlds may blur. While this can offer enhanced experiences and capabilities, it also raises questions about authenticity, our reliance on virtual representations, and the potential for detachment from the physical environment. In fields like education or training, immersive digital twins can be invaluable. However, over-reliance could also diminish the importance of direct sensory experience and embodied learning. There is a need to foster a balanced relationship with these technologies, ensuring that they augment human experience rather than replace or distort it.

Finally, the principle of
responsible innovation must guide the entire development and deployment process. This means embedding ethical considerations from the earliest stages of design, conducting thorough impact assessments, and engaging in ongoing dialogue with stakeholders, including the public. It involves a commitment to transparency, fairness, and accountability, and a willingness to adapt and evolve

as new ethical challenges emerge. Fostering a culture of ethical awareness within organizations developing and utilizing digital twins is paramount. This could involve establishing internal ethics boards, providing ethics training for engineers and developers, and creating mechanisms for whistleblowing or raising concerns about potentially harmful applications. The proactive development of ethical guidelines and best practices by industry consortia and international bodies is also essential to provide a common framework for responsible digital twin development. By prioritizing these ethical and societal considerations, we can steer the evolution of digital twins towards a future that is not only technologically advanced but also equitable, secure, and beneficial for all.

Chapter 15: Getting Started with Digital Twins

Before embarking on the journey of digital twin implementation, it is crucial for any organization to conduct a comprehensive assessment of its readiness. This initial diagnostic phase is not merely a procedural step; it is a strategic imperative that lays the foundation for success, mitigates risks, and ensures that the organization is poised to capitalize on the transformative potential of this technology. A haphazard or ill-prepared approach can lead to significant wasted resources, missed opportunities, and ultimately, the failure to realize the intended benefits of digital twins. Therefore, a detailed evaluation of several key areas is essential to gauge an organization's preparedness.

One of the foremost areas to scrutinize is the **existing data infrastructure**. Digital twins are, at their core, data-driven entities. They thrive on accurate, comprehensive, and readily accessible data streams from their physical counterparts. This necessitates an evaluation of the organization's current data collection capabilities. Are sensors adequately deployed on physical assets to capture the required parameters? Is the data being collected reliable, clean, and in a format that can be easily ingested by digital twin platforms? Furthermore, the organization's data storage and management systems must be examined. Can current systems handle the sheer volume and velocity of data that digital twins generate? Are there robust data governance policies in place that ensure data quality, integrity, security, and compliance with relevant regulations? The architecture of the data infrastructure, including its scalability and interoperability, will profoundly impact the effectiveness and efficiency of a digital twin implementation. Organizations must consider whether their existing databases, data lakes, or data warehouses are capable of supporting the real-time or near-real-time data requirements of a digital twin. Moreover, the ability to integrate data from disparate sources – operational technology (OT) systems, information technology (IT) systems, enterprise resource planning (ERP) systems, and even external data sources – is a critical determinant of success. A fragmented or siloed data landscape will present a formidable obstacle to creating a holistic and functional digital twin. The assessment should also look at the connectivity and bandwidth available to transmit this data from the physical world to the digital realm, especially for geographically dispersed assets.

Concurrently, a thorough assessment of

technological capabilities is indispensable. This involves evaluating the organization's existing technology stack and its suitability for supporting digital twin technologies. Does the organization possess the necessary hardware, such as high-performance computing resources, robust network infrastructure, and edge computing capabilities if real-time processing at the source is required? Software infrastructure is equally critical. Are there existing platforms for data analytics, simulation, visualization, and artificial intelligence (AI) or machine learning (ML) that can be leveraged or integrated with digital twin solutions? The organization's cloud strategy, if any, also plays a significant role, as many digital twin deployments are cloud-native or cloud-enabled. Understanding the current state of IT infrastructure, including its security posture and ability to support new applications, is paramount. The assessment should also consider the organization's experience with advanced technologies such as IoT platforms, AI/ML frameworks, simulation software, and immersive technologies like augmented reality (AR) or virtual reality (VR), which often complement digital twin applications. The maturity of these technologies within the organization will dictate the complexity of the digital twin implementation and the potential need for significant upgrades or new investments.

The
workforce skills and organizational culture represent another vital dimension of readiness. Implementing and managing digital twins requires a workforce with specialized skills. Does the organization have personnel proficient in data science, AI/ML, IoT engineering, cybersecurity, simulation modeling, and domain-specific expertise relevant to the assets or processes being twinned? A skills gap analysis is therefore essential. Identifying current skill proficiencies and pinpointing areas where upskilling or reskilling is necessary will inform training and recruitment strategies. Beyond technical skills, the organizational culture must be conducive to innovation and data-driven decision-making. Are employees open to new technologies and ways of working? Is there a willingness to embrace change and collaborate across different departments and disciplines? A culture that is resistant to change or operates in rigid silos can undermine even the most technically sound digital twin project. The assessment should also consider leadership buy-in and a clear understanding of the strategic objectives that digital twins are intended to support. Without strong leadership sponsorship and a shared vision, initiatives can falter. The capacity for cross-functional

collaboration between IT, OT, operations, engineering, and management is a critical cultural indicator of readiness.

Furthermore, assessing
organizational maturity provides a holistic view of the enterprise's preparedness. This involves evaluating the organization's strategic alignment, project management capabilities, change management processes, and overall operational discipline. Is there a clear digital transformation strategy in place, and how do digital twins fit within that roadmap? What is the organization's track record with implementing complex technological projects? Are there established processes for managing change, mitigating risks, and ensuring adoption? The maturity of the organization's governance structures and decision-making processes will also impact the speed and effectiveness of digital twin deployment. A mature organization will likely have well-defined processes for technology selection, vendor management, and intellectual property protection. The readiness assessment should also consider the organization's financial capacity to invest in digital twin technology, which can include software licenses, hardware, implementation services, and ongoing maintenance. Understanding the return on investment (ROI) expectations and having a realistic budget allocation is crucial. Finally, the assessment should gauge the organization's understanding of the ethical and regulatory implications associated with digital twins, as discussed in previous sections, and whether appropriate policies and procedures are in place to address them. This might include data privacy policies, cybersecurity protocols, and compliance frameworks.

A structured approach to this readiness assessment can involve a combination of self-assessments, workshops with key stakeholders, and potentially external expert consultations. The output of this assessment should not be a simple pass/fail but a detailed report that highlights strengths, identifies weaknesses, and provides actionable recommendations. These recommendations can then inform the development of a phased implementation strategy, prioritize specific digital twin use cases, guide technology selection, and shape the necessary investment in workforce development and cultural change initiatives. By thoroughly understanding its starting point, an organization can move forward with confidence, embarking on its digital twin journey with a clear roadmap and a significantly higher probability of achieving its desired outcomes. This proactive diligence ensures that digital twin technology is adopted not as a novelty, but as a strategic enabler of enhanced performance, innovation, and competitive advantage.

The inception of any successful digital twin initiative hinges on a foundational understanding of *why* it is being undertaken. Before delving into the technical intricacies of data streams, modeling, or visualization, it is paramount to crystallize the core purpose. This involves meticulously defining a clear use case and articulating specific, measurable, achievable, relevant, and time-bound (SMART) objectives. Without this clarity, the endeavor risks becoming a technologically impressive but strategically aimless exercise, consuming resources without delivering tangible value.

The process of identifying a high-value problem that a digital twin can effectively address is the cornerstone of this initial phase. This requires a deep dive into the organization's operations, identifying pain points, inefficiencies, or opportunities for significant improvement. These might manifest as recurring equipment failures, suboptimal process performance, excessive energy consumption, safety concerns, or the inability to accurately predict future outcomes. The key is to pinpoint a challenge that is both significant enough to warrant the investment in digital twin technology and for which a digital twin can offer a unique or superior solution compared to existing methods. Consider, for instance, a manufacturing plant experiencing frequent downtime on a critical production line. A digital twin could be used to monitor the health of each machine on that line in real-time, predict potential failures before they occur, and optimize maintenance schedules. This would directly address the pain point of unplanned downtime and its associated costs. Alternatively, an energy utility might identify that it struggles to accurately predict load demand in specific regions, leading to inefficient power generation and distribution. A digital twin of the energy grid, incorporating real-time weather data, historical consumption patterns, and event triggers, could provide more accurate predictions, thereby optimizing resource allocation and reducing waste.

Once a potential problem area is identified, the next critical step is to translate this into a well-defined use case. A use case is essentially a narrative that describes how the digital twin will be used to solve the identified problem. It should outline the specific functionalities the digital twin will provide, the users who will interact with it, and the expected outcomes. For the manufacturing plant example, the use case might be: "To develop a digital twin of the XYZ production line's critical machinery to enable predictive maintenance, thereby reducing unplanned downtime by 20% within the next 12 months." This use case clearly states the asset (XYZ production line's critical machinery), the technology (digital twin), the primary function (predictive maintenance), and a quantifiable goal.

Articulating clear, measurable objectives is inextricably linked to defining the use case. These objectives provide the benchmarks against which the success of the digital twin implementation will be measured. Simply stating "improve efficiency" is too vague. Instead, objectives should be specific. For the manufacturing example, this could translate into objectives such as: "Reduce unscheduled maintenance events on the XYZ production line by 20% within 12 months," "Decrease mean time to repair (MTTR) for critical components by 15% within six months," or "Increase overall equipment effectiveness (OEE) of the XYZ production line by 5% within 18 months." These objectives are not only measurable but also provide a clear target for the project team and stakeholders. They allow for objective evaluation of the digital twin's impact and help justify the ongoing investment.

For an energy utility aiming to improve load forecasting, the objectives might be: "Improve the accuracy of day-ahead electricity demand forecasts by 10% within nine months," "Reduce the instances of over-generation by 15% within 12 months," or "Decrease the operational costs associated with grid balancing by 8% within 18 months." The specificity of these objectives ensures that the project team remains focused on delivering tangible results that align with the overarching business goals.

It is often more effective for initial implementations to focus on a well-defined scope, such as optimizing a single critical asset or process, rather than attempting a large-scale deployment across an entire enterprise. This approach, often referred to as a pilot project or a Minimum Viable Product (MVP), allows organizations to learn, iterate, and demonstrate value with a manageable investment and a reduced risk profile. Attempting to build a digital twin for every asset or process simultaneously can lead to an unwieldy project, stretched resources, and a diluted focus, making it difficult to achieve success.

Consider a large petrochemical complex with thousands of individual assets. Embarking on a project to twin every single pump, valve, reactor, and pipeline from the outset would be an immense undertaking, fraught with complexity. Instead, a more prudent approach would be to select a single, critical distillation column that is known to be a bottleneck in the process or is prone to performance degradation. A digital twin of this specific column could be developed to monitor key operational parameters like temperature, pressure, and flow rates, simulate different operating conditions, and predict the onset of fouling or other issues that impact efficiency. The objectives for this focused pilot would be clear: "Improve the yield of the target product from the XYZ distillation column by 3% within six months," or "Reduce energy consumption of the XYZ distillation column by 5% within nine months."

The success of this focused pilot project would then provide invaluable insights and demonstrate the tangible benefits of digital twin technology. These insights could include lessons learned about data acquisition from specific types of sensors, the effectiveness of particular modeling techniques for that process, the usability of the chosen visualization tools, and the skills required from the operational and engineering teams. The proven success and demonstrated ROI from this pilot can then be leveraged to secure further investment and support for expanding the digital twin implementation to other critical assets or processes, gradually building a more comprehensive digital twin ecosystem.

This phased approach also allows for the iterative refinement of the digital twin itself. Initial models might be simplified, and the data inputs might be limited. As the project progresses and understanding deepens, the models can be made more sophisticated, incorporating more complex physics or chemical processes, and additional data streams can be integrated. For the distillation column example, the initial twin might focus on predicting throughput and energy consumption. Later iterations could incorporate predictive maintenance for critical components like reboilers and condensers, or even simulate the impact of feedstock variations on product quality.

Furthermore, focusing on a single asset or process helps to clarify the data requirements and the necessary integrations. For a pilot project, the data sources might be limited to a few key sensors and the existing supervisory control and data acquisition (SCADA) system. This makes the data integration task more manageable. As the project scales, the organization will need to address the integration of data from enterprise resource planning (ERP) systems, advanced process control (APC) systems, and potentially external data sources like weather forecasts or market prices. Starting small allows the organization to tackle these integration challenges incrementally.

The benefits of this focused approach extend to organizational readiness as well. A pilot project requires a dedicated, cross-functional team, typically comprising subject matter experts from operations and engineering, data scientists or analysts, and IT specialists. This concentrated effort allows for intensive collaboration and knowledge transfer within a smaller group. It also provides an opportunity to identify and address skills gaps within this core team, facilitating targeted training and development. The experience gained from a successful pilot can then be disseminated throughout the organization as the digital twin initiative expands.

Defining a clear use case and objectives is not a one-time activity but an ongoing process. As the digital twin evolves and new opportunities arise, the use case and objectives may need to be revisited and refined. For instance, an initial objective might be to improve operational efficiency. However, as the digital twin matures and provides deeper insights into asset behavior, new use cases might emerge, such as optimizing product quality, enhancing safety protocols, or enabling new business models.

In essence, the journey of implementing a digital twin should be guided by a clear destination. This destination is defined by a well-articulated use case that addresses a significant business problem and a set of SMART objectives that provide a quantifiable measure of success. By focusing on a manageable scope for initial implementation, organizations can de-risk the endeavor, accelerate time-to-value, and build the necessary expertise and organizational buy-in to scale their digital twin capabilities effectively. This strategic clarity at the outset is the most crucial determinant of whether a digital twin initiative will deliver on its transformative promise or become another costly, underutilized technological investment.

The successful adoption of digital twin technology is rarely an instantaneous leap; rather, it is a strategic journey best navigated through a carefully constructed phased implementation roadmap. This approach acknowledges that digital twins are complex systems, requiring iterative development, continuous learning, and gradual integration into existing operational frameworks. By breaking down the overarching vision into a series of manageable stages, organizations can effectively mitigate risks, demonstrate value incrementally, and build the necessary momentum and expertise to achieve a comprehensive and impactful digital twin ecosystem.

The foundational principle of a phased implementation is to begin with focused, high-impact pilot projects. These initial undertakings serve as crucial learning opportunities, allowing teams to gain practical experience with the technology, validate chosen methodologies, and identify potential challenges in a controlled environment. The selection of a pilot project should be guided by the clear use cases and SMART objectives established in the preceding stages. Ideally, the pilot should target a specific asset, process, or system that offers a significant opportunity for improvement and provides a strong potential for demonstrating tangible benefits relatively quickly. For instance, in a manufacturing setting, a pilot might focus on a single critical machine known for its frequent breakdowns or a specific production line that is experiencing performance bottlenecks. In the energy sector, it could involve developing a digital twin for a particular substation to improve local fault detection or a specific wind turbine to optimize its energy generation based on real-time wind conditions. The key is to select a scope that is sufficiently complex to yield meaningful insights but constrained enough to be manageable within a defined timeline and budget.

Once a pilot project is selected, the roadmap must clearly delineate the stages involved in its execution. This typically begins with the detailed design and architecture phase, where the specific requirements for the pilot twin are fleshed out. This includes identifying all necessary data sources, defining the required data granularity and frequency, selecting appropriate modeling techniques (e.g., physics-based, data-driven, or hybrid), and choosing the visualization and user interface tools. For the manufacturing machine pilot, this might involve identifying sensors for vibration, temperature, and pressure, specifying the data protocols for their extraction, and defining the simulation models that will predict component wear. Similarly, for the wind turbine twin, it would involve incorporating data from anemometers, pitch sensors, and generator load, and selecting aerodynamic and structural models. This detailed planning phase is critical for ensuring that the pilot project is built on a solid foundation, minimizing the need for extensive rework later on.

Following the design phase, the implementation of the pilot project proceeds through data acquisition and integration, model development and validation, and the deployment of the digital twin for operational use. Data acquisition involves setting up the infrastructure to collect, clean, and pre-process data from the chosen sources. This stage often reveals unforeseen challenges related to data quality, connectivity, or compatibility, underscoring the value of a phased approach that allows for problem-solving in a smaller context. Model development involves building the mathematical and computational representations of the physical asset or process. This is where subject matter experts collaborate closely with data scientists and simulation engineers to ensure the models accurately reflect the behavior of the real-world system. Model validation is a crucial step, where the digital twin's predictions and behaviors are compared against historical data and real-time performance metrics to ensure fidelity and accuracy. Once validated, the digital twin is deployed for its intended purpose, whether it's for real-time monitoring, predictive analytics, or scenario simulation.

The success of the pilot project is not merely measured by its technical completion but by the tangible value it delivers and the lessons learned. This evaluation phase is a critical part of the roadmap, informing the next steps. Key performance indicators (KPIs) defined earlier, such as reduced downtime, improved efficiency, or enhanced prediction accuracy, are rigorously assessed. Beyond quantitative results, qualitative insights are equally important. This includes understanding the usability of the digital twin interface, the effectiveness of the training provided to users, and the impact on operational workflows. The team also identifies what worked well, what didn't, and what challenges remain. For the manufacturing machine pilot, a successful outcome might be a documented reduction in unscheduled maintenance events by 15% and valuable feedback from maintenance technicians on the early warning alerts provided by the twin. For the wind turbine, it could be an increase in energy output by 2% through optimized pitch control and insights into the most effective parameters for performance tuning.

Armed with the learnings from the pilot, the roadmap then outlines the expansion phase. This is where the scope of the digital twin implementation begins to broaden. This expansion can take several forms: deepening the functionality of the existing twin, extending it to related assets or processes, or replicating the successful pilot to other similar environments. For the manufacturing example, expansion might involve integrating the predictive maintenance capabilities for the initial machine into a broader asset management system, or extending the twin to encompass the entire production line, linking the performance of individual machines. In the energy sector, it could mean building upon the substation twin to include its upstream and downstream connections, or scaling the wind turbine twin to cover an entire wind farm, enabling coordinated control and performance optimization across multiple units. This expansion phase requires careful planning to ensure that the growing complexity of the digital twin ecosystem is managed effectively.

The scaling phase of the roadmap involves progressively increasing the breadth and depth of the digital twin implementation across the organization. This could mean developing twins for more critical assets or complex processes, integrating additional data sources (e.g., enterprise resource planning (ERP) systems, supply chain data, or customer feedback), or enhancing the analytical capabilities with more advanced AI and machine learning algorithms. For example, a digital twin initially used for operational monitoring of a chemical plant might be expanded to include simulations for optimizing chemical reactions, predicting product quality, or assessing the impact of different feedstock compositions. The integration of ERP data could enable the digital twin to forecast spare parts demand or optimize production schedules based on inventory levels and market demand. This scaling must be accompanied by robust governance frameworks, standardized data management practices, and a clear strategy for ongoing maintenance and evolution of the digital twin assets.

Throughout this phased journey, organizational change management and capability building are paramount. Each stage of the roadmap should include provisions for training and upskilling employees, fostering a culture of data-driven decision-making, and ensuring buy-in from all stakeholders. The initial pilot project provides an excellent opportunity to identify key champions and early adopters who can help drive broader acceptance. As the implementation progresses, formal training programs, workshops, and knowledge-sharing sessions become increasingly important. This ensures that the workforce can effectively interact with, utilize, and contribute to the evolving digital twin ecosystem. The roadmap should also consider how new roles and responsibilities might emerge, such as digital twin managers, data stewards, or simulation specialists, and outline plans for recruiting or developing talent for these positions.

The iterative nature of the phased implementation allows for continuous refinement and optimization. As more data is collected and more operational experience is gained, the digital twin models can be improved, their accuracy enhanced, and their predictive power strengthened. New use cases may emerge as the organization becomes more adept at leveraging the insights provided by the digital twin. For instance, a digital twin initially designed for predictive maintenance might later be repurposed for optimizing energy efficiency, or for training new operators in a safe, simulated environment. This adaptability is a core strength of the phased approach, allowing the digital twin to evolve alongside the organization's needs and technological advancements.

Furthermore, a phased roadmap provides a structured mechanism for managing investment and demonstrating return on investment (ROI) at each step. By focusing on delivering value through clearly defined milestones, organizations can justify ongoing funding and build confidence among leadership and other stakeholders. The success of early stages can be leveraged to secure resources for more ambitious later phases. This incremental funding approach reduces the financial risk associated with large, upfront investments in complex technologies like digital twins. The roadmap should therefore include clear financial projections and metrics for evaluating the economic benefits realized at each stage, ensuring that the digital twin initiative remains aligned with the organization's strategic financial objectives.

Finally, a well-defined phased implementation roadmap for digital twins is not a rigid, inflexible plan but a dynamic guide. It should be periodically reviewed and updated to reflect changing business priorities, technological advancements, and lessons learned throughout the implementation process. This agility ensures that the digital twin initiative remains relevant and continues to deliver maximum value over time. The journey from a single pilot to a comprehensive digital twin ecosystem is one of continuous learning, adaptation, and strategic evolution, with the phased roadmap serving as the essential compass and itinerary for this transformative endeavor.

The journey toward realizing the full potential of digital twins hinges significantly on the judicious selection of the underlying technologies and, where appropriate, the strategic engagement of implementation partners. This decision-making process is not a mere technical exercise; it is a strategic imperative that can profoundly influence the project's trajectory, its ultimate success, and its long-term viability. A meticulously chosen technology stack and a robust partnership ecosystem can accelerate deployment, enhance capabilities, and foster innovation, while a misstep in either domain can lead to costly rework, performance limitations, and ultimately, a failure to achieve desired outcomes. Therefore, a systematic and thorough evaluation is paramount before committing significant resources.

When considering the technology landscape for digital twins, it is essential to recognize that it is not a monolithic entity but rather a convergence of various specialized domains. At its core, a digital twin requires robust data acquisition capabilities. This often involves a range of sensors, actuators, and edge devices capable of capturing real-time information from the physical asset or process. The selection of this hardware is dictated by the nature of the asset being twinned, the criticality of the data points, and the environmental conditions. For instance, a harsh industrial environment might necessitate ruggedized sensors resistant to extreme temperatures, vibration, or corrosive elements. Similarly, the required data granularity and frequency will influence the choice between simple analog sensors and sophisticated multi-parameter digital probes. The proliferation of the Internet of Things (IoT) has brought forth a vast array of such devices, each with its own communication protocols, power requirements, and data output formats. Compatibility and integration with the chosen platform become critical considerations at this stage.

Beyond data capture, the effective management and processing of this deluge of information are fundamental. This is where digital twin platforms come into play. These platforms serve as the central nervous system, ingesting data, facilitating its transformation, enabling its analysis, and driving its visualization. The market offers a diverse spectrum of platforms, ranging from comprehensive, end-to-end solutions provided by major software vendors to specialized modules that can be integrated into existing IT infrastructures. When evaluating these platforms, several key criteria should be considered. Scalability is perhaps the most crucial. The chosen platform must be capable of handling the anticipated volume and velocity of data, not just for the initial pilot project but also for future expansions as the digital twin initiative grows across the organization. A platform that struggles to cope with increased data loads will quickly become a bottleneck, hindering performance and potentially requiring a costly replacement down the line.

Interoperability is another critical factor. Digital twins rarely exist in a vacuum. They must seamlessly integrate with existing enterprise systems, such as Enterprise Resource Planning (ERP), Manufacturing Execution Systems (MES), Product Lifecycle Management (PLM), and Computerized Maintenance Management Systems (CMMS). This integration allows for a holistic view of operations, where data from the digital twin can inform and be informed by other business processes. A platform that offers robust APIs (Application Programming Interfaces) and adheres to industry standards for data exchange (like OPC UA for industrial automation) will significantly simplify this integration effort. Conversely, a platform that operates in a closed ecosystem may create data silos and limit the overall value proposition of the digital twin.

The analytical capabilities of a digital twin platform are central to its value. This includes the ability to perform real-time monitoring, conduct historical analysis, and, most importantly, enable predictive and prescriptive analytics. The platform should support a variety of modeling techniques, from physics-based simulations to data-driven machine learning algorithms. The sophistication of these analytical tools will determine the types of insights that can be extracted from the digital twin. For example, a digital twin intended for predictive maintenance will require advanced algorithms capable of identifying subtle patterns indicative of impending equipment failure. Similarly, a twin focused on process optimization might need sophisticated simulation engines that can model complex cause-and-effect relationships. The ease with which users can develop, deploy, and manage these analytical models is also an important consideration, often influenced by the platform's user interface and development tools.

Vendor support and the overall ecosystem surrounding the technology are often overlooked but are vital for long-term success. When selecting a platform or technology provider, it is essential to assess the quality and responsiveness of their technical support. This includes the availability of documentation, training resources, and expert assistance. The vendor's commitment to ongoing research and development is also important, ensuring that the platform will evolve with new technologies and capabilities. A vibrant community of users and developers can also be a significant asset, providing a valuable source of shared knowledge, best practices, and readily available extensions or add-ons. The financial stability and long-term vision of the vendor should also be evaluated to ensure a reliable partnership.

Cost-effectiveness is, of course, a primary driver for any technology investment.

However, it is crucial to look beyond the initial purchase price and consider the total cost of ownership (TCO). This includes the costs associated with hardware, software licenses, implementation, integration, training, ongoing maintenance, and potential upgrades. Cloud-based platforms often offer a more predictable subscription-based pricing model, which can be attractive for managing operational expenses. On-premises solutions might involve higher upfront capital expenditure but can offer greater control over data and infrastructure. A thorough total cost of ownership analysis, factoring in potential ROI from the digital twin initiative, will provide a more accurate picture of the financial implications. It is also important to consider licensing models that allow for flexibility and growth, avoiding models that penalize expansion.

Beyond selecting the core digital twin platform, organizations must also consider the supporting technologies that enable its functionality. This includes data storage solutions, which must be capable of handling large volumes of structured and unstructured data with appropriate access controls and disaster recovery mechanisms. Network infrastructure is equally critical, ensuring reliable and high-bandwidth connectivity between physical assets, edge devices, and the central platform, especially for real-time data streams. Cybersecurity is paramount, as digital twins can represent highly sensitive operational data and control systems. Robust security measures must be implemented at all layers, from the edge devices to the cloud or on-premises servers, to prevent unauthorized access, data breaches, or malicious manipulation. This might involve encryption, authentication protocols, intrusion detection systems, and regular security audits.

The visualization layer of a digital twin is what provides users with an intuitive and actionable understanding of the data and insights generated. This can range from simple dashboards and charts to immersive 3D models and augmented reality (AR) or virtual reality (VR) experiences. The choice of visualization tools should align with the intended users and their specific needs. For shop-floor operators, a simple, real-time dashboard might be sufficient. For engineers or maintenance teams, a detailed 3D model with drill-down capabilities and simulation overlays might be more beneficial. For strategic decision-makers, high-level trend analysis and scenario simulation visualizations could be key. The chosen tools should be user-friendly, customizable, and capable of rendering complex data in an easily digestible format. Integration with AR/VR hardware, if part of the strategy, requires careful consideration of compatibility and performance.

The decision to engage external implementation partners is another critical strategic choice. While some organizations may have the internal expertise and resources to manage the entire digital twin implementation lifecycle, many will benefit from collaborating with specialized firms. These partners can bring a wealth of experience, deep technical knowledge, and a proven track record in areas such as IoT integration, data science, simulation modeling, cloud architecture, and change management. When selecting a partner, it is crucial to conduct thorough due diligence. This includes evaluating their understanding of your specific industry, their familiarity with the chosen technology stack, their methodology for project delivery, and their client references.

Key considerations when selecting an implementation partner include their technical capabilities and expertise. Do they have a demonstrated history of successfully deploying digital twins for similar use cases or in your industry? What is their approach to data integration, model development, and system architecture? Look for partners who can provide end-to-end services, from strategy and design to implementation and ongoing support. Their ability to work collaboratively with your internal teams is also vital. A successful partnership is one where the external experts act as an extension of your organization, fostering knowledge transfer and building internal capabilities.

The partner's project management methodology and approach to risk mitigation should also be thoroughly assessed. How do they plan and execute projects? What measures do they have in place to identify and address potential risks and challenges? A partner who employs agile methodologies and maintains transparent communication throughout the project lifecycle will likely lead to a smoother and more successful implementation. Understanding their contractual terms, including intellectual property rights, service level agreements (SLAs), and pricing models, is also essential. A clear and comprehensive contract will help prevent misunderstandings and ensure alignment of expectations.

Consider the partner's long-term vision and their ability to support your ongoing needs. Digital twins are not static deployments; they require continuous evolution and improvement. A good partner will not only help you get started but will also be a valuable resource for future enhancements, upgrades, and the exploration of new use cases. This might involve ongoing managed services, strategic consulting, or access to specialized expertise as your digital twin program matures. Building a long-term strategic relationship with a trusted partner can be more beneficial than a series of one-off engagements.

In summary, the selection of appropriate technologies and implementation partners forms the bedrock upon which a successful digital twin initiative is built. It requires a deep understanding of organizational needs, a thorough evaluation of available options, and a strategic approach to collaboration. By carefully considering factors such as scalability, interoperability, analytical capabilities, vendor support, cost-effectiveness, partner expertise, and long-term viability, organizations can make informed decisions that pave the way for a robust, adaptable, and value-generating digital twin ecosystem. This deliberate and strategic approach ensures that the technological foundation and collaborative efforts align perfectly with the overarching business objectives, setting the stage for transformative outcomes.

The true power of digital twins, once meticulously selected and integrated, is not solely in their technological sophistication but in the organizational culture that embraces and leverages them. A digital twin is more than just a digital replica; it is a catalyst for a profound shift in how an organization operates, makes decisions, and innovates. To unlock its full potential, a deliberate cultivation of a data-driven culture is paramount. This involves fostering an environment where data is not merely collected and stored but is actively sought, understood, and acted upon to drive continuous improvement and innovation. Without this cultural underpinning, even the most advanced digital twin will remain an underutilized asset, a sophisticated piece of technology observing rather than transforming.

At the heart of this cultural transformation lies a comprehensive and ongoing commitment to education and skill development. The introduction of digital twins necessitates new ways of working and new skill sets across various departments. It is crucial to invest in training programs that equip employees at all levels with the knowledge and abilities to interact with, interpret, and utilize the insights generated by digital twins. For operational teams, this might mean understanding how to interpret real-time performance data, identify anomalies flagged by predictive analytics, and respond to prescriptive recommendations for optimizing asset performance or maintenance schedules. For engineering and design teams, it could involve leveraging the twin for scenario testing, design validation, and faster iteration cycles, moving from theoretical models to data-backed simulations.

Furthermore, the data scientists and analysts who will be the primary custodians of the digital twin's analytical power require specialized training. This encompasses not only advanced data analytics techniques and machine learning algorithms but also a deep understanding of the physical domain being twinned. A data scientist unfamiliar with the operational realities of a manufacturing plant or the intricacies of an energy grid will struggle to build truly insightful models. Therefore, training should emphasize cross-disciplinary learning, encouraging these professionals to spend time with their operational and engineering counterparts, gaining firsthand knowledge of the physical assets and processes. This fusion of data science expertise with domain knowledge is what elevates a digital twin from a data repository to a powerful engine of insight.

Beyond formal training, the establishment of accessible resources and continuous learning opportunities is vital. This could include internal knowledge bases populated with best practices, case studies, and guides on using the digital twin platform. Regular workshops, webinars, and lunch-and-learn sessions can provide platforms for employees to share their experiences, discuss challenges, and learn from each other. Fostering a community of practice around digital twins, where individuals with shared interests and challenges can connect, collaborate, and innovate, can significantly accelerate the adoption and effectiveness of this technology. This community can serve as an organic mechanism for knowledge dissemination and problem-solving, reducing reliance on centralized support and empowering individuals to become digital twin champions within their respective teams.

However, the human element extends beyond formal training; it requires a strategic approach to change management. The introduction of digital twins often represents a significant departure from established workflows and decision-making processes. This transition can be met with resistance if not managed effectively. Change management strategies should focus on clearly articulating the value proposition of digital twins, not just at a strategic level but also for the individuals whose daily work will be affected. Understanding and addressing the "what's in it for me?" question for each stakeholder group is crucial for gaining buy-in. This might involve highlighting how digital twins can reduce manual effort, improve safety, enhance job satisfaction by enabling more informed decision-making, or lead to more fulfilling projects.

Effective change management also involves early and consistent engagement with all relevant stakeholders. This means bringing together individuals from diverse departments – Information Technology (IT), Operational Technology (OT), engineering, maintenance, product development, sales, and executive leadership – from the outset of the digital twin initiative. These cross-functional teams are essential for identifying potential challenges, defining requirements, and co-creating solutions that are practical and beneficial for all. The traditional divide between IT and OT, often characterized by different priorities, systems, and even cultures, needs to be bridged. Digital twins, by their very nature, sit at the intersection of these two domains, requiring a unified approach to data governance, security, and operational management.

Fostering collaboration between IT and OT is not merely about technical integration; it is about cultural alignment. IT professionals are typically concerned with data security, system scalability, and enterprise-wide integration, while OT professionals focus on real-time operational performance, safety, and the reliability of physical assets. Digital twins require both perspectives to be valued and integrated. Collaborative workshops, joint training sessions, and the establishment of shared governance frameworks can help break down silos and build mutual understanding and respect. This collaborative spirit is crucial for ensuring that the digital twin platform is not only technically sound but also aligns with operational needs and constraints, and that OT data is protected and managed according to IT best practices.

Moreover, the insights derived from digital twins need to be translated into actionable strategies and organizational improvements. This requires a commitment from leadership to empower teams to act on these insights. If a digital twin identifies an opportunity for process optimization, the organization must have the agility and willingness to implement the necessary changes. This might involve reconfiguring production lines, updating maintenance procedures, or investing in new equipment. A culture of innovation thrives when data-driven recommendations are not met with bureaucratic inertia but are seen as opportunities for growth and efficiency.

This often necessitates a revision of performance metrics and incentive structures. If employees are rewarded solely on traditional metrics that do not account for the benefits of data-driven insights, they may have little motivation to adopt new practices. Introducing metrics that reward proactive problem-solving, the adoption of optimized processes, or the successful utilization of digital twin insights can help drive the desired cultural shift. This requires a holistic view of performance, where the long-term benefits of digital twin adoption are recognized and incentivized.

The concept of continuous improvement, central to many quality management philosophies, finds a powerful ally in digital twins. A digital twin provides a dynamic and data-rich environment for identifying areas of inefficiency, suboptimal performance, or potential risks. By continuously monitoring and analyzing the digital twin, organizations can identify trends, pinpoint root causes of issues, and test potential solutions in a risk-free virtual environment before implementing them in the physical world. This iterative process of measure, analyze, improve, and verify is significantly accelerated and enhanced by the capabilities of digital twins.

To truly embed this culture of continuous improvement, organizations must actively solicit feedback from all users of the digital twin. What is working well? What are the pain points? Are the insights generated truly actionable and valuable? Establishing clear channels for feedback and demonstrating that this feedback is being heard and acted upon is critical for maintaining momentum and ensuring that the digital twin continues to evolve in alignment with user needs and business objectives. This feedback loop is also essential for identifying new use cases and opportunities for innovation that may not have been apparent during the initial implementation.

Ultimately, cultivating a culture of data-driven innovation around digital twins is an ongoing journey, not a destination. It requires persistent effort, strategic investment in people and processes, and a genuine commitment from leadership to embrace a more informed, agile, and forward-thinking way of operating. When this culture is successfully nurtured, the digital twin transforms from a technological marvel into a deeply integrated enabler of operational excellence and a powerful engine for sustainable innovation. It becomes the digital heartbeat of the organization, guiding decisions, predicting futures, and continuously pushing the boundaries of what is possible. The successful integration of digital twins is therefore not just a technical feat; it is a testament to an organization's ability to adapt, learn, and thrive in an increasingly data-centric world. This shift requires patience, perseverance, and a clear vision of how data, coupled with a supportive organizational culture, can drive transformative change. The journey to fully leverage digital twins is intrinsically linked to the organization's capacity to evolve its mindset, skills, and collaborative practices, ensuring that technology serves as an amplifier of human ingenuity and strategic foresight, rather than merely a complex tool.

Digital Twin: A virtual representation of a physical asset, process, or system, updated in real-time by data from its physical counterpart, used for monitoring, analysis, simulation, and prediction.

IoT (Internet of Things): A network of physical objects embedded with sensors, software, and other technologies that enable them to collect and exchange data.

Predictive Maintenance: A maintenance strategy that uses data analysis and machine learning to predict when equipment failure might occur, allowing for maintenance to be scheduled proactively.

Simulation: The process of imitating the behavior of a real-world process or system over time, often used to test hypotheses or predict outcomes.

Data Governance: The overall management of the availability, usability, integrity, and security of the data employed in an enterprise.

OT (Operational Technology): Hardware and software that detect or cause a change, or monitor and control the operation of physical processes, devices, or events.

IT (Information Technology): The use of computers, storage, networking, and other physical devices, infrastructure, and processes to create, process, transmit, and store information.

Cross-functional Teams: Groups of people with different functional expertise who work together toward a common goal.

www.ingramcontent.com/pod-product-compliance
Lightning Source LLC
LaVergne TN
LVHW052026200926
848481LV00005B/1593